King Cohn

The Life and Times of
Hollywood Mogul Harry Cohn

Bob Thomas

NEW MILLENNIUM PRESS

Beverly Hills

To my wife, Patricia

Original hardcover publication in 1967 by G. P. Putnam's Sons. Published in paperback in 1968 by Bantam Books and in 1990 by McGraw Hill. First New Millennium Press edition 2000.

Library of Congress Cataloging-in-Publication Data

Thomas, Bob, 1922–
    King Cohn : the life and times of Hollywood mogul Harry Cohn / Bob Thomas.--
1st New Millennium Press ed.
      p. cm.
    Originally published: King Cohn : the life and times of Harry Cohn. New York :
Putman, [1967]. With new pref. and a restored final chapter that had been
removed from the original ed.
    Includes index.
    ISBN 1-893224-07-4 (trade pbk.)
    1. Cohn, Harry, 1891–1958. 2. Motion picture producers and directors--United
States--Biography. I. Title.

PN1998.3.C665 T47 2000
791.43'0232'092--dc21
[B]   99-087100

New Millennium Press
A division of NM WorldMedia, Inc.
350 South Beverly Drive
Suite 315
Beverly Hills, California 90212

DOUGLAS WHITNEY: "Harry, why are you so rough on the people who work for you?"

HARRY COHN: "I am the king here. Whoever eats my bread sings my song."

Author's Note

Harry Cohn left no writings, made virtually no speeches, scarcely ever submitted to an interview. Personal publicity was of no moment to him; all that mattered was what appeared on the screen.

Research into his life, therefore, had to be conducted largely through interviews with his onetime employees, competitors, friends, associates, and enemies. I extend my thanks to the more than 300 individuals who gave willingly of their memories of Cohn.

Two notes about conversational passages:

1. No dialogue was invented. Conversations are reproduced as they were recalled by participants.

2. Cohn's speech abounded with Anglo-Saxon words that have long been exiled from polite usage. To paraphrase them would dilute the essence of the man; to print them would offend certain readers. I have supplied blank spaces, which the more literal-minded may fill in according to their own vocabularies.

The account of Jack Cohn's adventure with *Traffic in Souls* was taken from Terry Ramsaye's monumental *A Million and One Nights* (copyright 1926 by Simon and Schuster, Inc.; copyright renewed 1954 by Terry Ramsaye). I am grateful to Simon and Schuster, Inc., for permission to use it, as well as permission to quote from Ezra Goodman's *The Fifty Year Decline and Fall of Hollywood* (copyright 1961 by Simon and Schuster, Inc.). I am also indebted to the library of the Academy of Motion Picture Arts and Sciences for use of its facilities.

CONTENTS

Foreword

A figure like Harry Cohn assumes mythic proportions when viewed from the perspective of present-day Hollywood. Cohn was the ultimate rough-and-tumble pioneer, an uneducated immigrant who built Columbia Pictures virtually brick by brick. Cohn relished his tough-guy image and celebrated his feuds with his rivals as well as with the stars and filmmakers under contract to Columbia. He was coarse and ferocious, and that was exactly the way he wanted to come across.

Given this style, Cohn would seem almost like a cave man were he to materialize in today's "corporate" Hollywood, a town controlled by glibly sophisticated "suits" who serve as apparchiks for the multinational media corporations. Today's Hollywood runs on budgets and business plans. Its bosses dedicate themselves to supplying "content" for the vast distribution mechanisms owned by the Rupert Murdochs, Sumner Redstones, and Edgar Bronfman Jrs.

Harry Cohn's dream was to build a vast inventory of talent—writers, directors, and stars who worked under contract to the studio. Today's studios are intent mainly on building an inventory of filmed fodder that can be sliced and diced for the parent company's diverse enterprises that span video, music, cable and satellite TV, retail stores, and theme parks. Cohn had to make movies to make money. Most of today's movies lose money but are produced nonetheless as pricey loss leaders to feed other enterprises. Cohn had to appease his bankers. Today's multinationals must cater to investors around the world whose fixation is on quarterly earnings and share prices, not on a broader blueprint for building an entertainment company.

Harry Cohn spent money as though it were his own, and arguably it was. He was gratified to close a deal with a "hot" young film maker like Stanley Kramer, but nonetheless demanded that Kramer's movies cost no more than $980,000.

When Kramer bought an extraordinary book called *The Caine Mutiny* and told Cohn that his movie would cost easily three times his budgetary limit, Cohn went crazy. In the end, Kramer brought it in for $2.4 million and it turned out to be a big hit, but Cohn was nonetheless relieved when Kramer left the lot.

"You cost the studio a lot of money," Cohn gruffly told him. "I'm glad to see you go."

"I'm glad to be going," Kramer replied, and he meant it. He went on to make many celebrated pictures, most of them for later regimes at Columbia.

It is unimaginable how Cohn would react to the hallucinatory costs of present-day Hollywood, where film makers calmly submit budgets of $100 million or more and studios spend as much as $50 million merely to advertise the launch of a movie. A meeting between Cohn and a film maker like *Titanic*'s James Cameron would likely end in homicide. Cohn enjoyed banning adversaries from his lot almost as much as Cameron relishes barring studio executives from his set.

Cohn would similarly be apoplectic over the way today's studios treat writers. The old studio chief seemed to enjoy screaming at hapless writers and dismissing their ideas almost before they could complete their pitches. "Seventy-five percent of the ideas that people try to sell me are no good, so if I turn them down at the outset that makes me right seventy-five percent of the time," he would boast. Aides would try to explain that patience was required in nurturing talent, but Cohn was dismissive. "I kiss the feet of talent," he intoned. "If you've got talent, I'll kiss your ass; if you haven't, I'll kick it."

And he did. With regularity. Surely Cohn would not be one to listen to lengthy pitches from writers and then reward those he liked with sums ranging from $1 million to $3 million, as is regularly done at studios nowadays. Indeed, the new breed of million-dollar writers would receive a chilly reception in Cohn's Columbia.

With all their limitations, of course, the old goniffs of the Cohn era built an extraordinary industry. The golden era of Hollywood endured through the years of World War II, finally crashing down with the advent of television in the 1950's and 1960's. The studios owned the stars and owned the theaters as well. An extraordinary "habit" audience could be counted on to give most new releases a hospitable reception. In their heyday, the baronial studio chiefs were the highest-paid executives in America.

To be sure, they were ruthless. They were mean spirited. They cared not at all for the impact of their product on pop culture. But in their own arch, vulgar way, the Harry Cohns of that era had an amazing instinct for reading the public's changing tastes. And their sheer ferocity managed to sustain an economic balancing act between the demands of the talent and the needs of the companies—a balance that today's multinational corporations have been unable to preserve.

Harry Cohn may have created a reign of terror, but his movies by and large hold their own. More and more, the films of today seem to have lost their sense of scale with the appetites of the film makers overwhelming those of their corporate handlers.

Given all this, Bob Thomas's perceptive examination of the life of "King Cohn" takes on all the more interest today. Harry Cohn was an improbable dreamer. But his dream factory lives on.

Peter Bart
Vice President, *Variety*
Los Angeles

PREFACE

It's good to see *King Cohn* back in print. More than three decades after it was first published, strangers still say to me, "Bob Thomas? Oh, yes, you wrote *King Cohn*." After writing fifteen subsequent biographies, it remains my favorite, perhaps because it was the first. Harry Cohn was the biographer's dream: brash, profane, outrageous, a primitive who helped create an important segment of America's culture. Without Cohn there might never have been such film classics as *It Happened One Night, Mr. Deeds Goes to Town, Lost Horizon, The Jolson Story, Gilda, All the King's Men, Born Yesterday, From Here to Eternity*, or *The Caine Mutiny*.

King Cohn came about through a happy accident. Harvey Ginsberg, then an editor at Putnam's, came to Hollywood on a book-hunting expedition. He and I met in the coffee shop of the Beverly Wilshire Hotel, and he expressed interest in two subjects: Harry Cohn and Irving Thalberg. After some discussion, he came to the conclusion that a Cohn biography would be impossible to do.

I agreed. Cohn had been the most secretive of studio bosses—"the Jewish Howard Hughes," he was termed by one of his studio publicists, Bob Yeager. I decided to investigate the possibility of doing a Thalberg biography, but the widow Thalberg, Norma Shearer, told me that she was writing a book of her own about Irving. So I gave up the idea. (Miss Shearer's book was never published, and I later wrote *Thalberg*.)

Discouraged, I explained my plight to Bob Yeager, who could have been a borscht belt comedian if he hadn't become a press agent. He told me story after story about Harry Cohn, all of them hilarious. I resolved to pursue Cohn's life despite the inherent difficulties. Putnam's offered me a $4,000 advance for what would become a two-year project.

To my surprise, those who feared talking about Harry Cohn during his lifetime proved free and open a decade after his death.

My research dovetailed conveniently with my duties as a Holly-wood reporter. Whenever I finished an interview, I asked, "Did you know Harry Cohn?" Quite often the question evoked a flood of memories. Frequently I heard a comment such as, "He was a tough son of a bitch, but by God, I did my best work for him."

The mosaic gradually took shape, but I lacked a comprehensive pattern. That was supplied by a rare gentleman, Sidney Buchman.

For a dozen years, Buchman served as the writing genius behind many of Columbia's most important films. Cohn respected him as he did no other studio employee. One of the tragedies of Cohn's life was being forced to fire Buchman in the wake of the blacklist. Buchman vanished from public view. When the McCarthy era ended, Charlie Feldman hired Buchman to produce *The Group*. I met him in New York during that period, and we had three four-hour lunches at the Carlyle Hotel, where he was staying. A remarkably sensitive, insightful man, Buchman poured out his memories of "the man with the danc-ing china-blue eyes." The enigma of this most private man began to dissipate, and I could see him whole. Tragically, Buchman's career never recovered, and he retired to Cannes, where he died virtually penniless in 1975.

The most bizarre of my interviews for *King Cohn* took place in the empty bar of the Friars Club in Beverly Hills. Johnny Roselli, who had been the Chicago mob's West Coast ambassa-dor since bootlegging days, had heard of my project and had asked to see me. He was a devilishly handsome man with a tanned face and white hair (he was called "the Silver Fox" by his fellow mobsters), and he spoke in quiet but persuasive tones.

"I want to tell you about Harry Cohn," he said, and for two hours he related his tale of friendship and betrayal. Roselli's story appears in Part V, Chapter 6, with his name changed to Charlie Lombard; he'd requested anonymity because at the time he was courting a famous singer whose parents disapproved of him.

Johnny's colorful history continued after our meeting. He was revealed as one of the Mafia figures hired by the CIA to assassinate Fidel Castro. Johnny was later nailed by the feds for taking part in a card-cheating scam at the Friars Club. After serving time, he ended up in Florida, where he incurred the disfavor of the mob. His body was found in an oil drum floating in Biscayne Bay.

One of my later interviews for *King Cohn* was with Danny Kaye, who had eulogized Harry at the funeral. We spoke in the rehearsal room for Kaye's CBS television show, and I confessed to being unable to know when to stop in my research.

"How many people have you interviewed?" Kaye demanded.

"Two hundred and fifty," I replied.

"You've got the story. Write it."

I did. I wrote 500 pages, then edited out a third, so the narrative would move as briskly as a Columbia picture. Kaye had been right. After *King Cohn* was published, many people told me: "You should have talked to me before you wrote the book." But only once did I hear a story that I wished I had included, and it was to me by Mary Martin.

Mary had had an interview with Cohn after she had created a sensation singing at the Trocadero, then Hollywood's most popular nightspot. She sang number after number for Cohn in his office while he spent most of the time on the telephone. "Okay, okay," he said, "you sing fine, but you gotta get your nose fixed. It's too round, like W. C. Fields'."

Declining surgery, Mary went to New York and was cast in a Cole Porter musical, *Leave It to Me*, in which she became an immediate star with her show-stopping number, "My Heart Belongs to Daddy." One night she spotted Harry Cohn in the front row. She came to her exit line, "He treats it and treats it and then he repeats it . . . my Daddy he treats it so well." As she reached the side curtain, she circled her nose with her thumb and forefinger and pointed it directly at Harry Cohn.

The reaction to *King Cohn* was almost evenly split between those who thought I was too harsh on Harry and those who believed I was too soft. Budd Schulberg, whose film pioneer father had been humiliated by Cohn, wrote in *Life* magazine: " . . . Thomas may be too nice a guy to write the definitive book on Cohn. His efforts to immortalize him leave this jaundiced reader dry-eyed and wishing for more indignation and eager to give form and impact to the memorabilia."

The critical pro and con, the word-of-mouth retelling of the book's jokes, and the dedicated work of Putnam's publicist Eilleen Lottman helped create brisk sales of *King Cohn*—and then it all stopped. Putnam's ran out of books. I asked the publisher, Walter Minton, what had happened. He explained that he once met with Harry Cohn to discuss a book prize contest to be sponsored by Columbia. Cohn's comment: "What's in it for me?"

Minton told me: "I figured, 'Who'd want to read a book about such a son of a bitch?' So I ordered a modest printing." *King Cohn* was out of stock for six weeks, losing its sales momentum. However, Bantam had no such prejudice against Cohn, and the paperback sales zoomed.

Over the years Harry Cohn appears to have attracted the fame he never sought for himself. He is perceived as the epitome of the hard-driving, man-eating, buccaneering studio boss. Yet some of his old employees still bear respect for him. Says Jack Lemmon: "He may have been a tyrant, but by God, he loved movies and he knew how to make them. We could use a Harry Cohn today."

Some of the Cohn stories seem to have become part of the American legend. Red Skelton's funeral crack ("Give the people what they want, and they'll come out for it") is oft repeated. The Lord's Prayer story turned up in the play *Ma Rainey's Black Bottom*. I am sometimes asked, "Did Harry Cohn really wake up with a horse's head in his bed?" The confusion with the movie mogul in *The Godfather* is natural. Mario Puzo told me, "I didn't know anything about Hollywood, so I did my research in *King Cohn*."

And what would Harry Cohn think of Columbia Pictures today? The Gower Street studio that he created from the depths of Poverty Row now rents space to television series and independent films. Columbia Pictures is now owned by the Japanese and resides in the Culver City studio once ruled with absolute power by Cohn's old enemy, Louis B. Mayer. Is that a whirring we hear underground at Hollywood Cemetery?

This New Millennium edition contains two elements that had been removed from the first edition by Putnam's lawyers. First, they declined a list of the persons I interviewed for *King Cohn*, reasoning that those persons perhaps would not want to be associated with such a book. I have corrected that omission with a list that appears below.

In the final manuscript I had included a chapter I called "Rosebud," in which I offered some evidence that might help explain how Harry Cohn happened to turn out the way that he did. The chapter has been restored as this edition's Epilogue.

I remain in great debt to the following who contributed their memories to this portrait of Harry Cohn (some interview subjects requested that their names be withheld):

Edie Adams, Wilma Addie, Eddie Albert, Robert Aldrich, Richard Arlen, Max Arnow, Robert Arthur, Dorothy Arzner, Fred Astaire, George Axelrod, Lauren Bacall, Lucille Ball, Binnie Barnes, Ralph Bellamy, Jack Benny, Sam Bischoff, Dorothy Blair, Janet Blair, Michael Blankfort, Whitney Bolton, Ernest Borgnine, Bill Bowers, Lee Bowman, Mary Brandt, Jerry Bresler, Sam Briskin, Richard Brooks, Harry Joe Brown, Sidney Buchman, Larry Butler, Edward Buzzell, Irving Caesar, Frank Capra, Duncan Cassell, Bill Castle, Gower Champion, Marge Champion, Saul Chaplin, George Chasin, Mae Clarke, Jeanette Cohn, Robert Cohn, Claudette Colbert, Jack Cooper, Broderick Crawford, Bing Crosby, George Cukor, Robert Cummings, Tony Curtis, Bill Davidson, Muriel Davidson, John Derek, Walt Disney, Edward Dmytryk, D.A. Doran, Gordon Douglas, Bill Dozier, Eddie Dukoff, Irene Dunne, Mel Durslag, Elmer Dyer, Blake Edwards, Neely Edwards, Vince Edwards, Julius Epstein, William Fadiman, Peter Falk, Milt Feldman, Jose Ferrer, Jack Fiers, Glenn Ford, John Ford, Harry Foster, Y. Frank Freeman, Don Friedling, Mrs. Kramer Gaines, Martin Gang, George Glass, William Goetz, Phil Goldstone, Michael Gordon, Alex Gottlieb, Arnold Grant, Cary Grant, Kathryn Grant, William Haines, Barbara Hale, Al Hart, Howard Hawks, Mrs. Ben Hecht, Van Heflin, Alfred Hitchcock, Jerry Hoffman, Dona Holloway, Moe Howard, Rock Hudson, Helen Hunt, George Jessel, Garson

Kanin, Fred Karger, Harry Karl, Phil Karlson, Beldon Katleman, Sam Katzman, Millard Kaufman, Danny Kaye, Elia Kazan, Gene Kelly, Deborah Kerr, Richard Kline, Stanley Kramer, Norman Krasna, Mac Krim, Sue Carol Ladd, Evelyn Lane, Abe Lastfogel, Irving Lazar, Paul Lazarus, Charles Lederer, Jack Lemmon, Mervyn Leroy, D. Ross Letterman, Dorothy Lewis, Jerry Lewis, Anita Loos, Robert Lord, Jean Louis, Ida Lupino, Fred Mac-Murray, Morgan Maree, Frances Marion, Groucho Marx, Mary McCall Jr., Leo McCarey, Joel McCrea, Rouben Mamoulian, Wilt Melnick, Ann Miller, Irving Mills, Robert Mitchum, Chester Morris, George Murphy, Kim Novak, Edmond O'Brien, Pat Offer, Dennis O'Keefe, Tony Owens, Larry Parks, Joe Pasternak, Bill Perlberg, Milt Pickman, James Poe, Otto Preminger, Connie Wald Prinzmetal, Lew Rachmil, Luise Rainer, Aldo Ray, Donna Reed, Debbie Reynolds, Ted Richmond, Irving Riskin, Stanley Roberts, Cliff Robertson, Eugene Rodney, Sid Rogell, John Roselli, Robert Rossen, Lester Roth, Harry Ruby, Rosalind Russell, Oscar Saul, Mildred Missic Schermer, Joe Schoenfeld, Budd Schulberg, George Seaton, Rosalind Shaffer, Artie Shaw, Walter Shenson, Victor Sherman, Louis Shur, George Sidney, Lillian Burns Sidney, Phil Silvers, Frank Sinatra, Sid Skolsky, Edward Small, Lou Smith, Ann Sothern, Sam Spiegel, Barbara Stanwyck, Ralph Staub, Rod Steiger, Doris Stein, Herb Stein, Herb Stern, George Stevens, Inger Stevens, James Stewart, Morris Stoloff, John Strauss, John Sturges, Gloria Swanson, Jo Swerling Jr., Jonie Tapps, Dan Taradash, Bill Thomas, Danny Thomas, Lee Tracy, Virginia Van Upp, King Vidor, Peter Viertel, Josef von Sternberg, Joseph Walker, John Wayne, Bill West, Douglas Whitney, Arthur Wilde, Cornel Wilde, Billy Wilder, Fay Wray, Jane Wyatt, Bob Yeager, Loretta Young, Fred Zinnemann, and Adolph Zukor.

Bob Thomas
Encino, California
January 2000

PROLOGUE

*F*ebruary 27, 1958. Midmorning routine in the executive building of Columbia Studios. The clack of typewriter keys cutting stencils as secretaries copied dialogue created an hour earlier. In subterranean projection booths, the whirr of machines unreeling evidence of the previous day's filming. Writers gossiping with other writers and sipping cardboard-tasting coffee. Executives scanning *Daily Variety* and *Hollywood Reporter* for items outlined in red, those concerning Columbia. Messenger boys padding from office to office with intra-studio mail. Outside on Gower Street, a shining day.

A scream echoed through the halls.

"He's dead!"

Down the corridors, from one floor to the next, the scream and cry repeated: "He's dead!" Secretaries sobbing, unbelieving. Executives meeting in the hall, faces ashen. Was it true? Yes, the news had just come from Phoenix: Harry Cohn was dead. Heart attack. It was incomprehensible. For thirty-five years Harry Cohn was Columbia and Columbia was Harry Cohn. Now he was dead.

A friend called Rita Hayworth at her home in Beverly Hills. She had fought with Cohn over the years, but now she could feel only sorrow and regret. Frank Sinatra, whose career had been given new life by Cohn, heard the news at a film studio. "I can't believe it," said Sinatra. "I knew Harry was sick. But he was so strong, so vital—"

Jack Lemmon tuned in his car radio as he drove to an interview at Lucey's restaurant. He commented after his arrival, "I suppose a lot of people will be saying, 'There goes the last of the ogres.' I want to tell you something: I had great respect and fondness for Harry. I'm going to miss him. And the studio is going to miss him—deeply."

News of Cohn's death reached Aldo Ray at his home in the San Fernando Valley. He was greatly concerned. Had he helped weaken Cohn's heart during a violent encounter in the studio barbershop?

Lew Meltzer, a writer whose association with Cohn had been both intimate and violent, was paged at the Chicago airport. Ben Kahane, a Columbia executive, was on the telephone: "I want you to know before you hear it on the radio."

"Charlie's dead?" said Meltzer, meaning Cohn's great antagonist Charles Vidor.

"No—Harry."

Meltzer had no heart to continue to New York, where he was to research a movie. Kahane urged him: "Keep going. Don't even come back for the funeral. It would only embarrass you."

Glenn Ford picked up a newspaper in Paris, where he was finishing a film. "I thought Harry was indestructible," he said incredulously. That night he flew to Hollywood for the funeral. William Holden received a telephone call from Columbia's man in Hong Kong. Holden's reaction: shock and disbelief.

Sidney Buchman, the one film maker Cohn trusted above all others, was now exiled in New York. He bought a newspaper and saw the portrait of Harry Cohn on the front page. It was the official photograph, the only one Cohn would allow to be issued by the studio. The vitality shone through, especially in the eyes. The Man with the Dancing China-Blue Eyes, Buchman had always called him, and those eyes could utterly beguile or flash like lightning.

An executive brought the news to John Ford on the set of *The Last Hurrah*. Ford was near collapse. "I'm dismissing the company," he said.

"But you can't do that; it's never been done at Columbia!" the executive protested.

"It's being done now," said Ford.

Kim Novak was on a nearby stage, acting in *Bell, Book and Candle* with James Stewart. When she heard of Cohn's death, she rushed in tears to her dressing room. Production was halted until after the lunch break. Then the director, Richard Quine, addressed the company: "If I knew Harry Cohn—and I believe I did—I think the one thing he would want us to do is to go on working."

In the executive building, Michael Blankfort had heard the screams of the secretaries. With other writers he had discussed the grave news; then he returned to his own office for reflection. He could not conceive that this electric force, with whom he had contended over a dozen screenplays, was gone. He thought he might gain some perspective by visiting Cohn's office.

Incredibly, the outer office was empty. Even during Cohn's rare absences from the studio, it had always been occupied by two or three secretaries. Now the desks were unoccupied; the room was silent. Even more surprising, the massive door to Cohn's office, which bore no knob on the outside and could be opened only by a buzzer signal, was unlocked.

Blankfort walked inside. The long, intimidating office was the same as he had seen it hundreds of times before. The ancient piano by the door, where Cole Porter and Jerome Kern had tried out their melodies for Cohn, the former song plugger. To the left, the door to Cohn's favorite sanctum, his projection room. To the right, the windows through which he checked on departures of his employees.

The long walk to the upraised, semicircular desk—many an agent or actor had been defeated before he had traveled its length, just as Cohn had been whipped as he approached the desk of Mussolini, from whom he got the idea for the office. On the desk, the telephones and the interoffice speaker keyboard, which, a Columbia worker observed, Cohn played like a carillon. Behind the desk, row on row of gold statuettes, representing the uncommon amount of Academy Awards bestowed on Columbia films.

Blankfort sat in the chair he usually occupied during story conferences. He contemplated the empty seat behind the massive desk.

The silence of the immense office was profound. The passing of one who was not an ordinary man, thought Blankfort, creates a great emptiness. And Harry Cohn was not an ordinary man.

On the day of the funeral the leaden March sky weighed heavily on the Hollywood Hills, and by early afternoon, when the mourners were arriving in large numbers, a steady rain was falling. A field of umbrellas bobbed before the entrance to the newly completed Stages 12 and 14, where the memorial services were being held.

The event had been scheduled for Sunday, which served the dual purpose of allowing the largest possible attendance while not interfering with production at the studio. Columbia press agents were stationed at strategic locations to direct more important personages to favored positions and to issue fact sheets to members of the press.

The mourners came in numbers, the famous and the unknown. There were Cohn's fellow pioneers of the film industry, men who had striven to destroy little Columbia in its vulnerable years. There were directors and stars, those who had performed their best work for Cohn, only to be alienated by his fierceness. There were craftsmen from the back lots and the shops, secretaries and makeup men and seamstresses, workers from whom Cohn had exacted intense loyalty to Columbia Pictures. Their faces mirrored bewilderment and concern; some had known no other boss for thirty years, and they worried for their futures. (Their fears were real; many were swept out of the studio by the new administration.)

The crowd filed into the combined Stages 12 and 14—there was no Stage 13 at Columbia—to witness a study in Hollywood Gothic. Folding chairs filled the vast length of floor space. A stage rose at one end, and on it rested the casket, blanketed with white orchids. Hundreds of floral displays formed a fragrant wall fifteen feet high. Each had been inspected for freshness upon arrival at the studio gate. The reason for this was a comment by Cohn as he sat before the bier of another film pioneer, L. K. Sidney, five days before. "Look at those wilted flowers," Cohn muttered to his wife. "Those florists shouldn't be allowed to get away with that. When I go, make sure the flowers are fresh."

Near the casket stood a heroic replica of the Columbia Pictures trademark, a draped maiden in a Statue of Liberty pose.

The widow Cohn sat closest to the casket, accompanied by her two young sons, backs stiff in their blue military-school uniforms, and her daughter.

Schubert's *Ave Maria* was sung by a handsome soprano who was unknown to most of her listeners. She had been under contract to Columbia, undergoing extensive vocal training with the prospect of starring in a remake of *One Night of Love*. Month after month, year after year, she had continued trilling in the Columbia music department, but the film was never made. Harry Cohn's funeral was to be her first and last performance at the studio, and her name was lost to history.

After the song came the solemnities. They were conducted by two comedians.

First, Danny Kaye stepped to the microphone, his face grave. He had been asked by the widow to deliver the eulogy, and he agreed, if he could enlist expert help in preparing it. Help came from Clifford Odets, whose portrait of a megalomaniacal studio boss in *The Big Knife* was believed to be based on Harry Cohn; in later years he had written the script of the unfilmed *Joseph and His Brethren* for Cohn. Odets and Kaye had collaborated for five hours the night before the funeral, and this is what was said:

How short is the time of man.

We've come here today, dressed in solemnity, both in body and mind, in a final tribute to an unusual and remarkable man named Harry Cohn.

We sit here on this great stage, perhaps very fittingly, we sit here on this great stage of the studio that Harry built, in itself a monument to some of his more remarkable qualities.

Without irreverence, this was Harry Cohn's cathedral. This is where he lived, and worked, and dreamed, and this is where his energies, ambition, and vision gave reality to those dreams. This is where the fierceness of the flame that was within him burned some and warmed others.

The story is well known—even legend—in its way of how Harry Cohn came from the sidewalks of New York and entering some remote back door of Hollywood and with nothing—nothing but his two bare hands—quickly took his part and place in the making of motion picture history.

The pictures he made along the way, the stars he found and developed—these are parts of the legend already familiar to most of us here today.

Harry performed most of what he proposed to perform in life. As tragically brief as life is, he lived nevertheless for two-thirds of a century; he lived long enough to enjoy the fruits of his extraordinary labor. I think few men enjoyed life so fully as Harry did.

His was truly a lust for life. Probably there was not an hour of his life that he did not live deeply and fully with an energy and a zest which, in themselves, are usually the distinguishing marks of a gifted person.

Men cannot be all things to all men.

They cannot, unfortunately, be all things even to themselves, but in this constant battle of man with himself, Harry emerged with a true sense of what you are and let the chips fall where they may.

Harry was always himself—always. He was a large-scale businessman and if, like most businessmen, he did not choose to succumb or go under, he was sometimes capable of reacting strongly—even harshly.

We have felt his anger, his defiance, his stubbornness, his pride, but many of us have felt his warmth, his understanding, his gentleness—and some of us even his love.

The activity of developing stars, producers, and directors was a matter of immense personal solace to Harry. Himself little educated, he admired, almost to a fanatic degree, talent. Talent itself was a quality which bred in him a deep respect, almost as though the gifted human being was set aside, as if God had put a special mark on his forehead.

Harry was, in his trade, a master—and a master in business, art, or whatnot is one who masters, and Harry Cohn was not afraid to master.

It doesn't mean that he didn't listen to those who were expert in their field. The attitude of Harry behind his desk—lips pursed, head half bent, listening shrewdly—is a very very familiar one.

We remember, too, his lack of posturing, his frequent self-deprecation, his wry humor, and his sudden flashes of tender concern for others, which he chose to cover with a bulldog gruffness, rather than reveal a strong streak of sentiment in his nature.

Yes, Harry was a complex and gifted man. It was bracing to know him—stimulating. His appetite for anything under the sun quickened yours. It cannot have been easy for a man of Harry Cohn's joy of life to reconcile himself to mortality. It cannot have been easy.

But long ago, sensing man's essential loneliness—man's need—man's need of family, of love, Harry married a woman he loved and respected and from that marriage will come his true immortality, for from that marriage have come three beautiful children, intelligent and maturing, who will carry some parts of their father and mother wherever they go. This is the legacy that he leaves—far beyond the legacy of wealth and fame. This is the legacy of his immortality.

Harry Cohn's breadth and size were of an older day that we shall not see again. I am glad that I knew Harry Cohn and his brawny vigor—he was an unforgettable man.

Kaye's eulogy had been unannounced. John Ford, seated in the front row, turned to Abe Lastfogel, head of the William Morris talent agency, and inquired, "Who is that intelligent young rabbi?"

Next, Danny Thomas approached the microphone. He had been asked by Mrs. Cohn to deliver some religious sentiments for a ceremony that was designed as nondenominational. Thomas, a Roman Catholic of deep religious conviction, consulted his parish priest, who granted permission for reading of the Catholic burial service, with the omission of the name of Jesus Christ. Thomas also delivered the Twenty-third Psalm.

No reference had been made in any of the ceremonies of the fact that Harry Cohn had been born a Jew.

It was over. The casket was removed to nearby Hollywood Cemetery, which Cohn had selected for his tomb only two weeks before. The crowd milled out of the huge sound-stage doors, raising umbrellas against the unfriendly sky. Now a torrent was falling, and the clouds crackled with lightning.

Two thousand persons had come to Columbia that day, March 2, 1958. It was the largest crowd ever to attend a funeral in Hollywood. On his television program that week, Red Skelton made the comment that was to become legend: "Well, it only proves what they always say—give the public something they want to see, and they'll come out for it."

The event had been held against Cohn's wishes. The first stipulation of his Last Will and Testament, which was dated thirteen days before his death, stated: "I direct and request that no funeral services be held at the time of my death." Columbia executives convinced Mrs. Cohn to authorize the services, arguing that the passing of a man of her husband's stature in the community should not go unmarked. Only in death could an order of Harry Cohn's be countermanded.

Who was this man with the fierce inner flame that "burned some and warmed others"? He was a thousand men to a thousand persons.

He was the last of the pirates (Everett Riskin, producer). He was a lovable old pirate (Artie Shaw, clarinetist, producer). He was a pirate, but he got things done (Richard Brooks, director, writer). He was a pirate with everything that implies except the romantic appeal; yet he was more likable than many of those in Hollywood who weren't piratical (Rouben Mamoulian, director). He was gruff, but not unfair (Ann Sothern, actress). He was a tough adversary, but everybody's got to fight in this business (William Holden, actor). He felt the guilt and fears of an uneducated man (Garson Kanin, writer, director). He had a ruthless contempt for manners, which was basic in the East Side philosophy (Michael Blankfort, writer). He was a great showman, and he was a son of a bitch (George Jessel, comedian). He was a sadistic son of a bitch (Hedda Hopper, columnist). For all his crusty ways, he had a soft heart (Wilma Addie, telephone operator). He was sensitive, like a little boy (Mervyn Le Roy, director). He was the kind of a man whose nod and handshake were worth more than a contract drawn up by a score of Philadelphia lawyers (John Ford, director). He liked to live (Jack Fier, production manager). He never learned how to live (Samuel Goldwyn, producer). He was the meanest man I ever knew—an unreconstructed dinosaur (Budd Schulberg, writer). His toughness was a facade, part of a big act (Gene Kelly, actor, director). He enjoyed playing Harry Cohn; he liked to be the biggest bug in the manure pile (Elia Kazan, director). He could be the most terrifying tyrant, or he could be a petulant child (Janet Blair, actress). He was absolutely ice-cold in his self-interest, but could reasonably charm someone in his inelegant way (Norman Krasna, writer). He was a square shooter (Ida Lupino, actress, director). He was straight across the board (Cliff Robertson, actor). He was rough and tough, but you always knew where you stood with him (José Ferrer, actor). He was a friend, a real friend (Frank Sinatra, actor). He was a great friend and a great enemy (Louis Shurr, agent). He had a great knack for making you dislike him, but also a great quality for making you forgive and forget (Leo McCarey, director). He was a real buccaneer, with enormous aggressiveness (Dore Schary, producer). He was a song plugger and a louse; later he became a multimillionaire, and success didn't change him (Lou Holtz, comedian). He was not all good and not all bad; he had star quality (Lewis Milestone, director). He wanted to pull everyone down to his level (Edward Dmytryk, director). He could be rude, crude, overbearing and seemingly insensitive, but he helped others (Jack Lemmon, actor). He gambled on people, never on himself (Frank Capra, director). He was very active as a young man, very ambitious; obviously he was going to get someplace (Adolph Zukor, executive). He was rough, but he had tremendous heart (José Iturbi, pianist). He was crude and hard, but something underneath was very human (Lew Ayres, actor). He had great taste—it was blind, instinctive—but it was taste (Rosalind Russell, actress). He was the Wandering Jew; he had no soul (Sam Bischoff, producer). He was a Jekyll-Hyde; socially he could be charming (Moe Howard, comedian). He was an entertaining fellow, very light on his feet and always on the run (Bing Crosby, actor). He could be cruel, kind, giving, taking, despicable, benevolent, compassionate, and malevolent, all at the same time (Glenn Ford, actor). He was a great showman; he had guts (Otto Preminger, director). In many ways he was an impossible man, but he had complete belief in himself (Darryl Zanuck, company president). He was an okay guy (John Huston, director). He was a son of a bitch (John Wayne, actor).

Harry Cohn was all these things, and more.

I

Beginnings:
1891–1920

• • • • •

IN THE BEGINNING IS A SNEEZE. Thomas Alva Edison takes a motion picture of Fred Ott's sneeze, and an industry is born. Drop in a penny, turn the crank, and see the funny man sneeze. The public crowds into kinetoscope parlors to peep for a minute at pictures that move. Besides *The Sneeze*, they see Sandow the Strong Man, Annie Oakley, trained bears, a tooth extraction, and *How the Porto Rico Girls Entertain Uncle Sam's Soldiers*.

Koster and Bial's Music Hall on Herald Square accompanies its vaudeville with Mr. Edison's latest marvel, the vitascope, which actually projects moving pictures on a screen. The date: April 20, 1896.

In 1902, T. L. Talley opens his Electric Theater at 262 South Main Street in Los Angeles. He advertises: "An Hour's Amusement and Genuine Fun for 10 CENTS ADMISSION. Evenings 7:30 to 10:30." The following year Edwin Porter tells a story with moving pictures: *The Great Train Robbery*. When George Barnes appears on the screen and fires his six-shooter into the theater, men and women scream.

The same year: the advent of commerce. The first film exchange is established to act as middleman in shipping movies from producer to exhibitor. By 1907 there are 100 exchanges.

There is gold to be won. Edison, Biograph, and Vitagraph stake first claim; they form the Motion Picture Patents Company, which controls cameras and projectors. The Patents Company exacts a royalty from all producers and exhibitors using motion picture equipment. The films made by Edison, Biograph, and Vitagraph are rented at high rates.

The gold is too alluring, and some refuse to pay tribute. Cameras are stolen. Projectors are bootlegged. Negatives are duplicated and sold at cut-rate prices. Prints are bicycled from theater to theater while only one rental fee is remitted.

The Patents Company strikes back—midnight raids, sabotage, subpoena.

Solution for independent producers lay in escaping the trust. They flee to California, where the Patents Company detectives can't find them. Anyway, it's only a hop across the border to the safety of Mexico, if the detectives do come. Each week new film makers arrive in Los Angeles, their luggage heavy with pirated movie gear. They disperse to Edendale, to Universal City, to Culver City, to Hollywood.

A Democrat enters the White House in 1913, and the trust is broken by government action. The film makers stay in California. They have sunshine and scenery, and the New York office is 3,000 miles away. It seems like paradise.

The fetching lass with corkscrew curls is known only as the Biograph Girl in the films she makes, two each week. Then Carl Laemmle of Independent Motion Picture (IMP) Company spirits her away and proclaims her to be Florence Lawrence, now the IMP Girl. For better or worse, the star system is born.

The system grows fast. Adolph Zukor pays Mary Pickford $1,000 a week, then $2,000 a week. Everyone is bidding for Charlie Chaplin. Mutual Film Corporation wins by handing him a check for $10,000 every Saturday for a year, with an added $150,000 for writing his name on the contract. Zukor makes a new two-year deal for America's Sweetheart: $10,000 every Monday, a $300,000 bonus on profits, her own studio, choice in scripts and casting, her name in the biggest type in all ads, plus passage by parlor car across the continent for her and her mother.

This is not a business for the dilettante, the aesthete, the penny-ante player. They are shouldered aside by a new breed: Carl Laemmle, the German-born bookkeeper for an Oshkosh clothing store; Adolph Zukor from Hungary, once a sweeper in a fur store; Samuel Goldfish, late of Warsaw, glove salesman; William Fox, a cloth sponger from Hungary; the Schenck brothers from Russia, Nick and Joe, who ran drugstores in the Bronx; Marcus Loew, a furrier born of immigrant parents in Manhattan; Lewis Selznick from Kiev, a jewelry salesman; Louis B. Mayer, junk dealer, born near Minsk.

They have at least two things in common: they know what the public wants; they are tough. Any pretender to their ranks would require the same degree of toughness.

● ● ● ● ●

I

AN ACCOUNT OF THE ORIGINS
AND EARLY YEARS OF HARRY COHN

*T*he immigrant hordes that packed into Manhattan's East
Side during the closing decades of the nineteenth century produced millionaires on both sides of the law; hoodlum empires
and industrial fortunes were spawned amid the tumult of the city
streets. Harry Cohn, born in New York City on July 23, 1891,
chose to operate in a legal manner. Although in later years he
enjoyed entertaining Frank Costello and other mobsters in his
New York hotel suite and often hinted darkly of underworld
connections, Cohn was impeccable in his business dealings. His
income tax return was a model of rectitude. His stewardship of
Columbia Pictures Corporation, of which he was founder, largest
stockholder, and chief officer, was thoroughly honest. When disgruntled stockholders charged mismanagement in a lawsuit,
Cohn satisfactorily answered each of the accusations.

Cohn adopted the speech and mannerisms of a gangster, but
he could not operate like one. The reason was that he could not
face the possibility of being caught. He was the son of immigrant parents who believed in unceasing toil and scrupulous honesty. If a Cohn son swerved from that code, he was thrashed
severely by his father or mother, or both.

Joseph Cohn came from Germany, his wife, Bella, from a village in Russia, near the Polish border. They met in the New
World, married, and produced four sons—Max, Jacob, Harry,
and Nathaniel—and then a daughter, Anna. They lived in a four-
room apartment on Eighty-eighth Street, across from Joseph
Cohn's tailoring shop. The mothers of both parents shared the
apartment.

Like most immigrant families, the Cohns knew hardship.
Jack Cohn recalled late in life that he and other members of the
family had shared mush from a common pot. Harry Cohn, who

rarely spoke of his early years, once explained why he worked so hard as a studio boss: "So *my* sons won't have to sleep with their grandmother."

The Cohn household was matriarchal, but not because Bella Cohn dominated her husband. Joseph Cohn was a stern, uncommunicative man whose life seemed devoted to the piles of clothing that lay in his dimly lighted shop. His children knew him but distantly or in flashes of temper; he was quick to discipline his sons for breaking family rules. Bella Cohn tried to protect the boys from undue beatings by their father, but she did not stand in the way of proper discipline; nor was she reluctant to administer it herself.

Joseph Cohn could not be reached by his children, but between him and Bella Cohn there was understanding and devotion. She deferred to him in most matters, not merely because she was his wife but because of her station. She was a Russian; he was a German; in the strata of Jewry in America, his homeland held preeminence. The Germans were educated, well spoken, the first to emigrate; they ran their own businesses, even entered the professions, and lived on the upper East Side. The Russians were unschooled peasants, who spoke Yiddish and worked at menial jobs; they were relegated to the downtown slums.

"But of course you're right," Bella Cohn often told her husband. "You're high-class. You're from Germany." This attitude also extended to the two grandmothers during the sixteen years they dwelled with the Cohn family.

Joseph Cohn's shop specialized in tailoring and altering uniforms for the policemen who worked out of the Yorkville station around the corner. The Cohns knew scores of policemen by name, and this was also a factor in keeping the sons on the right side of the law. Cops lounged about the shop day and night and sometimes were caught at it. When he was head of the New York City Police Board from 1895 to 1897, Theodore Roosevelt made a practice of prowling streets on rainy nights to find officers who were under shelter when they should have been patrolling. More than once he flushed out a gathering in Joe Cohn's tailoring shop.

Bella helped in the shop and also supplied the business acumen that her husband lacked. He was content to carry the policemen's accounts indefinitely. Not Bella.

"Where are you going, Mama?" Joseph Cohn asked as his wife mounted a bicycle at the curb.

She explained that since it was the first of the month, the day policemen were paid, she was going to make her rounds to collect the accounts receivable. When her husband urged her to leave the delinquent customers alone, she replied, "And who will feed your children?"

Off she flew, tracking down every Yorkville officer whose account was overdue. She knew where each lived, and she was not reluctant to storm into a bedroom and demand payment, rousing a policeman from sleep after his night shift.

The Cohn home was immaculate. Aided by the two grandmothers, Bella Cohn kept the floors spotless and the furniture without a trace of dust. As the family fortunes improved, so did the cuisine. The Cohn apartment was pungent with the smell of spicy stews. A mountain of dough remained on the kitchen table. When the Cohn sons returned from school, Bella Cohn baked fresh coffee cakes for them.

Like most Jewish immigrants of their generation, Joe and Bella Cohn wanted their sons to be educated. It was a severe disappointment to the parents that only Max, the eldest, continued into high school. Ironically, he was the least successful of the brothers in later life.

Bella Cohn assumed the task of trying to instill a religious spirit in her children; her husband, being German, had less concern for Orthodoxy. As a concession to his wife, he attended 7 A.M. services at temple before opening his shop on Saturday. Bella attended both Friday night and Saturday, and she insisted that her children take instruction in the faith. At the age of thirteen, each son had his Bar Mitzvah.

For Max, Jack, Harry, and Nat, the procedure was the same. Friends and relatives gathered at temple in their best Sabbath clothes. Mama Cohn beamed from the front row, her reluctant husband at her side. As her son stood before the congregation and proclaimed his manhood, she wept softly.

Afterward the Cohn apartment rang with shouts of joy. Guests came laden with presents, which formed stacks on the big bed in Mama's bedroom. Cousins moved through the throng offering sweet cakes and steaming black coffee. Bella Cohn shushed the gathering and brought her son to the center of the living room. At her insistence he donned the prayer shawl, the tallis, and repeated in Hebrew his profession of faith for those who had missed the temple ceremony: "Hear, O Israel, the Lord is our God, the Lord is one. . . ."

For Harry Cohn, his Bar Mitzvah was to be the apex of his religious experience. To his mother's despair, he avoided attending temple in later years. He was more concerned with secular matters.

A year after his Bar Mitzvah, Harry Cohn was impatient to join the world of commerce. His brother Jack, two years older and his rival in all things, left school at fourteen. Harry reached his decision to follow Jack's example one day as he walked home from school bearing a report card blemished by poor grades. He knew what would happen when his father saw them. So he dropped the card down a sewer and altered his course to find a job.

His tenor voice, clear if unsure, was sufficient to win him a position as a choir singer in a play, *The Fatal Wedding*, produced by Al Woods. Harry returned home that evening and faced his father's demand that he produce his report card. Harry confessed he had thrown it away.

"But you can't hit me," he added quickly. "I got a job."

His work as choir singer lasted a short time, and Harry Cohn proceeded to other employment. He was shipping clerk for a music publishing house, Francis, Day and Hunter. He sold furs— "hot" furs, he claimed later in his life. He hustled pool at Bergman's Pool Hall at 116th Street and Lenox Avenue. He and his brother Jack, both expert bowlers, sometimes picked up money as bowling hustlers. Visiting bowling alleys where they weren't known, they posed as beginners, sometimes acting drunk. Their skill suddenly improved when local bowlers invited them to a match at a sizable wager.

During this period Harry Cohn often absented himself from home for long periods. But always he returned to tell Bella Cohn of his adventures, to be nourished by her robust meals, and to be admonished to walk in the paths of righteousness.

All her sons paid tribute to Bella. One of Jack Cohn's first jobs was as delivery boy for Regal Shoes. He pocketed the change given to him for carfare and walked long blocks to deliver packages of shoes. His aim was to save enough to buy his mother a lavaliere. When he had amassed $4, he went shopping at jewelry stores and found a necklace with an amethyst pendant. It cost $5, and Harry Cohn happily supplied the extra dollar.

The presentation was to be made at Bella's coffee klatch, which she held in the apartment each afternoon at four. All the nearby female relatives appeared in their starched white aprons, and even Joseph Cohn closed his shop early.

"A lavaliere? What is a lavaliere?" asked Cousin Yetta. When it was explained to her, she nodded her head and said, "So *that* is a lavaliere!"

Bella Cohn opened the package amid expectant eyes. Her own eyes brimmed as she caught a glimpse of the violet stone and then held it to her throat. It was a rare and golden moment in her life. Even though they hadn't finished school and refused to go to temple, her sons were beginning to achieve.

2

THE BRIEF CAREER OF EDWARDS AND RUBY: THEIR ADVENTURES, AND A LATER MEETING THAT BEARS SIGNIFICANCE

CLAREMONT THEATER
174th Street and Third Avenue

Those Two Clever and Popular Vaudeville Entertainers

EDWARDS	and	RUBY
Harry Cohn		Harry Rubinstein

Will Play and Sing All of the Very
Latest Selections and Song Hits
of the Big Publishers

Mr. Rubinstein is the best PIANO MAN in his line, and he would rather play than eat. And the same can be said of Mr. Cohn— only that he is a singer that can sing, and he is not a bit backward about it.

Don't forget we also have a few of the
very latest Photoplays

Admission All Seats 5 Cents

*T*he 1912 playbill advertised an unequal partnership. Edwards was indeed a singer who could sing, but not well. Ruby, although no virtuoso, could maintain the rhythm of the ragtime tunes, and his repertoire was enormous. As Harry Rubinstein, he had been a popular figure in the social pattern of his Bronx neighborhood. He was often invited to weddings, Bar Mitzvahs, and parties, which he enlivened with his piano playing. Cohn, who was living in the area with a married couple, heard of Rubinstein and sought him out. Cohn proposed a partnership, and Rubinstein, having no other immediate prospects, agreed.

Ruby, as he was to call himself thereafter, heard that a pianist was needed at the Claremont Theater. Like many nickelodeons of the period, it was a converted store seating 300, the maximum allowed under city licensing. Ruby applied for the job, proposing that his partner be hired to sing along with the tinted song slides that interspersed the two- and three-reelers, affording the projectionist time to load the cans of film. The proprietor agreed to a tryout.

Cohn decided the fate of the new partnership should not rest solely on the artistic whim of the proprietor. Both Cohn and Ruby were affiliate members of the Wendover Avenue Gang, a band of local toughs. Cohn induced members of the gang to infiltrate the Claremont on the day of the audition. Ruby's piano received the acclaim of a Paderewski, and Edwards' songs drew enough applause to satisfy Chauncey Olcott. Not only did the gang members respond lustily, but they also elbowed customers sitting next to them into a similar response. Edwards and Ruby were hired.

Although Edwards received first billing, Ruby did most of the work. He labored at the piano during most of the afternoon and evening; Cohn dropped in four or five times to sing with the illustrated slides. Their pay was $28 per week—$17 for the pianist, $11 for the singer. From the start of the relationship, Cohn assumed the managerial capacity. He dealt with the management of the Claremont. And he decided the team should leave the nickelodeon after five months to venture into the show world.

Cohn and Ruby combined their resources for train fare to Baltimore, arriving with only a few dollars. Cohn took over the task of finding work. It was a rare instance in which his salesmanship brought negative results, possibly because of the nature of what he was selling.

Cohn sought means to husband their dwindling dollars. He discovered a cafeteria-style restaurant, named Buck's, where patrons declared what they had eaten as they exited, and the cashier charged them accordingly. Cohn consumed meals costing as much as 35 cents, but his parting comment to the cashier was: "Cup of coffee and a piece of pie." The charge was 10 cents. Ruby ate more frugally and paid the correct amount.

"You're a soft son of a bitch," Cohn told Ruby one evening as they returned to their room after another fruitless day of job seeking. "You're never going to get anywhere unless you learn to be tough. You've been spending too goddam much on dinner, and you gotta stop it. Now look. Tonight we're going to eat at Buck's, and you do exactly what I do."

They returned to the restaurant, and Ruby reasoned that if he were going to jail, he might as well eat his fill. Both he and Cohn consumed dinners that would have cost 45 cents. When they finished, Cohn muttered, "Follow me and do exactly what I do."

Cohn strode confidently to the cashier's stand. "I just had a drink of water," he announced, and he walked past.

Ruby followed and gulped, "Me, too." Miraculously, the cashier raised no issue. Ruby had almost reached the door when he felt a hand grasp his shoulder.

He turned around and stared at the stern face of a detective. Another had accosted Cohn. The two young men were drawn aside, and one of the detectives told them, "Look, fellows, we saw exactly what you did. We're not going to run you in now. But if we ever catch you inside that door again, we're going to put you in jail."

The fortunes of Edwards and Ruby became more bleak. Their funds had all but vanished, their source of cheap meals had been cut off, and no job was in sight. Cohn came to the room one day to find Ruby holding a $5 bill in one hand and a letter in the other.

"It's from my father," Ruby announced.

Cohn was jubilant until his partner added, "I'm sending it back."

"Sending it back!" exclaimed Cohn.

"That's right, Harry. My father can't afford to send me five dollars; he's living in a room over a Yiddish theater at two dollars a week. This five-spot means a lot to him. Besides, I want to show him I can make it on my own."

No amount of argument could dissuade him, and Cohn roared, "You'll never amount to anything."

"Maybe not, Harry," said Ruby. "But I'm still sending it back."

Suddenly their position brightened. Cohn located a job in the cabaret of the Hotel Plaza. They were to play and sing from 8 in the evening until 2 A.M. for the payment of $12 apiece and a club sandwich at midnight.

The cabaret manager was a bibulous man who enjoyed telling long, unfunny jokes. Cohn would shake with laughter at each fumbled punch line, but Ruby remained unamused until his partner muttered, "You son of a bitch, laugh your head off!" Ruby then feigned hilarity while Cohn roared, slapping the manager on the shoulder.

The engagement continued for three weeks and might have stretched longer except that the manager showed up sober one night and listened with care to the pair of entertainers he had hired. So ended the career of Edwards and Ruby.

When Cohn and Ruby returned to New York, they dissolved their partnership. But they still met each day. Ruby was hired to accompany the singing waiters at Gilligan's Historic Inn at Clason Point, the Bronx. He traveled to the job by trolley, boarding at 174th Street and Third Avenue. The conductor on the trolley was Harry Cohn.

When Ruby offered his nickel fare, his former partner refused it with a gesture that was to be characteristic of Cohn throughout his lifetime. It was a swift chop away from the body of the forearm, wrist straight and fingers joined. It communicated much in one sudden movement: put that nickel back in your pocket, Ruby; still playing the sucker, aren't you?; don't you know I can avoid ringing up your fare?; you're soft; you're never going to amount to anything.

Despite Cohn's predictions, Harry Ruby became one of the most successful song creators of his era, combining with Bert Kalmar to produce scores for many Broadway musicals. With the advent of the musical film, Kalmar and Ruby shifted to Hollywood, where they fashioned songs for all the leading companies, except Columbia.

Once Cohn sent for Ruby and offered him a song-writing contract. The terms were satisfactory, and Ruby almost signed. But memories returned of the Claremont Theater and Buck's in Baltimore and the Hotel Plaza cabaret. He returned the contract unsigned. He knew that working for Harry Cohn would produce misery.

The two old partners remained friends, and Cohn would often call Ruby from his Columbia office and command, "Come on, you son of a bitch, get your ass down here for lunch."

One evening Ruby received a telephone call at his Beverly Hills home. "Hey, pal," said Cohn in his warmest tones, "I want you to meet my girl; her name is Joan. How about inviting us for dinner tonight?"

"Sure, come on over," said Ruby. He had heard that Cohn, long separated from his wife, had been escorting a young actress named Joan Perry.

When Cohn arrived, Ruby instantly recognized his pride in the green-eyed beauty. Nor could there be doubt that she was genuinely fond of Cohn. After she had been introduced to Ruby and his wife, the two couples went to the living room for cocktails. Cohn could scarcely remove his eyes from Joan.

"Harry has been telling me all the things that happened when you and he were partners," she said to Ruby.

"Oh, yes?" Ruby replied. "'What did he tell you?"

"How the two of you got caught trying to get out of your bill in that restaurant in Baltimore." The mention of it brought laugher from all four.

"What else did he tell you?" Ruby asked.

"How you used to ride the streetcar when he was conductor," she said.

"Did he tell you that he wouldn't let me pay my fare?"

"Yes," she said, and again they laughed, Cohn most heartily of all.

"Did he tell you," added Ruby, "how much we were paid at the Claremont Theater?"

The smile disappeared from Cohn's face. He shot an annoyed glance at Ruby.

"No, he didn't," said Joan.

"Well, I'll tell you," Ruby continued. "Together we drew twenty-eight dollars a week. Harry got eleven, and I got seventeen."

"You're a goddam liar!" snapped Cohn, with no trace of levity in his voice.

Ruby took up the challenge: "Just a minute, Harry. You got eleven, and I got seventeen. I'll tell you why. I sat glued to that piano from one in the afternoon until eleven at night, with an hour off for what we called supper."

"Yeah, what about it?" Cohn said gruffly.

"What about it? You came by a few times during the day and night and sang some songs. And one night you had a girl up in Crotona Park and you came in so late the title slides melted."

"Very funny!" Cohn growled.

The discomfort of the moment was relieved when the butler appeared to announce that dinner was served. The two ladies led the way to the dining room. As the men followed them, Cohn tightened a grip on Ruby's arm and whispered threateningly, "Don't you *ever* tell her or anyone you made more money than I did!"

3
JACK COHN ENTERS THE INFANT INDUSTRY AND LEARNS THE VALUE OF
TRAFFIC IN SOULS

*J*ack was the first of the Cohn sons to join the motion picture business. He had been educated by Bella Cohn, as was brother Harry after him, in the benefits of hustle, and he applied those lessons in his first important job, at the Hampton Advertising Agency. He impressed his employers with his energy and his eagerness, and he soon advanced to more important positions.

But advertising held only temporary fascination for Jack Cohn. Like many New Yorkers, he had become addicted to the nickelodeons that had sprung up along Broadway and all around the town. His enthusiasm was shared by a fellow employee, Joseph Brandt.

Totally unalike, Jack Cohn and Joe Brandt became fast friends. Jack was stocky, pugnacious, accustomed to the language and tactics of the street. Joe was lean and ascetic. He was also the son of immigrants, but he had grown up in the less aggressive environment of Troy, New York. He had followed his parents' dictates and continued his schooling. While working at Hampton's from 1902 to 1906, he was studying law at New York University.

The two young advertising men talked long hours about the exciting possibilities to be found in the fast-growing movie business. But Joe Brandt aimed to practice law, and after qualifying for the New York Bar in 1906, he left his job at Hampton's and opened a law office. Jack Cohn remained at the agency until 1908, when he announced he was quitting. He had acquired a new job in the laboratory of Carl Laemmle's IMP Company.

Those were exciting times for a young man to be joining Laemmle. Bulbous, nearsighted, avuncular, the German-accented movie boss seemed like a village burgomaster. But Uncle Carl was in reality a fierce competitor, as the Motion Picture Patents Company was discovering. He pirated stars from the trust and fought it in the theaters and in the courts, eventually winning the battle.

Broad-shouldered Jack Cohn was an ideal candidate for bustling young IMP. He was destined not to remain in the lab; soon he was moving from department to department, absorbing everything he could learn about the functioning of a film studio. One of his achievements was the founding of the newsreel. As editor and producer of *Universal Weekly*, he conceived the idea of a regular quota of film based on news events around the world. His plan was to maintain photographers in key news-producing areas and have them report the events on film as they occurred.

As editor of IMP films, Jack Cohn provided an invaluable service to the economy-minded Laemmle. IMP directors were led to believe they were shooting one-reel films and hence were encouraged to be niggardly with film stock and production time. Through chicanery by the executives, the movies were actually released as two-reelers.

Jack Cohn discussed scenarios with directors and suggested expanded scenes. By judicious cutting, he could provide a finished product that would be double the length the directors originally intended. Thus, Laemmle got two reels for the price of one.

Jack Cohn's work brought him in close association with George Loane Tucker, an actor-director who had been making films for IMP release. Tucker had been impressed by racy Broadway plays, and he confided in Cohn his idea of making a picture about the white-slave trade. Cohn was enthusiastic. He was familiar with the subject; in his youth he had witnessed bordello raids by policemen who patronized his father's shop.

Tucker broached his idea to Laemmle. But Laemmle was more concerned with fighting the trust and his own rebelling partners, and he was not enthusiastic about Tucker's suggestion. He was especially dour when the director suggested a budget of $5,000, enough to film a dozen two-reelers. Laemmle waved Tucker away.

The idea of a white-slave picture still burned in Tucker's creative mind. He formed a conspiracy with four others in the company, including Jack Cohn. Tucker would shoot the film without the knowledge of Laemmle and his lieutenants. Each of the five plotters guaranteed $1,000 to a fund for purchase of the film if the IMP brass did not accept the finished product.

The plot was aided when the regular IMP studio manager was called to Europe, and a producer named Mark M. Dintenfass took over in his stead. Dintenfass was too distracted by squabbles between Laemmle and his partners to detect that *Traffic in Souls* was being filmed at the studio. Jack Cohn cast the film, and George Loane Tucker directed it, shooting scenes when no executives were around. Production on the shorter films continued to grind away during the four weeks *Traffic in Souls* was being shot *sub rosa*. Tucker ended with ten reels of film, gross extravagance in 1913.

The ruse remained uncovered, but Tucker quit IMP after a quarrel with Dintenfass. The director sailed off to a job in London with a warning to Cohn not to cut *Traffic in Souls* under seven reels.

Working behind a locked door at night, Jack Cohn trimmed the film down to a fast-moving six reels, including titles. Then he was faced with the task of showing it to Laemmle.

While *Traffic in Souls* was being unreeled in a studio projection room, Uncle Carl argued with an aide over the latest strategy in the warfare with dissident board members of IMP. Jack Cohn was downcast. The boss' indifference made it appear that Cohn would be liable for his $1,000 guarantee, which he could ill afford.

The situation demanded desperate action.

Cohn called at Laemmle's house late at night and declared, "I've come about *Traffic in Souls*. You talked all through the picture, and you didn't see it. Nobody can look at a picture and talk business all the time. Won't you come down now and really see it?"

A second viewing of *Traffic in Souls* convinced Laemmle of its value. Now he faced the task of selling it to fellow board members of his releasing company, Universal. They were scandalized that the film had cost a monumental $5,700. Furthermore, it was six reels, and Universal had never released anything longer than a two-reeler. The only long pictures had been spectacles like *Fall of Troy*, *Quo Vadis*, and *Queen Elizabeth*, and they had been exhibited in prestigious theaters, not movie houses.

The board of directors was in an uproar when release of *Traffic in Souls* was proposed.

"All right," Laemmle shouted, "I'll take the picture off the company's hands and pay ten thousand dollars for it."

That sobered the other directors. If the canny German was willing to buy the film, it must have great value. Universal released it.

Traffic in Souls was shown to the Shubert theater magnates, who paid $33,000 for a third interest and assumed exploitation of the film. It opened on Monday afternoon, November 24, 1913, with the advertisement:

> TRAFFIC IN SOULS—The sensational motion picture dramatization based on the Rockefeller White Slavery Report and on the investigation of the Vice Trust by District Attorney Whitman—A $200,000 spectacle in 700 scenes with 800 players, showing the traps cunningly laid for young girls by vice agents—Don't miss the most thrilling scene ever staged, the smashing of the Vice Trust.

Thirty thousand patrons packed into Joe Weber's Theater during the first week, paying 25 cents apiece. Soon *Traffic in Souls* was appearing in twenty-eight theaters in the New York area. Total receipts for the film were $450,000.

Traffic in Souls was a landmark in motion picture history. It demonstrated the commercial value of the feature film. It brought to light what producers have realized ever since: that sex can mean box office. It also provided the corollary to that formula: sexy films can bring censorship. The success of *Traffic in Souls* created a wave of white-slave films and a subsequent cry by moralists that movies were corrupting Amenca.

His judgment vindicated, Jack Cohn felt enough encouraged of his future to marry his childhood sweetheart, Jeanette Lesser. He also induced Laemmle to hire his friend from the Hampton

Advertising Agency, Joe Brandt. After two hapless years as an attorney, Joe had been working for theatrical journals. He rose swiftly to become general manager of Universal.

While working for Uncle Carl, Jack Cohn and Joe Brandt harbored dreams of starting their own movie company. Those dreams were not to be realized until the arrival of the third member of a triumvirate.

4
ENTER HARRY COHN, SINGING

*H*arry Cohn's career as a trolley conductor was short-lived. The tolerant company expected conductors normally to pocket 15 percent of the fares. Young Cohn reversed the formula, allowing the company 15 percent. It was a joke among his associates that the company thanked him for bringing the trolley car back each night.

After the trolley concern decided it could no longer afford his services, Harry Cohn returned to a career in music. With the realism that marked his character throughout his lifetime, he concluded that audiences would not pay to hear him sing. The failure of Edwards and Ruby had proved that. But there was another field of endeavor for his voice: song plugging.

The music industry was flourishing in the second decade of the twentieth century. Americans felt more lyrical than ever before, and music racks of parlor pianos were filled with the latest hits from Tin Pan Alley. The making of a hit was a problem that occupied all music publishers, and that was why they hired song pluggers.

The life of a song plugger called for energy, resourcefulness, and nerve; hence, Harry Cohn was ideally suited for it. His day began in the morning, when he reported to his employer, Waterson, Berlin and Snyder. Along with a score of other pluggers, he learned which songs were being pushed by the company; they might have been *I Hear the Voice of Belgium, Becky Do the Bombashay*, or other tunes by the prolific partner of the firm, Irving Berlin.

Cohn's daytime beat was the five-and-ten-cent stores. He walked from Kresge to Woolworth to Grant to Grand, striding to the music counter and handing his song sheet to the pianist-salesgirl. After an opening spiel extolling the popularity of his song, he delivered it in his uncertain tenor, singing loudly to attract customers from other counters.

In the evening Cohn began his tour of nickelodeons. There were 500 in New York, and each offered a ready, submissive audience. Theater managers appreciated the free addition to the evening's entertainment and stopped projection of the movie with the arrival of the plugger.

Cohn handed glass slides to the projectionist and gave the sheet music to the nickelodeon pianist. Cohn stood at the side of the screen and sang as the illustrated lyrics were flashed before the audience. The song was repeated, and the patrons were encouraged to join in the singing.

Next came calls on vaudeville houses, and Cohn traveled as far as Coney Island to visit backstage with musical acts, leaving copies of the latest plug behind. By eleven o'clock it was time to drop in at various cabarets and attempt to sell singing stars on the coming hit.

Harry Cohn thrived on such a life. He savored the backstage smells, the flash of spotlights, the knowledgeable talk that show people reserved solely for insiders. Performing offered no great attraction for him, but it held no terror, either. He sang on cue, without pride; it was part of the job. The elements that appealed most to him were the wheedling, the dealing, the selling of songs by pleas or coercion.

A significant sidelight of his profession was the accessibility to actresses, dancers, and show girls whom he met and dated backstage. Patterns of the later Harry Cohn emerged in this formative period. Aggressiveness in business was accompanied by a natural counterpart, sexual athleticism. Cohn became adept in the ways of winning a woman.

He presented a compelling figure to the opposite sex. He was brawny, but with a light-footedness that made him a dream to dance with. He was invariably clean and well groomed, sporting the snappiest new styles from Broadway haberdashers. He had a large, classically featured face, dominated by large, intensely blue eyes.

Harry Cohn's career in music was interrupted when he was drafted into the United States Army. He served uneventfully in the Cavalry at Fort Slocum, where Bella Cohn often visited him. He chafed under the inactivity of Army life and pleaded with his mother, "You've got to get me out of here, Mama; you need me to help support you."

Joseph Cohn had died at forty-nine after a life of hard work, and his widow relied on her sons for support. Bella Cohn made the proper representations, and her son Harry was relieved of military service. America was not yet involved in the war in Europe.

The turning point in Harry Cohn's career came after the office manager of Waterson, Berlin and Snyder assigned him to cover a singing act of three sisters at the Alhambra Theater. Cohn exerted his charm on the sisters, who promised to visit the publishing house the next day and audition songs for their repertoire.

Cohn bragged of his accomplishment to the office manager. But the Cohn charm apparently did not function as well in triplicate as it did with individual females. The sisters failed to appear, and Cohn was fired.

"Dammit, Mama, it isn't fair!" he complained to Bella Cohn. "If I can get fired for a simple thing like that, I don't want to work for anyone. I'm going to be my own boss."

He had been harboring an idea to improve song plugging in theaters: substitute movies for song slides. Expending most of his savings, he hired a one-room office in the Strand Building, in the heart of Tin Pan Alley. Jack Cohn came by from the Universal office to visit his brother's new enterprise on the first day of operation.

"Hey, look at this, Jack," said Harry, displaying a newly purchased ledger. The first entry read: "Harry Cohn—$500."

"Have you got that much money?" Jack asked.

"No, but it looks swell, doesn't it?" said Harry, beaming.

Soon he was able to make bona fide entries in the ledger. Louis Bernstein of Shapiro, Bernstein placed an order for a film to plug *I'm on My Way to Dublin Bay*. Harry Cohn relied on his military experience to illustrate the martial song. The entire reel consisted of an Army platoon executing march maneuvers. Cohn's total expenses were $25. He sold the film to Bernstein for $200.

His next order came from his former employer, Waterson, Berlin and Snyder, a fact that gave him great pride. As his enterprise improved, the films became more sophisticated in content. Soon he was producing vignettes to fit the lyrics of the songs, and theater owners found them an entertaining part of the program.

Cohn reasoned that if theaters were so eager to have his song films on their bills, they might pay for them. Through his brother Jack, he sold Carl Laemmle on undertaking a series of song shorts employing Universal stars.

The shorts proved a success, and Uncle Carl was impressed by the energy and resourcefulness of the younger Cohn brother. In 1918 Laemmle hired Harry Cohn to be his secretary at the studio in Universal City, just over the hill from Hollywood. Jack Cohn and Joe Brandt remained in New York.

Now Cohn, Brandt, and Cohn were employed by Laemmle, but they were soon to depart on a new and independent course of their own.

II

Flicker and a Voice:
The Twenties

• • • • •

THE INFANT INDUSTRY BECOMES A VIGOROUS ADOLESCENT, capturing the world market as European film making languishes in the war. The time of bigness has arrived. Cathedrals are erected for the worship of the screen. The public can share the prosperity; film company issues are now sold on the New York Stock Exchange. It is 1920, and 35,000,000 Americans are going to the movies every week.

Boom begets corruption. The quick-buck artists are at work. Film companies rise overnight, then disappear, along with investors' money. Stars are hired at immense salaries, only to kick back a third to producers. Writers channel a portion of their fees to their directors. Movie budgets are looted. Nepotism, the permanent plague of the film business, runs rampant.

No one cares. There is money for all.

Or is there? The money seems to flow into fewer hands. Independent producers find it more and more difficult to compete with the big combines, which have found a new way to annihilate opposition. Zukor is buying theaters by the hundreds. Loew acquires Metro to supply product for his theaters. Chains spread across the continent to link producing companies with ready markets. Who controls theaters controls production. Woe to the independents!

There is trouble in paradise. William Desmond Taylor, the director, is murdered in his Los Angeles home, and his alliances with Mary Miles Minter and Mabel Normand add scandal to the mystery. A binge in the St. Francis Hotel of San Francisco brings rape-death charges against Fatty Arbuckle; he is acquitted, but not by the club-women of America. Wallace Reid, portrayer of the all-American boy, dies at thirty of drink and dope.

Sex and seduction abound in Hollywood films, and Baptists and editorial writers take up the cry against the new Gomorrah. The clamor bruises the film companies where it hurts most: at the box office. They move to regulate themselves before the government does it for them. The policeman: Will Hays, the big-eared Hoosier who helped put Warren Gamaliel Harding in the White House.

The sanctimonious Postmaster General helps rebuild confidence. Sex in films is toned down, and morality clauses are included in actors' contracts.

The big companies regain equilibrium and consolidate their advantage. Not only do they own their own theaters to provide prime playing time for their movies, but they also institute block booking, making independent theater owners buy pictures in bunches, the good with the bad.

Now the positions of power seem entrenched. But the essence of the movie business is change, and those Warner brothers have been tinkering with sound. In 1926 Will Hays makes one of his arid speeches from the screen of the Manhattan Opera House, where *Don Juan* is playing with sound effects. A year later Al Jolson flashes his eyes and bawls, "Come on, Ma! Listen to this," as he goes into his song.

William Fox scoffs, "I don't think that there will be the much-dreamed-of talking pictures on a large scale." The public disagrees. The clamor for talkies boosts weekly theater attendance from 57,000,000 in 1927 to 80,000,000 in 1929.

Film makers are astonished and happy. But they don't know that the best is yet to come.

● ● ● ● ●

I

UNCLE CARL LAEMMLE SUFFERS
THREE DESERTIONS, AND C.B.C.
IS BORN ON POVERTY ROW

*J*ack Cohn was the first to leave. After a dozen years in a variety of positions at Universal he had grown impatient to launch his own film enterprise. Leafing through some of the fan magazines that had proliferated as movies tightened their hold on the American public, he conceived the idea of *Screen Snapshots*. It was to be a series of shorts that would report the off-screen doings of film stars. Jack handed his notice to Laemmle and launched *Screen Snapshots* with a partner.

The shorts were successful; the partnership was not. Jack severed the relationship after six months and sought someone more congenial to his mode of operation. Quite naturally he thought of Joe Brandt, his comrade-in-arms at Hampton's and Universal. A conservative man, Brandt nonetheless succumbed to Jack Cohn's enthusiasm and joined the new enterprise.

Both men felt the need for another partner with production knowledge. They invited Edward Small to join them. Small, agent for many of the top film stars and thus familiar with production problems, chose to remain in the agency business. Jack Cohn brought forth a second suggestion: his brother Harry.

Harry Cohn was eager to join the entrepreneurs, and he was recalled from Universal City to help form the C.B.C. Film Sales Company in New York.

In searching for new properties to augment *Screen Snapshots*, the partners discovered the *Hall Room Boys*. H. A. McGill had drawn a comic strip of that name in the New York *Telegram*. Its popularity had prompted the vaudeville team of Flanagan and Edwards to create a new act about the pair of bums who tried to crash New York society. C.B.C. signed a contract with McGill, paying him $300 for three one-reel films with an option for others at $100 apiece. The new company hired Edward Flanagan and Neeley Edwards to repeat their roles on the screen and arranged for a reputable director to shoot the films in California at $10,000 apiece.

When the first three films arrived in New York, they were screened immediately by the expectant partners. Their hopes were shattered. The films were so inept as to be scarcely releasable. Harry Cohn dispatched a message to a friend in Hollywood. The friend investigated and discovered why the comedies were of such poor quality: the director had been making them for $2,000 and pocketing the rest of his budget.

Their company almost ruined before it could get started, Cohn, Brandt, and Cohn concluded they could no longer trust outsiders with their dwindling capital. One of them would have to go to California to watch over production. By all logic it had to be Harry Cohn, who had previous experience in Hollywood.

Harry Cohn returned in a new guise. No longer was he a Laemmle underling. He was now a full-fledged partner of a production company. He could drop in at the Alexandria Hotel in downtown Los Angeles and watch the fabled figures discussing deals as they stood on the lobby's $1,000,000 rug—Mack Sennett, Thomas Ince, Cecil B. DeMille, Jesse Lasky, Gloria Swanson, Charlie Chaplin, D. W. Griffith, Mary and Doug.

"Someday I'm going to live like that," he vowed as he watched Samuel Goldwyn and Nicholas Schenck drive into Goldwyn's studio in a chauffeured Pierce Arrow limousine.

First came survival. A. P. Giannini, the shrewd boss of the Bank of Italy, had lent C.B.C. $100,000 to get started. The capital was depleted, and there was little chance of getting more. Harry Cohn had to start producing, and the place to do it was Poverty Row.

No one knew how the name originated, but it fit perfectly. Like a slum quarter on the edge of a prosperous city, Poverty Row had affixed itself to the boomtown of Hollywood. There dwelt the fly-by-nights and the hopefuls, the shoestring producers who aimed to collect whatever movie market was left over after the big companies amassed their share.

Poverty Row stretched for a block along Beachwood Drive and around the corner of Sunset Boulevard. With small offices facing on the street every few steps, the area looked like a red-light district. Inside each office was a producer-promoter, often working solo, exploring every conceivable device for making films at the lowest cost. Behind the offices were four-wall stages, which the producers could rent from studio owners for interior scenes.

By 1920, when Harry Cohn arrived, the procedure of a Poverty Row producer had been ritualized. The foremost consideration was money with which to begin the enterprise. Bankers like Giannini advanced the financing, or it came from the releasing company that contracted for the film.

A star was next. If the producer was lucky, he uncovered a name player who was down on his luck and willing to work in a quickie on a deferred salary. Lacking a recognized actor, the producer created his own star. He could pick one from the cowboys who loitered in "Gower Gulch," the area around the drugstore at Sunset Boulevard and Gower Street, one block west.

With backing and a star assured, the producer composed a script. It might have been a detailed plan of the action. More than likely, it was a rough sketch of how the plot was to proceed, with the details to be filled in during the progress of the shooting. In either case, the script was planned logistically to achieve the greatest scenic results at the lowest possible cost. Outdoor films were a virtual necessity, since sets cost money.

Sets were sometimes borrowed. If Paramount had just completed an epic on the sinking of the Titanic, the Poverty Row producer hastily composed the scenario of a shipboard drama and rented the set from Paramount at a fraction of its cost. Or the producer could enhance the appearance of a film by purchasing stock footage from major studios, perhaps a cattle stampede or an Indian charge.

Having rented a camera and other equipment and arranged for credit at the film lab, the producer was ready to begin shooting. His film crew was compact. He hired a director or did the directing himself. An assistant was needed to cue horses and do odd jobs. Also, the cameraman, who did his own lighting, and an assistant, who loaded the camera, took still photographs and shot action scenes.

The California sun provided light for the film. It was focused on the scene by a grip who adjusted the gold- or silver-foiled reflectors that illuminated the actors. Metallic tins, used on the background only, provided too intense a light for human eyes. One wrangler handled the horses. Wardrobe men and makeup men were seldom needed unless an actress was on the location; hence, the actress' scenes were usually filmed at the studio. Cowboys didn't wear makeup; the star did, but he brought a kit and applied his own.

The shooting day began early. Actors and crew left before dawn to be on location in the first glow of photographable daylight. Western scenery near Hollywood was favored, to cut down on traveling time; the Lasky ranch, which had a Western street, was often used, as was the pig farm that later became Warner Brothers studio.

Cowboys were hired for $7.50 a day. Fat Jones supplied horses at $5 a day, and a stagecoach was available at $15. Producers made the most of the horsemen. It was a common practice for a director to order a dozen cowboys to gallop their steeds in a wide arc around the camera, thus creating the illusion of an immense posse.

Actors were often required to play two or three different roles in one film, adopting adequate disguises. If a crowd scene were needed, it might well have included grips, makeup man, the director, the producer, and his secretary.

Filming of Poverty Row pictures was generally done in brief takes. Producers often bought short ends—fifty feet or so of unexposed negative that had been discarded at the end of reels by less thrifty studios.

The shooting day lasted as long as the sun, and a canny director continued his filming up a mountainside to catch the last rays of sunset. Production continued in any weather; in case of rain a subtitle of dialogue commenting on the rain was inserted, and the action continued.

Poverty Row crews were accustomed to stealth when they filmed modern stories in Los Angeles streets. The city had long since become inured to the novelty of film companies; a license costing $400 was required for shooting on public thoroughfares. Camera crews were trained to set up fast, complete the street scenes quickly, and vanish before police arrived to check for a license.

Grab shots were common. When the Barnum and Bailey Circus came to Los Angeles, an enterprising producer filmed its arrival from a hidden camera in a nearby building. He then fashioned a carnival story and began his film with the Barnum and Bailey footage. The main story began after the title: "You have seen The Greatest Show on Earth—now look at the smallest one."

A favorite action sequence was the transfer of an actor from a motorcycle or automobile to a moving train. The best place to film it was in Pasadena, where the Santa Fe passed along blocks of paved streets. A director and cameraman boarded the train in Pasadena, carrying their heavy luggage to the observation car. As soon as the train pulled out of the station, they hauled a camera and tripod out of the bags. The motorcycle or automobile appeared at the designated spot, and the actor made the daring transfer as the camera cranked. The conductor generally came along to throw the film makers off the train at the next stop.

Harry Cohn was to learn such tricks of the trade in quick order. Indeed, the newest member would teach the Poverty Row fraternity some brand-new marvels of economy.

2

THE PILGRIM'S PROGRESS
IN THE NEW LAND:
FROM THE *HALL ROOM BOYS*
TO *MORE TO BE PITIED*
THAN SCORNED

*H*arry Cohn formed an alliance with Morris Schlank, who operated a tiny studio on Sunset Boulevard between Gower Street and Beachwood Drive. Having a base of operations, Cohn now sought a director for the *Hall Room Boys*. He instituted the policy he was to apply ever after: hire the best talent available at the best possible price. His director was Alfred Santell, a former architect who had turned to fashioning comedies for Kalem and Sennett. He provided the comedic skill that Cohn needed, and the first *Hall Room Boys* comedy of the Harry Cohn regime was filmed and shipped to New York.

Jack Cohn and Joe Brandt eagerly received the print and screened it. The film possessed the quality they had been seeking, and they quickly sold it to provide funds for the next *Hall Room Boys* two-reeler.

This procedure continued for months, each new film providing the financial impetus for the next. In addition, Jack and Harry Cohn instituted a fiscal policy that was to sustain their tiny enterprise in its formative period. All checks for salaries, rentals, and other expenses in California were drawn on the C.B.C. bank account in New York. All New York expenses were paid via check from a Hollywood bank. The lapse of four or five days as the checks traveled across country provided time to husband the bank accounts. Cohn later remarked that if air mail had been instituted, there would have been no Columbia Pictures.

Harry Cohn devised other means of economizing. All movie scenery backdrops were painted on one side, the reverse being blank. "Why not paint the other side, too?" theorized the new producer. The scenic artist did so, and C.B.C. companies filmed on both sides of backdrops.

When Estelle Taylor was starring in an early Cohn film, production was delayed one morning while she was being made up. Cohn rushed up and instructed the makeup man, "Just make up one side of her face; we'll make it a side shot."

Another actress was cast in a C.B.C. Western that required her to ride in several scenes. Her ignorance of horsemanship was total. For one key sequence she was supposed to gallop across the plain to a telegraph station, dispatching word that outlaws were marauding her father's ranch. Each time the director called for action, the actress rode a short distance and then fell off the horse.

Exasperated by the delay, Cohn ordered the propman to attach a telephone to a post. The actress phoned the alarm.

Besides the *Hall Room Boys*, *Screen Snapshots*, and Westerns, Harry Cohn was producing comedies and had particular success with a series starring Billy West. The formula was simple: West performed a precise imitation of Charlie Chaplin, even to the twitch of the brush moustache. The comedies found a ready market; audiences clamored for Chaplin, real or phony.

Harry Cohn realized the fledgling company would not progress by manufacturing two-reel staples and counterfeit Chaplins. The big money was in features, and he proposed that C.B.C. make them. Jack Cohn concurred, and Joe Brandt grudgingly agreed. New financing was necessary, and five new partners were recruited.

In 1922 Harry Cohn fashioned his first feature film, *More to Be Pitied Than Scorned*. It was produced for a total cost of $20,000.

The finished product was shipped to New York, and Jack Cohn and Joe Brandt showed it to the all-powerful Marcus Loew, who could bestow prosperity on any film by booking it into his chain of theaters. The wholesome schmaltz of *More to*

Be Pitied Than Scorned appealed to Loew, and he offered $65,000 for the negative print. Cohn and Brandt were joyful that the millionaire showman would wish to buy a C.B.C. picture outright, but their joy was tempered with self-interest. If Marcus Loew would offer $65,000, the film might be worth considerably more. Would he bid $100,000? Loew shook his head.

Jack Cohn and Joe Brandt returned in defeat to their offices at 1600 Broadway. They had to report their failure to the five new partners, who were agitated over the turn of events. Cohn and Brandt went to work immediately to transform *More to Be Pitied Than Scorned* into hard cash. They sold it in the states' rights market—the system by which distributors would purchase rights to a film in certain states or combination of states, leasing it to theaters for their own profit. C.B.C. not only realized $130,000 in sales but was also awarded a contract for five more features.

The five new partners collected their profits and withdrew, foreseeing no future prosperity with Cohn, Brandt, and Cohn. With outside support gone, the three founders faced the shooting of a second feature with only $5,000 in the treasury. The film was produced, and at its conclusion the company still possessed $5,000. The miracle was accomplished by steadfast thrift, postponing payments, and continuing the flow of checks from one coast to the other by the slowest mail possible.

The enterprise was growing in distinction, and hence it required a new name. C.B.C. was now universally recognized in the trade by its sobriquet, Corned Beef and Cabbage. A company could scarcely prosper under such a handicap. On January 10, 1924, C.B.C. became Columbia Pictures.

The division of duties among the corporation executives fell naturally into place. Joe Brandt, professorial-looking, a man conversant with law and finance, was president. Jack Cohn, vital, tough, a formidable negotiator, became vice-president in charge of sales. The post of vice-president in charge of production remained with Harry Cohn.

By the end of 1924 Columbia Pictures was proceeding at a steady pace and could advertise in *Motion Picture News*:

A 100% Picture
Loudly Proclaimed by the Critics

THE MIDNIGHT EXPRESS
The Story of a Railroad Man
Who Would Not Be Sidetracked
Featuring
Elaine Hammerstein and an All-Star Cast

The advertisement also featured a row of books that purported to be titles of forthcoming Columbia attractions: *After Business Hours, The Foolish Virgin, Fighting the Flames, The Price She Paid, One Glorious Night, A Fool and His Money,* and *Who Cares?*

Columbia was obviously becoming the pride of Poverty Row. Now it was Harry Cohn who felt secure enough in his position to take a wife. As with most everything else in his life, he did so in a highly individualistic way.

3

A Brief Account of How Harry Cohn Courted a Wife — Not His Own — and of the Salutary Events That Ensued

*H*er name was Rose Barker, and she was a pretty little thing—pretty, but not beautiful. Her attractiveness was not so much facial as it was internal; she possessed a warm Italian soul that men found enchanting.

She was an actress, though not a very good one. But her profession afforded her a degree of prominence, and she never lacked for gentlemen friends. One of them was Harry Cohn. His boss at Waterson, Berlin and Snyder had been Max Winslow, who was married to Rose's sister. Max introduced his sister-in-law to the hustling young song plugger. For several months he lavished his salary on her. He took her to Ziegfeld's *Midnight Frolics* on the New Amsterdam Roof, and they danced the tango at the Palais Royal.

Rose could have fallen in love with the vital young man with the intense blue eyes, and perhaps she did. But Harry Cohn was too much on the move to become encumbered. While enjoying the present, he spoke nothing of their future together.

A girl had to look out for herself. One of her other gentlemen friends was a man somewhat older and far richer. His name was Cromwell, and he was a partner in the distinguished law firm of Sullivan and Cromwell. He was more ardent in his pursuit than Harry Cohn, and he promised a happy life for Rose if she would marry him. She did.

Harry Cohn's career as a song plugger ended, and he moved into the movie business. He continued from girl to girl, scarcely remembering one six months after each encounter. But he never forgot Rose.

She lingered in his mind during the time he was struggling to elevate C.B.C. from Poverty Row. Whenever he traveled East to confer with his two partners, he called her. At first she protested that he must not try to see her, since she was now married. But Harry Cohn had overwhelming powers of persuasion, and soon they were meeting in out-of-the-way Manhattan cafés. Rose could not escape the fact that she was utterly fascinated by him.

"Come out and visit me in California," he urged. "It's exciting out there. I want you to see how I make movies."

At first she dismissed the proposal as too dangerous. Cohn persisted. He made the trip sound so attractive that she decided to take the chance. She told her husband that since he was extremely busy in a court case, she would like to take a holiday to California with a lady friend. Cromwell, distracted by demands of the law, allowed her to go.

Rose had chosen an unmarried friend she deemed worthy of trust. The pair set out for California.

Harry Cohn treated Rose like a visiting maharani. He filled her hotel suite with long-stemmed roses. He provided a throne-like seat from which she could observe the making of his movies. He introduced her to as much Hollywood society as a Poverty Row producer could. Together they glided over the ballroom floor of the Garden Court Hotel, brushing past Rudolph Valentino and Pola Negri.

Rose was greatly impressed by her California holiday, although she returned to New York with all intentions of resuming her role as Mrs. Cromwell. But her confidante and traveling companion proved not as trustworthy as Rose had supposed. The friend blurted the entire story to Cromwell.

He was enough of a gentleman to award her $250,000 in the divorce settlement. Rose became Mrs. Harry Cohn as soon as the decree was final.

Despite the scandal, the episode ended happily for most of the parties involved. Rose had Harry Cohn—for a while. He had Rose, and her dowry from Cromwell was transfused as lifeblood into his anemic company.

The traveling companion also prospered. She became the new Mrs. Cromwell.

4
1926: YEAR OF DECISION

*B*y the mid-1920's the corporative patterns of Columbia Pictures were beginning to solidify. A double dynasty was in the making, with the Cohn brothers at the top and the Briskin-Schneider family occupying the secondary level. Sam Briskin had joined C.B.C. as an auditor at $45 a week; he became second in command to Harry Cohn at the studio. Abe Schneider, Briskin's brother-in-law, had delivered newspapers to the C.B.C. New York office before joining the bookkeeping department; he soon moved up in the company.

Later in Columbia's history an alert employee counted twenty-nine Cohns and Briskin-Schneiders in the corporation. Robert Benchley once termed Columbia the Pine Tree Studio "because it has so many Cohns."

During these early years of Columbia, Jack and Harry Cohn established the intercompany relationship that continued until death parted them. They battled continuously. What once had been a sibling rivalry developed into an all-consuming warfare.

The two Cohns exemplified in the extreme the factor that plagued every large-scale motion picture company: the gulf between East and West. Production had centered in California because of the need to escape the Patents Company and to employ the sunshine and scenery. Economic necessity dictated that the parent companies, including the distribution apparatus, remain headquartered in New York, close to the center of finance and near the major population areas.

The distance between the two major arms of the film companies was more than geographical. To the West, the East was comprised of pencil-pushing accountants who fretted over every penny spent on production and sold movies like so much salami. To the East, the West was filled with dreamers and profligates who ground out movies that were next to impossible to sell. The two ends of the continent were constantly at odds over budgets, film subjects, treatment of stars, etc. Each was quick to blame the other for reverses suffered by the company.

In most companies the East had the upper hand; the president was located in New York, close to stockholder control, and he presumably had the power to hire and fire. But his power could be offset by the performance of the production chief. If the movies were successful and the studio's stars were luminous, then the studio head presented a formidable figure. But a succession of flops could bring him disaster.

Warfare between the opposing coasts debilitated some of the movie companies, pushing them to the edge of bankruptcy. Oddly, such conflict proved a stimulus to the growth of Columbia. Because Harry Cohn dearly loved to catch his brother in an error, Jack honed the Eastern operation to the sharp edge of efficiency. Since Jack was ever alert to point out where Harry had failed, Harry devoted all his energies to making the studio succeed.

Joe Brandt was caught in the middle. As president of the company, he was forced to act as mediator between the two brothers; as a result, he absorbed abuse from each side. He also strove to act as a stabilizer against what he felt were the excesses of the ambitious Cohns.

By 1926 Columbia had grown to such a degree that the course of its future history had to be charted. Expansion was needed if the small company was to compete with the unlimited resources of the major studios. Columbia could no longer struggle from picture to picture, scraping together financing from whatever sources could be found. The partners agreed that Columbia should offer shares to the public on the stock market.

Columbia could not progress under its early system of selling franchises for films on the states' rights market. The company then collected flat fees and could not realize the profits when a picture captured the public's fancy. So in 1926 the first four film exchanges were opened by Columbia. More exchanges were opened as franchises expired, until the whole nation was marketed directly by Columbia sales branches. Later, the world.

Joe Brandt viewed such developments with caution. He

refused to permit one expansionist plan. "We will not buy theaters," he decreed.

This decision was also crucial to Columbia's history. In one respect, Joe Brandt seemed shortsighted. The big companies were flourishing in the 1920's because they were able to ensure a market for their product. All owned hundreds of theaters in which their movies were accorded prime playing time. Even when the studio product turned sour, theater chains could turn a profit by playing movies of other companies and thus offset losses on production.

But Joe Brandt foresaw a time when a chain of theaters would not prove an asset to a production company. That time came after 1929, when Paramount and RKO were carried down to bankruptcy by the weight of empty theaters.

Whether beneficent or not, Brandt's decision was to establish the essential nature of Columbia as a movie company. Columbia never enjoyed the cushion of guaranteed playing time. It was required to gamble on quality films that would so engage the public that theaters would be forced to book Columbia movies.

And when the United States decreed separation of film making from theater owning in the 1940's, Columbia escaped the paroxysms of those studios that could not function without the bulwark of their theater chains.

Another decision in 1926 that was to help chart Columbia's future was the purchase of a studio. Harry Cohn insisted on it. He felt it was time for Columbia to escape the stigma of renting space on Poverty Row. He had been eyeing some property around the corner on Gower Street, a small plot that included two stages and a small office building. The place was being used by Sam Bischoff, an enterprising producer who had been a certified public accountant in New England.

Cohn learned that although Bischoff owned the studio, it was heavily mortgaged to a Boston firm. Cohn went to Boston and bought the mortgage for $150,000. Then he returned to announce to Bischoff that he was being evicted to make way for Columbia Pictures.

"I guess there's nothing I can do about it." Bischoff sighed.

"That's right," Cohn replied triumphantly.

"But what are you going to do about my stage?" Bischoff asked.

Cohn eyed him with suspicion. "What stage?"

"The big stage. If you investigate, you'll find it's my property. I built it."

Cohn found out Bischoff was reporting the truth. The producer had paid for construction of the sturdy stage, which measured 30 by 100 feet.

"You outsmarted me," said Bischoff. "You bought the studio out from under me. But no hard feelings. I'll make you a deal. That stage cost me twenty-six thousand dollars. That kind of steel structure would cost you fifty thousand to build today. You can have it at my cost."

Cohn shook his head. "I'll give you seventy-five hundred dollars," he said.

Bischoff exploded. "You think you're going to steal it from me? Well, you're wrong. I'll move it."

Cohn laughed. "What are you going to do—fly it out of there?" He knew that the stage was too big to move along Gower Street.

Cohn gloated over his triumph. But when he came to his new studio the next day, the stage was gone. Bischoff had purchased a lot across the street on Beachwood Drive, removed a bungalow, and transferred the stage to the new location.

Nothing perturbed Cohn more than to have someone get the better of him in a deal. When he encountered Bischoff months later, he inquired unhappily, "I heard you sold your stage; how much did you get for it?"

"Seventy-five thousand," Bischoff announced. Cohn grunted morosely.

"I don't need to talk to you," Bischoff remarked, puffing on a cigar. "I'm a rich man."

'Oh, you'll talk to me," Cohn retorted. "You're going to work for me someday."

Bischoff hooted at the idea, but two years later he was hired as production supervisor of Columbia. He held the post for three years, then resigned to become production head of Tiffany because Cohn refused to give him a raise in salary.

"I'm sorry to be leaving, but I'll be back," he told Cohn.

"When?" Cohn asked.

"When you pay me more money than you or any other son of a bitch at the studio is making."

5

Two Important Triumphs for Harry Cohn: Columbia Makes the Roxy, and Bella Cohn Pays a Visit to California

The Port of Missing Stars: that was the epithet tossed at Columbia by a local critic, and Hollywood chuckled over it.

"Maybe we are the Port of Missing Stars," Harry Cohn said in defense. "We give stars who are free-lancing vehicles that we believe they will fit into best, and we prolong their screen lives by so doing. We are exceedingly careful in casting our pictures, and with only three players under contract we do not have to rush into production with a star who is miscast or give a picture to a director who doesn't want to make it."

As a riposte, he added, "The big studios may be Ports of Missing Stars also, because they miss when they give stars stories not suited to them."

This defensive thrust at the majors revealed another Columbia strategy. Lacking a Clara Bow or a John Gilbert, Columbia relied on castoffs from the big studios: stars who had been let go because their box office appeal had seemingly been drained. With the passé stars, Cohn combined newcomers, often borrowed at a bargain from major studios. "We get 'em on the way up and the way down," he said. It was this technique he used for Columbia's first venture into the big time, *The Blood Ship*.

Hobart Bosworth had been a handsome leading man who had starred in the first movie made in Los Angeles, *The Sultan's Power*, in 1909. Later he specialized in sea films, such as *The Sea Wolf, Behind the Door*, and *Below the Surface*. In 1927 he was a spare white-haired man of sixty, whom the major studios would no longer consider for leading roles.

Still, Bosworth harbored dreams of returned glory. He had purchased an adventure novel, *The Blood Ship*, which he peddled from studio to studio. Bosworth came to the end of the trail at Columbia. He offered *The Blood Ship* free—on the condition that he play the starring role. Harry Cohn agreed.

Cohn signed Jacqueline Logan for the feminine role. To play the younger man in the story, he sought a Paramount contract player, Richard Arlen, who had recently made impressive appearances in a series of films. Paramount officials told the young actor to pay Cohn a courtesy call on his lunch hour.

The distance between Paramount and Columbia was more than the geographic mile up Gower Street. Arlen left his bustling, prosperous home studio to enter the world of Harry Cohn: a rickety building on the fringe of Poverty Row, where the silence was broken only by the strong, clear voice of Cohn.

"Damn nice of you to come up here on your lunch hour," Cohn said. "I know what they told you before you left Paramount: don't make any commitments. Right?"

The young actor grinned. "You're right," he admitted.

"You like boats?" Cohn asked.

"Yes."

"I want you to read this script. See what you think of it." Cohn handed Arlen the script of *The Blood Ship*, and the interview was over.

Arlen received a telephone call at his house at nine o'clock that night. It was Cohn. "How'd you like the script?" he asked.

"Fine," said Arlen.

"Like to do the picture?"

"Sure."

The Paramount hierarchy was furious because Cohn had exacted a commitment from Arlen, but the executives could do nothing except honor it.

Cohn hired George B. Seitz as director and rented a three-masted schooner, the *Indiana*. The film was shot mostly at sea, and Harry Cohn directed part of it. Because of the immense expenditure, Jack Cohn came out from New York to help oversee the film, adding further irritation to his relations with Harry.

The Blood Ship justified Harry Cohn's gamble, winning an engagement at the nation's biggest and most prestigious movie house, the Roxy in New York. It marked a great stride forward for Columbia.

The burgeoning fortunes of Columbia Pictures brought more notice to its aggressive studio boss, and this both pleased and concerned him. He was pleased to be winning some recognition from an industry that had treated his studio as a slum. But he was concerned lest his plain speech make him sound like an illiterate in print. His publicity directors shared that fear; throughout his career they shielded him from interviewers.* Harry Cohn never acquired the knack of most studio bosses for uttering platitudes for the press. On the rare occasions when he issued pronouncements, they were recorded and watered down by publicity department writers.

One such "interview" was transcribed on March 26, 1928, and it reveals the film-making philosophy of Harry Cohn at that juncture in his career. Excerpts:

> We are growing at Columbia, because we haven't put up a false front. We haven't wasted much and are able to progress because we have been able to correct most of our mistakes early in the game and make the kind of pictures our returns prove theater men want. Just plain common sense, determination, and concentration—that's the Columbia motto. . . .
>
> We have found that aside from an occasional book or play, original stories are the best. With all his resources and entrée, the big producer doesn't get many real good stories; he buys ideas. So we have concentrated on ideas and we have created most of our pictures right here in the studio. . . .
>
> What is art in pictures?
>
> I believe the real art in pictures is the acting.

---

* A few months before his death, Cohn was caught in a candid moment by a *New York Post* reporter who was touring the studio. Cohn, who was sitting in a barber's chair while being shaved, was asked how he liked being president of a large studio for twenty-five years. His reply: "It's better than being a pimp."

What about close-ups?

We don't like them in our pictures. On very rare occasions do we use single close-ups. When action takes place between two or three people, we show them all in the close-up. . . .

We don't have temperament in our studio. We don't tolerate it. There is no reason why an actor should be more temperamental than a doctor or lawyer or teacher or preacher. . . .

What about the cost of pictures?

The cost of pictures isn't important to the public anymore. There was a time when the so-called million-dollar picture seemed to assure the public that it must be good. However, you can't fool all of the people all of the time. There is only one thing the public demands—a picture must be good. The public is fickle to a certain degree, and it is difficult to predict accurately how any new picture will go. However, if your story has novelty, human appeal, humor, and pathos without being too morbid, your chances are very good.

What about distribution?

The producer who makes a good picture can always get distribution for it. Good pictures will always be in demand. The big-line producer cannot possibly make every picture a hit. Exhibitors realize this, and they are always on the lookout for the picture that can pinch-hit for a mediocre one. We feel that our pictures must be better than the other fellow's to gain a consistent play on the market. That is why we work on our stories a long time before we put them into production. We build our pictures on showmanship, studying the market continually and not waiting to slide into favor by following some other producer's lead.

We have learned, too, that big circuit bookers look at a reel or two of a picture, and if they are not astounded by the revelations of the early footage, they never finish looking at the picture. The result is that, like newspaper writers, we put a punch in the first reel of our picture that demands immediate respect and attention, and then go on with our story, building, building, building. . . .

Our scenarios run about two hundred and seventy-five scenes. The big studios use five hundred scenes in their scripts. We never waste time and money filming scenes we don't really need. . . .

The most important point I can stress is that any man with a normal degree of intelligence knows as much as the other fellow in six months. It is an open business.

Thus, in a rare display of public candor, Harry Cohn outlined the elements that were to propel him to the status he so obviously envied: that of the big producer. Those elements were economy of operation; attention to exhibitors' needs; stress on original stories (which were cheaper than books and plays); avoidance of artiness; quelling of temperament; shunning of trends; compactness of well-prepared scripts; grabbing the film buyer (hence, the audience) in the first reel; concentration on "novelty, human appeal, humor, and pathos without being too morbid."

By 1928 Harry Cohn's work habits had also developed into the pattern he was to follow. He explained them:

I come to work about noon, and you'll find me at my desk or in the projection room almost every night until midnight. The reason I work that way is because I need to concentrate on our progress. I can't concentrate on a picture, story, or an idea if I am interrupted by the routine of daily business.

So I come to work when the day's work is pretty well organized by the department heads and consult with them when the daily routine is done and can give them concentrated attention and the value of a fresh viewpoint.

The engagement of *The Blood Ship* at the Roxy brought Harry Cohn recognition by his peers, but he needed something more. He needed to demonstrate to Bella Cohn his position of growing importance.

For years he had been urging his mother to come out to California to see the enterprise that was thrusting him and brother Jack into position and wealth. For years Bella Cohn had put him off, not wanting to leave the comfort of her East Side surroundings. And she was the one person Harry Cohn could not overwhelm with his persuasiveness.

He persisted, and finally, Bella Cohn could find no honest reason why she shouldn't go to California. "But I can't go without my down pillow," she protested. Her son assured her she could take her favorite goose-down pillow along on the trip, and he arranged to accompany her.

Her departure from Grand Central Station was a memorable family event. All the relatives, including Cousin Yetta and many neighbors from Eighty-eighth Street, were at the station to wish her farewell, and there were presents, tears, and speeches. Bella Cohn, who had scarcely traveled out of Manhattan since her arrival from Russia as a girl, clutched her goose-down pillow and viewed the train with uncertainty. Harry assured her she had nothing to fear.

Bella Cohn continued across the plains with apprehension, as if she were expecting an Indian raid. She was happy to arrive in Los Angeles and to be received in Harry's home by the warmhearted Rose. Bella, who had cooked kosher-style all her life, didn't even mind when she was served ham.

"In your home, Rose dear," she said, "it tastes like chicken."

The long-anticipated day arrived, and Harry Cohn drove his mother to the studio. He took her on a movie stage to watch the shooting. He showed her the progress of construction of a new stage and where future ones would be located. He took her through every department until Bella began to complain that her feet were hurting.

"Then we can sit down in the projection room and watch the film we shot yesterday," her son said. He escorted her to the room and instructed the projectionist to run the day's rushes of two-reel comedy.

The room darkened, and onto the screen flickered a series of scenes that were to constitute a comedy chase. Harry Cohn was pleased that his mother chuckled at the antic performance.

Suddenly the door to the projection room flew open, admitting a flash of sunlight that whitened the screen. Standing in the doorway was the unmistakably squat figure of the star of the comedy.

"Who the hell is running my rushes without letting me know?" the comic demanded.

He gazed down at the seats and was startled to see the studio boss, his face turning a dark red.

The comic never worked at Columbia again.

6
THE ADVENT OF CAPRA

*H*e was a small man, thin-muscled, with a swarthy skin and a profusion of hair like electric wire. At times when he spoke, it was with an intensity that seemed to preclude interruption or comment. There were times when he remained silent, as if in brooding contemplation of some thorny problem. He was constantly engrossed with problems, whether a formula for a hydraulic lift or the proper stance preparatory to a pratfall.

He was a Sicilian mystic named Frank Capra, whose coming to Columbia can be marked as the real beginning of Harry Cohn's ascent to first rank among Hollywood producers.

Capra had a curious preparation for his historic role in Columbia's fortunes. His parents brought him at the age of three from Palermo to California, where his father found work as an orange picker. A poor boy, one of seven children, young Frank sold newspapers and plunked a banjo in Los Angeles honkytonks. He worked his way through the California Institute of Technology, graduating as a chemical engineer in 1918, when he enlisted in the Army.

After the war Capra discovered there was no work for chemical engineers. Then began his period in the wilderness, when he wandered about the West, selling volumes of Elbert Hubbard, as well as mining stocks, some of them bona fide. He slept in flophouses and in culverts, encountering in his travels a wide range of the American character.

Wandering palled on him in 1924, when he had been earning his livelihood playing draw poker in San Francisco. Employing the skill with which he sold questionable securities to farmers, Capra bamboozled himself into a job as a movie director. Using actors with no more experience than his own, he created a one-reeler of waterfront life, *Fultah Fisher's Boardinghouse*, based on a Rudyard Kipling ballad. It was good enough to sell for more than double its cost, $1,700, and it earned $75 for Capra.

Encouraged by his success in the new art, Capra migrated back to his home city and found a job writing gags for Our Gang at Hal Roach Studios. He did the same for Harry Langdon at Mack Sennett's, winning the confidence of the baby-faced comedian. When Langdon moved to First National, he took Capra with him as director.

Capra directed Langdon in three films—*The Strong Man; Tramp, Tramp, Tramp;* and *Long Pants*—all of them minor masterpieces. Langdon had previously bumbled his way through successions of sight gags, in which the Sennett factory was expert. Capra defined Langdon's character in three-dimensional terms: the guileless, open-faced ninny who was victimized by a flinthearted world. An infant in an adult world, he was enormously appealing.

After three hits Langdon suffered the occupational ailment of comedians: he believed his genius was self-created. He fired Capra and began directing himself, thus commencing his descent to oblivion. Further, he broadcast the untruth that it had been he, not Capra, who had actually supplied the directing genius of the three hit films.

Producers chose to believe Langdon, and Capra found studio doors closed to him. He was able to find an assignment in New York, directing *Love o' Mike* with a stage actress, Claudette Colbert. The picture was a total loss for its investors. Director and star ended the film hating each other, and she returned to the stage in despair.

The disaster compounded Capra's unemployability, and he couldn't find a job for a year. One day he encountered his old boss, Mack Sennett, on Hollywood Boulevard.

"Why don't you come back to work for me?" Sennett asked.

"All right," said Capra with heavy heart.

Sennett, who admired comedy and thrift with equal fervor, rehired Capra at $75 a week. The director had been earning $600. He returned to grinding out two-reelers at Sennett's Edendale, where his fellow workers taunted him as a man who had tried to make it on the outside and had failed.

One day Capra's agent called him at Sennett's with instructions to report to Columbia for an interview about a picture. Capra drove to Gower Street and was received by Sam Briskin. Operating under the code of Poverty Row, the negotiator began by denigrating the interviewee.

"Your last picture wasn't very good, was it?" muttered Briskin.

Capra bristled. "What *was* my last picture?" he demanded.

"You know—that picture you made," Briskin answered feebly.

The Sicilian temper erupted. "You son of a bitch," he growled, "you don't even know what the picture was!"

He stalked out of the office, slamming the door behind him as Briskin stared in astonishment.

A few days later Capra's agent called again and pleaded with him to return for another talk with Briskin. Capra agreed, and he faced the executive with fighting stance.

"What the hell was the matter with you the other day?" Briskin asked.

Capra shrugged off the inquiry. "What do you want of me?" he demanded.

"We want you to make a picture."

"Okay."

"How much do you want?"

"That's up to you."

"Name your price."

"You want me to direct?"

"Yes."

"Write?"

"Yes."

"How about a thousand dollars?"

"Sold."

Briskin explained that the deal would be subject to the approval of the boss, Harry Cohn. Briskin took Capra to Cohn's office. They walked in to find Cohn talking explosively into the telephone. Briskin mentioned Capra's price.

"Okay, okay," bellowed Cohn, continuing his telephone conversation as he waved the two men out of the office.

Thus began the decade-long marriage that brought undreamed-of fame and prosperity to Frank Capra and Columbia Pictures.

In his first week of filming his initial Columbia picture, *That Certain Thing*, Frank Capra learned the universal verity in successful dealing with Harry Cohn. It was true when Cohn was hacking out the beginnings of C.B.C. on Poverty Row; it was true when Cohn was president of an immense, worldwide enterprise. The rule was simply this: aggressiveness was the only tactic Cohn understood or respected.

One day Capra strode off the set of *That Certain Thing* and stormed into Cohn's office. The director slammed his hand on the desk and shouted, "I want to know how many goddam extras I have to order to get fifteen."

Cohn looked up with astonishment. "What's the matter with you?" he asked.

"I ordered fifteen extras, and I got five," Capra ranted. "Now just tell me what the hell I have to do—order fifty in order to get fifteen?"

Cohn convinced the furious director to return to work. Shortly afterward ten more extras appeared on the set.

Capra had been the victim of the Poverty Row heritage in which all Columbia employees were trained: cut expenses wherever possible. But at the outset of his Columbia relationship Capra established his own rule: he did things his way or not at all. Harry Cohn respected that. As long as Capra produced results—and he continued to do so—Cohn would not interfere. The director enjoyed virtual autonomy during his ten years at Columbia.

Cohn recognized Capra's uncommon touch in *That Certain Thing*, which starred Viola Dana and Ralph Graves. The film was good enough to be sold as a special picture instead of being marketed in a block of films, as most Columbia movies were. Cohn gave Capra a $1,500 bonus and a contract for three more films at $2,500 apiece. Capra never asked for a raise in the years that followed; Cohn always advanced his salary satisfactorily.

So This Is Love, Matinee Idol, Way of the Strong, and *Say It with Sables* continued the promise that Capra had shown with *That Certain Thing*. Most were comedies into which he injected flashes of human behavior that brought recognition from the audience.

One night Capra was attending a premiere at Grauman's Chinese when he saw the boss waving to him from the other side of the theater. Capra gathered from Cohn's vehement gestures what he wanted: return to the studio after the premiere was over.

Capra escorted his companion to her home, then drove to Columbia. He found Cohn and Briskin in a state of concern. Cohn was talking on the telephone to San Pedro, and he interrupted the conversation to instruct Capra, "Go to the projection room and look at a couple of reels of film I've got there." Capra did so, and he saw some edited film of Columbia's most ambitious movie, *Submarine*, starring Jack Holt and Ralph Graves. It had been shooting for a few weeks at Los Angeles Harbor under the direction of Irvin Willat, an expert on sea pictures.

Capra returned to Cohn's office.

"What do you think of the film?" Cohn demanded.

"I'm not going to judge another director's work," Capra replied.

"Do you think you could finish the picture?"

"I don't think so. I'd have to start all over again."

"Why?"

"Because what I saw isn't mine; it belongs to him. I know nothing of the story. Why don't you let him finish it?"

Briskin agreed that Willat should complete *Submarine*.

"Take the script," Cohn instructed Capra. "Go down to San Pedro tomorrow morning. You're directing the picture."

"All right," Capra replied. "But I'll have to shoot the whole thing over."

"Go!" Cohn commanded.

The conference took place on Saturday night. Capra reached the location the following morning and had a day to study the script and plan his strategy. On Monday morning he was told by the assistant director that the company was verging on mutiny.

Actors and crew alike felt an intense loyalty to the deposed Willat, and they resented the upstart gagman from Mack Sennett's who was taking over the intense melodrama. Capra realized he would have to act fast to gain control of the company.

"Get all the actors on the dock—without makeup," he instructed the assistant.

"What?" said the unbelieving assistant.

"You heard me."

Capra arrived on the dock to face what had all the aspects of a lynching party. Jack Holt, the stiff-backed, gimlet-eyed veteran of films, tugged at his tapered moustache and demanded, "What's this crap about no makeup?"

"That's right: no makeup," Capra said firmly. "I saw the film you shot so far, and you look like a bunch of fairies."

Holt recoiled at the suggestion. "I never played without makeup in my life, and I'm not going to start now," he snapped. "I'm going to call Harry Cohn."

"Go right ahead," Capra replied.

Holt found a telephone on the dock and put in a call to Columbia Studios. He explained the situation to Cohn, who replied, "I don't care if he tells you to play the scene with your fly open. You take direction, or you're on suspension!"

Capra further instructed the actors to rumple and soil their freshly starched Navy uniforms. "You look like you're ready to go into a song and dance," he said.

The actors grumbled through the first day's work, during which Capra deviated from the script to inject comedy touches that would relieve the melodrama. Capra captured the company when the first rushes were shown. All realized they were participating in the making of a hit. Once recalcitrant, Holt and Graves now declared they wanted to make all their films with Capra.

The success of *Submarine* brought Capra a new contract for $25,000 a year, by far the most Columbia had paid to a film maker.

Submarine was the biggest money-maker in Columbia's history until then. It was also the studio's first film with sound. Al Jolson had heralded the new era, and exhibitors sent up the clamor for talkies. The transitional films had only sound effects, and one in *Submarine* proved memorable.

It came when Jack Holt, a deep-sea diver, tapped on the side of a sunken submarine in an effort to determine if anyone inside were alive. One of the crew members was his brother, Ralph Graves.

To the relief of millions of moviegoers, a faint tap-tap-tap could be heard from inside the submarine.

7

NOTES ON THE DEVELOPING
CHARACTER OF HARRY COHN,
STUDIO BOSS

*H*arry Cohn was nearing forty years of age as he prepared to meet the challenge of sound. Columbia was far from achieving its full growth, but Cohn had developed the habits of work that were to prevail throughout his history with the studio.

He was a thorough autocrat. He made decisions instantly, and underlings carried them out or they were dismissed. He insisted on knowing everything that was going on in the studio. He was omnipresent, speeding from department to department, always ascending stairways two or three steps at a time. No employee knew when he might look up and find Harry Cohn staring down at him. If a worker left a light burning in his office when he departed for the day, Harry Cohn extinguished the light himself, then summoned the miscreant to his office for a dressing down the following day. This policy continued well after the time when Columbia had become a major studio.

What information Cohn did not obtain from personal observation he acquired by other means. The Cohn spy system was the subject of a wealth of legends, some of them spurious, many of them true.

The making of movies was the obsessive force in Cohn's life, to the exclusion of all other activities save one: gambling.

It was natural that Cohn would be an intense gambler. He gambled every hour of the business day—on the hiring of talent, the purchase of stories, the expense of sets, etc. With the decisions, he put his own prosperity and position on the line. For although he was a principal stockholder of Columbia Pictures, there prevailed the threat from the East. If he failed in his performance as chief studio officer, Jack Cohn and Joe Brandt possessed the theoretical power to depose him.

Harry Cohn gambled extensively on horse races. He formed a fast friendship with Buzzy Appleton, a shadowy figure who supplied information to major bettors. At one time Cohn was paying Appleton $25,000 annually for racing tips.

"Why on earth would you spend twenty-five grand for dope on horses?" asked one of Cohn's executives, D. A. Doran.

"It cuts down my losses," replied Cohn.

The association of Harry and Buzzy was initiated in a typically Cohnian manner. It was Cohn's custom to take a house at Saratoga during the racing season and spend his days at the racetrack. One day he attended the races with Joe Schenck, who enjoyed the counsel of Buzzy Appleton in his betting endeavors. Cohn had long known of Appleton but had never met him. Schenck supplied the introduction.

It was the day of the classic match race between Equipoise and Omar Kiam. As the racing card progressed, Cohn tried to find out Appleton's feelings about the feature race. Appleton had a natural wariness of strangers, no matter how distinguished, and remained noncommittal.

As the match race approached, Cohn remarked that he favored Omar Kiam, which was being offered at four to one odds. Appleton commented dryly that no scientific bettor would wager against the blood lines of an Equipoise, no matter what the odds. Cohn switched his bet and placed several thousand dollars on Equipoise at odds of three to five.

Equipoise galloped home the winner. But then the foul-claim flag was raised. The judges ruled that Equipoise's jockey was guilty of a foul, and Omar Kiam was pronounced the winner.

Buzzy Appleton was distraught that his chance remark had robbed Cohn of his winnings. Cohn was inwardly delighted. He had lost the bet but he had incurred the obligation of the most noted betting counselor in the nation. The association proved highly profitable for Harry Cohn, though not because of racing wagers. Buzzy became valuable at a time when Cohn needed to consolidate his corporate power.

Harry Cohn was not unique among film executives in his fondness for gambling. All were instinctive gamblers, and bookmakers roamed freely in studio administration buildings. No Hollywood figure wagered more than Harry Cohn, a fact that gave him considerable pride.

Although he professed to care nothing for public recognition, Cohn's standing in the community was a matter of intense personal concern. Cohn envied the bosses of M-G-M, Paramount, and Fox—producers who could support a vast stable of stars and directors and turn out a year's program in elegant style, realizing that the Loew's, Paramount, and Fox theaters were awaiting the product. Columbia still scrambled for every play date. All the perfumes of Araby would not erase the odor of Poverty Row.

Gradually, Harry Cohn's position changed. As Columbia prospered, his prestige grew. But Cohn never changed. He had risen from beginnings similar to those of all the hard-driving film pioneers, yet he avoided their metamorphoses. He did not adopt the statesman's toga of Sam Goldwyn, the spiritual robes of Cecil B. DeMille, the clown's costume of Jack L. Warner, or Louis B. Mayer's cloak of paternalism.

He remained Harry Cohn. He spoke in the language of the streets, employing the ancient Anglo-Saxonism for the sex act as often as any other word. Friends and foes alike were ——s, and women were ——.

Despite his earthiness, Cohn betrayed some yearnings for the trappings of his growing eminence. He dressed in natty style, though without flamboyance, and he drove the most expensive car in town. In 1926 he began regular trips to Europe, traveling in the most elegant accommodations.

He became a Republican—not out of any conviction, because he was completely apolitical. All rich men were Republicans; hence, Harry Cohn was a Republican.

Harry and Rose Cohn moved into a house in a private residential park on Wilshire Boulevard named Fremont Place. Here they lived among affluent members of Los Angeles society. Although Cohn mingled with none of them, the proximity of established wealth seemed to be of comfort to him.

The marriage to Rose was not going well. Although she was enormously warmhearted, she lacked the social grace and the attractiveness that seemed necessary in the consort of an ascending figure in the industry. To her great sorrow, she was barren. For a man of Harry Cohn's intensive drive, the lack of the symbol of his masculinity—a son—was a matter of deep concern.

One day Rose Cohn and her sister-in-law Jeanette Cohn went to Pasadena to visit the two daughters of Max Cohn, oldest of the brothers. Max had gone into the textile business, was prosperous for a time, then failed. Harry gave him a job in the studio casting department. Max's wife died, leaving him with two small daughters he was unable to care for. He deposited them in a Pasadena school.

Leonore was five, and Judith was three and a half. When Rose saw the forlorn little girls in the unfriendly school, she cried.

"Jeanette," she told her sister-in-law on the drive back to Los Angeles, "I'm not going to leave those two children in that school."

When Harry Cohn arrived home from the studio that night, Rose announced her intention to take Leonore and Judith into her home.

Her husband scowled. "All right, goddammit," he replied, "but it's your decision, not mine. I'll pay all the bills for them, but I won't be involved in any of their problems. Keep them away from me. Is that understood?"

Rose said that it was. Predictably, Harry Cohn assumed control of the lives of his two nieces, rearing them as his own daughters. So great was his possessiveness that when Max tried to interfere in their upbringing, Harry transferred his brother to the New York office. He tried to guide the lives of Leonore and Judith even into their adulthood, and his efforts resulted in estrangement.

The acquiring of daughters did not materially alter the course of Cohn's marriage to Rose. His sexual drive was intense, and his position as studio boss provided ample opportunities for fulfillment. He neglected none of them.

Convenient for Cohn was a passageway that led directly from his office to a dressing room occupied by a succession of actresses. The route was to continue until later years.

Once Cohn absentmindedly walked from his office into the dressing room. He came face to face with the stern visage of Bette Davis, who was making a film on the lot. Struck with embarrassment, Cohn made a hasty retreat.

8

THE SPECTER OF SOUND: AND A
LITTLE MOUSE SHALL LEAD THEM

*E*xcept for the Warner brothers, all those in positions of power within the film industry were disquieted by the coming of sound motion pictures. Many of the leaders issued brave, wrong-headed statements that sound was a fancy that would soon pass, returning films to their blissful, mute form.

Harry Cohn was less certain that sound films were a temporary fad, but he was not prepared to leap into the new medium. Columbia, as always, was geared to the desires of the exhibitors, and they were reluctant to undergo the expense of wiring for sound. Cohn had witnessed the value that sound effects had contributed to *Submarine*. But there was a great difference between adding boat whistles and gun noises to a film and making one in which the actors spoke complete sentences.

Frank Capra, always seeking new tools with which to improve his craft, was convinced of the efficacy of sound. He was more sure than ever when he saw a film made by a cartoonist friend, Walt Disney.

Disney, who had created animated films in Kansas City and Hollywood, had had a previous encounter with Columbia Pictures. He had concocted a new cartoon figure, a large-eared mouse, and was trying vainly to interest a studio in releasing a series of shorts. An executive of Columbia saw the test film and admitted he liked it.

"But I'm not going to buy it," he said.

"Why not?" the young cartoonist asked.

The executive held up a package of Life Savers. "This is what I'm looking for: an identifiable product," he declared.

"But if you'll only release my cartoons, they'll become identifiable," Disney protested.

"Not interested," was the answer.

Finding all studio doors shut to him, Disney set about making his Mickey Mouse an identifiable product. He released two films on a states' rights basis, realizing enough returns to keep his tiny enterprise in business. Meanwhile, sound was arriving. Disney recognized it as a splendid addition to the art of animation. He made a third Mickey Mouse cartoon, *Steamboat Willie*, in which he coordinated action with music and sounds of Mickey's whistling, pigs' oinking, etc. It created a sensation at the Colony Theater in New York, but Disney was still unable to interest a studio in backing a series.

Capra induced Cohn to see *Steamboat Willie*, and Cohn was properly impressed. Columbia released the *Mickey Mouse* and *Silly Symphony* cartoons for two years—until Disney discovered that salesmen were using his shorts as loss leaders in order to sell the company's features.

Cohn decided Columbia was ready for the plunge into sound. The man to direct the company's first all-talkie was Capra, of course. The subject had to be carefully chosen, because the primitive sound equipment allowed no flexibility. Cameras were encased in soundproofed booths to prevent interference with the dialogue by the whirring of film. Outdoor scenes were precluded because of extraneous noises.

Capra selected *The Donovan Affair*, a standard murder mystery in which the detective gathered all the suspects in the living room at the last reel for a denouement. The star: Jack Holt.

Columbia was unequipped for sound as yet, so the film had to be shot at a nearby studio with padded stage walls. Capra, with his scientific mind, was intrigued by the problems involved in shooting a sound film. Cohn, being more practical, was not. He remained on the sidelines, alternating between querulousness and silent fury. He was at the mercy of mechanics.

The sound man was a newly deified god. The actors performed long exchanges of dialogue, acting as in a stage play, with the encased camera as an audience. The words were recorded on a wax disc, and the slightest untoward sound could ruin the take.

"No good for sound," the sound man announced over and over again, plunging Harry Cohn into despair. He had long imposed the studio code that every company must complete a take by 9 A.M. each shooting day. On *The Donovan Affair* there was often no printable take until late afternoon. It meant nothing to Cohn that the take was lengthy enough to constitute an average day's shooting.

By the time *The Donovan Affair* was released—in April, 1929—the prophets of doom for sound had ceased their auguries. Talkies were permanent, and the film industry found itself in a state of chaos. Columbia, like all other studios, discovered many of its stars could not make the change to the new order.

Film companies scrambled desperately for sound equipment, without which they could not function in the shifting marketplace. Being one of the minor studios, Columbia had to wait for sound apparatus until the major studios had theirs. Columbia strove to improve its position by any means possible. Production supervisor Sam Bischoff managed to hijack a pair of movieolas destined for Pathé; a $500 tip to the truck driver was responsible.

Technicians struggled to lessen the unwieldiness of the sound camera, which permitted little more than filmed stage plays. Paramount developed a portable camera, but it required eight strong men to lift.

Joe Walker, who photographed all of Capra's Columbia films except the off-the-lot *Donovan Affair*, was convinced that a more practical camera could be devised. He refused to shoot from a camera booth, which necessitated filming through glass with the resultant loss of clarity. Walker invented a padded wooden blimp, which permitted camera mobility while eliminating mechanical noises.

Just as stars and technique changed with the advent of talkies, so did content. In a less-sophisticated era Harry Cohn had been able to hand his producers and directors a list of thirty titles and instruct them, "Here—find me stories to go with these titles." Thus, Columbia's yearly program was created, largely from original stories.

That was not possible in the sound era. Movies were no longer simple allegories of good and evil. Dialogue brought a new sophistication, a need for greater reality.

Cohn hired D. A. Doran, who was acquainted with the stage and literary scene, to scout literary properties. Doran went to New York and in eight weeks bought plays and books for a year's supply of screen stories. Included were *The Criminal Code*, which starred Walter Huston and Constance Cummings, and *Rain or Shine*, in which Joe Cook repeated his Broadway role.

Columbia was maturing. It was outgrowing the Jack Holt-Ralph Graves heroics, which took place on land (*War Correspondent*), on sea (*Hell's Island*), and in the air (*Flight* and *Dirigible*). Columbia was seeking a style, which it would find in the golden decade ahead.

III

The Golden Time:
The Thirties

• • • • •

THE UPHEAVAL OF SOUND COINCIDES WITH DEPRESSION. Curiously, the film industry thrives. "Forget your troubles—see a movie." Every week 90,000,000 tickets are sold.

The old order gives way. Silent stars, astonished by the change in their fortunes, retire to their Beverly Hills aeries and sniff at the new-found noise. Each week brings a new wave of stage actors, their diction practiced on the journey across the continent. Britons arrive in large numbers.

Depression comes late to Hollywood. In 1933 almost a third of the nation's 16,000 theaters are dark. The novelty of sound is long past, and directors have not yet mastered the idiom of the talking picture. Americans are disenchanted with movies.

The film industry responds with salary cuts and better pictures. It creates a new American folk hero, the gangster. It discovers the musical, and audiences marvel at the geometric patterns Busby Berkeley can create with a few hundred feminine legs.

The industry also realizes the salability of sophisticated actors delivering sophisticated dialogue.

But sophistication can be carried too far in puritan America. Archbishops decry the corruption of the innocent by immoral films, and Hollywood is scared into self-censorship. Joe Breen wields the scissors and whitewash, prohibiting the use of such terms as cripes, fanny, (the) finger, Gawd, goose, hell or damn (except when justified), hold your hat, in your hat, madam (relating to prostitution), nance, nerts, nuts (except when meaning crazy), pansy, razzberry (the sound), SOB, son-of-a, tart, tomcat (applied to a man), and whore, as well as traveling salesman and farmer's daughter jokes.

Industry censors even find fault with a Disney cow. The udder is erased.

The rules preclude reality in films. But Americans aren't seeking reality; they want dreams. Hollywood can supply them in vast quantity.

It is the time of the big studios. Each becomes a suzerainty, sufficient unto itself. To ship a finished film to New York every week, a studio must operate like a factory, with legions of producers, directors, writers, and stars. M-G-M boasts that it has more stars than there are in the heavens.

The big companies conquer all. No independent can prevail against them—except the unconquerable Sam Goldwyn. Block booking is now in full flower, and exhibitors must buy in quantity or not at all. FDR's trustbusters are looking into this.

Bank night and bingo help support the theater business, which remains good for five years. Then the 1938 recession brings a brief dislocation. The industry, ever responsive to crisis, spends $1,000,000 to convince the public that "Motion Pictures Are Better Than Ever."

And so they are. A host of accomplished directors, some schooled in the silents, some newly arrived from Broadway, are providing an explosion of creativity in comedy and drama.

War approaches as the decade ends, but Hollywood still cherishes its dreams. For the climax, David Selznick produces the supermovie *Gone with the Wind*. Such is the euphoria in Hollywood that Joe Breen permits Rhett Butler to say as his curtain line, "Frankly, my dear, I don't give a damn."

●　●　●　●　●

I
TOWARD STYLE

*D*uring the flowering period of the 1930's each of the studios was to develop its particular style and flavor.

M-G-M, the Grand Hotel of the studios, was distinctly feminine. The gentle, gifted Irving Thalberg and Louis B. Mayer, with his appreciation of women, fostered the idealized woman: the divine Garbo; the regal Norma Shearer; Joan Crawford, the graduated shopgirl; Myrna Loy, the improbable wife; Jean Harlow, the tart's tart; lyrical Jeanette MacDonald; tragic Luise Rainer; brittle Rosalind Russell. Even the formidable M-G-M men—Clark Gable, Spencer Tracy, Robert Taylor, William Powell, Nelson Eddy—seemed to function largely to enhance the ladies.

Paramount was the college campus, with such stalwarts as Richard Arlen, Jack Oakie, Bing Crosby, and Fred MacMurray playing on the varsity. Life seemed a game, whether it was played for Yale University, the Bengal Lancers, or *Beau Geste*.

Warner Brothers was the studio that spoke in the jargon of the big city—fast, breezy, faintly cynical. Jimmy Cagney set the pace with his rat-a-tat-tat style, and all was set to Leo Forbstein's loud, brassy orchestrations.

Fox was folksy and sentimental, with Janet Gaynor, Shirley Temple, and Will Rogers eliciting tears and grins. The pace accelerated when Darryl Zanuck swept into the studio on a polo pony in mid-decade. The new Twentieth Century-Fox specialized in leggy musicals and glossy evocations of America's recent past.

Fred Astaire and Ginger Rogers established the tone for RKO: smart, witty, up-to-date.

Universal, divested of Uncle Carl Laemmle and saved from extinction by Deanna Durbin, followed an escapist course—sunny musicals, Westerns, horror films.

And Columbia. Its features seemed to be peopled by beauties in long gowns and handsome men in dinner jackets. They thrust themselves into outrageous situations, always maintaining their *savoir faire.* Columbia became the home of the sophisticated film, an eventuality that astounded the many people in Hollywood who considered Harry Cohn the compleat vulgarian.

A studio's style did not develop overnight, nor did it come by chance. Columbia's style was born in the 1920's, and it grew to a large degree out of necessity. But style must also be nurtured and directed, and that was done at Columbia by the man who guided its every move.

Born in Poverty Row, Columbia never moved its location. It resisted the impulse to transfer to more spacious quarters in outlying areas, as had bigger studios. Instead, it merely swallowed up Poverty Row, parcel by parcel, until it occupied most of the long block between Sunset Boulevard and Fountain Avenue and between Gower Street and Beachwood Drive. The area was small by major-studio standards, but it was crammed with sound stages, offices, and shops. The compactness provided a double advantage: working in proximity, Columbia employees developed an *esprit de corps*; also, Harry Cohn could easily reconnoiter their activities by foot. In 1935, as the studio prospered and developed more need for exteriors, Columbia bought the first forty acres of an eventual eighty-acre ranch for outdoor sets in nearby Burbank.

Except for the program Westerns—eight a year starring Buck Jones, another eight with Tim McCoy—Columbia's movies were largely filmed on interior sets. Thus, directors were not subject to costly delays of sun and weather.

Columbia films were mostly contemporary in content. This was also a matter of economics. Period pictures required expensive costumes and sets.

Also, Harry Cohn was contemporary in his outlook. He felt insecure when he ventured away from modern subjects, and with good reason. A cherished tale among his screenwriters concerned the time when Cohn was perusing the script of an Arabian Nights fantasy. Suddenly he began pushing buttons to summon the writer and producer of the film, as well as his executive assistants.

The men stood in an anxious semicircle before Cohn's desk. With an eloquent scowl he began his interrogation.

"You college men!" he snapped. "I pay you bastards thousands of dollars a week to know something, and what do I get? Ignorance!"

His listeners continued in silence, awaiting the attack.

"You there," Cohn said, stabbing a finger toward the scriptwriter. "How far did you get in college?"

"I graduated, Mr. Cohn," was the reply.

"Graduated, huh? Well, tell me this: about when would you say this picture takes place?"

"I'd say about 1200 A.D."

"Aha! Well, I never went to college like you sons of bitches, but I can tell you one thing: they didn't say 'yes, sirree' in 1200."

The producer and writer gazed at each other in perplexity.

"It's all through this script, goddammit," Cohn continued.

"You've got 'em all saying, 'Yes, sirree.'"

"Could I see where you mean, Harry?" the producer asked.

"Sure—right here!"

Cohn shoved the script across the desk, pointing to a passage. The producer read it and said, "But, Harry, that's 'Yes, sire'!"

Harry Cohn dealt more adequately with modern subjects, and although he was seldom an innovator, he had a gift for recognizing what was true and what was phony in a script. There was nothing obscure or obtuse in Columbia films.

This quality dated back to the company's earliest days. While reviewing the final print of one of his first features, Cohn came across a three-syllable word in a title. He ordered the film stopped.

"What does that word mean?" he demanded.

The writer of the script told him.

"Take it out," said Cohn. "If I don't know what it means, the average guy in a movie theater sure as hell won't."

Although Columbia films possessed clarity, they were not aimed at the twelve-year-old mind. Cohn hired the brightest writers and the most accomplished directors he could find. Again, this was a matter of economics. Little Columbia could not afford the mammoth star lists of M-G-M and Paramount. Cohn had to borrow stars from the major studios or hire the top free-lancers.

He knew they could be lured only by good scripts and crack directors.

Columbia films had taste. Despite Cohn's personal habits of speech, he allowed nothing vulgar or salacious on the screen. It was simply not good for business. He checked every costume worn by leading ladies and vetoed deep necklines and other suggestions of sex. He had a sharp eye for double entendres; they were excised.

When Ralph Graves was a contract player, he was eager to direct a film. Cohn gave him an assignment. One of Graves' first scenes showed the leading man in a nightclub watching a shimmy dancer. On the table before him was a mound of Jello. He ordered another dish of Jello and jiggled the pair as the dancer continued her shimmy. Graves was removed from the film as soon as Cohn saw the scene.

Columbia films had the feel of having been hand-tailored, while those of the major studios seemed mass-produced. This quality extended not merely to the content of Columbia pictures, but to the physical aspects as well. The film itself seemed brighter, more luminous than the product of other studios.

The unique pictorial quality of Columbia films found its origins in a 1928 melodrama, *The Warning*. Joseph Walker, a devotee of the art of D. W. Griffith, was photographing the film as his first assignment on the lot. He came to work one morning to find he was required to shoot a waterfront scene in which the principal feature was a large, inept model of a sailing ship.

"I can't shoot it that way," Walker complained to the director, George Seitz. "We ought to cover up that ship somehow. Why not make it a night scene with fog?"

"It's all right with me," said Seitz. "But Harry Cohn doesn't like anyone to make changes without asking him."

Walker had misgivings. "Maybe I should just shoot what they put in front of me," he said.

"Oh, well," added Seitz, "Cohn probably won't like the first day's work, and he'll fire you anyway. Might as well do it the way you want."

The scene was photographed with lights and shadows, so that only the outlines of the sailing vessel were visible. The next day Seitz and Walker waited with apprehension as Cohn viewed what had been filmed. With him was Dorothy Howell, first of a series of women assistants on whom he relied for the feminine viewpoint.

"Where's that boat?" Cohn demanded. "I paid four hundred dollars for that boat!"

He was prepared to fire the cameraman when Miss Howell intervened: "Wait a minute. I liked the way it was shot. This is the first time we've had exciting photography. Why not give him a chance?"

Cohn grudgingly agreed to do so. *The Warning* received the best reviews of any Columbia picture to that time, largely because of the arresting pictorial quality.

During the same year Walker began his long, fruitful collaboration with Frank Capra. Walker photographed other Columbia films as well, and his diffused portraiture of Grace Moore, Irene Dunne, Loretta Young, Jean Arthur, and Rosalind Russell set the standard for glamour in the industry.

Harry Cohn recognized the value of expert photography and also realized that sloppy developing and printing could negate a cameraman's efforts. Columbia became the first studio to establish its own film laboratory. The Columbia lab handled each print with utmost care and developed the technique of achieving a brilliance in the whiteness before the white "choked up" and went dull, Cohn decreed that every print had to leave the studio in immaculate condition, and more than one lab technician was fired for having allowed scratched or dirty film to be released.

He expected the same standard of excellence in every department. Columbia sound was the best in the industry. The prop department, the mill, the location department, makeup, hairdressing, wardrobe—all were models of efficiency—because of constant, nagging supervision by Harry Cohn.

"Every time you spend a dollar, twenty-five cents of it is mine," he said repeatedly, citing his approximate share of the company.

Those who played by his rules could remain at Columbia for thirty years. Those who did not were swiftly removed from the payroll.

2

JOE BRANDT WITHDRAWS FROM THE FRAY; ALSO, THE COUP D'ETAT THAT FAILED

*A*s Columbia approached the edge of success, it experienced the defection of one of the founding partners. Joe Brandt, the conservative president of the corporation, had found his position increasingly uncomfortable. He had served the corporation well during its formative years, steering it through the shoals of insolvency that had sunk many another Poverty Row company. His knowledge of law and his businesslike manner had reassured investors who might otherwise have been frightened away by the volatile nature of the movie business and moviemakers.

But Brandt had none of the gambling instinct of Harry and Jack Cohn. He was constantly urging his partners to play safe.

"Make more Westerns," he urged. "We can always sell Westerns."

Harry Cohn argued that Westerns were a cheap item that any two-bit producer could make. The only way C.B.C.—later Columbia—could progress would be to invade the field occupied by the majors: the making of first-class attractions. Jack Cohn agreed, but there was little else the brothers agreed on. Harry and Jack fought constantly.

Joe Brandt wearied of it all. His wife urged him to quit Columbia.

"You're forty-one-and-a-half years old," she argued. "We could have thirty years of wonderful living ahead of us. With the portfolio of stocks that I have invested for you, we have two million dollars. With that and what you could get for your Columbia stock, we could travel all over the world and enjoy ourselves for the rest of our lives."

Brandt was swayed, but he was not yet willing to leave the company he had helped found and build. He felt he could manage Jack if only he could get Harry out of the way. Seated in a position of growing power as boss of the studio, Harry Cohn had absolutely no intention of selling out.

Jack Cohn was acutely aware of the dangers in a shift of power. He and Joe Brandt sometimes disagreed on procedural matters, but the two New York-based officers of the corporation generally presented a united front in opposition to the vice-president in charge of production. With Brandt gone, it would be Jack versus Harry, a situation that the older brother did not relish. He decided to make his move.

Jack made a clandestine journey to California. He paid a call on A. P. Giannini, the leonine founder of the Bank of Italy—now the Bank of America—who enjoyed the adventure and profit of investing in motion picture companies. Giannini was a member of the board of directors of Columbia because of his large investment in the company.

The banker listened carefully to Jack's argument: Harry Cohn was irresponsible and profligate and incapable of managing a motion picture studio.

As soon as Jack Cohn left his office, Giannini placed a call to Columbia Studio.

"Harry," said Giannini, "I think you should know who just visited me."

Jack Cohn's power play failed; Giannini's faith in Harry as a moviemaker could not be shaken.

Seeing no hope of relief from the brotherly warfare, Brandt decided to heed his wife's advice and sell out. His price was $500,000.

Now it was Harry Cohn's chance to execute a power play. If he could acquire Brandt's stock, he would be in a more formidable position to ward off further attacks by his brother. But where could he find $500,000 in a hurry?

He knew of only one person who dealt in such amounts and might lend him $500,000: his betting adviser, Buzzy Appleton. Buzzy came through.

Harry Cohn assumed the presidency of Columbia Pictures Corporation in 1932. He retained his position as chief of production, becoming the only film company head to hold both positions. Jack Cohn became vice-president and treasurer.

The storm between the two brothers never abated. Each spoke violently of the other, in or out of the other's hearing. Each strove mightily to achieve an advantage.

Harry perused business contracts made by the East, and he ordered studio lawyers to study every clause. He was ever hopeful of uncovering at least one tiny loophole that might redound against the corporation. If he succeeded, then he could castigate and berate his brother for permitting such incompetence.

Jack, on the other hand, lay in wait for studio errors. Since every movie made by the West was a potential mistake, he acquired much ammunition for his charges that the studio administration was inept. This constant surveillance by Jack prompted Harry to strive ever harder to eliminate studio waste and create better pictures.

But it was an uneven battle after 1932. As president and major stockholder, Harry Cohn occupied the position of power. There could be no real threat to him as long as he continued producing movies the East could sell. Most of the time he was able to do so.

Jack Cohn underwent a change of personality after his thrust for control of Columbia had failed. He seemed to have lost the fire that he had displayed when he had maneuvered the *Damaged Goods* deal at Universal, the consuming drive he possessed during the early years of C.B.C. and Columbia.

The decisive defeat by Harry eroded the flinty edge of Jack's personality. He became more gentle with his underlings in the New York office and with his wife and three sons, Ralph, Joseph, and Robert. Before, Columbia Pictures had been the abiding interest of his life. Now he acquired 350 acres in Connecticut and enjoyed spending long weekends on the farm, riding horseback over the meadows and rolling hills. He initiated the formation of the Motion Picture Pioneers, a benevolent organization that helped support needy old-timers.

The failure of Jack to devote his entire life to Columbia Pictures irritated Harry. As studio boss, Harry worked all day Sat-

urday at the studio and often part of Sunday. It pained him to
think of Jack rusticating at his Connecticut acreage. Harry often
timed his Friday afternoon telephone calls to the East at five
o'clock New York time. He engaged Jack in a long and often
violent conversation, thus postponing Jack's departure to the
country.

The ambivalence of the brothers' relationship provided legends that were cherished by their employees. During his early
tenure at Columbia, Frank Capra was witness to a violent quarrel between Harry and Jack in Harry's studio office. The language was profane and vituperative, and Capra feared that the
brothers would come to blows.

As both reached a red-faced fury, the jingling bells of the
Good Humor ice-cream truck were heard outside on Gower
Street.

"Just a minute," Harry said, striding to the window. He
swung it open and issued a blasting whistle to stop the ice-cream
salesman.

"What do you want, Jack?" Harry asked. "They got a good
vanilla stick with crunchy chocolate on the outside."

"Okay, I'll take that," said Jack.

"What about you, Frank?" Harry asked.

"Nothing for me, thanks," replied the astonished Capra.

Harry yelled down to the street, "One vanilla with the
chocolate crunch and one plain chocolate." The salesman tossed
the two bars to the second-floor window, and Harry threw down
two dimes. He handed Jack his ice cream and then resumed:
"Now listen, you son of a bitch."

On any threat to Columbia from the outside, Harry and Jack
Cohn presented a united and sometimes savage defense. But on
most intercorporation matters they were at odds.

During one Western visit of Jack and his New York executives, Harry succeeded in uncovering an error by the East. He proceeded into a fifteen-minute tirade, assailing the intelligence of
the entire sales force and Jack in particular. He ended by shaking
his finger in Jack's face.

Having unburdened himself, Harry turned to resume his
position behind his desk. As he did so, Jack delivered an eloquent

rebuttal in full view of everyone in the room except Harry. Jack stuck out his tongue.

Joe Brandt had left Columbia to escape the brotherly conflict. But his wife's hopes for a long and peaceful life together failed to come true. Joe Brandt succumbed in 1939, preceding the Cohns in death by almost twenty years.

3
HARRY COHN AND THE WRITERS: BEGINNINGS OF THE LONG, PRODUCTIVE WAR

*H*arry Cohn paid one of his rare morning visits to the studio. He strode into the courtyard around which arose the writers' offices, and he noticed something that disturbed him greatly: silence.

No sound emerged from the tiers of rooms wherein scenarios were produced. The scent of freshly made coffee hovered in the air, adding further evidence of the midmorning lull of activity.

"Where are the writers?" Cohn shouted. "Why aren't they working? I don't hear a sound. I am paying you big salaries, and you do nothing. You are stealing my money!"

Suddenly, from a score of windows, came the clacking of typewriter keys.

"*Liars!*" Harry Cohn bawled.

The incident demonstrated Cohn's relationship with the craftsmen of movie scripts. With the sound era he began his thirty years' war with writers, a conflict that produced a remarkable contribution to the literature of the screen.

Talkies placed the writer in ascendancy. In the silent era the writer merely outlined the action and created the titles; the director fleshed out the story in the shooting. The director remained the dominant figure in the making of sound pictures, but he could not function without the skillful collaboration of the writer.

Harry Cohn realized that talkies required a new breed of writer. He sent scouting expeditions to New York and sometimes went himself to interview prospects among playwrights, novelists, short-story writers, and journalists. Those who displayed promise were shipped West to try their talents on scenarios. If they proved adept at creating action and dialogue, they remained at Columbia. If not, their services were terminated.

Most important of the early importations was Jo Swerling, Russian-born, a onetime reporter and magazine writer who had turned to vaudeville sketches and Broadway plays. He was a prodigious worker; during his first eleven months at Columbia he produced thirteen scripts, including several for Frank Capra.

One morning in 1932, as be was filming *The Bitter Tea of General Yen*, Capra expressed dissatisfaction with an upcoming scene. Swerling returned in an hour with four completely different versions of the scene.

"If you don't like those, I'll write some others," he said.

Robert Riskin had arrived in 1931. A New Yorker, he had sold original screen stories to Paramount at the age of seventeen. He became Swerling's successor as writer for Capra and set the standard for writing excellence at Columbia.

A man whose gentle humanity was reflected in the Capra scripts, Riskin did his writing in longhand as he sat on the porch of the Columbia office building. He wrote each script as if he were telling a story, completing a final version in two weeks. He never reread the first draft, never rewrote. Other writers often popped out of their offices to seek Riskin's advice on a story point or a line of dialogue. He delivered his opinion, then returned to his own project.

The exchange of ideas and technique was an essential quality of the Columbia writing staff. The members formed an alliance, united in a spirit of cooperation and in opposition to Harry Cohn.

Oddly, Cohn had an affinity for writers. This was not true of his relations with other creative people.

He treated most of his producers with contempt. Directors— the better ones—received more consideration. He permitted the best of them to work without interference, if they so demanded; his attitude toward mediocre directors could be indifferent or brutal. Actors whose fame had been achieved at Columbia were considered possessions by Cohn.

All three—producers, directors, stars—experienced eventual and often violent estrangement from Cohn and Columbia. Writers remained. Many were to know lengthy tenure, by Hollywood standards.

The writing process was something Cohn could not comprehend. He secretly viewed it with awe and wonder, although he never betrayed those feelings to writers.

His treatment of a new writer at Columbia became standard. The same charade was repeated hundreds of times with little variation.

After the writer had been working on a script for two weeks, he received a telephone call from Cohn's secretary.

"Mr. Cohn would like to see what you've written so far," the secretary said. "Seventy-five pages will do."

Protests that the work was not in proper condition for perusal were unavailing. The script had to be delivered to Cohn's office. A day later the writer received a summons to appear before Mr. Cohn.

The script rested on Cohn's desk. As the writer approached, Cohn ranted, "That's the worst piece of———I've ever read. You call yourself a writer? What the———am I paying you for?"

The next few seconds determined whether the writer stayed at Columbia or vanished from the payroll. His days would be numbered if he replied, "I'll admit, Mr. Cohn, that the script is not my best writing, but I think there are some playable scenes."

Those who remained were the ones who replied heatedly, "'What the hell do you mean, that's a piece of———? It's goddam good. Now you take that scene where the girl meets the guy. . .'"

Cohn then listened. The writer could score an additional advantage if he could uncover the fact that Cohn had not even read the script. He was merely testing the writer's faith and conviction in his material.

This procedure was emotionally exhausting for writers, and some good ones left Columbia rather than face the ordeal. But many stayed, and they were to set the tone for the Columbia product: vigorous, contemporary, imaginative.

Many writers who worked at Columbia felt distaste for Cohn and his methods. Principal among them was Ben Hecht, who applied a lasting epithet to Cohn: White Fang.

Many others, with the writer's appreciation of a unique and formidable character, were stimulated by their encounters with

Cohn. Some admitted to a feeling of love-hate, which character-
ized the relationships of many people to Harry Cohn.

As a class, writers did not accord Cohn the deference he
received from most other Columbia employees. He endured writers' jibes with a tolerance he extended to no one else.

Once Cohn summoned Swerling and complained with bitterness that Swerling's wife had driven into Cohn's Rolls-Royce in
the Columbia parking lot. Swerling's explanation: "She must
have thought you were in it."

Norman Krasna proved the most bothersome gadfly to
Cohn. Once a press agent at Warner Brothers, Krasna had written a successful play, *Louder, Please*, and had been enlisted for
the Columbia writing staff. After completing a few scripts, he felt
he was being underpaid. Since he was firmly tied to a contract he
reasoned that his only instrument of escape was his wit.

The principal producers, directors, writers, and production
aides met each day for lunch with Cohn in the executive dining
room. Krasna chose these occasions for cracking jokes he hoped
would provoke Cohn into firing him.

Cohn entered the dining room one day with a wide smile on
his face, a rare happening at Columbia. "Where do you think I
was last night?" he asked expansively.

"Night school?" Krasna inquired.

Cohn once assumed his seat at the head of the table and
announced, "Gentlemen, I am going to England next week."

Krasna, at the far end of the table, took up the cue immediately: "Gee, Mr. Cohn, can I go along with you?"

Cohn stared down the table scornfully. "Go with me!" he
snorted. "Now why the hell would I take a punk like you to England with me?"

"As interpreter?"

When Cohn was leaving for a trip to New York, Krasna
again volunteered himself as traveling companion. He expressed
fear that Cohn might starve to death on the train without someone to write his meal order.

Following a series of successes, Cohn delivered a pep talk to
his staff, declaring that Columbia was going to be the greatest

studio in Hollywood. His enthusiasm mounted, and he began spelling out the studio name like a college cheerleader: "C-O-L-O-M-B-I-A."

His listeners sat in uneasy silence. Krasna seized the opportunity to remark, "You know, Mr. Cohn, if you're going to remain as president of the company, you really ought to learn that it's spelled C-O-L-U-M-B-I-A." (The occurrence was to have a sequel a decade later.)

Krasna was striking at an area of extreme sensitivity by deriding Cohn before his underlings. But economic considerations remained preeminent; Krasna was too good a bargain to fire.

The writer reasoned that he might achieve his goal by holding Cohn up to ridicule before the community. His tactic was sound. William Wilkerson, the powerful publisher of *Hollywood Reporter*, was engaged in one of his periodic feuds with Columbia, and he delighted in printing Krasna's wisecracks about Cohn in the trade paper.

The climax of the campaign arrived when *Hollywood Reporter* conveyed the news that Norman Krasna had drawn up a new will. His executors were instructed that he was to be cremated and the ashes were to be thrown in Cohn's face.

Krasna won his release from the Columbia contract.

In December 1932, Harry Cohn was in New York interviewing prospective writers. He had been assisted in his search by Walter Wanger, a bookish graduate of Dartmouth who had become a vice-president of Columbia. Wanger helped sift through literary material submitted by applicants.

Wanger had suggested to Cohn, "When you go to New York look up a writer named Dore Schary. She's got a lot of guts in her writing."

One morning Dore Schary was ushered into the presence of Harry Cohn in Columbia's New York offices. Cohn glanced up from some papers he was perusing and muttered to an aide, "Is this one of them?"

"Yes, sir," said the aide.

"What's your name?" Cohn demanded.

"Dore Schary," replied the slender young man.

"Dore Schary!" Cohn broke out laughing as Schary stared in puzzlement.

"That stupid son of a bitch, Wanger," Cohn continued. "He thought Dore Schary was a dame. I ought to send you out there as a gag."

He began interrogating the writer.

"How many plays have you had produced?" Cohn asked.

"None," Schary admitted.

"Then you haven't made a living from writing yet?"

"No, sir."

"Do you want to go to Hollywood?"

"Yes."

"Do you think you can write pictures?"

"I know I can."

"When can you leave?"

"Tomorrow."

"Okay, I'll let you know."

"Thank you." Schary stood up to leave.

"Wait a minute," said Cohn. "You didn't ask me how much I would pay you."

"I figured it would be enough to take care of me."

Cohn slapped the desk and said, "Just because you said that, you're on your way."

Later the terms were telephoned to Schary. He would be paid $100 a week and his fare to California. No fare was provided for transportation of his wife, but the sum was advanced, to be collected from future paychecks. Since Schary was then averaging $28 a week from occasional acting jobs, selling greeting cards and soda jerking at the YMHA, he considered the offer entirely adequate.

Schary reported to the studio and was assigned a cell in the writers' building, where newcomers were installed amid such established scenarists as Swerling, Riskin, James Cain, and Sidney Kingsley.

At five o'clock in the afternoon Schary was summoned to appear in Cohn's office. He and three other newcomers were told to sit on a long couch that faced Cohn's desk. They were also confronted by Capra, Briskin, Wanger, and Riskin.

Cohn conducted the entire proceedings. First he asked a former newspaper reporter what kind of screenwriting he thought he could do.

"Sports stories, gangland murders—hard-hitting stuff," the prospect answered jauntily. "The kind of thing you fellows call cops and robbers."

Next, an effeminate writer of magazine stories declared that he wanted to specialize in dramatic material with artistic quality. Then a novelist in London-tailored clothes spoke at great length of how he intended to write sophisticated comedy.

"What about you, Schary?" Cohn asked, pointing to the young man at the end of the couch. "What can you write?"

"I don't know," Schary replied.

The room seemed more silent than before. "What's that?" Cohn asked unbelievingly.

"I'm sort of like a bottle of milk left on your doorstep," Schary continued. "Give me something to write, and I'll try to do it."

"You're a pretty snotty kid," Cohn said.

"No writer can give you an impression of what he can do," Schary insisted. "You'll have to see for yourself in the writing."

Riskin interjected, "That makes sense to me."

Cohn grew impatient. "All of you get out of here," he ordered. As the new men left, he turned to Wanger and began, "Now I want to tell you something, big brain—"

Of the four candidates for screenwriting, only Schary survived.

4

THE FLOWERING OF CAPRA
AND COLUMBIA:
IT HAPPENED ONE NIGHT

*D*uring the early years of sound films Frank Capra was engaged in a quest for style. He continued pouring forth films to meet the exigencies of the Columbia program, investing each film with touches of imagination.

Continuing with the Jack Holt-Ralph Graves service cycle, Capra directed *Flight* and *Dirigible*, both commendable action films. *Dirigible* provided a milestone: the first Columbia picture to appear at the august Grauman's Chinese Theater. Capra directed Barbara Stanwyck in *Ladies of Leisure* and thus created a new contract star for Columbia. Jean Harlow, who had been seen briefly in *Hell's Angels*, achieved stardom in *Platinum Blonde*, which Capra directed for Columbia. But the profit went to the Caddo Company, which held her contract.

In *American Madness*, which starred Walter Huston and Constance Cummings in 1932, Capra made his most studied effort to inject pieces of business that underlined character. "To my mind, plot is unimportant," he commented later. "I am interested most in characterizations. The people must be real."

Critics found reality in his Oriental drama, *The Bitter Tea of General Yen*, with Barbara Stanwyck and Nils Asther playing the leads. It was selected as the first feature to appear on the immense screen of the Radio City Music Hall.

The emergence of Capra as a movie stylist came with *Lady for a Day* in 1933. The director had found the material in a short story by Damon Runyon, and it was purchased for $1,500, marking the first of many sales to the studios by Runyon.

Riskin's script caught the slangy, hard-boiled sentiment of Runyon's Broadway characters. The plot concerned Apple

Annie, a frowzy Times Square peddler who was thrown into a panic by the impending visit of her daughter. The girl, who had been well supported by Annie, was long separated from her mother, who claimed to be a society matron in her letters. Now the daughter was bringing her future husband, a Spanish noble-man, and his family to meet Annie. By a conspiracy of Annie's friends of the demiworld, plus the assistance of the mayor of New York City and the governor of the state, Annie was trans-formed into a lady, captivating the Spanish visitors.

Shortly before *Lady for a Day* was to go into production, Capra lay in bed one night contemplating the project. Suddenly he sat upright. He reached for the telephone and called Harry Cohn.

"Harry, we've got a problem," said Capra. "I've got to see you about it in the morning."

Capra entered Cohn's office with worry rumpling his Sicilian face. *Lady for a Day* was scheduled to cost $300,000, making it one of the most expensive Columbia films to that time.

"Harry," said Capra, "you've got to face the fact that you're spending three hundred thousand dollars on a picture in which the heroine is seventy years old."

Cohn stared at the director, then took a stick of chewing gum from his desk drawer, unwrapped it, and put it in his mouth. He walked to the window and gazed down at the traffic on Gower Street, chewing intently.

He turned and faced Capra. "All I know is the thing's got a wallop," said Cohn. "Go ahead."

May Robson was superb as Apple Annie, and her splendid hamming was supported by the assemblage of Runyon charac-ters. Never before had a Columbia film attracted such laudatory reviews or such box office returns. Capra, May Robson, and *Lady for a Day* were nominated for Academy Awards, marking the first time Columbia achievements had been cited.

The most prestigious movie made by Columbia came from a short story called "Night Bus," written by Samuel Hopkins Adams. Capra was intrigued by the tale of the newspaperman who accompanied an heiress on a cross-country disappearance, his indifference winning her away from a playboy fiancé. Columbia bought the film rights for $5,000. Bob Riskin fashioned a screenplay that stressed the unique relationship between the man and woman, creating brilliant comedy scenes, such as the hitchhiking lesson and the motel sequence in which woolen "Walls of Jericho" protected the heiress' honor.

Casting was all-important to the success of *It Happened One Night*, which was the title selected for the film. Columbia's scant contract list could provide no one suitable for the leading roles. Harry Cohn had to find help from the major studios.

He had long sought the favor of Louis B. Mayer, who had scores of stars at M-G-M. Because of *Lady for a Day*, Frank Capra was in demand as a director, and Cohn used him for bargaining power. Cohn offered Mayer the services of Capra for one picture in exchange for the loan of Robert Montgomery. Mayer agreed, since Montgomery was getting difficult about his film roles and needed the discipline of being sent to a minor studio.

Montgomery refused to go. Capra asked for Clark Gable, and Mayer agreed to lend him. Cohn grumbled about having to settle for a lesser name.

Gable thought he had been betrayed. He complained of being lent "to a little independent on Poverty Row—Siberia for me." It seemed a reversal for his ascending career.

For the heiress role, Capra wanted Myrna Loy, who refused it. Then he sought Claudette Colbert, with whom he had contended on her first film, *Love o' Mike*. She was unimpressed by the script, but it offered her a departure from the tearful heroines she had been playing at Paramount. Most of all, she savored the prospect of appearing with Clark Gable. So she accepted the role, exercising her option for one picture annually outside her Paramount contract. Columbia paid her $40,000.

Both Gable and Colbert reported to Capra in faintly hostile moods. Capra, who had known many bus rides during his wandering years, dwelled at length on the bus sequence at the beginning of the picture. He wanted to picture the sociability of the passengers as they traveled through the stormy night, contrasting with the aloofness of the fleeing heiress. He tried out three teams of hillbilly musicians, liked them so much he included all in the scene. For a song, he resurrected a forgotten ditty, *The Daring Young Man on the Flying Trapeze.* All the bus riders joined in the singing.

Miss Colbert thought the scene corny and unbelievable.

"How could everyone in the bus know all the words to the song?" she rationalized.

"Don't worry about it," Capra said assuringly. "If the scene doesn't work, it can come right out of the picture without interfering with the plot."

Miss Colbert remained dubious until she noticed the rare delight on the face of her colored maid as she watched the singing by the rollicking passengers.

During the first fortnight of filming the two stars were unaware that they were engaged in anything remarkable. Then one morning, as they drove to the location site in a limousine, Gable turned to his costar and commented, "You know, I think this wop's got something." Miss Colbert agreed.

What Capra had discovered was to be the touchstone for himself and for other film creators at Columbia during the decade of the thirties. Other studios tried to duplicate their success, but they generally failed for lack of the important ingredient. The formula was profound, yet simple: you can explore any comic possibility as long as your characters remain human beings. Capra alternated scenes of pure comedy with others that delineated character. Even as they enacted the hilarious "Walls of Jericho" scene, Gable was espousing his ideals and Colbert was countering with her narrower point of view.

It Happened One Night was filmed in four weeks at a cost under $300,000. Cohn and his staff attended the first preview, at which the audience reaction was highly favorable. The entire group returned to Cohn's office to discuss the film. Several underlings expressed the belief that it was overlong at more than two hours, and possible cuts were weighed. Capra listened without comment.

Cohn finally turned to Capra and asked, "Well, Frank, what are you going to do?"

Capra took a puff from his pipe and replied, "I'm going to cut the negative and ship it to New York without a change."

Cohn slammed the desk and ordered, "Ship it!"

It Happened One Night struck the film market with an astonishing impact. It continued for months in theaters that seldom played a movie more than two or three weeks. Critics praised it to the skies.

The industry's accolade came on February 27, 1935, the date when the stigma of Poverty Row was erased from Harry Cohn and Columbia.

It was the night of the Academy Awards, and Claudette Colbert was so certain she had no chance of winning that she scheduled a departure to New York that evening. As she was boarding the Santa Fé Chief, Academy officials dashed up to inform her that she had been named best actress of 1934. A motorcycle escort rushed her to the Biltmore Bowl, where she entered the formal gathering in a traveling suit and brown felt hat.

Clark Gable was selected best actor, marking the only instance in Academy history when costars won the major awards. The Academy proclaimed *It Happened One Night* the outstanding picture of 1934, Capra the best director, and Riskin the best writer of an adaptation.

For Harry Cohn, the triumph was without parallel. Not only did it legitimatize his claim to acceptance in the film industry, but it also strengthened his position versus the East, giving him a long supply of ammunition for the continuing warfare.

And *It Happened One Night* was converted into new and impressive wealth for the growing Cohn fortune. The film played more theater engagements than any attraction in movie history. The profits were enormous, though uncalculated. *It Happened One Night* was sold along with the rest of the Columbia program; thus, it buoyed the entire product.

As the major stockholder of Columbia Pictures Corporation, Harry Cohn was the principal recipient of this prosperity. But his happiness was tempered with sorrow. Shortly before *It Happened One Night* worked its triumph, Bella Cohn died.

5
VICISSITUDES OF A STUDIO BOSS:
THE RECALCITRANT SOPRANO AND
THE ALCOHOLIC VOYAGE

*G*race Moore had eaten herself out of one movie career.

She was a Tennessee choir girl who had climbed her way by one means or another into a singing career that vacillated between the popular and the classical. After appearing in Broadway revues, she was befriended by the millionaire music patron Otto Kahn. He urged her to study opera, and she made her debut in *La Bohème* at the Metropolitan Opera House in 1928.

Hers was a lyrical but uneven soprano. Operagoers were inclined to overlook her faulty tones because of her splendid appearance. Her fiery presence and blond good looks illuminated the operatic stage in an era when most divas were stolid heavyweights. Miss Moore's small frame was also inclined to obesity, but she seemed sylphlike in comparison to her operatic contemporaries.

Grace Moore was among the multitude of dramatic and musical personalities scooped up in New York by the studios during the early days of talkies. Metro-Goldwyn-Mayer signed her to a contract, and she went West in style. She traveled in a private railroad car, the result of a liaison with a Pullman heir. Among her entourage were her collegiate brother, three members of his fraternity, and Beatrice Lillie, who was reporting to Hollywood for a contract with Fox.

Miss Moore's first M-G-M film was an inept pastiche, *A Lady's Morals*, based on the life of Jenny Lind. Unshaken by failure of the American public to embrace the singing star, Irving Thalberg next cast her in a Sigmund Romberg operetta, *New Moon*, with Lawrence Tibbett, who had been successful in *The Rogue Song*. Miss Moore, distressed by her initial failure and discontented with her treatment by the studio, began overeating.

M-G-M boss Louis B. Mayer grew alarmed as he watched his leading lady balloon with each day's rushes. He made repeated visits to the *New Moon* set, shaking his finger at Miss Moore and insisting that she contain herself to no more than 135 pounds. She refused his order to step on his office scales, knowing that she had already exceeded the limit.

Even the robust Tibbett could not adequately carry a chubby costar, and *New Moon* hastened the end of his brief movie career. It finished Miss Moore's.

She returned to the concert stage, discovering that the flop in Hollywood had sliced her fee in half. Her bitterness was edged with determination.

"I'm going to show that crowd," she told an interviewer after returning East. "You just watch. It may take a year; it may take five years. But I'm going back there one day, and when I do, I am going to bring Hollywood to my feet."

She achieved her resolve within three years.

Harry Cohn had been in the opening night audience when Grace Moore starred on Broadway in *The DuBarry*, a musical that helped restore her fame. After the show closed its successful run, she returned to California for an appearance at the Hollywood Bowl. Edmund Goulding, the director, gave a party in her honor, and among the guests was Harry Cohn.

"How would you like to make a picture over at Columbia?" he asked. "Why don't you come to see me tomorrow at eleven?"

Miss Moore agreed, but she overslept the following morning. The telephone aroused her.

"Where the hell are you?" demanded Harry Cohn. "You're supposed to be in my office."

She hurried to Columbia Studios, and Cohn offered her a contract for $25,000 per film. She said she would consider it.

Meanwhile, she knew that Maurice Chevalier wanted her to costar with him in his first film under a new contract with M-G-M, *The Merry Widow*. So great was her desire to erase her previous failure at the studio that she offered to make the film for nothing. Thalberg declared that Miss Moore was fat and unphotographable; he cast Jeanette MacDonald as the Merry Widow. Defeated, Grace Moore signed the contract with little Columbia.

Harry Cohn experienced misgivings almost immediately. He could find no vehicle that suited a soprano. Brother Jack and other powers of the East declared it would be madness to attempt a film with operatic music; it would never get playing time in the sticks.

Columbia's chief negotiator in uneasy situations, Sam Briskin, was directed to get the company out of the contract.

He summoned Miss Moore and told her the deal was off; Columbia would buy out her contract. She responded with what was to be recognized as the Moore style. She screamed her refusal and stalked out of the office, slamming the door hard enough to shatter the glass.

Unable to dispose of his soprano, Cohn canvassed his producers in an effort to find a vehicle for her. Only one was willing to undertake the assignment: Robert Riskin's brother Everett, who had accepted a producing job at Columbia against his brother's advice.

"Boy, did I stick your brother with a lemon!" Cohn crowed to Bob Riskin.

The new producer went to work on a romantic story about an American girl who studied opera in Italy under a stern taskmaster and finally achieved success at the Metropolitan. It was a fluffy tale, but Riskin calculated that it might be supported by Miss Moore's ebullience and her renditions of familiar arias.

She had her own notions about what she wanted to sing, and she worked her persuasion on Cohn.

"Harry, darling, I must sing *Butterfly*," she urged.

"That old thing? You really want it?" said Cohn.

"Yes—please."

The former song plugger buzzed the head of the music department on the intercom. "Find out how much they want for *Poor Butterfly*," he ordered.

"No, no," corrected Miss Moore. "I mean the *Butterfly* by Puccini."

"You mean he stole it?" asked Cohn.

Madame Butterfly was acquired for the film, as well as *Carmen* and *Ciribiribin*, which attached itself to Miss Moore as a trademark. The music was carefully supervised by the director,

Victor Schertzinger, himself a composer, and by conductor-arranger Morris Stoloff. Theirs was a sensitive function. Not only were they introducing grand opera to the screen, but they were also dealing with a voice that could fluctuate in quality from day to day.

When Miss Moore recorded *One Fine Day* with Stoloff leading a full symphony orchestra, the notes wouldn't come. Even the bottle of champagne that she always brought to recording sessions did not help. She shouted that the orchestra was not playing correctly and strode off to her dressing room. No amount of cajoling could induce her to emerge.

Stoloff went in desperation to Cohn's office and related what had happened.

"Is she at fault or are you?" Cohn demanded.

"There's nothing wrong with the orchestra," Stoloff replied. "Those are the original Puccini orchestrations."

"Go to her dressing room," Cohn ordered. "Tell her I said she has to return to the recording stage, or she'll have to pay the day's salaries for the entire orchestra."

Miss Moore returned.

The recordings turned out to everyone's satisfaction. Now it remained for Joe Walker's camera skill to make Miss Moore appear attractive on the screen. At Cohn's insistence she had continued paring down her weight. She nibbled on celery stalks, and constant hunger contributed to her temperament; she caused the firing of five workers during the first week of shooting. Even though her figure had achieved proper proportions for the screen, her features remained heavy. Walker solved this with lens diffusion, effecting a softness that made her seem as beautiful as her voice.

One Night of Love was filmed while Harry Cohn was in New York for one of his regular face-to-face combats with the East. He was constantly under attack for approving a film that contained opera, and he dispatched worried memorandums to producer Riskin at the studio. "Why are you spending so much money?" Cohn inquired.

Riskin proceeded at a deliberate pace. The entire film, including six arias, was made for $185,000, with retakes bringing the cost up to $200,000.

When Cohn returned from New York and saw *One Night of Love*, he continued to question the wisdom of his judgment. A preview in Glendale brought scattered applause, and he drew some encouragement from this. The Santa Barbara preview was better.

Still, Cohn was unconvinced. He escorted Miss Moore and her Spanish husband, Valentin Parera, to the Hollywood preview and listened in astonishment as the audience interrupted the film with applause and shouts of delight. The ending signaled a thunderous ovation, and Cohn recognized his vindication over the taunts of the East.

So great was his elation that he bent down to plant a kiss on Miss Moore's cheek. In the confusion he missed her and kissed her husband instead.

"My God," he worried afterward, "this will ruin my reputation as a he-man."

One Night of Love was an immense hit, winning a mass audience for operatic music for the first time in America. Grace Moore was nominated for best performance by an actress in 1934 by the Academy of Motion Picture Arts and Sciences. The film was nominated for best picture and best direction and won awards for its recording and score.

The venerable Society of Arts and Sciences of New York bestowed on Miss Moore its gold medal for "raising the standard of cinema entertainment"; it was the first time a film figure had been given the award, which had previously gone to such figures as Thomas Alva Edison, Robert A. Millikan, and John Philip Sousa.

The British royal family selected *One Night of Love* for a command performance on New Year's.

Such honors were gratifying to Harry Cohn. More important, the film broke records for long-run engagements in major cities of the United States and Europe. True to the predictions of the East, failed in the small towns. But it was the first Columbia film to win important bookings in the powerful Loew's chain of theaters, and that was a milestone in Columbia's progress.

Cohn spared no expense in the next Grace Moore film, *Love*

Me Forever. Instead of three singers to accompany her in the quartet from *Rigoletto*, he provided thirty.

Miss Moore starred in three more Columbia films: *The King Steps Out*, a period piece with Franchot Tone as a young Franz Josef; *When You're in Love*, in which she sang *Minnie the Moocher* as Cary Grant played piano; and *I'll Take Romance* with Melvyn Douglas as costar.

By 1937 the operatic vogue in films had passed, and Grace Moore ended her Hollywood career. On the strength of her movie reputation she was able to draw crowds with her singing for a decade afterward. She died on January 26, 1947, when a Royal Dutch Airlines DC-3 crashed and burned on the runway of Copenhagen's airport.

The triumph of *One Night of Love* provided Harry Cohn with an exquisite note of pleasure: he had made a star of a performer who had been tried and rejected by Metro-Goldwyn-Mayer. Never was Cohn more satisfied than when he could score some such victory over M-G-M. The reason was basic. Coming from Poverty Row, he always considered M-G-M the House on the Hill. He envied the way Louis Mayer, with the riches of Loew's Incorporated to support him, could maneuver vast resources in stars, stories, directors, and producers with the ease of a freight handler. He also envied Mayer's baronial mode of living and tried to emulate him.

Cohn's constant desire to best M-G-M led him to hire John Gilbert for *The Captain Hates the Sea* in 1934. The idea had come from Lewis Milestone, one of the topnotch directors Cohn had lured to Columbia with the promise of 50 percent of film profits.

Gilbert, M-G-M's most important star of silent films, had been laughed out of talkies because his high-pitched voice seemed at odds with his image as a screen lover. Milestone theorized correctly that the actor's voice had risen in pitch because of tension and fast talking.

"Look—I know Jack very well," Milestone told Cohn. "There's nothing wrong with his voice. I'm convinced he can come through with a performance. We can make a test, if you want. It's a gamble, but a good gamble. Everybody in town is kicking Jack, now that he's down. Here's a chance to prove them wrong."

The idea of proving M-G-M wrong appealed to Cohn, and he approved Milestone's proposal of a test. Now the director had to sell the idea to Gilbert.

The star had been locked in his hilltop mansion, drinking to assuage his lost fame. At first he scorned Milestone's proposal.

"If you don't want a second chance, don't listen to me," said Milestone. "But if you want to show this town you're not washed up, then you've got to help me. I'll do everything I can to make it easier for you in this test. If you want, I'll shoot it at six in the morning. We'll be finished by eight o'clock, and you can be out of the studio before anyone knows about it."

The conditions appealed to Gilbert, and he delivered an excellent performance in the test. Cohn was impressed, and he agreed to hire Gilbert for the film. He told the actor, "If you keep your nose clean on this picture, I'll see that you get work. I'll go to bat for you with every producer in town."

The grateful actor reported for *The Captain Hates the Sea* in sober condition, and his conduct was exemplary for a week. Then the doubts began to gnaw, and he stupefied himself with drink. A day's bender was followed by remorse—and a flare-up of ulcers that precluded his work.

Milestone had to admit that he couldn't control Gilbert.

"It's too goddam bad," said Cohn, "but if a man wants to go to hell, I can't stop him. Shoot around him as much as you can. But keep the picture moving!"

Milestone tried to do so. When the company went on location at Los Angeles Harbor, he convinced maritime unions to allow the rented ship to sail, despite a strike on all shipping. The director reasoned that Gilbert could be better controlled at sea, where liquor would be less readily available.

He failed to calculate the ingenuity of the rest of the cast, who provided Gilbert with drinks from their own supplies. The cast included such imbibers as Walter Connelly, Victor McLaglen, Walter Catlett, and Leon Errol.

Production of the film grew slower. Skies were overcast and Milestone maneuvered the ship about the Southern California waters in search of sun. Often he found some, only to discover the wind too fierce or the actors too drunk for the dialogue to be heard.

Exposed film dribbled into the studio, and Harry Cohn was fuming. In desperation he fired off a cable to Milestone: "Hurry up. The cost is staggering."

Milestone cabled back: "So is the cast."

6

A Visit to Il Duce, and How It Affected the Cohn Style

*J*n 1933 Columbia released a documentary feature called *Mussolini Speaks*. It originated when Jack Cohn acquired two reels of film showing a speech by the Italian dictator, Benito Mussolini, on the occasion of the tenth anniversary of his march on Rome. A young worker in the New York office of Columbia, Harry Foster, proposed illustrating the speech with footage of the Mussolini accomplishments. The feature was assembled for $10,000, with a narration by Lowell Thomas. It grossed $1,000,000 at a time when America was still impressed by the statement that Mussolini made the trains run on time.

The effectiveness of the publicity was not lost on *Il Duce*, and he proposed decorating the president of Columbia Pictures. Harry Cohn traveled to Rome for the ceremony. The event made a profound impression on him. He had no comprehension of the Mussolini ideology, but he could understand and appreciate the Mussolini style.

Harry Cohn returned to Hollywood with an autographed photograph of Il Duce that remained on his office wall until admiration of the Fascist dictator became unfashionable. Cohn spoke awesomely of the legendary Mussolini office chamber, with its vast length and platform on which the dictator sat. "By the time I arrived at his desk, I was whipped," said Cohn.

If it worked for the premier of Italy, it could work for the president of Columbia Pictures. And so Harry Cohn created the structure that was to be the seat of his power to the end of his years.

The outer office was occupied by a receptionist, who admitted visitors to the inner office, where the head secretary and an assistant or two were located. It was here that visitors waited for admittance to the Cohn chamber. The length of the wait was judiciously calculated by Cohn. A writer, director, producer, or actor in disfavor might be detained for two or three hours. One who was being wooed by Cohn to sign with Columbia was admitted immediately.

Cohn was kept informed at all times of who was waiting to see him and on what mission. None could be admitted unless he knew the purpose of the visit; it was basic in his code that Cohn should not be confronted with surprise proposals. He often supplemented his intelligence of visitors' purposes by a personal look. He accomplished this by bustling through the waiting room on some imaginary mission and returning swiftly to his office before he could be accosted. Or he sometimes tiptoed down an outer hall and peeked in a side door. A quick glance told him whether a negotiator was determined or docile. Solicitors of Cohn's favor, particularly agents, might be kept waiting for two or three days before Cohn would see them. Often they would not be admitted at all.

The portal to the position of power was a massive sound proofed door that had no knob and no keyhole on the outside. It could be opened only by a buzzer operated from Cohn's or his secretary's desk. He announced to the head secretary who was to be admitted and pressed the buzzer. If the visitor did not respond immediately, the buzzing had to be repeated, and this was not calculated to improve Cohn's humor. In later years Glenn Ford noted discoloration of the doorjamb at mid-level; it had been soiled by the sweat of innumerable palms of those who had passed through to an audience with Harry Cohn.

In keeping with the Mussolini tradition, the Cohn office was massive and elongated, with the desk at the far end. The visitor marched down the thick carpet to the huge semicircular desk, slightly raised above floor level. Cohn remained in the shadows while the visitor was clearly lighted. Behind Cohn rose the gleaming symbols of his achievements: the Academy Awards, eventually numbering fifty-two, won by Columbia films.

Cohn often appeared to be poring over documents as the visitor approached his desk; in reality, he might well have been studying the racing form. Meek individuals were kept waiting a minute or two before Cohn lifted his eyes from the papers. Others who were aware of the Cohn tactics and were unafraid of him employed a simple gambit: they began talking as soon as they entered the door, thus combating the immensity of the office and Cohn's inattention.

The ganglia of studio control centered on the intercommunications switchboard that remained within Cohn's easy reach. It connected him directly to his executives, producers, department heads and other key personnel. The crackle of the intercom could incite terror in the hearts of the more timid Columbia employees. Cohn delivered his messages in blunt style. No one was requested to report to his office. The usual command was: "Get your ass down here!"

The telephone was an essential instrument of the Cohn power. Secretaries did not handle his telephone calls; all went through the studio switchboard. Cohn demanded fast action from his operators, and they were skilled in reaching anyone Cohn wanted to talk to, usually locating the party within seconds. Cohn employed the technique of lifting the receiver with an added rattle against the cradle button when he wanted to make a call; that informed the operator he was on the wire and ready to talk.

Cohn was equally demanding of his secretaries. He was intolerant of mistakes unless they were quickly admitted.

Surprisingly, Cohn secretaries often lasted for years at a time. He seldom complained, as long as they remained efficient and loyal. Cohn's demands for efficiency were made known immediately. A secretary learned to enter the Cohn office with pencil and notebook at the ready, because he generally began dictating as soon as the door opened.

Cohn secretaries were both male and female. Although he conducted most of his business negotiations in obscene language, he seldom used it within the hearing of female secretaries. Once Mildred Missic was present during a conversation with Gregory Ratoff, whose use of obscenities was prolific.

"Do I have to remind you that Miss Missic is here next to me and she is not accustomed to such language?" Cohn said reprovingly.

Adjoining the Cohn office were other areas of his personal domain. A door led to the projection room, where an operator was on duty at all times while Cohn was at the studio. An adjacent room was occupied by his New York liaison, Nate Spingold, when he was in Hollywood; Cohn used this entrance when he didn't want to be seen by those waiting outside his office. The passageway also led to the dressing room occupied by female stars. Behind the desk was a door to Cohn's private bath. It contained a barber's chair, in which he received shaves and haircuts and also had his dental work done. Cohn never permitted anesthesia under the dentist's drill; he had learned that Mussolini endured such pain as a form of self-discipline.

Beside the entrance to the office was a battered piano that was the despair of the Columbia music department. Despite complaints, Cohn refused to part with it.

"Don't knock that piano," said Cohn, whose musical education had been gained in five-and-ten-cent stores. "I paid three hundred dollars for it thirty years ago, and it's still good."

Near Cohn's desk was a bay window, which afforded a view of the Gower Street entrance to the studio and of the parking lot across the street. From this point of vantage Cohn observed the comings and goings of his employees. Most of them didn't dare to leave the studio before six o'clock, the end of the working day, but there were a few exceptions.

One producer maintained an air of independence, bolstered by the fact that he had made a series of hits for Columbia. His office hours were casual. One day Cohn spotted the producer leaving the front entrance at three in the afternoon.

Cohn leaned out the window and shouted, "It's three o'clock; where the hell are you going?"

"I'm going to get laid," the producer replied.

"The hell you are!" Cohn replied. "You're going to play tennis."

"Then why did you ask me?" responded the producer, continuing on his way to a tennis match.

Cohn himself didn't arrive in his office until noon, but he expected all studio workers to be at their posts by nine o'clock. Cohn's first order of business upon arrival in his office was to scan a sheet of legal-sized paper on which the front-entrance security officer, Cap Duncan, charted the arrivals of all executives and creative workers. During conferences he confronted offenders with their tardiness, interrupting discussion of production matters with: "Why the hell can't you get to work on time?"

Another Cohn technique was to telephone the studio at nine-thirty in the morning and find out what executives had not arrived. He then telephoned the latecomers' offices and asked to speak to them. When told they hadn't arrived yet, he left a message for them to call him.

The tardy ones arrived to receive the ominous instruction: "Call Mr. Cohn." He refused their telephone calls all day, allowing them to suffer the agony of fear and perplexity over what the boss had called about.

Dealing as he did with creative persons, Cohn naturally encountered opposition to his Mussolini-like methods. The high point of organized discontent came with the underground Writers' Revolt of 1935.

The revolt grew out of a chance remark by Dorothy Parker, who was one of the important writers enlisted by Columbia during the expansion of the 1930's. Returning from an exasperating conference with Cohn, she muttered to Jo Swerling, "For four cents I would buy the bastard out and put Cap Duncan in charge of the studio."

The preposterous statement appealed to Swerling's sense of the absurd. He went immediately to the porch where Riskin was writing a script in longhand.

"Got four pennies?" Swerling asked.

Riskin examined his pockets. "Yes," he replied.

"Fine. I want to match you for them."

"Four cents? That's silly. Why not a quarter?"

"No, it has to be four cents," Swerling insisted. "I'll tell you about it afterward."

The two writers matched the coins, and Swerling won. Then he outlined his plan: they would continue matching coins with other Columbia workers. If they won, nothing would be said. If they lost, the others would be told the purpose of the fund. When enough money was accumulated, it would be used to finance production of a play. The success of the play would provide the funds with which to buy Columbia, force Harry Cohn out of office, and install Cap Duncan as head of the studio.

The campaign was heartily received. Writers, directors, and actors contributed to it. Ben Hecht and Charles MacArthur promised to channel a portion of the royalties from their next play into the fund. Carole Lombard was an euthusiastic contributor.

Swerling and Riskin decided on a daring scheme: they would induce Cohn to add money to the money for his own deposing. They invaded a conference Cohn and Sam Briskin were having with Michael Balcon, visiting head of Gaumont-British.

"How about matching me for half a dollar, boss?" asked Swerling.

Cohn, anxious to avoid a scene in front of the foreign dignitary, agreed to do so. He lost. Briskin was also brought in on the game. He lost, too.

"My, you're running a very comfortable studio here," said the admiring Balcon.

"Oh, yes," said the mystified Cohn. "We're just one big happy family."

Swerling and Riskin were beginning to lose their bravado. The fund had swollen to $350, and they were afraid that their lark was getting out of hand. They proposed one final fling.

The two writers were spending a week in Palm Springs, where a gambling establishment called the Dunes was operating without interference from the law.

"Let's see if the Lord is with us," suggested Riskin.

He and Swerling decided to visit the Dunes and place the fund on the black in the roulette game. When they placed the curious assemblage of coins and bills on the table, the proprietor asked. "What is all that crazy money?"

Swerling and Riskin explained their purpose to him—to buy out Harry Cohn. The owner replied, "That's holy money. Let the wheel spin. If you win, okay. If not, I'll match it."

The spin came up red, and the owner contributed another $350.

The writers' revolt ended short of its goal. Soon after the escapade at the Dunes, Harry Cohn was informed of the plot. He moved swiftly to end it.

"The worst part of it," Cohn complained bitterly, "was that those bastards were using some of my own money."

7
DEALINGS WITH ACTORS:
JOHN WAYNE, ROBERT YOUNG,
BARBARA STANWYCK,
RALPH BELLAMY, LEE TRACY,
GLORIA SWANSON

*J*ohn Wayne, formerly Marion (Duke) Morrison of the University of Southern California varsity, had ascended from set worker to star of *The Big Trail*, directed by Raoul Walsh in 1931. A descent came just as rapidly when the public expressed no interest in Westerns, big or small. Lacking any more promising opportunity, Wayne signed a contract with Columbia.

He appeared in one film with Laura LaPlante, *Men Are Like That*. It was a modest but promising start at Columbia for the young actor. But the promise was never fulfilled, because the virile Wayne collided headlong with the boss's libido.

Cohn was convinced that Wayne was romancing a Columbia starlet in whom Cohn was enjoying a proprietary interest. He once accosted Wayne and admonished him, "When you're at this studio, you keep your pants buttoned."

Wayne was mystified, since he had no particular interest in the starlet. Nothing further was said, but the actor felt the Cohn rebuke. In his next film, *Maker of Men*, he was demoted to the heavy role while Jack Holt and Richard Cromwell played the leads. Then Wayne didn't work at all.

His contract was extended for a second six-month period, but Cohn would neither cast him in a film nor allow him to be lent to other studios. At the end of his first year at Columbia, Wayne was dropped.

Because of his flop in *The Big Trail* and his poor record at Columbia, Wayne was unable to find work at other studios.

Finally, Sid Rogell agreed to hire him for a series of cheap Westerns to be called *The Three Mesquiteers*. Later Rogell told him the deal was off.

"Why?" Wayne demanded.

"Well, I heard you drank on the set and were difficult," Rogell admitted. "Do you drink?"

"Hell, yes," answered Wayne, sensing that the tale had originated with Cohn. "But just show me anybody who says I ever drank on a set and I'll knock his teeth down his throat."

Rogell was convinced enough to hire Wayne after all.

When Wayne became a valuable star in later years, his services were sought by every studio, including Columbia. It was his pleasure to decline Columbia's offers in terms that Harry Cohn could easily understand.

Robert Young, a handsome, genteel young man newly graduated from the Pasadena Playhouse, had been accorded polite treatment at M-G-M, where he was under contract. For his second film, he was lent to Columbia. He was to appear opposite Constance Cummings in *Guilty Generation*, a Romeo and Juliet story of gangsterdom, with Leo Carrillo and Boris Karloff portraying the fathers of the young couple.

After the first day of shooting, Young was summoned to the office of Harry Cohn, president of Columbia Pictures.

"Why, you cheap son of a bitch!" Cohn ranted. "I'm paying M-G-M more goddam money than you're worth, and you show up looking like a ——ing bum. You're supposed to be a gangster's son. But you're not dressed like a gangster's son. You're dressed like a ——ing bum!"

Cohn continued at length in the same manner. Young, who owned two suits and was unaware that an actor was required to supply his own wardrobe in a modern-dress film, left the office in a daze. It required half an hour's persuasion by the director, Rowland V. Lee, to convince Young not to quit the picture and the movie business as well.

Young brooded over the incident long afterward, but he later viewed it as a lesson in film making by Cohn: the picture was all that mattered. And Young never again lacked the proper wardrobe.

Barbara Stanwyck had come to Hollywood during the early talkie period with her husband Frank Fay, who was in demand as a master of ceremonies for revues and as a light comedian. She had starred on Broadway; but her one film, *The Locked Door*, was a failure, and the studios declined to hire her.

Miss Stanwyck assisted Fay in a sketch at a benefit sponsored by the Los Angeles *Examiner*. Harry Cohn was in the audience. He was searching for an actress to star in Capra's *Ladies of Leisure* and asked Miss Stanwyck to test for it.

"No, thanks," she replied. "I've had my experience with tests: I made one at Warner Brothers. If you want to see me on film, send for it."

She had reported to a Warner Brothers stage one evening to find no one present. A cameraman, Alexander Korda, appeared, but he was unprepared with material for the young actress. She volunteered a scene for a play she had done, *The Noose*. Since there was no script, she delivered the leading man's lines, as well as her own.

Cohn saw the Warner Brothers test and was sufficiently impressed to sign Miss Stanwyck to a contract. Three Capra films brought her increasing recognition—and offers. Warner Brothers now sought her at $50,000 a picture. She told Cohn he would have to match the figure.

"What would you do if you don't get the fifty thousand?" he asked.

"I'd go to Europe," she replied.

"There are ten boats a day and nothing stopping you," he said.

When she balked at working, Cohn took her to court and won the suit. As soon as she returned home after the verdict, she received a telephone call from Cohn.

"What did you prove?" he asked.

"Nothing," she admitted.

"Okay, you're at your house and I'm in my office," he said. "I've got scripts for you. How about returning to work?"

"All right."

"How much money would make you happy?"

"Fifty thousand a picture."

"You've got it."

Cohn was unhampered by union regulations in the early 1930's, with the result that actors worked long and hard in Columbia films. Most actors consented to the conditions; a few did not.

Ralph Bellamy was a workhorse of the Columbia lot; in one year he appeared in thirteen feature films. But he was schooled in the unionism of the legitimate stage, and he believed there were limits to the conditions an actor should endure.

Once he was assigned two Columbia films without a day's rest between. Bellamy said he would perform the work only if a stand-in was provided for both movies. The stipulation was reported to Harry Cohn. He summoned the actor to his office.

"What the hell is this —— about a stand-in?" Cohn demanded.

Bellamy explained that he could not be expected to deliver adequate performances in the two films unless he was relieved of the chore of standing under the hot lights as the set was prepared for filming.

"We've never had a stand-in on this lot, and we never will!" Cohn declared.

"All right, let's call the whole thing off," said Bellamy. He turned to leave.

"Wait a minute," Cohn said. He pondered for a moment.

"All right," he continued. "You can have your stand-in on one condition."

"What's that?" Bellamy asked.

"Don't tell Jack Holt."

Many studios had adopted a policy of working actors as late as midnight and then calling them for the regular morning start the next day. Some stars were beginning to rebel, and Bellamy was one of them. He instructed the assistant director, "Don't begin any elaborate shot after five-thirty, because I'm leaving at six."

Word of this reached Cohn, and once again he summoned Bellamy to his office.

"What the hell is going on?" Cohn demanded. "Do I understand that you are walking off a Columbia set?"

"I'm not walking off," the actor explained. "I arrive here early in the morning, and I deliver a full day's work. That's all you're entitled to—nothing more, nothing less."

"Listen, goddammit," Cohn fumed, "everybody on this lot works as long as I tell them to work!"

"I can't function that way," said Bellamy. "So why don't you call off my contract?"

He started to leave, and Cohn detained him.

"All right, dammit," said Cohn. "You can quit at six o'clock, but on one condition only."

"What's that?" Bellamy asked.

"Don't tell Jack Holt."

With his machine-gun delivery of sophisticated dialogue, Lee Tracy built a reputation as an electric performer in a series of talkies. He also became legendary for his drinking. Harry Cohn had both considerations in mind when he talked with Tracy about a contract after the actor had left Warner Brothers.

The two men arrived at satisfactory terms. Then Cohn introduced the matter of Tracy's drinking.

"Never in my life have I drunk during a picture," the actor declared.

"Will you give me your promise you'll never take a drink during a picture?" Cohn asked.

"No, I won't promise," Tracy replied.

Cohn eyed him suspiciously. "What do you mean, you won't promise?" he said.

"I'm telling you that I never drink when I'm doing a picture—except on Saturday night, and then I might not know my own name."

"I want your promise," Cohn insisted.

"I won't give it to you," Tracy declared. "Before she passed away, my own mother asked me to promise never to take a drink. I wouldn't do it. I didn't want to promise her something I couldn't keep. Now if I wouldn't promise my own mother, I'm certainly not going to promise you."

Cohn stared at Tracy for a moment. The injection of the note of motherhood had a curious effect on him.

"That's good enough for me," he said.

Lee Tracy made three films for Columbia—*Washington Merry-Go-Round*, *The Night Mayor*, and *Carnival*—all without mishap.

For years Gloria Swanson had been a commanding figure in Hollywood, but her career in talkies had not been going well. Irving Thalberg had promised important vehicles for her at M-G-M, but he died before he could provide them.

Harry Cohn lured her with the promise of a film to be called *The Second Mrs. Draper*. It offered a meaty role for her. Columbia had been producing more and more prestigious films, so the prospects seemed favorable. Besides, she believed Harry Cohn had reason to be grateful to her. Hadn't she helped introduce him to Hollywood society at a time when he still carried the aroma of Poverty Row? Indeed she had, inviting Cohn to join the glittering guests at her parties in his earlier days in Hollywood.

Two treatments were written of *The Second Mrs. Draper*, but Cohn expressed dissatisfaction with both of them.

"What is wrong with them?" Miss Swanson asked.

"You need a more sympathetic role," he said.

"Like *The Trespasser*?" she demanded, citing one of her most successful films, in which she played a woman undeserving of sympathy.

Her reasoning made no headway with Cohn. He told her he was hunting other stories for her. Miss Swanson herself located a number of stories that she deemed suitable, but Cohn approved of none of them.

One day she telephoned Cohn and reported she had found the most sympathetic role she had ever read. It was a story owned by David O. Selznick, who was willing to sell it.

"I'm not going to send it to you and let you use it as a prop to hide your phone to Santa Anita," she added. "I'm coming to your office and reading it to you myself."

She read the twenty-five pages to Cohn in his office. He said he would let her know his decision later.

"Why not now?" she demanded.

"I want to think about it," he replied.

On the following day Cohn telephoned Miss Swanson. He told her he didn't want to buy the story. His reasoning: "It can't be any good if Selznick wants to sell it."

Miss Swanson erupted in a tirade. How much of it Cohn heard was problematical, because at one point Miss Swanson pulled the telephone wire from the wall.

"I've got to get out of this place!" she screamed. "I've got to go back where people think!"

She closed her house and took up residence in New York, never returning to films until *Sunset Boulevard* in 1949. The story she had read to Cohn was later filmed as *Dark Victory*, starring Bette Davis.

Harry Cohn also played an indirect role in the flight from Hollywood of Maurice Chevalier. After Grace Moore's success with *One Night of Love*, M-G-M belatedly sought her services. Cohn agreed to lend her with the proviso that she receive top billing. Thalberg proposed a costarring film with Chevalier and outlined the terms to the Frenchman.

"But it says in my contract I must receive top billing," Chevalier protested. "I have had top billing for twenty-five years. Why should I change now?"

"Maurice, you're being difficult," Thalberg replied. "Cohn won't give us Grace Moore unless she gets top billing. Why don't you cooperate?"

Rather than endure such circumstances, Chevalier ended his Hollywood career and returned to Paris.

8

HARRY COHN PERFORMS A CONFIDENTIAL SERVICE FOR THE KING AND QUEEN OF ENGLAND AND IS REWARDED WITH ROYAL RAIMENT

*D*uring the 1930's Harry Cohn voyaged to Europe once each year to oversee the Columbia sales organization and to enjoy the fruits of his new wealth. The first thing he did upon entering a Columbia office was to inspect the portraits of the two remaining founders of the corporation. Managers of foreign branches learned, often after smarting rebukes, that the portrait of Harry Cohn must be placed to the left and at a higher level than that of Jack Cohn.

Harry Cohn believed that he should travel in a style befitting the president of a motion picture company, but this view was tempered by his basic thrift. On one occasion he sailed to England with Lewis Milestone. Cohn suggested they could share Milestone's valet, and Cohn succeeded in monopolizing the valet's services.

The two film makers stayed at the conservative Dorchester Hotel in London. Cohn had to return to Hollywood early, and he instructed Milestone, "When you pay your bill, tell the cashier that I made arrangements for a ten percent discount."

"But why would the Dorchester give you a discount?" Milestone asked.

"I made a deal," Cohn said.

When Milestone departed, the management told him that no such arrangement had been made. Furthermore, Mr. Cohn had been requested not to return to the Dorchester.

Cohn had his own methods of dealing with exclusive London shops. At Sulka's he told the clerk, "I want to order a lot of things, but first I want to have samples made. Make me up one of each—shorts, undershirts, shirts, pajamas, and robes. If I'm satisfied, I'll give you a big order."

Later he confided to Milestone, "I'll take their clothes and have a woman in New York duplicate them for half the cost."

Cohn bustled into Dunhill's and asked to see the cigarette lighters—gold ones. The white-coated clerk returned with a selection of designs, and Cohn chose five. He asked the prices.

"I want to buy a couple dozen for gifts," Cohn said. "What kind of a discount can you give me?"

The clerk repeated the prices.

"You don't understand," Cohn insisted. "I'm entitled to a discount because I'm a volume buyer."

"I'll be happy to refer your request to the governor," said the clerk. He disappeared into the inner offices and returned with the news that Dunhill's was willing to offer Mr. Cohn a discount of 2.5 percent.

Cohn grumblingly asked to see the Dunhill humidors he had heard about. He was ushered to a quiet oak-paneled room, where the clerk displayed the humidor samples. Cohn opened one, took out a cigar, and smelled it.

"Say, that's damned good," he remarked. "I want some of those."

"I'm sorry, sir," said the clerk. "Those are not for sale. They are reserved for our regular customers."

Cohn exploded. "What the hell does a guy have to do to get a cigar in this joint?" he demanded.

"Our regular supply of cigars is on the upper story," the clerk informed him. "If you were to become a resident of Great Britain, we could put you on the waiting list for our special line of cigars." Cohn stalked out in a rage.

During one of his visits to England, Cohn was accompanied by Nate Spingold, his close friend and a Columbia executive. Spingold was a man of culture and refinement, and he convinced Harry Cohn that he should have a set of tails made by a Savile Row haberdasher.

Spingold made an appointment at the tailor's and took Cohn there. Cohn rummaged through bolts of cloth until he found one that suited him.

"Oh, I'm terribly sorry, sir," said the clerk. "That bolt is reserved exclusively for the Duke of Kent. No one else may use it."

Cohn's reaction was apoplectic. "How do you like this goddam country!" he muttered to Spingold as they left the place. "I can't even get a set of tails made for me!"

One of the purposes of the Cohn-Spingold mission was to confer with Gilbert Miller about a film he was to produce for Columbia. Miller invited the two executives to a party for members of London society, and he harbored a natural concern over how Cohn would behave. Miller used diplomacy in instructing Cohn in the proper behavior at a formal dinner in an English manor house.

On the evening of the dinner Miller was relieved to find Cohn responding in a gentle manner as he was introduced to the guests, who included the Duke of Kent. The dinner proceeded without incident. Afterward Miller was alarmed when he saw Cohn and the duke walking arm in arm toward the library. He grew more concerned as the door closed behind the two men.

Inside the library the duke asked Cohn to take a seat, and after a few hesitant remarks he began: "Mr. Cohn, you are president of the Columbia Pictures Corporation in Hollywood, are you not?"

"Yes, sir," Cohn replied.

The son of George V cleared his throat. "This is a matter of some delicacy, and I would like you to keep it in the strictest confidence," he said. "You see, my brother, the Prince of Wales, has a wide and rather varied acquaintance, and sometimes he takes up with persons of whom my mother and father do not approve. At the present he is very friendly with a gentleman who appears to have had some gambling connections in your country—in Hollywood as a matter of fact." The duke mentioned the man's name and added, "I wondered if you could tell us whether he is a suitable companion for my brother."

Cohn smiled genially. "Sure, I know him," he said. "He's a square guy. You tell your mom and dad they've got nothing to worry about."

The Duke of Kent seemed greatly relieved. "They'll be very happy to hear that, Mr. Cohn," he said. "I must thank you. If there is anything I could possibly do for you during your visit in England, I hope you would tell me."

"As a matter of fact there is something you could do," Cohn replied. He told of his experience at the haberdashery.

"We're going back to California, Duke," said Cohn, "so your cloth won't be seen here. Do you suppose you could release that bolt?"

The Duke of Kent took out a card and wrote some instructions. Harry Cohn returned to Hollywood with a set of tails made from royal cloth.

9

FRANK CAPRA FINDS, THEN LOSES HIS SHANGRI-LA

*T*he film industry continued to be dazzled by the prolific talent of Frank Capra and Robert Riskin, who seemed able to turn out an imaginative, popular film every year. Following the immense hit of *It Happened One Night*, they returned to Damon Runyon for *Broadway Bill*, with Warner Baxter and Myrna Loy, plus the assemblage of Capra characters. It was a funny, sentimental tale of racetrack life, and audiences everywhere wept openly when the champion, Broadway Bill, collapsed and died at the finish line of the crucial handicap.

Mr. Deeds Goes to Town followed in 1936. This was Capra in full flower, exploring the Americana he had studied during his vagabondage. Riskin's script was taken from a Clarence Budington Kelland tale about a small-town man, named Longfellow Deeds, who inherited $2,000,000 from a playboy uncle. Deeds came to the big city to be derided by the slickers, including a girl reporter he fell in love with. Disillusioned, he was about to return to the country when he was accosted by an impoverished farmer who castigated him for not using his wealth to aid the poor. When the farmer threatened him with a gun, Deeds was shocked into a revolutionary course: buying farmland for the poor. The high point of the picture came when Deeds was charged with insanity, and two old ladies from his hometown testified that he was pixilated, as evidenced by his eccentric behavior. Deeds was vindicated in the end and reconciled to the girl reporter.

Capra insisted on casting the film properly. He delayed production six months to secure the services of Gary Cooper, and the lapse of time cost Columbia $100,000. For the reporter, he chose Jean Arthur.

Mr. Deeds Goes to Town was received with favor by both critics and the public. Americans, still rising out of the Depression, were attracted to its philosophy, which one writer termed "*Saturday Evening Post* Socialism."

The film marked the high point in the relations between Harry Cohn and Frank Capra. Cohn had sagaciously given the director his tether, allowing him to prepare his scripts without interference and to film them with scarcely a visit from the president of the company. Inevitably, the strains developed.

Cohn, proprietor and guiding force of Columbia Pictures, rankled under suggestions that Capra was solely responsible for the studio's ascent to prosperity. Capra, now possessor of his second Academy Award because of *Mr. Deeds*, sought even more creative freedom and relief from economic pressures. Cohn, with the lessons of Poverty Row still firm in his business philosophy, watched in unaccustomed silence as the costs of the Capra films mounted.

Capra was undecided about a vehicle to follow *Mr. Deeds* until he journeyed with Cohn on the overnight train to attend a college football game at Palo Alto. At the Los Angeles station Capra picked up a copy of James Hilton's romantic novel *Lost Horizon*. He finished the book that night.

When he met Cohn for breakfast in the diner, Capra held up the book and said, "Harry, that's my next picture."

Cohn scowled at the cover and asked, "What the hell is it?"

"You'll have to read it to find out," said the director. "I can't describe it to you."

"Okay, that's your next picture," said Cohn, proceeding with his breakfast.

Lost Horizon marked a departure for Capra. Except for *The Bitter Tea of General Yen*, he had not swerved from the American idiom. The Hilton tale concerned an Englishman who was chosen to head the idyllic community of Shangri-La, hidden in the remoteness of the Himalayas. Despite his belief in the place, he was convinced by his brother to leave, only to realize his tragic mistake.

Capra devoted long months to fashioning the script with Riskin. Ronald Colman was signed to play the Englishman, Conway, and his supporting cast included Jane Wyatt, H. B. Warner, Thomas Mitchell, John Howard, Margo, Edward Everett Horton, Isabel Jewell, and Sam Jaffe as the ancient High Lama. A massive Shangri-La rose on the Columbia ranch in Burbank.

Two years were consumed in the preparation and filming of *Lost Horizon*. Finally, Capra had cut the film from twenty-six reels to fourteen and was ready to submit it to public view. He and Cohn and their wives departed by car for the first preview in Santa Barbara.

The initial five minutes brought no reaction from the audience. Then came the first laugh where none was intended. The laughter grew. The Santa Barbarans sensed overtones of a comic Fu Manchu in what Capra intended to be a serious depiction of an ideal society.

Capra broke out in a cold sweat. He bolted from his seat and went into the lobby for a drink of water. One of the local patrons had exited with him, and Capra stood back to allow him the first drink.

"Have you ever seen such a goddam thing?" muttered the man, jerking his thumb in the direction of the theater.

Capra rushed out of the theater and into a downpour. Finding Cohn's car locked, he wandered the streets of Santa Barbara for three hours. He arrived back at the theater in time to find the patrons filtering out the doors, shaking their heads over what they had seen.

Cohn hailed Capra and hustled him and the wives to the car. Nothing was said as they began the journey homeward. Capra was distraught. He had attempted what he hoped would be his monument in the cinema art, and he had failed spectacularly. He knew that the abysmal reception of *Lost Horizon* meant as much to Cohn. The East had been clamoring against the enormous cost of the film—$2,000,000, half the entire cost of the Columbia product for a year! Furthermore, *Lost Horizon* had occupied two years of the precious time of Columbia's most valued asset: Capra.

The failure of *Lost Horizon* would seriously upset the balance between the West and East, perhaps disastrously for Harry Cohn.

After driving a few miles down the coast Cohn made the first remark: "Frank, I'll still give you that seven-year contract we've been talking about."

When he returned home, Capra told his wife he was going away for a while. He headed his car eastward and climbed the mountains to Lake Arrowhead. For days he walked alone amid the tall pines, searching for the riddle of the failure in Santa Barbara.

At last he returned to the studio.

"Harry, let's take the picture out again," Capra said.

"The same way?" Cohn asked.

"Yes, but let's throw out the first two reels. We'll start it at the third reel."

"Do you think that'll work?"

"I think it might."

They took the new version to Wilmington, near Los Angeles Harbor, and the preview was an enormous success. In its earlier form, *Lost Horizon* had dwelt too much on preliminaries; now the audience was captured by the bizarre tale from the start. Upon his return to Columbia, Capra personally hurled the original first two reels into the studio incinerator.

Lost Horizon proved to be a popular picture, though less so with the critics than previous Capra films. The damaging effects of the venture were demonstrated in Columbia earnings. The gross receipts had doubled to $20,000,000 between 1933 and 1938, but profits, which had reached a high of $1,815,267 in 1935, fell to a perilous $183,393 in 1938. Jack Cohn and other powers of the East seized the opportunity to exert new pressures on the production boss.

Cohn responded erratically.

Capra, whose salary had continually advanced during his years at Columbia, was earning $100,000 a year. He considered it his annual salary. But when he tried to collect the money after *Lost Horizon*, Cohn told him there would be no payment until he started another picture. He argued that Capra had expended too much time on *Lost Horizon*.

Capra was stunned. He couldn't conceive of such ingratitude after his contributions to Columbia's fortunes. He plunged into a depression and withdrew to his house at Malibu, where he brooded for weeks. Then he consulted his attorneys.

Fortunately for the Capra cause, Columbia had committed a sizable blunder. Company salesmen had long used the Capra films to help sell the rest of the year's program of pictures. In an excess of zeal, the sales department in England had advertised a film called *If You Could Only Cook* as a Capra picture. Capra had not directed it. His attorneys seized on this misdeed and sued to terminate Capra's contract with Columbia.

10

THE IRISH INVASION,
AND HOW IT ENDED WITH THE
EPITHET HEARD OVER THE OCEAN

*A*fter the defection of Capra, Harry Cohn was desperate to prove that Columbia's fortunes were not dependent on one brilliant director. He sought others to fill the void, among them Leo McCarey.

Son of a prizefight promoter, McCarey had learned comedy in the gag factory of Hal Roach. He progressed from Laurel and Hardy two-reelers to sophisticated comedies, then directed what he considered his greatest work, *Make Way for Tomorrow*. It was a tragicomedy about the neglect of elderly parents, and Adolph Zukor loved it—until he saw that the film was being neglected by the public. Zukor settled the remainder of McCarey's Paramount contract, and the director found himself without employment.

Always aware of who was being let out by other studios, Harry Cohn sent for McCarey.

"I understand Paramount just fired you," Cohn began.

"Is that why you sent for me?" asked the Irishman. "You wanted to rub it in about *Make Way for Tomorrow*?"

"No," said Cohn. "I liked it. It made me cry. But I've got a picture for you, and I want you to make people laugh."

Cohn gave McCarey the script of *The Awful Truth*. It had been a successful play in the 1920's, and D. A. Doran had purchased the film rights as a vehicle for Ina Claire at Pathé. When Pathé dissolved, Columbia bought its story properties for $35,000. Returning to Columbia after an absence, Doran found *The Awful Truth* in the Pathé inventory. Everett Riskin was assigned to produce, and Dwight Taylor had written a script.

McCarey and his agent returned to Cohn's office in two hours. McCarey said he had read the script, didn't like it, but would do the picture.

Cohn addressed the agent: "And what are you asking for him, now that he's just been fired?"

The agent gulped and said, "One hundred thousand."

Cohn's geniality vanished. "The conversation is at an end," he decreed.

McCarey rose to go, while his agent remained to argue with Cohn. As McCarey reached the door, he discovered the ancient piano. He always found it difficult to pass any piano without tinkling out a tune, and he sat down to play *Down among the Sheltering Palms*.

Cohn held up his hand to silence the agent's arguments. He strode down to the piano and demanded of McCarey, "What key are you playing that in?"

McCarey told him.

"Why, that's my key," said Cohn delightedly, and he began singing the song he had plugged in his New York days. The agent stared in astonishment.

Cohn finished the chorus and announced, "Anybody who likes music like that has got to be a talented man. I'll pay that exorbitant fee. Report to work tomorrow."

Everett Riskin withdrew from the film, because McCarey insisted on producing, as well as directing. He junked the script and began writing another one with Viña Delmar. Instead of reporting to the studio, the pair devised scenes as they sat in a car parked on Hollywood Boulevard. Such a procedure confounded Cohn. He was to learn more of McCarey's unique mode of operation.

The Awful Truth was being rushed to fulfill a commitment with Irene Dunne. She was to receive $40,000 for the film, and Cary Grant was signed at $50,000. Ralph Bellamy, who was under contract to Columbia, was designated for the role of the other man. All three were balky over their assignments. Miss Dunne could make little sense of her role from the script fragments presented by McCarey. Bellamy's role had originally been tailored for Roland Young and hence ill fitted a robust actor.

Grant, who had scarcely played comedy before, suggested that he switch to the Roland Young part. Barring that, Grant offered to give Cohn another commitment for nothing if he could be excused from *The Awful Truth*.

Cohn was equally confused by McCarey's script, but he was faced with paying Miss Dunne the $40,000 if the film did not proceed.

"Go ahead and make it," Cohn told McCarey. "I hope it looks better on film than it does on paper."

Both Miss Dunne and Bellamy were in a state of irritated perplexity as they reported for the first day of shooting. Neither had seen a complete script; neither was familiar with the improvisational style McCarey had learned at Roach.

"Can you play the piano?" the director asked Miss Dunne.

"Yes, but not very well," she replied.

"Can you sing?" he asked Bellamy.

"Not a note," the actor answered.

"Good!" said McCarey. "Now, Irene, I want you to play *Home on the Range*, and I want you to sing it, Ralph."

Entirely against their wills, the two performers played and sang *Home on the Range*. McCarey was so delighted with the results that he forgot to say, "Cut," at the end of the scene.

Shooting of *The Awful Truth* continued in the same impromptu manner. McCarey rode in a taxi to the studio each morning and often produced the day's script en route. Some days he arrived with a fragment of brown paper on which he had written an idea while walking on the beach the night before. On other days McCarey came with no notion of what to film. Cast and crew waited through most of the morning as he toyed with tunes on the piano.

"Why aren't you shooting?" Cohn demanded. "You're playing the piano all the time!"

"But I'm writing a song for the picture," answered the director, continuing to play.

Cohn was unimpressed by the film that was coming through. "I hired you to make a great comedy," he complained to McCarey, "so I could show up Frank Capra. The only one who's going to laugh at this picture is Capra!"

One day Cohn came on the set of *The Awful Truth* to find McCarey playing piano and telling jokes with his visitor, Harold Lloyd.

"What the hell is going on here?" Cohn exploded. "Clear the set of all visitors."

Harold Lloyd departed. So did Leo McCarey.

Cohn telephoned McCarey at his beach house and loosed a string of expletives and threats. The director was unmoved.

"I'm not coming back until you come on the set and apologize to the entire company—and send a copy of your remarks to Harold Lloyd," McCarey declarcd, ending the conversation.

Cohn pondered the ultimatum. He had never apologized to anyone at Columbia, much less an entire company. The thought of it repelled him. And yet it seemed impractical to replace McCarey on *The Awful Truth*. That would mean the loss of thousands of dollars. And who but McCarey could make any sense of what he had shot thus far?

On the following day Harry Cohn appeared on the set of *The Awful Truth*. He delivered the most perfunctory of apologies, then rushed back to his office. Production resumed.

When the thirty-seventh day of shooting arrived, Cohn came on the set at three in the afternoon to find McCarey serving drinks to the cast and crew.

"My God!" he exploded. "Are you trying to break me? This picture goes on and on, and now you're serving drinks in the afternoon!"

"Harry, tighten your bowels," McCarey replied with a grin on his Irish face. "I've got a surprise for you. We're finished."

Cohn continued to glower in disbelief; then he beamed. "In that case," he said, "pour me a drink."

Cohn had reason to be pleased. McCarey had finished *The Awful Truth* for $600,000—$200,000 under the budget. His technique was not as helter-skelter as it seemed. Although he lingered over the piano in the mornings and often finished shooting at three in the afternoon, his scenes were long and often filmed in one take to preserve spontaneity. Miss Dunne, Grant, and Bellamy were expert performers who responded quickly and skillfully to such direction. McCarey knew what he was seeking. He did retakes twice on a simple close-up between Miss Dunne and Grant, striving for expressions that indicated love still existed between the divorced couple.

The first preview went badly. The audience was unaccustomed to seeing the three stars in a comedy and wasn't entirely certain that laughter was expected. McCarey solved this by injecting an opening scene in which the divorce judge lectured Grant on the telephone about the joys of marriage while the judge's wife interjected bitter argument.

The Awful Truth brought roars of laughter at the next preview. Cohn was so overcome at having a new hit and a successor to Capra that he volunteered to bestow 25 percent of the profits to McCarey.

In the limousine returning to the studio, Cohn was engaged in serious conversation with two emissaries from the East, who had also attended the preview. McCarey could not overhear what they were saying, but he gathered the topic was his percentage.

Cohn poured drinks in his office and raised his glass. "Here's to Leo McCarey, who will be with Columbia for the next seven years," he saluted.

"But we have no contract," answered McCarey. "I signed for one picture only."

Cohn shot back, "You don't expect to get twenty-five percent of this picture unless you sign with us for at least five years, do you?"

McCarey's temper exploded. He threw his highball onto the floor and stormed out of the office.

When he reached home, he was still fuming. "Start packing," he said to his wife. "We're leaving Hollywood."

"Stay mad," she replied delightedly. "You've never taken me anywhere since we've been married."

The McCareys flew to New York and booked passage on a transatlantic liner. After three days at sea they were enjoying dinner together when a page approached their table.

"You're wanted on the radiophone, Mr. McCarey," the page reported.

McCarey went to the communications room and adjusted the earphones. He heard the voice of Harry Cohn.

"Can you hear me all right?" asked Cohn.

"Yes, I can hear you, Harry," the director replied.

"Leo, I've got good news for you. I talked to the board of directors, and you only have to put up with me for three years.

The news was received with silence.

"Did you hear that?" asked Cohn.

"Yes," said McCarey. "Can you hear me, Harry?"

"Just as clear as next door."

The last sound Harry Cohn heard over the radiophone was a loud, ripe "razzberry."

Leo McCarey won a 1937 Academy Award for his direction of *The Awful Truth*. He never again worked for Harry Cohn.

II

"Why Not Call It the
GOOD-BYE, ROSE?"

*H*arry Cohn's marriage to Rose continued to deteriorate. It became little more than an exercise in formalities as Cohn devoted more and more of his time and energies to the studio. Often he remained in his office or projection room until midnight or after. On nights when he returned home earlier, he arrived with his overcoat pockets filled with scripts. "Look at all this stuff I have to read!" he complained. He continued his reading until he was certain Rose had fallen asleep; then he went to bed.

He seemed incapable of maintaining a physical relationship with his wife. The pursuit and conquest of new, attractive women was of utmost importance in his life.

The source of his power over women stemmed not merely from the fact that he was head of a studio and hence could offer them wealth and renown. Many women found him genuinely attractive.

In middle age he retained a striking handsomeness. The thinning of hair served only to emphasize the almost heroic size of his head. The broad, square jaw was firm, and the shoulders were muscular, although he was chronically overweight. Most of all, there were the eyes, the intensely blue eyes that commanded fear and fascination.

Cohn demanded beauty. He liked to surround himself with beautiful things and beautiful people. He supervised with meticulous care the glamour trappings of his female stars; he would sometimes order three revisions of a simple hairdo. Many an expensive gown was scrapped because Cohn declared, "It looks cheap."

Ugliness was an affront to him. One of his secretaries was a maladroit cook who often appeared at work with burned and cut fingers. When she placed papers on his desk, he objected to the appearance of her fingers, and she learned to keep them hidden after kitchen mishaps.

Cohn himself was immaculate in his habits. He showered two or three times a day and splashed himself with has favorite scent, Carnival de Venise, which he bought by the gallon. He dressed in fashionable style, his only affectations being camelhair overcoats and Tyrolean-style hats.

He was capable of charming women of any age. He could be courtly with a distinguished actress like Ethel Barrymore, who bestowed on Cohn her high praise: "He knows the score."

With some women he attempted bluntness, to test their reactions. During early meetings with Katharine Hepburn he spoke roughly. The aristocratic actress pretended not to hear him, and he never tried such tactics again.

He applied the same technique with Margaret Sullavan. At the end of a private conference he remarked to her, "Willie Wyler tells me you're great in the hay." Wyler had once been married to the actress.

Miss Sullavan arose and replied scornfully, "You didn't hear that from Willie. He is too much of a gentleman to discuss such things with you."

She turned on her heel and marched the length of Cohn's office. Before she went out the door, she added, "But I am."

Many another woman was attracted by the sense of danger and the magnetism that Cohn exuded. A longtime admirer of Cohn, a woman who was never romantically involved with him, recalled attending a Hollywood party at which the majority of feminine eyes were focused on Harry Cohn. Also in the room were Clark Gable, Tyrone Power, and Robert Taylor.

Cohn continued to be disquieted that Rose could not bear him a son. On one occasion, according to a story he related to a confidant, he attempted a bold solution. This is how he told the sequence of events:

Cohn had brooded over the plan for weeks. He knew that if he attempted a frontal approach, he risked detection; the compactness of Columbia stimulated the swift flow of gossip. So he devised a ruse that he believed would be foolproof.

He visited the set of a nightclub film he had been observing for several days. A flip of the finger summoned the assistant director to his side.

"Who is that dame over there?" he demanded, pointing to a statuesque extra girl in an evening gown. "What's her name? I want to know. Why does the casting department hire dames like that?"

The worried assistant director determined the girl's name and reported it to Cohn. Returning to his office, Cohn could find no listing for her in the telephone book. He summoned an acquaintance with underworld connections.

"Find out her number by any means possible—as long as you don't reveal my name," Cohn instructed. The hoodlum returned with the number and was handed $50.

Cohn remained in his office until nine o'clock that evening. Then he dialed the number on his private telephone. Miss "Smith" answered.

"Miss 'Smith,' this is Harry Cohn."

"Yes, I'm sure," she replied scoffingly.

"No, I'm not fooling you," he insisted. "If you like, you can call me back on the studio switchboard."

Miss "Smith" seemed convinced. But she was also angry. "I don't want to talk to you," she said. "You got me fired today."

"I know. I did it on purpose and for a very special reason. I want to see you. On my solemn word of honor, I promise I will not molest you. I will not chase you around tables or anything like that. I beg you—and that is a word I seldom use—to see me. Do you live alone?"

"Yes. Why?"

"Because this is an extremely confidential matter. Would you please see me?"

"Mr. Cohn, I am accepting your word as a gentleman. You may come to my apartment."

Cohn arrived at precisely the appointed hour, ten o'clock. He entered the modest apartment, accepted an invitation to be seated and began his speech immediately.

"Miss 'Smith,' I don't wish to waste your time, so I will come directly to the point," he said. "I'll tell you as simply as I can, and all I ask is that you do not interrupt until I have finished. As you may know, I am a married man. I want very much to have an heir, and she cannot provide me with one. When I saw you on the set two days ago, I knew right away that you were a lady of good breeding and background. Now here is what I propose. I would like you to have a child by me. On the day that you are certified to be pregnant, I will put seventy-five thousand dollars in a bank under your name. If you give birth to a girl, I will pay you another fifty thousand. If it is a boy, I will pay you a hundred thousand. There is only one hitch."

"I can imagine what it is," she said.

"What do *you* think it is?"

"You will take the baby."

"That's right: I am buying a child. On the day the child is delivered to me, our relationship is over. And that is my proposition, put to you as gracefully as I can under the circumstances."

She paused a long moment. Then she said, "Mr. Cohn, you were right: I do come from a good background. And the very reasons you chose me are the same reasons I cannot accept your proposal."

As Cohn related the story, he caused Miss "Smith" to be restored to the Columbia casting rolls, and he never spoke to her again.

The formality of marriage proved too confining to Cohn, and he moved out of the Fremont Place home and into a penthouse of the El Royale Apartments on Rossmore Avenue. Rose declined his entreaties that he divorce her. Her pride would not permit her to admit the failure of her marriage. Besides, she still loved him.

Harry Cohn found a new diversion. Emulating Louis B. Mayer, he bought a yacht. He rarely sailed it, preferring to anchor at Santa Barbara or Catalina Island and entertain cronies and underlings. His pride in the gleaming white boat was immense, and he fretted for weeks over a proper name for it.

Day after day he plagued the creative minds of the studio for suggestions. During one lunch period he was particularly insistent, calling on each person for ideas. Finally, Sam Bischoff made the proposal that caused his banishment: "Why not call it the *Good-bye, Rose?*"

Cohn eventually named the boat himself. Significantly, he called it the *Jobella*, for his father and mother.

12
HOME COOKING AWAY FROM HOME

One hot September noon Harry Cohn and Sam Briskin strode the four short blocks from Columbia Studios to the Brown Derby restaurant on Vine Street near Hollywood Boulevard. They were denied admittance for lunch because they were in their shirt sleeves. The affront drew an immediate resolution by Cohn: he would institute a studio dining room so the Brown Derby would be denied the patronage of Columbia executives.

The dining room proved to be an important addition to the Cohn power structure. Once each day he was able to assemble his major underlings in one room and pick their brains, play one against the other, skewer them with scorn, make them entertain him, berate their efforts, and conduct all manner of devious dialectics that pertained to studio business.

A regular attendant of the Columbia lunches likened Cohn to Baron von Richthofen as he sat in icy silence at the head of the long table. He listened as the conversation proceeded warily among others at the table, none knowing when Cohn would strike. It might have come when a producer made a chance remark, "I saw a great picture last night."

"What the hell do you think was a great picture?" Cohn would reply. The others would sit back with relief to watch the one-sided duel. The producer would then have to defend the film he had seen, struggling vainly against the onslaught of Cohn's disdain. As Cohn moved in for the kill, others at the table might overcome their timidity and join in the attack.

The dining room was considered one of the hazards of working in an important post at Columbia, but that realization was of little comfort to those faced with the daily ordeal. More than one executive provided truth to the statement that Cohn proudly claimed to have originated: "I don't have ulcers; I *give* them!"

Cohn's fellow lunchers sought means to avoid Cohn's onslaught. One device was to eat as early as possible and thus gain minimum exposure to Cohn, who generally arrived at one o'clock. "The only safe time to arrive is for breakfast," observed one producer.

Early arrival provided another advantage: seating space at the end of the table. Cohn showed a preference for targets close at hand.

In the beginning years of the dining room it was limited to Columbia personnel. As Cohn gained in stature in the community, he entertained visiting dignitaries. This always pleased Columbia executives, who knew that Cohn would be on his best behavior before visitors.

Cohn also used the dining room as a place to woo new talent. This technique could backfire, as in the case of Groucho Marx. Cohn had been importuning Marx to come to Columbia as a producer of comedies. Marx was considering the proposal until he attended a lunch at Columbia. He was so appalled by the outpouring of sycophancy that he refused Cohn's offer.

Actors who worked at Columbia were seldom invited to the dining room. Cary Grant was included in the luncheon group, but he became so bored by the daily discussion of football that he asked to be excused.

Football and horse racing generally were the major topics of conversation, after picture making. Thousands of dollars changed hands on Mondays during the football season as bets were settled. The addition of new members to the table brought hopeful prospects of fresh victims for wager killings.

One such candidate was John Ford, who came to Columbia to direct *The Whole Town's Talking* with Edward G. Robinson. As an outsider, Ford appeared mystified as Cohn conducted the betting for the Saturday football games.

"I'll take USC," Cohn announced, siding with the team that was national champion. "I'll give you Pomona and twenty-two points. Bets up."

Cohn made the circuit of the table, beginning with Sam Briskin, who sat on his right hand. The lunchers lacked enthusiasm for the small college but nevertheless entered into bets with the studio boss. Finally, Cohn arrived at Ford, who was sitting on his left hand.

"What about you, Ford?" Cohn demanded. "I'll bet a thousand against your eight hundred. Okay?"

"Why should I bet?" Ford replied. "I never saw a football game. Rugby, perhaps. I know nothing about your football."

"Don't you have any sporting blood?" Cohn said indignantly.

"Tell me this: what is USC?" Ford asked.

"The University of Southern California, for crissake! You don't even know what USC is?"

Ford threw down his napkin. "Look, I'm getting sick and tired of all this blather," he snapped. "I'm going to find someplace else to eat. No, wait a minute. Give me that paper."

The director took the sports page and scrutinized it. He spelled out the name: "H-A-R-V-A-R-D, Harvard. And Holy Cross. What is Holy Cross?"

Cohn explained it was a Catholic college.

"What will you offer me on that game?" Ford asked.

Cohn sought the counsel of an aide with an odds sheet. Harvard was favored at ten to seven.

"How many points will you give me? Is that what you call them: points?" Ford asked.

Cohn offered seven points. Ford demanded twelve. He accepted eight. The bet was $1,500 versus $1,250. Others around the table clamored for similar bets with Ford. He accepted them all.

Cohn believed Ford was a native Irishman; in reality, Ford had been born in Portland, Maine, and had attended the University of Maine. The following Monday he collected $18,000 from inhabitants of the Columbia dining room.

They considered him lucky and attempted the same kind of coup against him the following week. Again he triumphed. When Ford remarked on the next Friday, "I'll take Iowa State and eight," Cohn replied, "The hell with you!"

A standard fixture in the dining room during the 1930's was an electrified chair, which was reserved for a newcomer to the group, preferably someone who was timid. Cohn waited until the victim was in the middle of a bite, then pressed a button with his foot, and roared with delight at the startled reaction. One night Frank Capra came into the dining room for some coffee at the end of a long cutting session and sat in the charged chair. The electricity was on, and he leaped out of the chair, picked it up, and hurled it to the floor, smashing it to pieces with his feet. Harry Cohn had another one built.

One day Cohn entered the dining room to find everyone at the table laughing.

"What's so goddam funny?" he demanded.

He was told that Dwight Taylor had just told a joke. Cohn turned on the writer and said, "All right, funnyman, tell me a joke. If you can make me laugh, I'll give you a hundred dollars."

Taylor contemplated as Cohn ordered his lunch. Then Taylor began his story:

> On a dark, rainy night in Paris, a hooded figure arrived at the door of a brothel. He pounded, and finally the door was opened to him. The madame inquired what he wanted.
>
> "Is this where I can find Fifi, the girl who will do anything?" he asked.
>
> "Yes," said the madame. She took him upstairs to a room where he found a frail girl with wild-looking eyes. The madame left them alone, and the man swept off his robe to reveal an incredibly cruel face. He was holding a black bullwhip in his hand.
>
> "Take off your clothes!" he commanded.
>
> "First the money," she insisted. "A thousand francs."
>
> He paid her, and she disrobed. He began whipping her again and again until her back was covered with welts. He stopped for a moment, and she asked, "Is that all?"
>
> "No" he said.
>
> "When are you going to quit?" she asked.
>
> He replied, "As soon as you give me back the thousand francs."

Cohn sat in stony silence, then burst out laughing. It was a joke he understood.

Cohn was so imperious about the dining room that he insisted on receiving the first copy of the typewritten menu; he was furious if he was handed a carbon copy. But he did not always command respect, as evidenced by the Norman Krasna barbs. On other occasions, writers on special assignments, hence not beholden to Cohn, responded in similar style. S. N. Behrman and Jed Harris spent one lunch period arguing back and forth about whether Cohn was a necrologist. Cohn, being unfamiliar with the word, was at a loss to comment.

The cuisine of the dining room was a special pride to Cohn. Knowing this, Garson Kanin found a device to needle him.

Kanin whispered to his wife, Ruth Gordon, "Don't eat too much of the soup." As he anticipated, Cohn overheard.

"What?" he asked. "What's wrong with the soup? There's nothing wrong with it."

Kanin feigned agreement and waited to whisper another obtuse remark about the food to his wife.

Nothing irritated Cohn more than having dieters at the table. Having been reared on Bella Cohn's cooking, he was a hearty eater all his life. If one or two lunchers ordered only salads, he grumbled through the meal, stabbing at the food with his fork.

When the dieting vogue became so prevalent among his executives that they eschewed desserts, Cohn ordered desserts banished from the menu as an economy measure. As a joke, several aides one day bought cheesecake at a delicatessen and had it stored in the dining room kitchen. At the end of the meal they ordered cheesecake, which was duly delivered. Cohn fired the dining-room manager for insubordination, rescinding his action only when the ruse was admitted.

The most famous incident in the Columbia dining room concerned an erratic genius named Herman J. Mankiewicz. He had been drama editor of *The New York Times* and *The New Yorker* before he turned to screenwriting. The freewheeling world of journalism seemed better suited to his temperament than did Hollywood. He possessed two failings that were inimical to the autocratic studio domains: he drank, and he was scornful of his bosses.

These faculties tumbled him from the position of a major screenwriter, and he had difficulty finding jobs. His agent, Charles Feldman, proposed a post at Columbia. Cohn was interested, since he enjoyed hiring bargain talent discarded by the major studios. Mankiewicz had previously earned $2,500 a week. Cohn agreed to employ him at $750 a week.

"I want to make good," said Mankiewicz when he reported to William Perlberg, then Columbia's executive producer.

"Fine," said the producer. "Go through the stories, and see if there is one you like. If you work hard, I'm sure there will be more work for you here. But there's just one thing to remember: don't go in the executive dining room. You know what will happen if you tangle with Cohn. So it's better to eliminate the temptation and stay away.

Mankiewicz concurred. He selected a story that seemed promising to him, and he was given permission to go ahead on a script. His work habits were exemplary, and he produced many pages a day.

But he began to feel a vague disquiet. His office was on the third floor, near the door to the executive dining room. As Riskin, Swerling, and other fellow writers emerged after lunch, he could hear them laughing over wisecracks and jokes that had been told inside. Mankiewicz himself was considered one of Hollywood's premier wits and raconteurs, and he rankled over his banishment.

One day Perlberg entered the dining room and was startled to find Mankiewicz sitting at the end of the table. The writer held a napkin to his mouth and promised, "I won't say a word."

When Cohn entered the room, he gave Mankiewicz a warm greeting, then assumed his monarchial position at the head of the table.

Cohn began the conversation: "Last night I saw the lousiest picture I've seen in years."

He mentioned the title, and one of the more courageous of his producers spoke up: "Why, I saw that picture at the Downtown Paramount, and the audience howled over it. Maybe you should have seen it with an audience."

"That doesn't make any difference," Cohn replied. "When I'm alone in a projection room, I have a foolproof device for judging whether a picture is good or bad. If my fanny squirms, it's bad. If my fanny doesn't squirm, it's good. It's as simple as that."

There was a momentary silence, which was filled by Mankiewicz at the end of the table: "Imagine—the whole world wired to Harry Cohn's ass!"

The employment of Herman J. Mankiewicz was terminated.

13
SIDNEY BUCHMAN, WHO SHALL BE CALLED INDISPENSABLE

*O*ne day when Harry Cohn was at his most imperious, his flinty eye fixed on each man at the lunch table as he asked, "All right, you ————-——, what did you do today to earn the money I'm paying you?"

The questions were answered in a jocular or a frightened manner, according to the executive's confidence in himself.

When Cohn aimed his inquisition at Sidney Buchman, he received this reply: "I'm too tired to play games, Harry. Drop it." Cohn dropped it.

The relationship of Harry Cohn and Sidney Buchman proved to be unique. Unlike Louis B. Mayer, who held tenaciously to his studio's talented individuals, Harry Cohn had a faculty for alienation. He discovered, hired, and developed many of the most accomplished film makers in Hollywood; all eventually left him, usually after violent disagreement. Sam Bischoff once suggested Cohn should erect a sign over the studio entrance reading: "Through these portals pass in—and out—the greatest talent in movies."

Buchman was the lone exception in Cohn's relations with film makers. Cohn battled with him as furiously as with any of his creative people, but Buchman was the one man Cohn could not part with. When Buchman was about to defect in later years, Cohn held onto him by doing something he had never before done as president of Columbia Pictures: he humbled himself. Their final parting was to come through a circumstance that neither could control.

Cohn and Buchman seemed entirely mismatched. Born in Duluth, Buchman took a degree at Columbia University, continued his studies at Oxford University, then traveled through England, France, and Italy for a year. He returned to London to gain employment as assistant stage director of the Old Vic. He began writing seriously and returned to New York to have two plays produced: *This One Man*, with Paul Muni, and *Storm Song*, with Francine Larrimore. Buchman was one of the scores of young dramatists lured to Hollywood in the talkie period. He labored at Paramount for three years, collaborating on such screenplays as *If I Had a Million* and *Sign of the Cross*.

After Buchman left Paramount, his agent, Sam Jaffe, negotiated an assignment at Columbia to write a script called *Whom the Gods Destroy*. He established no particular rapport with the studio boss at the outset.

Whom the Gods Destroy had been a favorite project of Cohn's, and he was disgruntled to hear Buchman say he thought the story was old hat. But Buchman agreed to work on the script. Calculating that his stay at Columbia might well be limited to one assignment, Buchman decided to write *Whom the Gods Destroy* to suit himself, not the prevailing formulas of Hollywood films. He wrote it quickly, without any consultation with Cohn, handed in the finished script, and checked off the lot.

Cohn telephoned him.

"I read your script," said Cohn. "It's pretty good."

"It's pretty different," Buchman remarked.

"Get your tail in here tomorrow," Cohn instructed.

Buchman knew enough of studio machinations to realize that Cohn had committed a tactical error in his comment that the script was "pretty good." It was a lapse that Cohn seldom permitted, and he was careful not to repeat it the following day in his office. He made no mention of Buchman's script.

Cohn began expansively: "Do you know of any other studio in town where you can walk right in the president's office whenever you have something on your mind?"

Buchman waited for Cohn to make his move. Eventually it came: an offer for a writing contract starting at $650 a week. Buchman accepted with the provision that he report directly to Cohn.

The first assignment under the contract demonstrated Cohn's regard for Buchman. Robert Riskin had gone off to Europe after he had written *Broadway Bill*, and Capra needed some rewriting on the location at Tanforan racetrack. Cohn sent Buchman.

Buchman also wrote a successful comedy for Claudette Colbert, *She Married Her Boss*, and a Grace Moore film, *Love Me Forever*. He established his reputation with *Theodora Goes Wild* in 1936.

The story concerned a small-town girl who went to the big city and returned home with a baby. Buchman felt that the first act of the film should aim for the shock when the girl stepped off the train with a baby in her arms. He wrote the earlier part of the script to be purposely dull, in order to build up to the comedy that was to follow. This went against Cohn's long-held precepts that a picture had to leap into its plot in the first reel.

"Let's risk dullness to make the train scene arresting," argued Buchman. With some misgivings, Cohn agreed.

Irene Dunne refused the film. So firm was her conviction that she departed for a six-week vacation in Europe rather than report to Columbia. Cohn suspended her salary. When she returned, he insisted that she carry out her commitment for *Theodora*.

Buchman completed the final script for *Theodora Goes Wild*. It was over long—180 pages, compared to the average 130—but Buchman preferred to write longer than necessary and edit later.

He submitted the script to Cohn. When he arrived in Cohn's office for a conference, the studio boss threw the script and hit him in the belly with it.

"Don't ever bring in a script with a hundred and eighty pages!" Cohn declared.

Buchman returned to the producer, Everett Riskin, and reported, "We're in!" Buchman interpreted the Cohn style well enough to know that the hurling of a script at the belly signified approval.

The script was sent to Richard Boleslavsky, a former member of the Moscow Art Theater who had been directing heavy dramas for M-G-M, notably *Rasputin*. He was elated to be offered a comedy. M-G-M agreed to lend him.

Miss Dunne's confidence in *Theodora* was not improved by the appointment of Boleslavsky. As a concession to her, Cohn agreed to remove him from the film after a week's time if she was dissatisfied with his work. She became enchanted with Boleslavsky, and he displayed a rare understanding of small-town America.

The preview indicated that Cohn had another comedy hit. Driving home from the theater, Cohn was expansive. He asked Buchman, "Pal, you ever had a screen card of your own?"

"No," said the writer.

"Well, you're going to get one now."

Buchman had received the accolade for a writer: to have his name appear alone on the screen during the credits. He continued his promise, as both a writer and a producer, and Cohn relied more and more on his judgment. Cohn often switched on the intercom and asked, "What are you doing, pal?"

"I'm writing," was Buchman's usual answer.

"Come on down here. I got a problem."

Buchman never entered the long, forbidding office without a sensation of excitement in the pit of his stomach. He knew he would be stimulated by another encounter with the man he considered the Devil's Advocate Supreme. Cohn's negative probing could be exasperating, but Buchman realized that Cohn used the technique to test the convictions of his writers. And when Cohn was not in a combative mood, he could be a miracle of charm. Buchman called him the Man with the Dancing China-Blue Eyes.

Buchman's position of favor with Cohn aroused the suspicions of his colleagues. He was accused of being a company man. The accusations proved false during the organizing campaign for the Screen Writers Guild. Three of the major organizers worked at Columbia: Robert Riskin, Mary McCall, Jr., and Sidney Buchman. While other studios coerced writers to drop their memberships and join company unions, Cohn did nothing to impede the guild.

Far from being a company man, Buchman adhered to his own working style, and this often irritated the president of Columbia Pictures. During a story conference Cohn gazed down at the check-in sheet for the morning and demanded of Buchman, "Who do you think you are, coming in late?"

"Harry," Buchman responded calmly, "if you really want to increase the productivity of the writers here, you will destroy that list."

He supported his thesis by citing the writer's daily routine at the studio: "He arrives at the studio depressed by the morning hour. Since all creative work is a torment, he does everything he can to avoid starting to write. He reads *Hollywood Reporter* and *Daily Variety*, taking them to the men's room. A bad review is cause for celebration, and he calls several friends at other studios to gloat over someone else's failure. Soon it is time for lunch, and he can stretch it to a couple of hours by kibbitzing with other writers as unwilling to write as he. He eats too much and goes back to his office with blood in his belly and unable to create. The solution is a nap. He awakes refreshed and full of resolves to go home and get a good sleep and then work like a maniac the following day.

"When a man is working on a script you should insist that he does not report to the studio," Buchman concluded.

Cohn was not amused. "Who do you think you are?" he repeated. "You conform to the rules around here. It sets a lousy example."

Buchman kept regular working hours during the next two days as he, Cohn, and others continued to agonize over a script that seemed to defy fixing.

"This is the third day," said the exasperated Cohn. "Why can't we get this problem solved?" He turned to Buchman and asked, "Have you got anything that will help?"

"Yes, but I can't tell you about it," Buchman replied.

"What?" said Cohn.

"You see, I got this idea at home as I was shaving. If I had got it at the studio, you could have it."

Cohn exploded. "You're a smart son of a bitch!"

"You're not the brightest man in the world," Buchman replied. "Now what do you choose: do you want only the ideas I get on company time, or do you want everything I think of?"

Buchman resumed his leisurely schedule.

14
EXIT CAPRA

*I*n 1938, Columbia Pictures was still striving to overcome the economic effects of *Lost Horizon*. Harry Cohn attempted a number of combinations of story and talent, but none produced that magical attraction that could buoy a whole season of Columbia films. Cohn's lifetime boast—that Columbia never showed a loss as long as he was president—was almost negated. Following the $1,000,000 plummet in profits in 1937, fiscal 1938 showed a net of only $2,046. Gross receipts continued near $20,000,000.

Jack Cohn and his salesmen of the East were in a state of alarm. Jack berated his brother for alienating Capra, even though it was a misdeed of the sales department on which the director based the suit to break his contract. The East brought pressures for settlement with Capra and restoration of his golden touch to the Columbia program.

Harry Cohn made peace. Capra, who had been given a new contract at $100,000 a picture after *It Happened One Night*, would henceforth earn double that amount. The money was not important to Cohn at that juncture in the company's fortunes. The essential thing was to get Capra back to work and reverse the two-year decline.

The immediate problem was finding a vehicle suited to Capra's unique talent.

You Can't Take It with You, the George S. Kaufman-Moss Hart comedy about the eccentric Vanderhof family, had been the big hit of the Broadway season. D. A. Doran, who scouted story properties for Columbia, saw it as an ideal subject for Capra and was hopeful of acquiring it for $75,000. That was far more than Columbia had ever paid for a property, but the need was urgent.

Doran went to New York to see the producer of *You Can't Take It with You*, Sam Harris. The news from Harris was chilling: "Kaufman says the first man to put up two hundred thousand dollars gets the property."

The price seemed beyond Columbia's means, and Doran returned to California in disappointment. He was hopeful that Kaufman might eventually lessen the figure, since no studio had ever paid $200,000 for a story property.

Doran received a telephone call from a New York agent, who was returning a favor. He reported seeing Louis B. Mayer in the office of Sam Harris that morning. Mayer planned to attend a performance of *You Can't Take It with You* that evening. If he liked the play, he would meet Kaufman's price the following day, Friday.

This intelligence was learned at eleven in the morning, when Harry Cohn had already departed for the Santa Anita racetrack. Doran rushed to suburban Arcadia, where he found Cohn in his racetrack box accompanied by his betting commissioner, Buzzy Appleton, and by Frank Capra.

Cohn's initial reaction to Doran's appearance was that of an indignant employer: "What the hell are you doing here?"

Doran attempted to explain his vital mission, but before he could communicate the news, he was instructed by Cohn to place $10 on the nose of a promising filly. The horse finished seventh, and then Doran explained the urgency of purchasing a Broadway play for $200,000.

Cohn turned to Capra and muttered, "This goddam fool is trying to sell me a property for two hundred thousand dollars."

Cohn returned to cataloguing the next race. After he had dispatched his bets, he asked Doran what the property was. Doran explained that it was *You Can't Take It with You*, the biggest hit on Broadway.

"I'd like to read it," said Capra.

"Can you get a copy?" Cohn asked Doran.

Doran believed he could. Cohn declared he would consider the matter at a meeting in his office that evening at eight o'clock.

A copy of the play was located and sent to Capra's house. At eight o'clock Cohn met with Doran and other executives in his studio office. By that time Louis B. Mayer had finished seeing *You Can't Take It with You*, had enjoyed it immensely, and was resolved to pay Kaufman's price the following day.

A telephone call was placed to Capra's home. Mrs. Capra answered. "Frank's in his room laughing his head off," reported Mrs. Capra.

"That's good enough for me," said Harry Cohn. He placed a call to his brother Jack in New York. Jack confirmed the immense success of *You Can't Take It with You* and agreed to the purchase.

The time for decision had arrived. It was 2:30 A.M. in New York. They would have to wake Sam Harris to make the deal. But no one knew his telephone number.

Harry Cohn knew that Buzzy Appleton also advised Sam Harris on his wagering. He called Appleton. Buzzy didn't have the Harris number, but he knew a Canadian mineowner who was staying at the same hotel and was acquainted with Harris.

Buzzy and the mining man arrived at Cohn's office shortly afterward with the number. The call was placed, and Harris answered sleepily.

"Look, Sam," shouted Harry Cohn. "Do I understand that the first person to put up two hundred thousand gets the movie rights to *You Can't Take It with You?*"

"That's right," Harris mumbled.

"You got a deal."

Harris awakened enough to add, "You'd better confirm this in a wire I can show to Kaufman and Hart."

"I will," assured Cohn. "Good-night."

Doran typed out a message for Western Union, and the deal was completed. Louis B. Mayer walked into the Sam Harris office that morning to discover that the play he wanted to buy had been snatched away by Harry Cohn. Cohn drew as much pleasure from beating out Louie Mayer as he did from the publicity that Columbia had paid the record high for a story property.

Robert Riskin turned out the script for *You Can't Take It with You*, and Cohn adhered to his promise to allow Capra complete creative freedom. Cohn borrowed Lionel Barrymore and newcomer James Stewart from M-G-M. The cast also included Jean Arthur, Edward Arnold, Mischa Auer, Ann Miller, Spring Byington, Halliwell Hobbes, Donald Meek, H. B. Warner, Samuel S. Hinds, and Eddie (Rochester) Anderson. Capra shot

329,000 feet of film for a final cut of 8,000 feet. The cost was $2,000,000, but Harry Cohn did not complain.

He was rewarded for his forbearance. *You Can't Take It with You* restored Columbia's fortunes. Box office returns were enormous, and the film was selected best picture of 1938 by the Academy of Motion Picture Arts and Sciences. Capra won his third award in five years for his direction.

By the end of 1938 both Jo Swerling and Robert Riskin had departed Columbia for more lucrative and less combative writing posts. Sidney Buchman was selected to write the next Capra film.

Lewis Foster had written a story about a guileless young politician who was hoodwinked by crooked businessmen and party leaders, then made a dramatic appeal for honesty and justice on the floor of Congress. The theme jibed with the Capra philosophy, and he agreed to undertake the project.

Buchman disappeared into the desert, locking himself in a room at the Desert Inn in Palm Springs. He labored day and night for a month and produced the first 100 pages of *Mr. Smith Goes to Washington*. He sent them off to Capra.

"Jesus, it's good!" said the director. "We're going to do all right."

Buchman wrote a first draft of 350 pages, then pared it down to 200. He had learned the trick of cutting down the number of pages by narrowing margins and eliminating descriptions. To play the idealistic young Congressman, Capra again sought James Stewart from M-G-M.

Mr. Smith Goes to Washington was another—and the last—Capra triumph at Columbia. Nominations for Academy Awards went to the film as best picture, to Capra, Stewart, Buchman, and Foster, and to Claude Rains and Harry Carey for supporting actor. None of the nominees was successful. This was 1939, the year of *Gone with the Wind*.

For his next film Capra wanted to veer from the Americana for which he was noted. He became enamored with the biography of Chopin, and Cohn purchased a German film for the basis of the story. Buchman composed a shooting script, and the film was cast and ready to begin production. Then came trouble with the East. Capra insisted that the film be made in color, which was then becoming more prevalent in big productions. Harry Cohn agreed, but Jack Cohn led the New York office in opposition. They were aghast at the prospect of trying to sell an expensive costume film about a piano player and a woman novelist who wore pants and smoked cigars. The opposition was strong enough to veto the project.

Capra was upset. He had poured a year's creative effort into the Chopin project, and now it had been wiped out by the book-keepers of the East. He left Columbia with the vow never to return.

Harry Cohn exerted every effort to lure Capra back. He dispatched Capra's longtime cameraman, Joe Walker, as an emissary, offering a deal Cohn had never proposed to anyone before: Columbia would pay all costs and split the profits fifty-fifty with Capra.

His efforts were overridden by a more munificent proposal: Warner Brothers was willing to pay Capra and Riskin $1,000,000 to make *Meet John Doe.*

Frank Capra was lost to Columbia Pictures. Harry Cohn did not lament. There were other directors besides Frank Capra.

15
THERE WERE OTHER DIRECTORS
BESIDES FRANK CAPRA

*T*n his search for creative talent Harry Cohn observed no restrictions, including sex. Other studios were virtually men's worlds, with only actresses and a few women writers and cutters among the important personnel. Over the years Cohn employed a succession of female executive assistants—not mere secretaries but women of accomplishment whose opinions he sought and respected.

During the early 1930's Cohn sought the services of Hollywood's only successful woman director, Dorothy Arzner. His persistence was such that he followed her home one night, hailing her on her doorstep.

"I'm Harry Cohn," he announced. "I want you to direct for Columbia."

"I'll work for you, Mr. Cohn—when your pictures start playing the first-run theaters," she replied.

After Frank Capra had accomplished that feat for Columbia, Cohn continued his pursuit of Miss Arzner. She had been committed to direct a film with Greta Garbo, but Irving Thalberg's death caused the assignment to be canceled. Miss Arzner sent her agent to see Harry Cohn, who reiterated his desire to hire her. But she wanted to function as producer, not director. Cohn agreed, although virtually no woman had succeeded as a producer in Hollywood.

Miss Arzner worked on two projects at Columbia, but neither developed to her satisfaction. Then she found *Craig's Wife*. The George Kelly play had been filmed as a silent by Pathé and had been acquired in Columbia's purchase of Pathé story properties. Miss Arzner was so intrigued by the story—how a woman becomes so obsessed with her house that she loses her husband—that she decided to direct it herself.

For the role of Mrs. Craig she chose a young M-G-M actress, Rosalind Russell, who had been playing second leads to Jean Harlow or first leads that had been refused by Myrna Loy. Still in her early twenties, Miss Russell seemed at first too young to play the meticulous Mrs. Craig. But she proved her maturity.

The living-room set was all-important to Miss Arzner. She had switched the locale from Philadelphia to Beverly Hills, but she wanted to retain the austere quality of a Greek tragedy in the set. Studio personnel decorated it three times, but she wasn't satisfied. She hired William Haines to complete the job. Harry Cohn threatened to fire her because of the expense, but he allowed her to continue.

Craig's Wife was filmed in four weeks at a cost of $280,000. It sent Rosalind Russell back to M-G-M as a star, and the film earned a handsome profit, convincing Harry Cohn anew of the wisdom of hiring women film makers.

Miss Arzner was awarded a new contract at Columbia. Fiercely independent, she insisted on a special clause: she could not be compelled to attend conferences aboard Cohn's yacht.

Rouben Mamoulian had been sought by Columbia since his successes had made him a top Broadway director. Like Dorothy Arzner, he considered Columbia an insignificant studio. Harry Cohn continued his wooing after Mamoulian had directed such films as *Song of Songs* and *Queen Christina*.

Having directed *Porgy and Bess* on the New York stage, Mamoulian was eager to make it into a film. But no studio would gamble on an all-Negro cast.

Harry Cohn sent for Mamoulian on the pretense of wanting to talk about a film of *Porgy and Bess*. The director quickly learned that Cohn had no interest in filming the Gershwin folk opera, and Mamoulian stalked out of the office.

Mamoulian was induced to return the next day. He told Cohn he was interested in only one Columbia property: *Golden*

Boy, the play by Clifford Odets. Cohn announced summarily that it had been assigned to another director.

But Mamoulian owned something that Cohn wanted: a short story that Frank Capra had admired. Mamoulian refused an offer of $75,000 to sell it. Finally, Cohn agreed to assign him to *Golden Boy* in return for the short story, which became the basis for *Mr. Smith Goes to Washington*. To Cohn's astonishment, Mamoulian would accept only what he paid for it: $1,500.

Mamoulian wanted Odets to adapt his play to the screen, but the dramatist had promised his bride, Luise Rainer, a European honeymoon. Mamoulian went to New York in search of writers with a feeling for the Odets saga. He found two, both in their mid-twenties, both unproved as writers. Daniel Taradash, a scion of wealth and a graduate of Harvard Law School, had won a national playwriting contest. Lewis Meltzer, a wry, unpredictable New Yorker, had actually had a play produced, but with small success.

"How much money do they want?" Cohn asked.

"At least a hundred dollars apiece," said Mamoulian.

"Are you crazy? This script needs a four-thousand-dollar-a-week writer."

"Then pay them two thousand apiece," suggested the director.

Cohn decided to pay them $200 apiece.

Taradash and Meltzer came to California, and Cohn had a first meeting with the two men who were to play important roles in his later life. Their age and salary prompted no respect from Cohn. He referred to them as "Hector MacArthur" or "those ——ing Theater Guild writers," although neither had ever been connected with the Guild. He urged them to make *Golden Boy* "sound like Capra." This irritated Mamoulian considerably.

Mamoulian spirited Meltzer and Taradash to an outpost on the Mojave Desert, where they fashioned the script beyond the interference of Harry Cohn. The script was completed in five weeks at a cost of $2,000.

Barbara Stanwyck, Adolphe Menjou, and Lee J. Cobb had been cast for leading roles, but Cohn lacked his Golden Boy. His prime choice was John Garfield, but Jack Warner was at odds with Cohn and would not permit a loan.*

Tested for the role were sixty-five actors, including many newcomers. Among them was William Holden, until recently Bill Beedle, a Paramount contract player who had yet to appear in a film. Cohn sent for him.

"Can you act?" Cohn demanded.

"I'm not sure," said the young man.

"Can you box?"

"No."

"Can you play the violin?"

"No."

"Then what the hell are you doing here?"

"I'm here because you sent for me."

The young man's candor appealed to Cohn, and he assigned him a test with an actress who was trying out for a minor role. She had appeared in several films, and she helped Holden understand camera technique.

The test started at five in the afternoon and continued into the evening. Holden said to the actress, "You've been so nice to me, I'd love to take you to dinner."

"Thanks," she replied with a smile. "But I have a date."

Harry Cohn and Sam Briskin came on the set to watch the two performers. Realizing that the two men held his fate in their hands, Holden commented to the actress, "I'd sure like to know what those two sons of bitches are thinking."

"They're thinking," she replied, "that you are going to be *Golden Boy.*"

---

*Harry Cohn once gave his version of the long-standing antagonism between himself and Warner Brothers: after Columbia had achieved prosperity, Cohn bought a large block of Warner Brothers stock. He professed no ulterior motive, and his relations with the Warners were cordial. Cohn was among the prominent mourners at the funeral of one of the Warners. As he was walking in the procession to the burial plot, Cohn overheard a female member of the family telling another to sell her Warner stock; a plan was under way to unload the stock to depress its market value, then to rebuy it at a low price. Cohn didn't wait for the deceased Warner to be lowered into the grave. He hurried to a telephone and instructed his broker to sell the Warner Brothers stock.

Holden didn't know how well informed she was until Cohn came over and said to her, "Sorry, dear, but I won't be able to have dinner with you until ten fifteen." The actress was Joan Perry.

The role did fall to William Holden, and he was immediately plunged into boxing, violin, and dramatic lessons. The weary actor asked for one evening off to attend his first movie premiere.

"No," decreed Harry Cohn. "If you're any good, there'll be plenty more premieres to go to. If you're no good, it won't make any difference."

Mamoulian was in a nervous state as the time approached to make the film with the untried actor, and the veteran cast shared his anxiety. Holden astonished them all by beginning *Golden Boy* with complete ease. But on the fourth day he was unable to report to the set; he was overcome with nerves.

With sensitive direction by Mamoulian and patient instruction by Miss Stanwyck, Holden managed a performance. But *Golden Boy* failed to achieve wide popularity. The nation in the late 1930's was bored with problems of the Great Depression.

The film was a disappointment for Harry Cohn, but he profited from it: he had created a new star. In exchange for bestowing *Golden Boy* on William Holden, Cohn exacted half of the actor's contract with Paramount.

Howard Hawks was another of the topflight directors Harry Cohn tried to enlist for Columbia Pictures. Cohn had succeeded twice before; Hawks had made *The Criminal Code* with Walter Huston and Constance Cummings in 1931 and *Twentieth Century* with John Barrymore and Carole Lombard in 1934.

One day in 1938, Hawks was visiting a friend on the Columbia lot. Cohn, who was informed of every important visitor to the studio, asked Hawks to visit his office.

"I've got commitments coming up with Cary Grant and Jean Arthur," Cohn said, "and I don't have a picture for them. Have you got any ideas?"

"Well, I might have," said the easygoing Hawks. "I was sitting around my swimming pool this morning, and I wrote out a six-page outline for a movie. It's based on some things I saw while flying the Andes. You can read it—if you can make out my writing."

Cohn eagerly accepted the manuscript. Two hours later he telephoned Hawks and said, "You've got a deal."

Besides Grant and Miss Arthur, the cast included Richard Barthelmess in a comeback try, Thomas Mitchell, Sig Ruman, John Carroll, and Allyn Joslyn. Hawks, who liked to discover and develop new female stars, searched for an unknown to play the wife of Barthelmess, a small but potentially showy role. He saw possibilities in a young brunette who was under contract to Columbia, Rita Hayworth.

Word of Hawks' interest reached Cohn. "Are you going to put Rita Hayworth in that part?" he asked.

"That's right" said Hawks.

"Have you tested her?"

"No, and I'm not going to. If I tested her, she'd freeze up; that's how scared she is. I'm going to test her in the picture."

With some misgivings, Cohn agreed to the casting. As Hawks anticipated, Rita Hayworth made a striking appearance in *Only Angels Have Wings*, and her more obvious attributes overshadowed her shortcomings as an actress.

"If you're smart," Hawks told Cohn, "you won't do anything with her until the picture comes out. No other movies, no publicity, nothing. Just wait until the public sees her. Then you'll know what you've got and you'll build up her self-confidence, too."

Again Cohn followed Hawks' suggestion. When *Only Angels Have Wings* was released in 1939, there was an undercurrent of excitement about the remarkably beautiful girl who played Barthelmess' wife.

The golden years were closing. Capra was gone, and so was the system by which Columbia could base its fortune on one or two or three immense hits each year. The order had changed, and Harry Cohn was required to change with it.

During the 1930's Columbia, along with Universal, United Artists, and Republic, had been one of the minors. The majors—M-G-M, Paramount, Twentieth Century-Fox, Warner Brothers, and RKO—commanded the industry and threatened to take an increasing share. With the Depression over and the nation preparing for war, entertainment would be in great demand during the decade to come. The time called for bigness.

It was a new and hazardous course for Harry Cohn. But he had the boldness for it. And he had found his star.

IV

Boomtown:
The Forties

• • • • •

JAMES STEWART WINS AN OSCAR and flies off to war. Clark Gable goes, too. And Tyrone Power, Robert Taylor, Robert Montgomery, Henry Fonda, Victor Mature, Gene Autry, Mickey Rooney, and Sabu.

Betty Grable peers cunningly over her shoulder, her round behind intriguing soldiers from Attu to Tangier. A pouting Jane Russell leans against a haystack in open challenge. Rita Hayworth, chest expanded, kneels in a negligee atop a silken bed.

Bing Crosby and his four sons sing Christmas carols at the Hollywood Canteen. Fort Hal Roach pours forth films to show fighting men how to survive on tropical islands and how to avoid venereal disease. Joe E. Brown, Ann Sheridan, and Bob Hope stand in jungle rains to tell jokes to boys far from home. Korean and Chinese actors find full enjoyment playing degenerate Japanese in animated war posters.

Hollywood is mobilized.

The war brings problems to the film industry. There are shortages of film, set-building materials, and leading men. A newly vocal segment of the population known as bobby-soxers helps create new male stars, notably Van Johnson and Frank Sinatra. Established stars are upset by government limitations of their earnings, and they limit the number of films they are willing to make. But the studio bosses do not suffer. Louis B. Mayer's salary in 1942 is $949,765.

Theaters prosper as never before. Managers need do little more than unlock the doors and stand aside. The public's indiscriminate need for entertainment encourages slackening of quality. Why try harder, when the yokels will buy anything?

War ends. Stewart, Gable, Power, Taylor, et al., come marching home, consigning ersatz leading men to oblivion. Hollywood swells with confidence. The British invasion by J. Arthur Rank is beaten off. Neorealistic films from Europe like *Open City* and *Shoe Shine* engage the intelligentsia, but the masses still prefer the glossy escapism that Hollywood produces peerlessly.

In 1946 canny old Sam Goldwyn makes *The Best Years of Our Lives*. It is a superlative year for films, with $1,500,000,000 pouring through American box offices. Although no one cares to believe so, the best years are over.

The whipped cream turns sour. Graustarkian visions have little pertinence to a nation that has been through a shooting war and is facing a cold one. Money that went for movies now buys baseball tickets. Bowling and boating take precedence over the local theater. And growing millions sit in darkened living rooms to watch Uncle Miltie in drag.

Movie profits slide from $90,000,000 to $55,000,000 between 1946 and 1948. And in 1948 comes the long-feared edict. The Supreme Court tells the movie companies to rid themselves of their theater chains within five years. The union of production and exhibition, which has stabilized the industry for twenty years, now will be forcibly dissolved in the name of the Sherman Antitrust Act.

More trouble in Washington. Politicians recognize the surefire box office of combining movie names with the nation's new paranoia. Stars parade before the House Committee on Un-American Activities to decry Red influence in Hollywood. Gary Cooper tells of rejecting scripts "tinged with Communistic ideas." The writers of those scripts appear before the committee, and they march off to jail as the Unfriendly Ten.

Cracks appear in the power structure. Nick Schenck imposes Dore Schary on Louis B. Mayer, who has preferred to rule M-G-M alone. Pressures from other New York offices increase as studio chiefs seem no longer able to perform miracles.

Nothing seems to stem the downward trend. Folksy, homespun Will Hays is succeeded by Eric Johnston, a stainless-steel product of the public relations mills. Johnston urges all to keep cool heads. He resists suggestions to loosen Joe Breen's hold on film morals; American movies should continue to condemn sin and uphold virtue, he argues, in contrast with those dirty pictures from Europe.

● ● ● ● ●

I
Onward and Upward with Columbia Pictures Corporation

*A*s Columbia entered its third decade, Harry Cohn was determined to elevate the company's status to a position of equality with the major studios. To do so, he had to abandon much of the company philosophy that dated back to its Poverty Row days. Cohn's attitude toward waste never changed; he still excoriated employees who did not turn off their office lights before leaving for the day. But he realized Columbia could no longer play a penny-ante game. To join the winners, he had to gamble for high stakes. That meant more first-class productions.

From the late thirties through the forties Columbia released from fifty to sixty-five features a year. Seventy percent of the films were program Westerns, serials, independent releases, and B pictures, including such series as *Blondie, Lone Wolf, Boston Blackie*, and *Crime Doctor*. Harry Cohn paid scant attention to such films. Much of the B unit was exiled to Columbia Sunset, an early-day studio that Columbia now operated two miles east of the Gower lot.

Cohn's prime concern was the A and AA pictures that provided Columbia its prosperity and reputation. During the ten-year period from 1937 to 1946 the AA and A product, although constituting 30 percent of the program, supplied 60 percent of the profits.

Cohn began lavishing more and more of the studio's talent and money on top films, and the results proved highly satisfactory. Six A films of the 1940–41 season brought profits of $424,000; a year later the same number of films cleared $2,000,000. Two years later, six films drew $3,500,000 in profits.

Still the only company president to boss production, Harry Cohn maintained his one-man rule. No studio knew such autocracy. But he realized that his own personality was not enough to attract talent.

"I kiss the feet of talent," Cohn said a thousand times. There were variations of this remark, notably: "If you've got talent, I'll kiss your ass; if you haven't got talent, I'll kick it." In truth, he did seem to possess at least a preliminary, perhaps grudging respect for the kind of talent that could make good pictures. With a paucity of star names and assets to lavish on productions, Columbia relied heavily on gifted film makers. And although Harry Cohn could not hold onto them, he did everything possible to woo them.

As an adjunct to his own persuasive powers, Cohn surrounded himself with executives who provided an air of distinction to the corporation. In contrast with the rough-hewn boss, they were well-read, educated men, smooth and capable in negotiation.

Nate Spingold occupied the delicate position as Harry Cohn's liaison in New York. Chicago-born, he had been a law student and newspaper reporter until an interview with William Morris led to a job as press agent for the talent agency. Profiting on investments, he had retired at forty-five. He was later convinced by Harry Cohn to become vice-president of Columbia Pictures. Spingold was married to a noted couturiere, Madame Frances, who was a heavy investor in Columbia Pictures, and both were patrons of the arts.

Spingold's wealth made him ideal for the role of Harry Cohn's man in the East. He was not subservient to Cohn, and indeed, he was one of the few people who could successfully reprove the company president for his excesses; Cohn listened. Jack Cohn and other executives of the East also respected Spingold and permitted him to share most of their confidences—but not all. Since they sometimes plotted how to gain an advantage over Harry, they did not care to risk the chance that Spingold might divulge their plans to the enemy. Spingold was circumspect in his confidences, but he would not condone any unfair treatment of Harry.

Ben Kahane was Cohn's strong right arm at the studio. He had practiced law in Chicago and New York before joining the

Orpheum Circuit as an executive. From 1932 to 1936 he was in charge of RKO Studios; then Harry Cohn invited him to join Columbia as vice-president.

Kahane was a kindly man, who acted as father confessor to actors and directors in their disputes with Cohn. Kahane performed the public functions of Columbia in its relations with the Academy, the Motion Picture Relief Fund, the Producers' Association, and the unions, performing ably in fields that failed to interest Cohn, who hadn't a shred of concern for public relations.

Mendel Silberberg, a distinguished Los Angeles attorney, was long Columbia's counsel and a member of the board of directors. Another top executive was Lester Roth, who had been a superior court judge and later sat on the district court of appeals. Cohn enjoyed the company of lawyers and delighted in catching them up in a point of law. His knowledge of the law was prolific, in contradiction with his reputation for being uneducated. He found pleasure in studying transcripts of famous trials and reread the Rosenberg treason case several times.

Harry Cohn realized the value of distinguished men to the stature of Columbia Pictures, yet his attitude toward them was ambivalent. In private he listened to and generally respected their judgments. But when others were present, he could be as harsh and abusive as he could be in addressing an erring actor.

"You smart college bastard," he would begin as prelude to an excoriation for some misstep. He delighted in using gutter language to educated men, and his delight was compounded if they answered in kind. Then they were on his level, and that pleased him.

After hearing Cohn laden Kahane with abuse during a production meeting, a witness asked, "Ben, why do you take it?"

"Harry doesn't mean it the way it sounds," answered Kahane wearily. "He makes it up to me in other ways."

Some executives had ways of combating the Cohn tirades. Everett Riskin began walking out of Cohn's office when the studio boss started berating two writers.

"Where are you going?" Cohn demanded.

"I'm leaving," said the producer. "You don't have enough money to make me sit and listen to you abuse another human being. And if you ever do that in front of me again, I'll beat the hell out of you." He left the office.

Two weeks later Cohn began to castigate another writer in a meeting. Riskin leaped to his feet, reached across the desk, and grabbed Cohn by the neck. Cohn never again attempted the tactic in the presence of Riskin.

Curiously, Cohn held no grudge over such a display of insubordination. Among the employees who stayed with him the longest were those who fought with him the hardest. Many stars, directors, and writers left Columbia amid threats by Cohn of recrimination, only to return a few years later. If they possessed talent that he needed, Cohn lured them back at any cost.

Cohn admitted this propensity in an oft-repeated statement. After a violent encounter Cohn would instruct his secretary, "I want that man barred from the lot. He is not to be allowed on studio property for any purpose. Tell the guards on the main entrance, the Beachwood Drive gate, and at the ranch, too. That man is not to be allowed in this studio—until I need him."

Cohn was combative in virtually all dealings with underlings. His normal reaction to any suggestion was: "You're full of ———." Then it was incumbent on the person making the suggestion to argue his case before Cohn, who deprecated each argument, often in abusive terms.

In the end came the decision: either a final no or an off-handed "All right, go ahead, but it's your skin if it doesn't work." That placed heavy responsibility on the person to make the suggestion succeed or suffer the wrath of Harry Cohn.

Cohn once confided the reasoning behind his technique: "Seventy-five percent of the ideas that people try to sell me are no good. If I turn down every idea at the outset, that makes me right seventy-five percent of the time. That's not a bad average."

Such negativism proved exasperating to many film creators, and they left Columbia rather than submit their ideas to the constant scorn of Harry Cohn. But others understood Cohn's method and found their talents were tempered by his annealing force. A surprising number of directors and writers gave Harry Cohn their best work and accomplished nothing of equal value after leaving him.

Also surprising was the innovation that could arise from such a system. Most producers, being frightened men, followed the trend. Harry Cohn, having none of the normal fears, did not hesitate to gamble on fresh ideas, once he was convinced they were worth the chance. As a result, Columbia often set movie trends.

It Happened One Night brought a flood of romantic comedies. After the success of *One Night of Love*, other studios imported such operatic stars as Lily Pons, Gladys Swarthout, and Nino Martini. *The Awful Truth* provoked a cycle of screwball farces.

The 1940's found Harry Cohn continuing his gambles on film subjects that other producers shunned, notably fantasy, musical biography, and political realism. It gave him pleasure to see his competitors rush to imitate his innovations, always with lesser success.

2

THE TRANSFIGURATION OF
MARGARITA CARMEN CANSINO

*A*lways there was a man.

In the beginning it was her father, the graceful, imperious Eduardo Cansino, late of Seville. His father had pressed him and his seven brothers and a sister into duty with the family dancing troupe. So it was only natural that Eduardo, who met and married Volga Haworth while both danced in the *Ziegfeld Follies*, would put his daughter Margarita to work at an early age. She was dancing professionally by the age of twelve.

Margarita developed early, and by fourteen she had the form and grace of a young woman. Since Eduardo's dancing school in Hollywood was languishing in the Depression years, he decided to return to performing. Margarita would be his partner. He drilled her for long weeks until she displayed the perfection of movement he demanded.

Their first engagement was at the Foreign Club in Agua Caliente, where Californians went for gambling, horse racing, and other pleasures that were denied them in their own cities. Eduardo and Margarita danced four shows a day, from noon to two in the morning. It was hard, unrewarding work, but Eduardo calculated that among the Hollywood figures that flocked to Agua Caliente, one might discover him and his daughter. He was proved correct, although it was Margarita who was chosen, not Eduardo.

Winfield Sheehan, the round-faced, fun-loving head of production at Fox, was the discoverer. He picked Margarita to dance in a gambling-ship sequence in *Dante's Inferno*. Her partner was Gary Leon, but Eduardo directed the dance. His daughter earned the amazing sum of $500 for a week's work.

Sheehan detected in the brief dance a quality that held promise of future achievements. Margarita was invited to test for a

Fox contract, and the results proved satisfactory. She was offered a starting salary of $75 a week. Eduardo said that would not do; Margarita must receive $200 a week. Sheehan reluctantly agreed.

Margarita Cansino again enacted a Latin dancer in *Under the Pampas Moon* with Warner Baxter, then recited her first lines in *Charlie Chan in Egypt*. Her dialogue was at first indistinct, but she improved in *Paddy O'Day*, a Jane Withers film. Again she was a Spanish dancer in *Human Cargo*.

Sheehan had plans for his discovery. He declared Miss Cansino would be starred in a remake of the California romance *Ramona*. Playing opposite Gilbert Roland, she performed in a test that was deemed highly satisfactory. But before the film could begin, Winfield Sheehan had been deposed as studio boss in the wake of a merger with Twentieth Century; all his projects had been countermanded by the new chief of production, Darryl F. Zanuck. Loretta Young was cast as Ramona, and Miss Cansino's contract was terminated.

The stirrings of ambition began to evidence themselves. After being fired, Margarita dashed home and cried in her mother's arms over the injustice of the new studio regime. The hurt turned to resolution as she vowed that the same men who fired her would someday regret their decision.

Margarita appeared in *Meet Nero Wolfe* at Columbia, then in some Westerns with George O'Brien at Universal. All were unrewarding, but she was learning how to work before a camera. And she continued to develop as a woman.

At seventeen Margarita Cansino knew little of men, having been sheltered in the Spanish tradition. Even if Eduardo had allowed her to date, her schedule of work and dancing practice scarcely allowed for it. But a man did enter Margarita's life. His name was Edward Judson. She had met him through co-workers at Fox, and he seemed profoundly interested in the ambitions of the radiant young beauty with the raven hair.

Eduardo protested loudly that Judson was as old as he himself, her own father. But Margarita was unconcerned. She was intrigued with the balding, round-faced Judson and his talk of how she could become a big star. The first date of her life was with him. She became Mrs. Edward C. Judson on May 29, 1937, when she was eighteen and he was forty. Eduardo was furious.

Margarita knew that her husband was a salesman—of automobiles, she believed. In reality, he displayed his greatest interest, as well as his most profound talent, in selling the film career of his new wife.

Judson helped acquire a term contract for Margarita at Columbia Studios. Harry Cohn took little notice of the new player, except to remark that her name would have to be changed. This found favor with Judson. As Margarita Cansino, the young actress had been limited to playing exotic dancers and vamps. The Latin quality of her name was minimized by shortening her given name and adopting a variation of her mother's maiden name.

But she needed more than the name of Rita Hayworth to avoid being typed. Judson sought the advice of Helen Hunt, hair stylist at Columbia Studios. "Tell me what we can do about Rita," he asked.

Miss Hunt suggested a change in hair color from Rita's natural black to a soft auburn. The girl's hairline extended too far down on her forehead. Miss Hunt had photographs taken of the face and consulted an electrolysis expert. Achieving a new design for Rita's forehead would entail a long and painful process. Each hair had to be removed individually, then the follicle deadened with a charge of electricity. Despite an acute sensitivity to pain, Rita agreed to undergo the ordeal, and in time she emerged with a broad, graceful brow.

Judson was determined that Rita would be noticed by those who could further her career, principally by Harry Cohn. Judson hired a press agent to inject Rita's name into the gossip columns. He escorted his wife to the Trocadero and Ciro's and to movie premieres. He promoted gowns of the latest fashion and employed a hairdresser to groom Rita before each excursion into Hollywood society.

In the end, it was the recalcitrance of Columbia's reigning female star that helped speed Rita's ascent, just as she was to prepare the advent of *her* successor.

Jean Arthur had known a career as an ingenue in silents and early talkies before making one of her characteristic disappearances from films. She returned for a contract with Columbia, where her blond good looks, smoky voice, and air of utter sincerity fitted her for the studio's sophisticated comedies—among them: *The Whole Town's Talking* with Edward G. Robinson; *If You Could Only Cook* with Herbert Marshall; *Mr. Deeds Goes to Town* with Gary Cooper; *You Can't Take It with You* with James Stewart.

Miss Arthur's was an evanescent personality, shining with brilliance before the camera and fading into timidity in her personal life. Harry Cohn's bluff manner frightened and upset her, with the result that they were repeatedly engaged in conflict and litigation.

Publicity was an anathema to Miss Arthur, and her refusal to cooperate produced frustration and discontent in the Columbia publicity staff. Lou Smith, head of the department, saw in the voluptuous Rita Hayworth a chance to recover some of the news space that had been lost by his inability to publicize Miss Arthur.

Rita, coached by Judson, was willing to follow the suggestions of Smith and his staff. She submitted to one photographic session after another in the studio gallery and at the beach, posing with giant firecrackers, turkey cutouts, or Easter bunnies, according to the season. Newspapers and magazines were flooded with the photographs.

The campaign produced the practical result of bringing Rita to the attention of Howard Hawks, who cast her in *Only Angels Have Wings*. Her appearance was brief, and Miss Arthur, who had the female lead in the film, was neither cognizant nor concerned that the attractive brunette would supplant her as the queen of Columbia. Miss Arthur's major interest then and for the next few years was how to escape her Columbia contract.

Despite a favorable reaction to Rita at the preview of *Only Angels Have Wings*, the Columbia hierarchy was undecided about exercising her next option, which would have lifted her salary from $250 a week to $300. Two of the executives were in favor; two wanted to retain her services only if she would forgo the $50 increase, a familiar tactic in all studios.

Rita's agents, Morris Small and George Chasin, suggested an alternative: her salary would remain at $250, but the $50 would be given to a dramatic coach, Grace Fogeler, in payment for lessons to Rita. Cohn accepted the proposal.

Harry Cohn proceeded cautiously. After being amid first-class talent in *Only Angels Have Wings*, Rita next found herself returned to potboilers: an RKO loan-out, *Special Inspector*; a minor musical with Tony Martin; *Blondie on a Budget*.

But the continuing publicity campaign was creating a demand for her services at other studios; for the first time Harry Cohn had brought forth a star who was valuable for loans to his competitors. M-G-M sought Rita for *Susan and God* with Joan Crawford. Rita was cast in the title role of *The Strawberry Blonde*, starring James Cagney at Warner Brothers; for the film, her hair acquired the coppery-red tone that was to be her trademark. She remained at Warner Brothers for *Affectionately Yours* with Dennis Morgan and Merle Oberon.

Rita's most satisfying triumph came when she was lent to Twentieth Century-Fox, the studio that had once fired her during a change in administrations. She saw none of the profit herself, but it satisfied her to know that Fox was paying Harry Cohn five times her normal salary so she could appear with Tyrone Power in a remake of *Blood and Sand*.

By now Cohn was eager to profit from Rita's services in a Columbia film. The war had created a need for escapist entertainment; hence, the revival of musicals. Cohn hired Fred Astaire, whose career had slumped since his breakup with Ginger Rogers, and costarred him with Rita in *You'll Never Get Rich*. This was to be her first costarring film at Columbia, and Cohn did everything possible to ensure its success. Cole Porter was engaged to write the songs.

Astaire was uneasy about working with Rita. He was concerned about the difference in their ages; thirty years before, he had appeared on vaudeville bills with her father, Eduardo. He also had reservations about her height. She was five feet, six inches, but by wearing low heels, she was comfortably shorter than Astaire. *You'll Never Get Rich* proved to be an entertaining musical comedy of Army life, advancing both their careers.

Rita's publicity remained a pace ahead of her screen endeavors. A *Life* magazine photograph by Robert Landry, displaying Rita crouched on a bed, captured the admiration of millions of men in military service. When she went to New York for the opening of *You'll Never Get Rich*, a resourceful publicity man in Columbia's New York office, Frank Rosenberg, suggested a stunt in the spirit of the times. Rita was to tour New York in the company of a soldier, a sailor, a marine, and a coast guardsman. Coverage of the stunt was displayed on front pages of newspapers in New York and elsewhere.

Ed Judson accompanied Rita to New York on that occasion, but he remained in the background. That was increasingly his position as Rita's career climbed and his function in it diminished. Judson's usefulness came to an end when his wife was lent to Twentieth Century-Fox once more for *My Gal Sal*, in which her costar was Victor Mature. A romance between Rita and Mature was rumored in the movie columns.

The divorce from Judson exhibited Rita's propensity for creating news. She charged that Judson demanded $30,000 to get out of her life; if she didn't pay, he threatened her with bodily harm and exposure to public contempt and ridicule. A $30,000 fee for managing her during their five-year marriage was ridiculous, said Rita.

"I didn't have any fun those five years," she declared. "I never was permitted to make any decisions. He robbed everything of excitement."

In the end, Edward Judson got his $30,000—from Harry Cohn. And Rita was to get her fun.

3

FILMS OF THE EARLY FORTIES: ANGELS, LADY REPORTERS, CHOPIN, ETC.

Here Comes Mr. Jordan derived from a play about a prize-fighter who died but was given permission to return to earth and settle his affairs. It was the type of subject that studios shunned, having witnessed the failures of *Outward Bound, Green Pastures*, and other adventures into the occult. But the subject intrigued Everett Riskin and Sidney Buchman, and Harry Cohn gave them permission to proceed with preparing the project.

After Buchman had completed his script of *Here Comes Mr. Jordan*, he received an urgent summons to the office of Harry Cohn.

"Pal, I got a helluva problem," said the long-faced Cohn. "The East is raising hell over *Mr. Jordan*. They say three kinds of pictures never make money: racetrack stories, backstage stories, and fantasies. I don't give a goddam what they think; but they're beating my brains in, and I gotta be damned sure we know what we're doing. What do you think?"

"Did you get a kick out of the script?" Buchman asked.

"Yes," Cohn admitted.

"Well, if you got a boot out of it, it must be good," said Buchman. "I'm not worried. If the audience gets the key to the fantasy, then there's no problem. If the Eastern boys are arguing this is a fantasy just because a man returns to earth, they're being too mechanical."

"You're right!" Cohn agreed. "They're mechanical bastards. All they want is what sold last year. Go ahead with the picture."

Again Columbia sought the services of Robert Montgomery, who had refused *It Happened One Night*. Since he was once more in poor grace with Louis B. Mayer, the loan was arranged from M-G-M. Montgomery grumblingly agreed to it.

Here Comes Mr. Jordan was a huge success, and it won Montgomery a nomination for best performance by an actor in 1941. The film was also nominated for best picture, direction (by Alexander Hall), and cinematography (by Joseph Walker). Buchman and his collaborator, Seton I. Miller, won Oscars for their screenplay.

The success of *Here Comes Mr. Jordan* later prompted Harry Cohn to cast Rita Hayworth as the goddess Terpsichore in *Down to Earth*. The film was a failure.

Years afterward George Axelrod was attempting to sell Cohn a fantasy he had written.

"Fantasies don't make money," Cohn stated flatly.

"But, Harry," the playwright protested, "you made a brilliant picture right here at your studio, *Here Comes Mr. Jordan*. It was a fantasy, and it made a lot of money."

"Sure," came the reply with Cohnian logic, "but think how much more it would have made if it hadn't been a fantasy!"

Harry Cohn once again sought the services of Howard Hawks.

"Have you got a story?" the director asked.

"No," Cohn admitted.

"I have: *The Front Page*," said Hawks.

At first Cohn didn't respond to the idea, since the Ben Hecht-Charles MacArthur play had been filmed less than ten years before, with Adolphe Menjou and Pat O'Brien as stars. But Cohn saw possibilities in a remake if a new approach could be achieved.

"How about casting it with Cary Grant and Walter Winchell?" he suggested.

"You're half right," Hawks replied. Then he told of an incident at a party at his house. Hawks had argued that Hecht and MacArthur wrote the best contemporary dialogue. To test his theory, he took a copy of the play and read the part of Walter Burns, city editor, inviting a girl to read the lines of the reporter, Hildy Johnson. Hawks was astounded to find the scene played even better between a man and woman.

"Why not have Grant play the city editor, get a girl for the reporter, and make them a divorced couple?" Hawks suggested. Cohn agreed.

Charles Lederer wrote the script, creating the role of another man in whom the divorced Hildy was interested. It was played by reliable Ralph Bellamy, who was soon to return to the stage to escape "Ralph Bellamy roles." Hawks assembled a fine supporting cast of Gene Lockhart, Porter Hall, Roscoe Karns, Frank Jenks, Regis Toomey, John Qualen, Ernest Truex, Cliff Edwards, Billy Gilbert, and Clarence Kolb.

But Hawks was stuck for a Hildy Johnson. Jean Arthur, Claudette Colbert, Ginger Rogers, and Irene Dunne declined the role of the regendered reporter. Searching the lists of available actresses, Cohn happened on the name of Rosalind Russell, who had ably performed for Columbia in *Craig's Wife*. Once more Louis B. Mayer was willing to lend her.

The choice wasn't popular with Hawks, and Miss Russell realized it. At their first meeting she commented, "You don't want me, do you? But you're stuck with me, so we might as well make the most of it."

They did. The talents of Grant and Miss Russell combined in crackling style, vying with each other for rapidity of dialogue. The film, which was called *His Girl Friday*, was said to possess the fastest dialogue in the history of talking pictures. Yet audiences had no difficulty in understanding the speeches, except when laughter overwhelmed the sound track.

After ending his collaboration with Charles MacArthur, Ben Hecht sought a career as a director. He had wearied of seeing his writings hacked by ignorant producers and misinterpreted by insensitive directors. He sought complete artistic control.

Hecht submitted to Columbia a theatrical story, *Angels over Broadway*, which seemed a suitable vehicle for Rita Hayworth. Harry Cohn permitted Hecht to produce and direct the film without interference. Douglas Fairbanks, Jr., appeared opposite Miss Hayworth.

When Cohn saw the finished product, he was distraught. *Angels over Broadway* was too gloomy a vehicle for his new star. He set about recutting the film to provide more pace and a lighter touch.

Word of the recutting reached Hecht. He rushed to Cohn's

office and pointed out that any tampering with the film was in direct violation of his contract.

"If you don't put it back the way I had it," Hecht threatened, "I'm going to put a title on the picture that will say: 'Written, Directed, and Produced by Ben Hecht, and Ruined by Harry Cohn.'"

Cohn restored the film to its original form. It failed to achieve success.

One of the topflight directors sought by Harry Cohn in the early 1940's was George Stevens. He had been a contemporary of Leo McCarey's at Hal Roach and had advanced from directing Laurel and Hardy comedies to such films as *Alice Adams*, Astaire and Rogers musicals, *Vivacious Lady*, and *Gunga Din*.

At first Stevens resisted the Cohn overtures, and this served to whet Cohn's eagerness to have the director under contract. Finally, a meeting was arranged. Cohn offered attractive terms, including a percentage of the profits, but still Stevens demurred.

"Mr. Cohn, I've heard that unpleasant things happen to directors at Columbia," Stevens remarked.

"I'll make you a deal," Cohn replied. "You make the pictures, and I won't talk to you.

The condition made the contract acceptable to Stevens, and he signed for three films for Columbia. Difficult though it was for him, Cohn adhered to his end of the agreement and never interfered with Stevens' picture making. Only once did he make a representation. He came on a set one day and said to Stevens, "Could I ask you a favor? Would you please not smoke on the set? I put signs all over the studio, and nobody believes them. If you'd set an example, maybe the others would follow."

As a courtesy, Stevens never smoked—whenever Cohn was in sight.

Stevens lacked a project until he read a short story in a magazine one evening. By eleven the following morning he had bought the story for $25,000 and by one in the afternoon he was at work on a script. The film was *Penny Serenade,* and it reteamed Cary Grant and Irene Dunne in a bittersweet romance. It was

Young film maker Harry Cohn flanked by his stars: Sid Smith (*left*) and Harry McCoy, successors to Flanagan and Edwards as the Hall Room Boys in the early 1920's.

The boss poses with two of his prize directors, Frank Borzage (*left*) and Frank Capra (*right*) in the early 1930's.

Hits of the mid-thirties:
Grace Moore in *One Night of Love* (1934)

Gary Cooper and Jean Arthur in
Mr. Deeds Goes to Town (1936).

Claudette Colbert and Clark Gable in the "Walls of Jericho" scene of
Cohn's breakthrough film *It Happened One Night* (1934).

Ronald Colman in
Lost Horizon (1937).

More hits:
Lionel
Barrymore,
James Stewart,
Jean Arthur,
Edward Arnold
in *You Can't
Take It with You*
(1938).

Cary Grant and
Irene Dunne in
The Awful Truth
(1937).

Claude Rains
and James
Stewart in
*Mr. Smith Goes
to Washington*
(1939).

Robert Montgomery in
Here Comes Mr. Jordan
(1941).

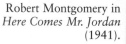

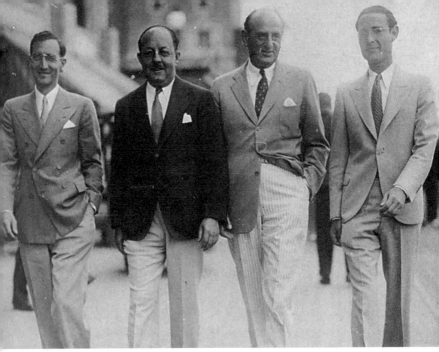

The East: Abe Montague, Jack Cohn, Nate Spingold, Abe Schneider on the boardwalk at Atlantic City.

Harry Cohn and bride Joan Perry pose in Hollywood on August 1, 1941, the day after their New York wedding (*AP/Wide World Photos*).

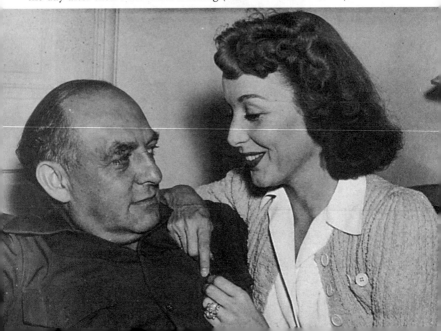

Sidney Buchman as a young
screenwriter.

Virginia Van Upp confers on the
script for *Gilda* with Glenn Ford.

The official studio
portrait, the only
photograph of himself
Harry Cohn allowed
to be issued.

The pose seen around the world: Rita Hayworth's pinup photo.

Rita's striptease in *Gilda*.

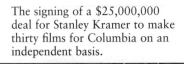

The signing of a $25,000,000 deal for Stanley Kramer to make thirty films for Columbia on an independent basis.

Harry Cohn, the humanitarian, receiving a check from Danny Thomas for the City of Hope.

Rod Steiger and Marlon Brando in a tense scene from *On the Waterfront* (1953).

Harry Cohn's two Love Goddesses, Kim Novak and Rita Hayworth, exert their wiles on Frank Sinatra in a dream sequence from *Pal Joey* (1957).

Cohn escorts Rita Hayworth (*left*) and
Mrs. Cohn to the Directors Guild awards
(*AP/Wide World Photos*).

Cohn's last appearance in
New York at the premiere of
The Bridge on the River Kwai
(1957) with Jack Cohn's widow
(*AP/Wide World Photos*).

Cohn's widow and sons, John (*left*)
and Harry Jr., arrive at the funeral,
March 2, 1958.

adroitly done, but it lacked the wide appeal of the Grant-Dunne comedies.

Next came *Talk of the Town*, a comedy with Ronald Colman, Jean Arthur, and Cary Grant. Cohn continued to leave Stevens alone, and the director conducted all his necessary studio business with Sam Briskin. Those who were able to joke with Cohn had sport with the situation. When Cohn offered a friendly greeting to Stevens one morning, Sidney Buchman chided, "Can't you live up to your agreement?"

Cohn faced his greatest challenge in adhering to the agreement when Stevens made his third film under the contract, *The More the Merrier.*

The story for *The More the Merrier* originated in one of Jean Arthur's periodic disagreements with Harry Cohn. She was distressed over the scripts he had submitted to her and fled to New York with her husband, Frank Ross. There she renewed her acquaintance with Carson Kanin, the director-writer who had been among the first prominent film makers to be drafted. He was serving in the Signal Corps at Fort Monmouth.

Miss Arthur complained of her treatment at the hands of Cohn, and Kanin suggested, "I'll write you a script; the next time Cohn sends you a lousy one, tell him you've got one you want to do instead."

Kanin returned to Fort Monmouth, where duty was light in the peacetime Army. He talked to a fellow draftee, Robert Russell, about a plot, and together they wrote a shooting script in two weeks. Miss Arthur was enthusiastic about it, and so was Ross. Kanin said he was giving it to them, since his contract with RKO precluded his writing for any other studio. They in turn could give the script to Harry Cohn under one condition: Kanin would have to read it to him.

The proposition was presented to Cohn, who was suspicious of it; he could not imagine acquiring something for nothing. But since he was coming to New York, he agreed to a meeting with Kanin.

The conference was arranged in the New York headquarters of Columbia Pictures. Cohn began by asking warily, "What's this bull—— about reading the script?"

"That's the only way you can grasp it," answered Kanin. "If Jean's crazy enough to give you this script, the least you can do is sit and listen to it."

Cohn agreed to the stipulation. Kanin began to read the script, which concerned a government girl who took a young scientist and an older tycoon into her Washington apartment because of the housing shortage. After he had listened to five minutes of reading, Cohn held up his hand and said, "Stop! That's enough. I'll take it."

"Just stay where you are," Kanin commanded. "I've only read the first scene."

"That's enough; I've heard all I need to hear."

"No, you'll hear it all through," Kanin insisted. "Sit down, you bum."

Cohn sat down. He remained through the entire reading, and he proved to be an excellent audience, laughing at the comedy and even crying in the love scenes. He had found, at an unbelievable bargain, the next vehicle for George Stevens and Jean Arthur.

A second reading—by the costars: Miss Arthur, Joel McCrea, and Charles Coburn—proved not so successful. At the rehearsal Miss Arthur recited her part with a wide-eyed flippancy. McCrea, who preferred roles on horseback, delivered a stolid performance. Coburn, who had trouped under every circumstance, made all he could of his lines. All three saw little promise in the script.

McCrea urged Cary Grant* for the role, but Stevens argued that he wanted an all-American type. The director was unconcerned about the actors' uneasiness. He had never placed stock in rehearsals, preferring to draw life from the script by on-the-set improvisation.

This was a tedious and time-consuming process, and Stevens' methods brought increasing concern to Cohn. Each day in the executive dining room he tried to interrogate McCrea about what was happening on the set.

---

* Grant was to play the Coburn role twenty-three years later in a remake, *Walk Do Not Run*.

"That Stevens exposes more film and shoots more angles than any director I've ever had on the lot" Cohn ranted. "What the hell is he doing?"

"Why the hell don't you ask him instead of me?" McCrea countered.

"I can't," Cohn said miserably. "It's part of the deal: I can't ask him any questions."

Stevens proceeded at his own deliberate pace to the conclusion of *The More the Merrier*. The result was a substantial hit that provided an Academy Award for Coburn as best supporting actor of 1943, as well as nominations for the picture, Stevens, Miss Arthur, and four writers, not including Garson Kanin. He received no credit for his contribution.

The More the Merrier was Stevens' last film before he departed for service in the Army. While the director was earning his small salary as a Signal Corps officer, Harry Cohn personally watched over Stevens' percentage of the hit film and determined that the remittances were sent promptly to him.

While searching for material to produce at Columbia, Lou Edelman encountered the script Sidney Buchman had written on the life of Chopin for Frank Capra. Edelman suggested making the film. The New York office was once more aghast at the prospect of trying to sell a movie about a classical composer, arguing that the market was geared for musical films of a more frivolous nature. When Edelman and Buchman estimated that the subject could be filmed for $700,000, Harry Cohn authorized production.

Buchman argued that the success of the film would depend to a large degree on the quality of the piano recordings, and Cohn agreed that a topflight pianist should be engaged. Morris Stoloff, music department head, entered into negotiations with Artur Rubinstein, who was invited to pay a visit to Columbia Studios.

Stoloff greeted Rubinstein at the studio entrance and ushered him to Cohn's office. As the eminent pianist began the long walk toward the desk, Cohn shouted the greeting. "Hiya, Ruby!"

The negotiations with Rubinstein came to naught and Stoloff approached Vladimir Horowitz. They had several meetings, and they were joined by Buchman and Edelman. Stoloff thought it best not to expose Horowitz to Harry Cohn, and Cohn became upset that he was not invited to meet the piano virtuoso.

Horowitz was to play a Rachmaninoff memorial concert at the Hollywood Bowl, and Stoloff reasoned that the occasion might provide the proper circumstances for a meeting of Cohn and Horowitz. The entire Columbia hierarchy occupied boxes for the concert, and all studied the reaction of Harry Cohn to the excursion into culture. He was sometimes attentive, sometimes bored.

Horowitz was exhausted after the long concert, but he graciously received well-wishers backstage. One gushing woman blurted, "You were marvelous, darling, but why do you play that dreary stuff?" Horowitz stiffened. The widow of Rachmaninoff stood at his side.

The pianist was so upset that he dismissed everyone and canceled the party for Cohn and Columbia executives at his house. Stoloff was faced with the task of telling Harry Cohn that Vladimir Horowitz would not see him.

Horowitz was persuaded to permit the party, but he gave no assurance he would make an appearance. Cohn and his executives waited downstairs until Horowitz descended. The moment of confrontation arrived, and Stoloff made the introduction.

"How do you do, Mr. Cohn," Horowitz said stiffly.

"Mr. Horowitz, you're terrific!" Cohn enthused. "Jeez, your piano playing tonight was great. Some of that slow stuff I don't understand, but that *brrrrrrrrr* up and down the keys is colossal!"

The two men conversed enthusiastically for the rest of the evening. Horowitz did not accept the assignment to record the sound track because he was artistically unable to cut the Chopin compositions to fit the film script. The solution was found in José Iturbi, a dynamic pianist with a sense of showmanship that allowed him to condense the musical passages.

Cohn took as much interest in the recordings as he did for a Rita Hayworth musical. Buchman had suggested to Stoloff and Iturbi that only the more popular of Chopin's compositions should be used. Iturbi came into the studio one day to report that he had made a three-minute version of the Scherzo in B Flat Minor.

He played the number on a recording stage. Buchman admired it but feared it was too technical and said, "Don't let Cohn hear it."

But Cohn had been at the rear of the stage, and he commented, "Jeez, that's pretty good." The number remained in the film and was applauded at the preview.

A Song to Remember, which starred a newcomer, Cornel Wilde, as Chopin, was filmed in Technicolor. As the costs mounted to $1,500,000, Eastern executives complained of the folly of the investment, arguing that a third of the nation's theaters would not play a film with serious music.

"You bastards said the same thing about *One Night of Love*," Cohn replied. "We're not making pictures for those towns along the Union Pacific tracks."

A Song to Remember was an overwhelming success. It won six Academy nominations and earned more money than had any other film with classical music. It created a Chopin boom and encouraged other producers to make films about serious composers. None of the films was successful.

4
LOVE FINDS HARRY COHN

$\mathcal{I}$t could have happened in a Columbia movie.

He was a movie mogul, she a fashion model. He saw her glide by on the floor of the Central Park Casino, dancing in another man's arms. The movie mogul found out the name of the lovely girl with the tawny hair and emerald eyes. Would she like to come to Hollywood and act in movies? She would.

Her name was Betty Miller, and she had been enjoying success as a model in New York, appearing on numerous magazine covers. She was ambitious, and she had been taking dramatic lessons from coaches in the theater. So when Harry Cohn made his offer of a Hollywood contract, she accepted eagerly. She yearned to succeed as an actress. And she was intrigued by this dynamic, persuasive man.

He was also intrigued with her. Cohn was forty-four, and his marriage to Rose had ended in all respects except legally. Betty Miller was twenty-one and divorced after a brief marriage to a photographer she had met while modeling. The year was 1935.

Betty Miller came to Hollywood accompanied by her mother. Harry Cohn aimed to create the girl in a new image, starting, of course, with a name; Betty Miller was obviously too prosaic for a potential star.

Cohn had admired an actress of the silent screen named Kathryn Perry. "What goes good with Perry?" he asked his chief aide, William Perlberg.

"How about Joan?" suggested Perlberg.

"Joan Perry—that's all right," Cohn mused.

The career of Joan Perry began with the rite of filling out the biographical form for the publicity department. The eight-page form was prefaced with a "Note to Artist: This may all sound sort of silly and nosey, but unfortunately the American and foreign motion picture public think they have an inalienable right to know about the private life of a screen personality. It is up to us to humor them."

Joan Perry recorded that she had been born in Pensacola, Florida, to a railroad executive; that she was a descendant of Robert E. Lee, as well as of the first settlers of western Florida, and that her family had been prominent in the political and cultural development of the South since the days of Lord Fairfax. She had attended public schools in Pensacola, then Plant, a girls' finishing school in Florida. Her favorite actresses were Norma Shearer, Katharine Hepburn, and Greta Garbo; she disliked spinach and wrote poetry, but not for publication; she had traveled throughout Europe and South America; she had lived through two or three hurricanes, "but they weren't anywhere near as exciting as the newspapers made them out to be."

The final question on the form asked: What business would you choose other than your present work? Joan Perry replied: "Matrimony."

Cohn ordered the makeup and hairdressing departments to give special attention to his new discovery. He then instructed Joe Walker to photograph some tests of Miss Perry. "Use your best lenses; take half a day," Cohn ordered. "Try anything you want. Make it good."

Walker employed his glamour technique on the tests and sent 1,200 feet of film to the laboratory for processing. The lab chief berated Walker for exposing so much film on the test of a starlet and refused to develop the negative. "I think you'd better," suggested Walker. The lab chief still refused. He received a blistering rebuke when Harry Cohn heard of it. The word spread through the studio that it would be advisable to handle with care all matters concerning Joan Perry.

She made her debut in a film called *The Case of the Missing Man* starring Roger Pryor, then played ingenues in B pictures and minor roles in the more important productions. Meanwhile, she became the most important woman in Harry Cohn's life.

As the years passed, Joan Perry became impatient for her career to develop beyond the starlet stage or for her romance with Harry Cohn to achieve a more permanent status.

But Rose would not submit to a divorce. There was no acrimony between her and Cohn, but there was no basis for continuing as husband and wife. He now lived in the penthouse of the Sunset Plaza, a luxury apartment house above the Sunset Strip, while she remained at the Fremont Place home. When she complained of being lonely and aimless, he suggested that she become a patron of the arts. She agreed to the suggestion, and therein lay his avenue of escape from the marriage.

Devoting herself to the furtherance of opera, she developed a fondness for a young Italian tenor. He, in turn, was both grateful and devoted to her. Private detectives uncovered this fact and so reported to the man who had hired them, Harry Cohn. He was furious; although he had long before abandoned any semblance of a marriage, the mere suggestion of the horned head was repugnant to his manhood.

But now he had his divorce. A property settlement was reached, bestowing riches deserved by the wife whose previous divorce had provided the funds to found Columbia Pictures. Her eighteen-year marriage to Harry Cohn came to an end in a Reno courtroom on July 28, 1941. Three days later he married Joan Perry in a room of the St. Regis Hotel in New York City.

His second marriage proved highly satisfactory to Harry Cohn. Now, at last, he was able to entertain in the grand manner, as did Louis B. Mayer. The Cohns first lived on Lexington Drive in Beverly Hills, later moved to the onetime John McCormack mansion at 1000 North Crescent Drive, across the Street from the Beverly Hills Hotel.

Joan became all that Cohn had hoped for in a wife. Gowned by Columbia's designer, Jean Louis, she looked stunning as she presided over dinner parties. She managed the servants with aplomb and entertained in quiet good taste, without ostentation. The Cohn dinners were formal and elegantly appointed. Joan sat at one end of the table, always beautifully groomed. Cohn was at the head of the table, with two telephones before him.

The telephone was so much an extension of his own being that he could not be parted from it, even at dinner. The telephone rang from six to a dozen times during the meal, and Cohn discussed business in a succinct manner. He also made calls himself; the two phones were connected to the studio switchboard. He often used the telephone to answer questions that arose in the dinner conversation, perhaps over the returns of another studio's film.

"Get me Nate Spingold in New York," Cohn instructed the operator. In less than a minute Spingold was on the line, and Cohn asked him about the latest figures on the competing movie.

Cohn was immensely proud of his wife. He displayed her oil paintings to visitors in his office and added glowingly, "She can speak French, too." To studio workers who had known her during her five years as an actress, he suggested, "It might sound better if you called her Mrs. Cohn instead of Joan." They complied with his suggestion.

Cohn's joy with his marriage was compounded when he discovered that his wife was pregnant. But his hopes were dashed when the baby, a girl, died half an hour after birth. She was named Jobella.

The obstetrician did not submit a bill for his services. When Cohn inquired why, the doctor told him it was not his custom to charge for his services in cases in which he was powerless to save the baby.

"Why did the baby die?" Cohn asked.

"We don't know, Mr. Cohn," the doctor replied. "There hasn't been enough research to determine the cause or how to avoid it." On the following day the doctor received a check from Cohn for $100,000, to be spent for research into causes of such infant mortalities.

After the death of Jobella, Cohn was subject to periods of depression, a phenomenon that none of those around him had witnessed before. But his spirits were lifted when Joan became pregnant again. This time the result was joyful: a son was born to Harry Cohn.

The baby was born at 5:45 A.M., and Cohn made one of his rare morning appearances at the studio that day to receive the congratulations of his employees. He gathered a dozen of his executives into his office. Amid expressions of felicitation, Cohn brought out a bottle of hundred-year-old brandy and poured each man a small glass. A department chief raised his glass and proposed an unctuous toast: "To the new baby—may he be just like his father!"

Cohn's genial manner vanished. He slapped the glass from the man s hand, and it crashed to the floor.

"Don't ever say that!" Cohn commanded. "I want my son to have friends."

The son was named John Perry Cohn; he was born on April 18, 1944. He was joined two years later by another son, Harrison Perry Cohn.* A few years later the Cohns adopted a daughter, Catherine Perry.

Rose Cohn never remarried. She remained devoted to Harry Cohn throughout her lifetime, and his concern for her surprised those who knew him. He advised her on all her investments and enlisted studio talent for her activities in providing entertainment for Army camps during the war. In his office and bedroom was a telephone line that could be called by only a handful of people. Rose Cohn was one of them.

---

* Later he asked his father's permission to be named Harry, Jr. Cohn was pleased, and the son's name was legally changed.

5

"Put Two Hundred to Win and Two Hundred to Show on Number Three in the Sixth Race"

*H*arry Cohn's gambling spirit had been nurtured in his boyhood, when he and brother Jack were bowling sharks. He never lost that spirit. When he and Edward Small were multi-millionaire producers, they happened to walk into a bowling alley in Palm Springs. The bowlers were Greek and Italian cooks and waiters from the resort hotels, and they challenged the two older men to matches. Cohn agreed to bowl, but only after wagers were laid. He won with ease but then refused to accept his winnings.

Cohn also participated in the studio bowling league, and once a year he joined in the locker-room poker game after the Columbia golf tournament; he competed fiercely in each. But he ordinarily disapproved of his employees' gambling. When a group of high-salaried writers engaged in a crap game after a Christmas party at the studio, Cohn notified the Los Angeles police to arrest the men. On another Christmas Eve, Cohn and William Perlberg came upon a group of carpenters and laborers in a nickel-and-dime crap game. Cohn ordered them all fired.

"But you can't do that on Christmas Eve," Perlberg protested.

"The hell I can't," Cohn replied.

The studio boss disapproved of his employees going to the racetracks—unless he invited them to accompany him—and Columbia workers learned to stay out of Cohn's sight at Santa Anita and Hollywood Park.

Cohn's own visits to the local tracks fell into a pattern. He insisted on a position in the grandstand befitting his position as president of a film company. For two years he hounded Mervyn Le Roy, president of Hollywood Park, for a suitable box. Le Roy finally passed over influential patrons to secure Cohn a box on the finish line. Cohn thereupon berated Le Roy in violent terms for acquiring only a four-seat box; Cohn insisted he needed six seats.

Cohn invariably attended the races on Saturday afternoon during the racing seasons. Saturday morning was spent at the studio, assembling information from sources in different parts of the nation. Cohn placed bets with bookmakers before leaving for the track and often stopped the limousine en route to Hollywood Park or Santa Anita and telephoned additional bets. Cohn disliked the racetrack food, and the limousine always carried lunches prepared in the studio dining room. He became disgruntled if his guests left his box for even a hot dog; in fact, he approved of no absences except for the placing of bets.

The composition of the Cohn box reflected who was in favor at Columbia. The current star, the hit director, the writer with a facile touch—these were ones invited to share the Saturday afternoons at the track with Harry Cohn. He tried to dominate their wagers, just as he tried to govern other elements of their lives.

One Saturday Cohn went to the racetrack with Robert Rossen, who was at the time the preeminent director on the Columbia lot. Rossen was ignorant of the intricacies of horse betting, but he had a friend who owned a horse in one of the races. The friend had advised Rossen to bet the horse, even though it was a twenty-to-one outsider.

When Cohn learned of Rossen's intention to place a wager on the horse, he was abusive. "I'm surprised you can make pictures," Cohn said derisively, "you're such a goddam fool at horses."

Nevertheless, the director went to the betting window and made his bet. When he returned to the box, Cohn demanded, "How much did you bet?"

"Twenty dollars on the nose," Rossen admitted.

"You're a goddam idiot," Cohn snorted.

Rossen's horse pulled away from the field at the start and finished the winner by ten lengths. Cohn was incensed. He turned to Rossen and snarled, "You son of a bitch—you knew something and you held it out on me!"

Like all horseplayers, Harry Cohn was acutely conscious of the value of inside intelligence, and he was ever alert for new sources. One day a new producer at Columbia heard the gruff voice of the company president on the intercom: "There's a wire here for you. It's a tip on a horse."

The producer, expecting a reprimand for using the studio telegraph line to receive racing tips, explained, "Yes, I have a friend who used to work at the tracks here. He went back to Chicago and sends me tips now and then."

Instead of chastising the producer, Cohn asked, "Do you think his information is any good?"

"I don't know," the producer replied. "But he has pretty good connections."

"How much are you going to bet?" Cohn asked.

"Five hundred," said the producer.

"Okay, bet five hundred for me."

The horse was a long shot that won and Cohn earned $12,000. He was elated, and he called the producer daily to ask if any more tips had been received. "Drop in and see me any time," Cohn remarked cordially.

One day the producer again heard Cohn's voice on the intercom: "Your friend in Chicago sent us another tip." He reported contents of the telegram and asked, "How much are you going to bet?"

"A thousand dollars," said the producer.

"Okay, make it a thousand for me, too," said Cohn.

The horse ran out of the money. Shortly after the race concluded, the producer received a message to report to Cohn's office.

Cohn was in a rage. "You're here to make pictures, not to play the horses," he shouted. "What the hell do you mean by having your tout send you messages on the Columbia telegraph? If that ever happens again, you'll be out on your ass. Now get the hell out of here, and go back to work!"

Cohn jealously guarded the information he received from Buzzy Appleton. Not only did he pay a high fee for it, but he also realized that disclosure of the tips could drive odds down.

One man coveted Cohn's racing tips more than any other: Sam Bischoff, the old adversary who had removed his stage from Cohn's property. Bischoff, who had become a successful producer at Warner Brothers, was an insatiable horseplayer, betting as many as forty races per day. Intrigued by reports that Cohn had amassed $250,000 in race winnings, Bischoff sought access to Cohn's information.

Bischoff found his source in a secretary who worked in Cohn's outer office. She intercepted the dispatches from Appleton and telephoned Bischoff at Warner Brothers. The system worked perfectly until the secretary caused a co-worker to be discharged from Columbia. The worker sought revenge by informing Cohn of his secretary's duplicity.

Cohn summoned Bischoff to his Columbia office. Bischoff suspected that something had gone awry when he was unable to reach his informant by telephone.

As soon as Bischoff entered the long office, Cohn began his tirade. Bischoff made no attempt to deny what he had done.

"You no-good son of a bitch, you'd —— a snake!" Cohn screamed.

"What would you stop at—a rat?" Bischoff replied.

The two men continued to hurl invectives until Cohn told Bischoff that the informing secretary had been locked in an office. Bischoff grabbed one of the Oscars from the display behind the desk and held it threateningly over Cohn's head.

"You let that girl out of there, or I'll kill you!" Bischoff shouted.

Cohn stared at him and then at the heavy base of the statuette poised above him. He pressed a switch on the intercom and ordered the release of the secretary.

Bischoff laid down the Oscar and stalked to the door. "And don't ever talk to me again as long as you live!" he commanded.

Two years later Bischoff received a telephone call from Harry Cohn.

"Sam, how are you?" said Cohn.

"What?" said the incredulous Bischoff.

"When are you coming home?" Cohn continued.

"Are you sure you've got the right guy?"

"I hear you're leaving Warner Brothers. I want you to come back to Columbia."

"You want to hire me after I threatened to kill you?"

"Oh, that was personal," said Cohn offhandedly. "This is business."

Bischoff went to Cohn's office to discuss the matter. He reminded Cohn: "When I left Columbia in 1931 because you wouldn't give me a raise, do you remember what I said?"

"Yes," said Cohn, "that you wouldn't come back until you were paid more than me or any other son of a bitch at the studio."

He pressed a button on the intercom and spoke to his secretary, Duncan Cassell: "Tell Mr. Bischoff what my salary is."

Cassell replied that it was $2,000 a week and $250 for expenses.

Cohn switched off the intercom and told Bischoff, "Nobody else at Columbia makes more than I do. I'll pay you twenty-five hundred dollars a week. Furthermore, I'll put it in your contract that you don't have to talk to me. Agreed?"

Bischoff agreed.

The betting career of Harry Cohn reached its peak in the 1940's, when his daily wagers totaled between $5,000 and $10,000 daily. When he could not attend the races, he placed bets through bookmakers or friends who were going to the track.

One of these was Franchot Tone, who arranged to have his scenes finished before noon so he could go to the races. This was possible, since he coproduced his films with Columbia. As Tone left the studio, Cohn would fling open his office window and shout, "Put two hundred to win and two hundred to show on number three in the sixth race."

Because he was head of a large corporation, Cohn tried to shield his betting activities from all but a few intimates. During story conferences, film makers often noted that Cohn sat stolidly behind his desk, staring into an open drawer. Few realized that inside the drawer was a dopesheet on which he studied his selections for the day. Despite this distraction, Cohn never lost track of what was being said.

Once a young director, John Sturges, was attempting to narrate the story line for a projected film. Cohn listened with little reaction and repeatedly lifted an earphone to his ear.

The exasperated director finally exclaimed, "What the hell are you doing?"

"I'm listening to the results at Santa Anita," Cohn shot back. "When you're as old as I am, you'll be able to listen to some goddam story like yours and the race results at the same time."

The end of Harry Cohn's racehorse betting came with the disastrous thirty-day drought at Saratoga during one summer in the late 1940's. For a full month of betting favorites, Cohn could not pick a winner. Disregarding the methods of his mentor Buzzy, who selected three or four horses during the day's racing, Cohn wagered on every race in a desperate attempt to recover his losses. The strategy failed, and his losses for the season were rumored to be as high as $400,000.

Informants carried news of the loss to Jack Cohn and the powers of the East. They issued the edict to the president of the company: end the horse betting, or suffer the loss of the presidency.

Harry Cohn realized the East might so embarrass him with the stockholders as to carry out the threat. He put an end to his career as a bettor on horses.

Gambling was too ingrained in the Cohn spirit for him to draw a complete halt to his wagers. He continued to play gin rummy, though never for the high stakes that other Hollywood executives competed for. Cohn also played bridge. He seldom gambled for more than a fortieth of a cent per point, but he was still a fierce competitor.

Cohn once telephoned Binnie Barnes, who had been making films at Columbia. He knew she was an expert bridge player, as was her new husband, Mike Frankovich, a sports announcer who had been a UCLA football star.

"I'm going to have dinner at my office," Cohn told the actress. "I'd like you and Mike to join me, and we can play a few hands of bridge afterward."

When Miss Barnes and her husband arrived, Cohn introduced them to an attractive woman he described as "a friend of mine." She seemed familiar to Miss Barnes. After a few hands of bridge she realized where she had met the woman: at a bridge tournament. She was a national champion.

"Harry, how can you do such a thing?" Miss Barnes asked.

"Well, I wanted to beat you," he said.

Bridge and gin rummy were mere diversions for Harry Cohn. With the close of his horse-betting years, he shifted his major interest to college football.

As with the horses, football became an obsession, although his bets never reached the same proportions. He was eager for expert advice, but football had no Buzzy Appleton. At one time Cohn sought Mike Frankovich as a source of information.

Cohn repeatedly telephoned the sports announcer in the early morning hours when he was pondering his bets for the week. Weary of being awakened, Frankovich replied to queries, "I don't know, Harry."

Incensed at being deprived of expert information, Cohn snapped, "Don't you ever come on the lot again!"

Cohn eventually found a source for football information and formed his only friendship with a newspaperman.

Always a reader of the sports pages of the Los Angeles newspapers, Cohn had admired the wry, spare prose and the cogent observations of Melvin Durslag, columnist of the Los Angeles *Examiner*. One day he invited Durslag to his office at Columbia. The sportswriter passed through the usual procedure of identifying himself to the Cohn attendants and was admitted to the inner office. Cohn was seated behind his desk. He waited until the secretary had withdrawn and then brought out a sheaf of papers from a desk drawer.

"I've been on the phone to Providence all morning," Cohn reported. "I've got some information that's sizzling: Brown over Harvard. What do you think?"

Durslag allowed that it was possible that Brown University could defeat Harvard, although the older school was favored. Brown emerged from the game with a 33–6 victory, and Harry Cohn was the winner of a $50 bet. He now considered Durslag an oracle for future bets.

During the football season Cohn telephoned the columnist

six and twelve times a week for advice on the chances of college competitors. Cohn expected Durslag to be available at all times and was upset when the columnist went on the road with a football team without leaving a telephone number.

Once Cohn was vacationing in Hawaii during the Christmas holidays, and he telephoned to the mainland to ask Durslag if he should hazard a bet on the Hula Bowl, a postseason encounter of college seniors. Cohn talked for half an hour at transpacific telephone rates before deciding not to bet $50 on the game.

On another occasion Cohn worried about the weather conditions for a professional football play-off between the San Francisco 49ers and the Detroit Lions. Durslag telephoned the San Francisco *Examiner* to determine that the field was dry, thus favoring the San Francisco team. Detroit won.

Cohn's remark to Durslag: "Between your information and mine, I'm losing the studio."

In reality Cohn was grateful to the sports reporter for his unbiased information, and he invited Durslag and his wife to dinner and movies at the Cohn mansion. Cohn sometimes attended football games with Durslag, traveling to the Los Angeles Coliseum in Cohn's chauffeured Rolls-Royce. As the limousine parked in the section reserved for the press, Durslag betrayed his embarrassment at such an appearance before his colleagues.

"So you think we look like a couple of four-flushers, eh?" said Cohn. "Well, next time we'll sit up front. People will figure we're pals of the chauffeur."

Cohn complained late one Saturday afternoon, "That goddam radio and TV—they don't give you the score until the game is over. You gotta wait until almost evening to find out how your bets went."

The newspaperman arranged with the *Examiner*'s wire desk to supply Cohn with scores whenever he telephoned. The deskmen answered Cohn's queries several times each Saturday afternoon, and he reported gleefully to Durslag, "I'm even getting quarter scores. This is sensational!"

As a showman, Harry Cohn enjoyed the suspense of anticipating the outcomes of scores of football contests, even though his wagers were a fraction of what he had once bet at Saratoga and Santa Anita. His greatest pleasure came on New Year's Day, when he watched three network channels telecasting Bowl football games, listened to radio accounts, and made frequent telephone calls to the sports desk of the Los Angeles *Examiner*.

6

CHARLIE LOMBARD DISCOVERS
THE PERILS OF FRIENDSHIP WITH
HARRY COHN

*I*n these pages he shall be called Charlie Lombard.

He met Harry Cohn in the mid-1930's, when Cohn was plunging on the horse races. Charlie was a very helpful young man to have around; he could see that bets were laid promptly. He even arranged for racing results to be transmitted by wire directly to Harry Cohn's office. Besides, Charlie was handsome, clever, and personable, an engaging fellow as a companion. Below the charm was an undercurrent of danger, and that was another factor that appealed to Harry Cohn.

The two men became fast friends. Charlie moved into the apartment building where Cohn lived, and they often took trips together. Cohn once offered to make Charlie a producer at Columbia.

"What would you pay me?" Charlie asked.

"Five hundred dollars a week," Cohn replied magnanimously.

Charlie laughed. "I get that much from waitresses who take bets for me," he said.

Charlie's enterprise continued to prosper, but he had ambitions for more legitimate endeavors. The opportunity arose for him to purchase a 26-percent interest in the Agua Caliente racetrack in Tijuana. His friend Harry Cohn supplied the necessary cash: $25,000.

Charlie was an honorable man, and he paid back the $25,000 in due time, adding a check for interest at 6 percent. Harry Cohn, in a grand gesture, tore up the interest check.

Charlie wanted to demonstrate his appreciation of his friend's beneficence. He bought two identical star rubies and set them into rings. He kept one for himself and presented the other to Harry Cohn. The gesture touched Cohn as he had seldom been touched before. He wore the ring everywhere.

Charlie eventually sold out his interest in Agua Caliente and sought to divorce himself from his onetime friends in the betting industry. He had managed to find himself a job with the Motion Picture Producers and Distributors of America—the Hays Office. Charlie became assistant to Pat Casey, who negotiated contracts with the labor unions. Charlie's persuasiveness and his underlying toughness helped make him an excellent negotiator, and he was being groomed as successor to Casey.

His new position suited Charlie. He was now married to a well-known movie actress, and he was being accepted as a respected member of the community. Unfortunately, his position placed him on collision course with a unique power in Hollywood labor, Willie Bioff.

Willie had the figure of a Greek wrestler and the morals of a panderer, which he once was. He had shared the noisome world of Al Capone, Big Jim Colosimo, and Dion O'Bannion in Chicago of the 1920's and was arrested for running a whorehouse in 1922. Somehow the papers remanding Bioff to six months in prison became lost, and he served none of it, a happenstance that later caused him embarrassment.

Willie edged away from the riskier endeavors and discovered a splendid outlet for his talents: labor unions. He moved in on the Chicago local of the International Association of Theatrical Stage Employees (IATSE), which represented the men who ran the projectors in movie houses. Willie was able to shake down theater owners for tribute with the mere threat of pulling the projectionists out of the booths.

The system worked with remarkable ease. Willie reasoned that if it could be done in Chicago, it could be managed on a larger scale, and he set his sights at control of the nationwide union. He reached his goal at the IATSE convention in Louisville in 1934, when he installed a Chicago pal, George Browne, as president of the union. Bioff had imported a platoon of burly assistants from Chicago to assure Browne's election, and they did their work well.

Browne's first act as president was to appoint Willie Bioff as international representative. Willie then headed West, where the gold was.

He found film industry labor in disarray. A ruinous strike in 1933 had decimated the American Federation of Labor craft unions to membership of a mere 159. Willie employed his muscle to reverse the trend. He surrounded himself with beefy lieutenants and, if necessary, sent off to Chicago for the reinforcements to convince dissident movie craftsmen to join the IATSE. Opposing unions were crushed by threats, beatings, or NLRB elections, according to which tactic was most certain of success.

Then Willie went to work on acquiring new contracts with the producers. He once explained his method to reporter Florabel Muir:

"I've found out that dickering with these picture producers goes about the same all the time. You get into a room with them, and they start yelling and hollering about how they're bein' held up and robbed. That goes on and on. Me, I'm a busy man and don't get too much sleep. After a while it dies down, and the quiet wakes me up, and I say, 'All right, gentlemen, do we get the money?'"

Willie Bioff was also doing some dickering with the picture producers on his own, not for the benefit of the rank-and-file members of the IATSE.

He continued his drive to organize all the studio craftsmen, collecting 12,000 to his control. The workers, except for a few who objected to Bioff's rule and were banished from studio employment, seemed to be content with his management of their union. There was some grumbling over an unexplained 2 percent assessment, which netted $1,500,000 and somehow vanished. But the studio employees were pleased that Bioff had achieved for them shorter hours and higher wages. Bioff had leverage in negotiations that was unbeatable: if the gentlemen didn't come across with the money, he could bring the film industry to a standstill by ordering the projectionists to strike the theaters of America.

Willie's kingdom might have continued to expand except that he grew too greedy. He wanted to control every union within the studios, and that included the actors. The thought of sharing the immense salaries of the stars held great fascination for him. He began making gestures to move in on the Screen Actors Guild. That was a mistake.

Bioff also made the error of taking on a crusty old editor named Arthur Ungar. As boss of *Daily Variety*, he could have been a support to Willie's dreams of conquest. The labor leader tried everything on Ungar: blandishments, bribes, threats. Ungar not only resisted, but also began campaigning against the high-living Bioff.

Robert Montgomery, who was president of the Screen Actors Guild, became alarmed at Bioff's attempts to dictate to the actors. Montgomery asked his board for a secret appropriation of $5,000, offering to pay the sum back later from his own pocket if its purpose were not deemed worthwhile. The request was granted, and Montgomery hired a detective agency to delve into the history of Willie Bioff.

The guild offered its information to the *Daily Variety* campaign with results that embarrassed Willie, especially with revelation of his unfulfilled sentence for pimping. But even more embarrassing was the disclosure that Willie Bioff had been extorting huge sums of money from virtually all the top leaders of the film industry, with the exception of Harry Cohn.

Willie Bioff paid a visit to Harry Cohn, as he had also called on Nicholas Schenck, Joseph Schenck, Harry Warner, Louis B. Mayer, and other heads of the film companies. The price for labor peace at Columbia would be $25,000 a year. It was a bargain price for a smaller studio; Nick Schenck had paid $200,000 for Loew's; Fox, Paramount, and Warners had been charged $100,000.

Cohn demurred. He put Willie off until he could call his good friend, Charlie Lombard.

"What should I do?" Cohn asked.

Charlie, who was familiar with the Bioff operation, told Cohn, "Don't give him a nickel."

Cohn announced his decision at a producers' meeting: "You guys do what you want; I've got someone taking care of me."

The other studio bosses wondered how Cohn could avoid paying the tribute, and their suspicions fell on Charlie Lombard, Cohn's close friend. This embarrassed Charlie with his superior, Pat Casey, and Charlie warned Cohn not to put him in the middle. Still, Cohn had faith that Charlie, with his old connections, could restrain Bioff from putting the heat on Columbia.

Willie moved against Harry Cohn on a crisp day in November, 1937. Cohn was in Palm Springs when he learned that pickets were marching around the studio entrance and production was at a standstill. He hurriedly called Charlie.

"What the hell should I do?" Cohn asked. Not only was the studio shut down, but Bioff had also caused a Columbia picture to be withdrawn from the Radio City Music Hall.

Charlie told Cohn he would try to get the strike canceled. He placed a telephone call to George Browne, the IATSE president, at his Chicago headquarters. Browne wasn't available. So Charlie drove to the IATSE office in Hollywood to accost Willie Bioff.

Willie was seated behind his desk with his hat and coat on, a cigar clamped between his teeth. A gun rested on the desk before him.

"Listen, Willie, I don't know what you're trying to prove, but it isn't going to work," said Charlie. "I want to talk to Browne. Get him on the phone."

Willie sullenly acquiesced. Browne told Charlie that the strike was Bioff's doing. Charlie told Bioff, "This is a spite thing, and you're not going to get away with it. You meet with Cohn and get it settled."

The strike lasted only one day. Willie's plan to force Cohn into submission had been defeated. Willie was to remember Charlie Lombard's part in causing that defeat.

The federal government became intrigued with Willie Bioff's affairs, particularly in the alleged payoffs to him by leaders of the film industry. Investigators questioned Joseph M. Schenck, who was president of the Motion Picture Producers and Distributors of America, as well as president of Twentieth Century-Fox. Schenck testified he had given Bioff $100,000—as a loan. The government questioned his truthfulness. When the facts were revealed, the president of the Producers' Association was convicted of perjury and sentenced to a year and a day in prison.

The facts of Willie's dealings began to tumble out as one president after another told of falsifying corporation ledgers in order to pay off the international representative of the IATSE. Nick Schenck testified that Willie originally asked for $2,000,000 from Loew's, scaled down his request to $1,000,000, and settled for $200,000. Some wondered whether the payments were aimed merely at forestalling labor trouble in the studios and the theaters. Did the company heads pay Bioff to prevent his rank and file from seeking better contracts? And did they plan to use his union to help destroy minor studios, such as Columbia?

Willie Bioff and George Browne were charged before a federal grand jury in New York on May 23, 1941, of extorting $550,000 from Loew's, Warner Brothers, Paramount, and Twentieth Century-Fox. The great names of motion picture finance came to testify against the two labor leaders. The defendants were found guilty, and Willie was sentenced to ten years in prison, Browne to eight.

Willie Bioff went off to Alcatraz, and he rankled under his imprisonment. He found the Department of Justice willing to assist his escape.

In 1943 Willie declared he would talk about the men behind his shakedown of the movie companies. He named six Chicago mobsters—and Charlie Lombard.

One of the seven, Frank (The Enforcer) Nitti, committed suicide the day the indictments were returned. The others stood trial in the United States Courthouse in New York. In view of his previous activities, Charlie Lombard didn't seem out of place in the company of such defendants as Charles (Cherry Nose) Gioe and Louis (Little New York) Campagna. But Charlie claimed he was innocent of the Bioff accusation.

There was one man who might be able to convince the jury: Harry Cohn.

Bioff's testimony seemed to substantiate the government's claim that Charlie was a Hollywood emissary of the Capone mob. Willie told of a series of meetings with Cohn and Lombard, with the result that Cohn had promised to pay Bioff $25,000 the following Saturday. No money arrived, said Willie, despite Cohn's promises.

The prosecutor asked if Willie ever collected from Harry Cohn or Columbia Pictures.

"No," Willie answered morosely, "I never got a dime."

The federal courtroom stirred with interest as the imposing figure of Harry Cohn advanced to the witness stand. He told how he and Charlie Lombard were close friends, lived in the same apartment building, and exchanged Christmas gifts. He also told of meeting Bioff and Browne at Charlie's table in the Brown Derby one evening.

A later confrontation with Bioff came in Charlie's apartment on the night of the strike. Bioff told Cohn the strike was over and the men would be back at work in the morning. Cohn testified, "I asked why the strike was called, and Bioff said it had something to do with makeup artists. I told him he knew that wasn't true, and he asked me what difference it made, that the strike was off."

The extent of Cohn's friendship with Charlie was brought out in cross-examination by Charlie's attorney:

Q—You made certain loans to Lombard?

A—I loaned him twenty thousand dollars in March, 1937. He wished to acquire an interest in the racetrack that was about to be reopened at Agua Caliente, Mexico.

Q—Was that twenty thousand repaid?

A—It certainly was, in September of the same year.

Q—Was there another loan of five thousand dollars?

A—There was, and it too was repaid.

Q—Do you recall an incident when you and Lombard were shooting pool at Palm Springs one time and someone wanted to wager on a horse but couldn't reach a bookmaker, so you two took the bet?

A—I do.

Q—And the horse lost, leaving you and Lombard something like fifteen hundred dollars ahead.

A—That is right.

Q—And wasn't that money used as a sort of pool upon which you both drew to make horse bets of your own?

A—It was.

Q—And you were fairly lucky, with the result that finally the pool grew to something like fifteen thousand dollars?

A—Something like that.

Q—And you divided that money with Lombard?

A—I gave him his half.

Q—Now let me ask you, Mr. Cohn, after Lombard repaid that twenty-thousand-dollar loan, didn't he present you with a ruby ring?

A—He did.

Q—Is that the same ruby ring you are wearing on your left hand right here in this courtroom?

The jurors strained for a look at Cohn's hand as he answered, "It is; it's the very same ring."

The defense attorney added one more question: "Now let me ask you, Mr. Cohn, do you still consider Mr. Lombard your friend?"

The reply came without hesitation: "I do."

Reporters thought they detected a twinkle in the eye of Charlie Lombard as Harry Cohn stepped off the stand. Cohn's testimony seemed to indicate that Charlie's friendship precluded any part in a conspiracy to extort money from Columbia Pictures.

But Charlie knew that Cohn hadn't told the complete story. He didn't say that it was Charlie who convinced Bioff to end the strike. Nor did Cohn testify that he had given Charlie no money for his services.

"Let me ask Cohn," urged Charlie's attorney.

"No, it would embarrass him," Charlie said resignedly.

All seven defendants were convicted and sentenced to ten years in prison. For his services to the Justice Department, Willie Bioff had his sentence commuted. He vanished into obscurity.

Charlie Lombard served his time and returned to Hollywood. Harry Cohn greeted him warmly and invited him to the house to see Joan and their two sons, who had been born while Charlie was in prison. Cohn agreed that Charlie had been wronged by the conviction.

Now Charlie wanted to put all his past associations behind him and pursue endeavors that would involve him in no trouble. He set up a dummy corporation to produce films through a new releasing company. He made several films, mostly of underworld and prison subjects, and they were well received. Harry Cohn was impressed. He gloated to his producers, "Here's a guy who can make good pictures for three hundred thousand, and you can't make anything as good for six hundred thousand."

Charlie couldn't elude his past. Senator Estes Kefauver came to town with his crime-busting road show. Charlie Lombard was among those subpoenaed to testify in secret before the investigating committee. The publicity made Charlie's position with the releasing company untenable.

The Kefauver appearance made him *persona non grata* with the studios. There was one person who could help him: Harry Cohn.

Charlie went first to his parish priest. He explained his situation: "I can't go on this way. I'm on parole, and I need a job. I remember once that Harry offered to make me a producer. He knows I'm capable. Shall I ask him if he would hire me?"

"I see no reason why you shouldn't," the priest replied.

Charlie, who knew Harry Cohn as well as anyone alive, pointed out the hazard: "I know this guy is tough. He's liable to turn me down."

The priest answered, "And who are you that you cannot be refused?"

Charlie also consulted his parole officer, who advised Charlie to see Cohn about a job. Charlie called for an appointment, and Cohn's reaction was friendly. "Come on up," he said.

The meeting of the two old friends seemed cordial at the outset. Cohn displayed photographs of his sons and talked of events at the studio. The ruby still gleamed on his left hand.

"Harry, I really need a favor," Charlie began. "I need a job."

Cohn looked pained. "Charlie, how could I give you a job?" he protested. "The stockholders would scalp me."

Charlie's temper flared at the sudden refusal. "You're a rotten ——," he snapped. "Did the stockholders complain when I got ten years in prison because of you?"

"Now wait a minute, wait a minute," Cohn said. "Charlie, I want to do something for you, but I can't hire you at the studio. I just can't. Let me put you in business with an agent. I'll see to it that you get the right clients, and I'll give you plenty of jobs for them at Columbia."

I don't want any tricky business," Charlie replied. "All I wanted was a job." He turned to leave.

"Don't go away mad," Cohn called to him.

Charlie wheeled and added, "Let me warn you about one thing. I want you to know that before I came here, I asked my priest and my parole officer. They know all about it, so nothing you can do can hurt me."

Charlie Lombard walked out of Harry Cohn's life. Charlie turned to other fields of endeavor, and he prospered without further interference from the law. As for Willie Bioff, he lived in Phoenix, Arizona, as William Nelson, grower and stock investor, until the morning of November 4, 1955. Willie was going downtown to check on his stocks at the brokerage. He turned the ignition key of his pickup truck and was blown to eternity. The police never discovered who put the dynamite under Willie's hood.

7
THE KING ADDS SOME FOOTNOTES
TO *THE PRINCE*

*N*o Hollywood mogul controlled a studio as did Harry Cohn. His power was complete and absolute.

The most notable illustration of Cohn's absolutism occurred when S. Sylvan Simon was his executive producer. Simon had been working with producer Buddy Adler and a young writer, Millard Kaufman, on a script that seemed to defy solution. Cohn had insisted on a story line that possessed no logic.

"It's impossible that way," Kaufman argued to Simon and Adler. The writer outlined his own solution to the plot situation.

"We know that's better," answered Simon, "but Harry wants it his way."

"Then why don't we go see him and show how much better it would be my way?" said Kaufman. Simon and Adler were so startled by the innocence of his suggestion that they agreed to ask for an appointment with Cohn.

Cohn grudgingly agreed to a meeting, and he listened as Kaufman related with enthusiasm his solution for the difficulty. When he finished, Simon remarked cheerfully, "We all think it would work. So you see, Harry, the vote is three to one."

Cohn gazed sourly at Simon and walked to the window. "You're wrong," he said. "I'll tell you what the score is. It's one to nothing."

He spat out the window and turned to Simon and added, "Simon, Gower Street is paved with the bones of my executive producers. Now get the hell out of here!" Kaufman was fired the next day.

The relationship of Cohn to his creative talent invariably followed a three-part pattern: the wooing and the honeymoon; the drive for control; the divorce.

Being wooed by Harry Cohn was an overwhelrning experience. The flash of the blue eyes, the persuasiveness of his imposing presence, the promises of concessions, and the vows not to interfere—the combined power of the Cohn personality melted the will to resist. The wooed ones may well have been warned by agents, colleagues, and scarred veterans of Cohn employ to fight off the blandishments of the Columbia president. But the siren call was irresistible.

Over and over again he recited the Cohn litany: "I kiss the feet of talent." Over and over again talent was persuaded.

If more persuasion was needed, Cohn was capable of bizarre proposals, such as those to George Stevens and Sam Bischoff that he would not even talk to them. Once he told a prospect for a writing post, "I'll do anything for you. You can't sleep with your wife anymore? You're crazy about a starlet? I'll let you take her down to Stage Eight, and I'll stand outside and guard the door." The proposal was fanciful, because Cohn forbade any romantic liaison between executives and actresses or secretaries at Columbia.

If promises failed to convince, Cohn brought out reinforcements from the closets of his back room. The shelves contained large supplies of the finest perfumes, cigars, liquors, and other luxuries for "trading with the natives," as one Cohn aide termed it. Cohn sometimes gifted favorite actresses with furs, always throwing them on the floor and stamping on them before the presentation. That a fur could survive such treatment was proof of its value, he explained; it was a technique he had learned in his early dealings in "hot" furs.

A honeymoon period followed the signing of the talent. During that time Cohn was solicitous of the new employee's office facilities. The newcomer was invited to the executive dining room for lunch and, if important enough, to the Cohn box at the racetrack and to dinner at the Cohn mansion. The honeymoon was generally of short duration.

Cohn could tolerate a relationship only when he could effect complete control. Life could become a misery for those who resisted that control. An example was Jean Arthur, who maintained her independence through ten violent, litigious years.

When she finally completed her contract in 1944, she ran through the Columbia streets shouting, "I'm free! I'm free!"

Most others succumbed, completely or in part, to Cohn's control. His customary weapon was money. As master of the economic destinies of his employees, he could wield exceptional power over them. If he wished them to perform extra services, he could hold out the promise of extra payments. If they misbehaved, he could withdraw their salaries: suspension. Over every single person within the studio walls he held the constant threat of dismissal.

But some independent souls could not be intimidated by the loss of a Columbia paycheck. For those, he was required to explore other areas of human frailty. Was it a short temper, which Cohn could trigger and reap the benefits of the ensuing remorse? Was it a checkered past, which Cohn could mention as the clincher to an argument? Was it a fondness for girls, which Cohn could arrange to be satisfied?

Symptomatic of Cohn's urge to control was a device he repeatedly employed in the signing of actors: he wanted to change their names. By so doing, he could cloud their former identities and create them, in name, if not in other respects, in a new image dictated by Harry Cohn.

Scores of actors bear names bestowed on them by Cohn. A few resisted. One of these was George Murphy, who was signed from Broadway musicals by Samuel Goldwyn, then shifted to a Columbia contract.

At their first meeting Cohn told the actor bluntly, "I'm going to change your name."

"What?" said Murphy.

"From now on you're going to be Gregory Marshall," Cohn announced. "'What do you think of that?"

"I think it's awful," replied Murphy, his Irish rising. "Nothing in the contract gives you the right to change my name. And you're not going to." He remained George Murphy.

Among those who worked closest to him, Cohn demanded constant attendance to his will. Such people were expected to notify the Columbia switchboard of their whereabouts at all times. They could be called by Cohn at any hour of the day or night. They could also be required to spend much of their non-studio time with Cohn, attending conferences in the boss' bedroom, watching hour after hour of rushes and finished film; Cohn viewed as many as 400 films a year, virtually the entire Hollywood product.

Being a Cohn assistant was an all-consuming job; many found the pace too exhausting and quit. Tony Owen was an agent Cohn had enlisted as his executive assistant. After a year and a half in the post Owen was issued an ultimatum by his wife, Donna Reed: "You'll have to decide whom you are married to—Harry Cohn or me." He resigned his position.

Few of those who worked intimately with Cohn departed from Columbia under amicable circumstances. For it followed, almost as night the day, that the period of productivity was succeeded by a time of estrangement and recrimination.

Why was this so?

This was a major puzzle to those who observed Cohn's behavior. The turnover of talent at Columbia was far more rapid than at any other studio, and the responsibility for that rested with Harry Cohn.

All the pioneering studio heads were egoists who required the subservience of their underlings. All cherished their positions of power and quashed those who might have pretensions to the throne. But in the case of Harry Cohn those tendencies seemed exaggerated. He appeared to nurture those who might achieve success, then to punish them for being too successful. Those who excelled at picturemaking were threats to his position.

Was the threat real, or did he react in a paranoidal fashion? Certainly the pressure of the East was omnipresent, and Harry Cohn had no doubt that his brother would try to depose him if the production end of the business should suffer two or three years of reverses. It behooved him to prevent such an eventuality; Columbia had bad years, but rarely two in a row.

The New York office repeatedly urged Harry Cohn to groom a second-in-command. Cohn did appoint a number of executive producers, from Walter Wanger to Jerry Wald; none remained.

Suspicion of motives was basic in Cohn's nature and dated back to his earliest days on the East Side. He had to be ahead of the other fellow. Most of all, he had an abhorrence of being played for a sucker.

This feeling was perceived in capsule form by Sidney Buchman on a flight with Cohn from Los Angeles to New York. During a stopover in Chicago, the two men walked to the terminal, where Cohn telephoned the studio. Buchman, a poor air traveler, wanted a Coca-Cola to ease his stomach, but he lacked change for the dispensing machine.

"Got a nickel?" Buchman asked. Cohn eyed him suspiciously.

"Didn't you hear me?" Buchman said. "I need a nickel for the Coke machine."

As he listened to messages from the studio, Cohn tossed Buchman a nickel. Returning with the drink, Buchman saw that Cohn was still gazing at him with suspicion.

"For crissake, I'll give you your nickel back!" said Buchman.

"Didn't you see the change machine?" Cohn demanded.

Buchman admitted that he hadn't. He was inwardly astounded that Cohn, a millionaire many times over, still reacted automatically to the threat that he might be cheated out of anything, even a nickel.

With the notable exception of Buchman, Cohn was unable to maintain a friendship with those who worked under him at the studio. The major reason was his terror of rejection. The thing he feared most in human relationships was placing his trust in someone, only to have that trust betrayed. Hence, he discarded others before they could discard him. The few viable relationships he could maintain were mostly with rich men who wanted nothing of him. One of these was Harry Karl, head of a large shoe enterprise.

Once Cohn remarked to Karl, "Harry, you're one of the few people I would let get close to me."

"But why?" Karl answered. "Why don't you let people get closer to you? You've got a reputation for being hard, rough, and uncouth, yet I know you can be a very warm individual. Why don't you change your image in the community and let people see this other side of you?"

Cohn replied flatly, "If you keep a fence around yourself, people can't hurt you." His eyes narrowed as he studied Karl. "I'm not even sure I haven't made a mistake with you," Cohn added. "You may hurt me, too."

Harry Cohn's control of Columbia Studios extended to every level of operation. His power was demonstrated in his management of the sneak previews. These were the first showings of a finished film, when the value of an immense investment was tested against the reactions of a normal audience, usually in some outlying community of Southern California. Later came the press preview, when the final product was presented for public review and evaluation.

On the night of the sneak preview the major production figures gathered for dinner in the executive dining room. They included Cohn and his executives, the producer of the film, the director, writers, and, rarely, the stars. After dinner they loaded into studio limousines for a destination known only to Harry Cohn.

Four blocks away from Sunset and Gower, Cohn announced to the driver, "Crystal Theater in Pasadena," or, "Warner Brothers, Huntington Park," or whatever previewing grounds he had chosen.

He had reason for the secrecy measures. Often Cohn was at odds with William R. Wilkerson, publisher of *Hollywood Reporter*, who delighted in sending his reviewers to sneak previews of Columbia films and printing raps before the product was to be officially reviewed. Also, actors and their agents were eager to achieve premature views of films to gain an advantage in contract negotiations.

Cohn's domination of his studio was nowhere more evident than in the area of communications. The telephone and the intercom were indispensable weapons for him, and he wielded them unerringly. He was notified of all long-distance telephone calls. The telegraph desk stood outside his office door, and he kept apprised of all communications.

His own office was equipped with a loudspeaker, over which he could broadcast conversations to others in the room. He used the facility to effect small exercises in power. He often called a department head or executive on the intercom and called a certain person, usually an agent, an obscene name. The employee generally agreed; then he was summoned to Cohn's office to encounter the slandered individual.

A variation: Cohn amplified telephone conversations while others were in his office. He responded to the caller in sincere terms while holding his nose or making other deprecatory gestures for the benefit of those in his presence.

Some of Cohn's callers were aware of this tactic and took steps to combat it. One was agent Irving Lazar, who prefaced his telephone conversations with salty language.

Cohn interrupted: "Wait a minute—don't you know there are ladies in the room?"

Lazar answered, "Then maybe you'd better turn off the loudspeaker."

The Cohn code required that he be master of every relationship within his studio. Anyone who ran counter to this was inevitably discharged. That happened with one of Columbia's publicity directors, Whitney Bolton, who committed the error of defending his boss.

At a press preview at the Pantages Theater in Hollywood, Bolton heard a Columbia producer ridicule Cohn. Bolton chastised the producer for his disloyalty, and the incident was reported to Cohn by Ben Kahane. Cohn sent for Bolton the following day.

"You're a schmuck," Cohn growled. "Who the —— told you to defend me?"

"Nobody," Bolton answered.

"You put me under obligation to you for something I didn't do," Cohn said. "I want you to quit. If you remained here, I would never be able to pass you on a studio street without knowing that I was obligated to you." Cohn paid Bolton $18,000 in future salary as settlement of his contract.

As a principal instrument in his system of power, Harry Cohn fostered the legend of the Cohn spy system. Much of the system existed in the minds of fearful Columbia employees.

Cohn did everything possible to bolster their beliefs, since he thus could strengthen his control over the studio.

In reality, Cohn was insatiable in his desire to know what was going on in the professional and private lives of those who worked for him. Few things gave him more pleasure than to be able to spring some information that was believed to be secret. Few things pained him more than to learn belatedly about some drastic development in the lives of those around him.

He absorbed information from every source possible. If he did have a spy system, it was staffed by volunteers. As in any organization, there were those at Columbia who sought favor with the boss by passing along pieces of gossip. No important event could occur at the studio without word of it reaching Harry Cohn via an informer within a matter of minutes.

During the 1930's Cohn informed himself of happenings on Columbia sets in a direct manner: microphones on movie stages were hooked up to a speaker in his office. By switching the dials, he could learn of the progress in shooting on every picture.

This device was generally known of by Columbia employees, but not by visiting actors. A rehearsal on a minor film was once interrupted by the disembodied voice of Harry Cohn saying, "That was lousy. Try it again."

"Who was that?" asked the startled actor, a free-lancer.

"God," replied the director, continuing with the rehearsal.

During his year tinder contract to Columbia, George Murphy tried to convince Cohn that he could perform in musicals; he had done so in Broadway plays but not in films. Cohn agreed to hear Murphy audition, and the actor prepared a number in a rehearsal hall. After a final run-through Murphy said to the pianist, "All right, let's go up to Cohn's office and try it on the old bastard."

"You don't have to," said the voice of Cohn over the loudspeaker. "I heard it, and it sounds okay."

The Orwellian technique faded with the invasion of Leo McCarey, Howard Hawks, George Stevens, and other independent directors. They delighted in broadcasting to the boss' office all kinds of scurrilous comments about Cohn, who then resorted to less direct means of informing himself of activities on sets.

Comings and goings were scrutinized by Cohn. When George Cukor was directing a film at Columbia, Cohn telephoned him one noon and said, "Your doctor visited you this morning, and your lawyer is coming this afternoon. What the hell is going on?"

Before one Christmas, Ralph Bellamy received a number of fur salesmen at the studio because he didn't have time to shop for a mink coat for his wife. Cohn called the actor to demand an explanation. When Bellamy explained, Cohn replied, "Why, you stupid son of a bitch, didn't you know I used to be in the fur business?" He arranged for a mink coat at a bargain price and even modeled it for Bellamy when the coat arrived.

Cohn tried to exercise complete sovereignty over actors he claimed to have discovered; having "created" them, he expected obeisance. He informed himself of the most intimate details of their personal lives and attempted to prevent them from committing mistakes that would endanger their careers and hence Columbia's investment.

One of the studio's stars of the 1940's was a married man with a talent for adultery. Cohn put up with the actor's transgressions until he made the error of conducting an affair with a Columbia starlet. Cohn immediately telephoned the actor's wife and asked, "Do you know what your chippy-chasing husband is up to?" The actor engaged in a violent scene with Cohn, during which he grabbed the miniature baseball bat that Cohn wielded in story conferences and broke it over the desk.

"You're finished; get off this lot," Cohn commanded. "You'll never enter this office again." The actor stormed out of the studio but was back at work soon afterwards. His relations with Cohn were as good as before, and he exercised more discretion in his extramarital affairs.

When William Holden was first at Columbia and unmarried, Cohn summoned him and remarked, "I hear you're going out with some dumb broad."

Holden was mystified until Cohn mentioned the name of an actress he had been dating. The young actor bristled.

"I think you're invading my private life," he retorted. "What I do after I leave the studio is my business."

Cohn didn't agree with such reasoning. "That dame is poison," he argued. "She's a dumb broad, and she's six years older than you are."

Holden discovered later that the actress, in whom he had only a passing interest, had concealed a previous marriage and had been involved in a scandal.

Cohn did not hesitate to use such information in an extremity. When one of his musical stars announced she was leaving her contract to marry a socialite, Cohn argued vehemently with her. He said that her husband-to-be was a sadist who had beaten up two girls, burning one with a cigar and causing brain damage to the other.

The actress refused to listen to Cohn's arguments. She turned her back on a career for a husband who threw her down a flight of stairs while she was pregnant.

8
THE INTERRUPTED SVENGALI

*T*he ascending stardom of Rita Hayworth provided a new and stimulating experience for Harry Cohn. Never before had he been able to discover and develop—and then to profit from—a star of top rank. Columbia had a sizable list of contract players, but they were serviceable actors and actresses who could be counted on to carry B pictures or to bolster the casts of the important product. For stars, Cohn depended on loans from the big studios or multipicture deals with prominent free-lancers. The latter were not entirely satisfactory, since they demanded high salaries and were so independent in temperament that they resisted the dictation of Harry Cohn. His faculty for alienation was such that Irene Dunne and Cary Grant, as well as Jean Arthur, refused to finish out their commitments for films with Columbia.

Rita was a bonanza. Every time Cohn lent her to another studio, she not only returned several times her normal salary; she also came back a bigger star. And the pictures she made for Columbia did not even have to be good in order to make money. The wartime clamor over the Love Goddess stimulated ticket sales.

She was perfect material for stardom, as malleable as gold. Trained since infancy as a dancer, she was an ideal leading lady for the musicals that were in demand during the war. It didn't matter that she could not sing; a succession of ghost voices supplied her songs.

Rita was also a remarkably good actress, when provided sensitive direction. Once instructed in what to do, she responded in skillful style, performing equally well in comedy and drama. Her figure was flawless, and she wore clothes marvelously well, moving with a dancer's grace.

Most of all, she was the quintessence of sex. She possessed the undefined quality that was required of all romantic stars: an emanation or fluorescence that was somehow communicated from the screen to onlookers in the darkened theater.

Harry Cohn recognized all this, and he did everything in his power to foster Rita's usefulness for Columbia Pictures. His efforts were successful as long as she remained unwed. But to Cohn's great sorrow, she had a habit of marrying.

After the expensive disposal of Ed Judson, Cohn enjoyed a period of noninterference in his control of Rita. As with all his important employees, he attempted to guide her personal life along the lines that would be most favorable for Columbia.

Rita's romance with Victor Mature continued after her divorce from Judson. When Mature entered the Coast Guard and was shipped to Connecticut, Rita planned to visit him. Cohn suspected her plans. He ordered the New York publicity head, Frank Rosenberg, to meet her at the train and dissuade her. Rosenberg spent an evening in solemn argument, and Rita agreed that it would be imprudent for her to join Mature in Connecticut. She felt differently in the morning and left to see Mature. Cohn fumed.

He was also incensed when Rita entertained a married leading man in her dressing room for cocktails after the day's shooting. The telephone rang every fifteen minutes.

"What the hell are you doing down there?" Cohn demanded.

"Just having a drink," said the leading man.

"Why don't you go home?" said Cohn. "I can't keep this studio open all hours of the night. It costs money. Now get the hell out. And don't forget to shut off the lights when you leave."

Enjoying Cohn's exasperation, Rita and the actor had another drink.

Cohn allowed no more loan-outs of his most valuable property after *Blood and Sand*. Henceforth Miss Hayworth would work only for Columbia. She returned for another musical with Fred Astaire, this one in color. Cohn had long resisted color films because of the added expense; now it was apparent that color was necessary to display Rita to full advantage. *You Were Never Lovelier*, with a lilting Jerome Kern score, continued her string of box office winners.

Next came *Cover Girl*, with which Cohn proved that wartime musicals could also contain quality.

Once again, the economics of the Columbia operation dictated the nature of the film. The studio had no choreography department, as did the big studios. It had no huge stages, on which could be filmed lavish numbers with hundreds of dancers. The dances were staged by Gene Kelly, who was borrowed from M-G-M to costar with Rita, and they were mostly solos and duets created with an imagination rare in movie musicals.

Once again, the story was uppermost in the planning of the film. *Cover Girl* was the creation of Sidney Buchman, who refused obeisance to the formulae of musicals.

Cover Girl, with another effective score by Jerome Kern, was a giant step forward in the career of Rita Hayworth. It was a vehicle of taste and quality that elevated her above the status of a pinup queen. Since Gene Kelly was new to films, Rita's name was the principal attraction. *Cover Girl* proved to Harry Cohn that she was a box office draw in her own right.

Cohn's joy at this revelation was tempered by a disturbing discovery: she had fallen in love. Moreover, the object of her love was a man likely to interfere with Cohn's guidance of Rita's career. He was Orson Welles.

They met at a dinner party given by Joseph Cotten. Rita was fascinated by the dynamic young man who had astounded the film world with *Citizen Kane*. He asked her to dinner the next evening, and she accepted.

Welles conversed brilliantly on matters of intellect to which Rita had never been exposed. He said nothing of her inadequacy; instead, he offered her a course of study for the elevation of her mind. She followed it eagerly. Cohn was upset by the courtship and barred Welles from Columbia, but she saw him anyway.

Rita appeared on the Mercury Theater radio show with Welles and Cotten. She also volunteered as an attendant in the magic show Welles was operating for the entertainment of servicemen. Their romance bloomed, and Rita married Welles on September 7, 1943.

Cohn was pleased that Welles did not intrude in Rita's career, the new husband being involved in his own activities. Rita was happy and hence did her work at Columbia without complications. She became pregnant, but her condition offered little interference with her schedule of films. She performed in *Tonight and Every Night*, a musical about entertainers during the London blitz, until two months before Rebecca Welles was born. Two months afterward she was rehearsing numbers for *Gilda*.

It was *Gilda* that placed Rita in the uppermost ranks of film stars. The story was fashioned to her talents by Virginia Van Upp. Costarring was Glenn Ford, newly returned from the Marines. The combination was electric. Rita's principal number, in which she simulated a striptease to *Put the Blame on Mame*, was a miracle of sexual provocation.

Inevitably, Rita grew restive under the dominance of Harry Cohn. The intellectual stimulus of Welles caused her to examine scripts more carefully and to weigh her value to Columbia Pictures against the salary she was being paid. Her agents made proposals for a new contract; Cohn rejected them.

Rita expressed her distaste for her next script, the fantasy *Down to Earth*; Cohn insisted that she make the film. Rita did, but the production schedule stretched to six months. She sometimes appeared in the early morning for hairdressing and makeup, but when the nine o'clock start of production arrived, she declared she was too ill to report.

On some days she merely telephoned the studio that she was unable to perform. Cohn dispatched his executive assistant Evelyn Lane to Rita's house to convince her to appear.

Cohn capitulated. He agreed to the suggestion by Rita's agents, the William Morris office, that she receive 25 percent of the profits from her films through her new corporation, the Beckworth company.

Rita's marriage to Welles began to deteriorate. Unable to recapture the brilliance he had exhibited with *Citizen Kane*, he sought escape from Hollywood to pursue artistic endeavors elsewhere. He and Rita announced a separation, and Welles went East to prepare a stage version of *Around the World in 80 Days*, produced by Mike Todd.

Todd ran out of money while the show was trying out in Boston. Faced with foreclosure because of a $50,000 costume bill, Welles was desperate for additional financing. He reasoned that the only man he knew who would gamble $50,000 on the basis of a telephone call was Harry Cohn. Welles placed a call to Columbia Studios from backstage.

Welles outlined his plight to Cohn and added, "Look, Harry, if you'll advance me the fifty thousand, I'll make a deal with you to write and direct a picture. I've got a suspense story that can be made inexpensively."

"Yeah? What is it?" asked Cohn.

Welles glanced at the cover of a paperback novel that a wardrobe mistress was reading nearby. "It's called *The Lady from Shanghai*," he said, reading the title.

"Okay," said Cohn. "You've got a deal. I'll send the fifty thousand."

The transfusion of Cohn money was not enough to make *Around the World in 80 Days* a success, and it closed after a brief run in New York. Welles returned to Hollywood to fulfill his commitment to Columbia. Now Cohn wanted a full-scale production instead of the modest film Welles had proposed. He also wanted the film to star Rita Hayworth. Cohn's persuasion was overwhelming, and a reconciliation was effected.

Welles aimed to create Rita in a new image, and he directed the transformation of her hair to a bleached bob. Cohn was apoplectic with rage. But he offered little interference with the production of *The Lady from Shanghai* during long weeks of expensive filming. Welles filmed a lengthy location in Acapulco but returned with little footage that was usable; he had neglected to shoot close-ups.

The sixty-day schedule stretched to ninety days; the cost soared from the $1,250,000 budget to $2,000,000. Welles ordered elaborate setups for scenes, then discarded them when he changed his mind. He ordered construction of a chamber of mirrors for a chase in an amusement park, then discovered it could not be lighted because of the mirrors.

The task of policing Welles' excesses fell to the aggressive little production manager, Jack Fier. A relentless man with a galvanic voice, Fier was in constant combat with Welles. As *The Lady from Shanghai* was drawing to a conclusion, Welles erected a sign that read: "THE ONLY THING WE HAVE TO FEAR IS FIER HIMSELF."

Fier countered with his own sign: "ALL'S WELL THAT ENDS WELLES."

With production completed, Welles set about the task of assembling a cohesive film from the mass of negative he had exposed. His efforts were unsuccessful. A meeting was held in Cohn's office early one morning, following a disastrous preview in Santa Barbara. Among those present were Cohn, Welles, and Virginia Van Upp, who had written Rita's best films. Welles had not consulted her on *The Lady from Shanghai.*

"All right, who's going to say it?" asked Cohn. As usual, he was not vindictive when previews went badly; he merely sought solutions.

"I'll say it," Welles volunteered. "There are things that are wrong with the picture."

"Can Virginia help you?" Cohn asked.

"I would appreciate it if she would," Welles replied. When the meeting ended, he and Miss Van Upp spread the script on the floor and spent the rest of the night devising methods of clarifying the muddled story. Scenes were reshot, and the entire film was recut. Long after its completion, *The Lady from Shanghai* was released. It showed flashes of the Welles talent; but the original concept had vanished, and the film was unsuccessful.

Rita's marriage to Welles came to an end after *The Lady from Shanghai.* He could find no solution to his continuing financial problems. He believed he could recapture his creativity and his solvency by working in Europe. Rita also wanted to make films in Europe, but Harry Cohn refused to allow her.

Rita divorced Welles on November 10, 1947, testifying: "Mr. Welles showed no interest in establishing a home. Mr. Welles told me he never should have married in the first place, as it interfered with his freedom in his way of life."

To reporters she added a comment that brought pain to Harry Cohn. "Certainly I'm going to marry again," she said.

9
"Folks, You Ain't Heard Nothin' Yet!"

*B*y the mid-1940's Al Jolson was a faded name in American show business. Virtually his only bookings were USC tours entertaining servicemen abroad. Jolson's voice was not what it had been, but the vibrancy and the style remained. Yet no one sought his services, not even for benefits. The times when he had ruled Broadway from the runway of the Winter Garden, when he had astounded the film world with his spoken words in *The Jazz Singer*—all seemed lost in the distant past.

Harry Cohn remembered. Al Jolson was the only man he ever idolized. When Cohn was in the music trade, every song plugger dreamed of placing a tune with Jolson. Cohn's opinion of Jolson as an entertainer never altered.

The idea for a film biography of Jolson originated with Sidney Skolsky. The movie columnist had been working at Warner Brothers as assistant to Mark Hellinger and had proposed the possibility of a film utilizing Jolson's singing voice and the face of a younger actor. Jack Warner refused to consider the idea.

Skolsky received rejections from other studios as well. Only Harry Cohn expressed an interest. Three months after their first conversation on the matter, Skolsky received a telephone call from Cohn.

"Get your ass over to the studio," Cohn ordered. "You're working on a picture."

"What picture?" Skolsky asked.

"The Jolson picture," Cohn replied.

Only after Skolsky had begun working on a story treatment did Cohn learn that the columnist had not apprised Jolson of his plan. Cohn telephoned his brother Jack to begin negotiations with Jolson, who was in New York. Jolson had just been replaced on radio by Judy Canova, and he was receptive to the suggestion of a trip to Hollywood to discuss a film biography.

Skolsky went to see Jolson after his arrival at the Beverly Hills Hotel.

"I've got the whole thing lined up except the terms, Jolie," said Skolsky.

"What are you doing at a crappy studio like Columbia?" Jolson asked. He then reported that he had encountered Jack Warner on the train to California. Learning of Jolson's mission, Warner saw a chance to beat Harry Cohn out of a deal. He offered Jolson $200,000 for the rights to his story, plus the services of the Epstein twins as writers and Michael Curtiz as director; they had recently made the hit biography of George M. Cohan, *Yankee Doodle Dandy*. Warner proposed that Jolson could play the leading role himself or let a younger actor do it. He further appealed to Jolson's proprietary interest as a major stockholder in Warner Brothers.

"Al," said Skolsky, "you go over to Warners, and yours will be one of many pictures. Besides, Jack Warner turned it down once. Harry Cohn is enthusiastic about the picture, and he'll give it the special treatment. At least go talk to Cohn."

Jolson agreed to do so. Since Cohn could not match Warners' terms, Skolsky offered a different formula: Columbia would pay Jolson no advance but would give him 50 percent of the profits.

Cohn approved. Jolson agreed with one condition: he be paid $25,000 for recording the songs. Cohn balked, then conceded. The deal brought a thunder of protest from the East, which argued that Jolson was a has-been who had been rejected by the American public.

The Eastern resistance solidified Cohn's resolve to make a success of the Jolson biography. He had only one choice for the man to lick the story: Sidney Buchman. But Buchman, who had been acting as executive producer, had grown weary of the studio pressure and yearned to establish himself as an independent producer. Cohn's persuasion was overwhelming; Buchman agreed to take on the Jolson project.

The key to the story eluded Buchman until he heard of an incident concerning the singer's marriage to Ruby Keeler. Jolson bought a house in rural Encino, where he expected to retire from show business. On the first night in the house he paced the living room and finally told his wife he was going out for a while. He returned in the early morning, having spent the time entertaining firemen at the local station.

"This story is a love affair," Buchman reasoned. "The lover is applause. Jolson's wife could handle another woman, but she was no match against the applause."

The script was developing promisingly, and Jolson began recording the songs. Morris Stoloff and Saul Chaplin of the Columbia music department had prepared the music with the repeated consultation of Cohn, who reveled in the songs of the Jolson period: *Rockabye Your Baby to a Dixie Melody; Mammy; You Made Me Love You; Toot Toot Tootsie; Sonny Boy; California, Here I Come; April Showers.*

The Jolson temperament revived during the recordings. Saul Chaplin had acquired all the old Jolson records and had studied them with care. After a rendition of *April Showers* everyone on the music stage except Chaplin cheered.

"Didn't you like it?" Jolson demanded.

"Yes, but you left out something," Chaplin replied, citing a passage that had been neglected. Jolson became incensed and argued that he could not sing the same as before because of the loss of a lung. To climax the argument, he brought out a roll of large-denomination currency.

"I made this in show business," Jolson shouted. "Where's yours?"

But his moments of pique were few, and Jolson genuinely enjoyed the rebirth of interest in his singing, at least within the confines of Columbia Studios. His voice was not up to the standards of his earlier recordings, his register having fallen with age. He had days of greatness before the microphone, other days when the recordings were not usable. The Columbia music department pieced together the tracks to achieve the best of the Jolson art.

The Cohn-Jolson relationship amazed Columbia workers. Jolson was the only person within memory who could be admitted to Cohn's office automatically. Jolson commenced singing as he approached down the hall. The secretary hurriedly announced his arrival to Cohn, and Jolson breezed through the knobless door to greet his great friend. His attitude was different from what it had been before the picture deal had been made; then Jolson had spoken of Cohn only in derogatory terms. When he was chided about the change of attitude by Virginia Van Upp, Jolson replied, "Whose bread I eat, his song I sing." Cohn was later to borrow the expression.

As Buchman continued fashioning the script, Cohn experienced occasional qualms about the wisdom of the project, especially in light of the East's repeated warnings of a fiasco. The low point of Cohn's confidence came when Jolson underwent major surgery at Cedars of Lebanon Hospital.

"He'll die before the picture gets out and ruin the box office," said Cohn fearfully.

Word of his forebodings reached Jolson in the hospital. He learned that Cohn and Ben Kahane were coming to visit him and check on his condition before they proceeded with the film biography.

Jolson induced his doctor to give him a hypodermic injection to blunt his pain. When the two executives entered the hospital room, Jolson leaped out of his bed. For half an hour he entertained Cohn and Kahane with jokes, snatches of songs, and bits of reminiscence. The two men went away convinced that Jolson would survive. His performance over, Jolson collapsed on the bed and was confined to an oxygen tent.

As production neared, Cohn wrestled with the issue of who could play Jolson. Cohn wanted James Cagney because of his success with *Yankee Doodle Dandy*, but Cagney wasn't interested in portraying another show business immortal. The role was offered to Danny Thomas, then a rising comedian, with the proviso that he submit to an operation to reduce the size of his nose; Thomas refused. Numerous other actors were considered, including José Ferrer and Richard Conte.

The first actor to test for the role was Larry Parks, who had appeared in dozens of B pictures while under contract to Columbia. He was also the last to test. He had been instructed in the Jolson style by Morris Stoloff and Max Arnow, both of whom had witnessed the mammy singer in his prime. Parks saw the Jolson movies, listened to all the records. Over and over again he played the recordings on a rehearsal stage, turning up the volume as loud as he could stand it.

When Parks made the final test, the results were uncanny. Even Jolson was disturbed that anyone could be so like Jolson.

Veteran director Alfred Green was assigned to the picture, and Evelyn Keyes was given the role of Jolson's wife. Shooting began without a completed script, and much of the time Buchman supplied scenes the day before they were to be filmed.

Before the film began, Cohn had decreed that it could cost no more than $1,500,000; anything more would be too great a risk. But after a week or two of film came through, he grew more defiant of the East. He removed the restrictions on the budget. Orchestrations were enlarged, and production values added. The final cost was $2,800,000.

Jolson maintained an aloofness from the filming; he was still upset that he hadn't been chosen to play himself. When *The Jolson Story* was three-quarters finished, his curiosity could not be contained. He had to see what was going on.

Now he was on the set constantly, watching the action and offering suggestions. When Parks rehearsed the Winter Garden sequence, he complained, "The kid just doesn't move like me."

And so, for one brief long shot, Al Jolson climbed onto the stage and performed the movements to one of his songs. For that occasion, Harry Cohn paid a rare visit to the sound stage.

Cohn was watching with rapt attention during a take when the cameraman, Joe Walker, called, "Cut!"

"What do you mean?" Cohn demanded. "You can't stop a scene when Al Jolson is singing!"

"Mr. Cohn, one of the arc lamps is flickering, and the shot is no good," said Walker.

Cohn continued to be indignant until he was reminded that the three-strip Technicolor film was costing 30 cents a second.

After filming had been completed, Buchman spent six months in the cutting room assembling the finished product. The first preview in Santa Barbara was a total success, but Cohn found one flaw in the film. Although Parks' rendition of *Sonny*

Boy proved to be one of the most poignant moments in the picture, Cohn felt that it interrupted the pace and distracted from the mood. The number was removed.

The impact of *The Jolson Story* was enormous. For a generation that had been reared on the gentle sounds of crooners, the full-voiced vitality of the Jolson voice was a revelation. The film grossed $8,000,000 and created a whole new career for Jolson. He became the highest paid guest star in radio, then signed to appear weekly on the *Kraft Music Hall* for $5,500 a week.

Cohn attempted a sequel, *Jolson Sings Again*, in 1949. Predictably, it was neither as good nor as successful as *The Jolson Story*, but it proved to be another profitable investment for Columbia. The sequel's most notable feature was a double-exposed scene in which Parks, as Jolson, met Parks, as Parks, the man who was to impersonate him in the film biography that would revive his career.

Harry Cohn continued to idolize Jolson. When the mammy singer died in San Francisco on October 23, 1950, after entertaining American troops in Korea, Cohn was at the Friars' Club. He wept unashamedly before the club members.

10
WORLD WAR II AND HARRY COHN

*T*he war evoked curious attitudes from Harry Cohn, as did all matters requiring an altruistic response. He resisted attempts to enlist him in worthy causes. One afternoon Louis B. Mayer spent an hour on the telephone before he was able to evoke a contribution from Cohn to Jewish Relief. Mayer used all his considerable powers of persuasion to appeal to Cohn's loyalties as a Jew, but Cohn had none. After he had committed himself to a sizable donation, Cohn complained to an aide, "Relief for the Jews! Somebody should start a fund for relief *from* the Jews. All the trouble in the world has been caused by Jews and Irishmen."

Likewise, Cohn was suspicious and difficult to reach for wartime charities. Once he received a delegation of film executives' wives who were raising funds for the entertainment of soldiers. Each of the major studios had agreed to contribute an important film to be premiered for the benefit of the fund. Cohn was asked if he would do so.

"No," he replied flatly.

The women were crestfallen. "Why not?" one of them asked.

"Because I am responsible to the stockholders of Columbia Pictures," he replied, "and they are entitled to every cent of revenue derived from our films."

His visitors, some of them indignant over his reply, prepared to leave.

"Wait a minute," Cohn said. "How much money do you expect to realize from one of these premieres?"

"Six thousand dollars," he was told.

Cohn wrote out a personal check for $6,000 and gave it to the women, adding, "If you ever tell anyone I gave you this money, I'll deny it."

When Hollywood Canteen was organized by Jules Stein and Bette Davis for the entertainment of servicemen, every studio was assigned a night on which to supply entertainment. Columbia had its night, but Harry Cohn never appeared. Mrs. Jules Stein asked him why.

He answered that he had sent a large supply of phonograph records to the canteen and had never been thanked for them. Mrs. Stein explained that the records had not been accompanied by a card, so she didn't know whom to thank; but the canteen was indeed grateful. Thus mollified, Cohn appeared every week on Columbia's night.

Cohn was as imperious at the canteen as he was at the studio. Once he ordered a sailor off the stage, accusing him of staring up the girls' dresses. A regular entertainer on Columbia night was Phil Silvers, who had appeared in *Cover Girl*. The comedian performed an act in which his accompanist, Saul Chaplin, interrupted Silvers' clarinet solo with cadenzas on the piano. When Silvers registered his mock indignation, Cohn thought it was real. He clapped his big hand on Chaplin's shoulder and ordered, "Let him play!"

It had been a tradition at the Hollywood Canteen that only servicemen were allowed to enter the front door. All entertainers and workers entered by the back door—all except Harry Cohn.

Every night when he arrived, he was stopped by attendants at the front door. Each time he bullied his way through. Doormen complained to Mrs. Stein, who sought a diplomatic means of informing the president of Columbia Pictures that he should enter by the rear door of the Hollywood Canteen.

One night Cohn invited Stein, who was head of the giant MCA talent agency, and his wife to dine at the studio before going to the canteen. After dinner Mrs. Stein suggested that she drive with Cohn to the canteen. When they neared the place, Mrs. Stein said, "Why don't you park on the back lot? It's so convenient to the rear door."

Cohn accompanied her through the rear door. But on the following Columbia night and every one after that, he continued to enter through the front door.

Cohn's attitude in bidding farewell to workers entering the service was not the usual one of a boss sending his employees off to war.

As William Holden was leaving for the Air Force, Cohn commented, "I hope this makes a man out of you." At least one of Holden's directors had complained of his youthful appearance. Cohn expressed the hope that war would make Holden a more mature actor and hence a greater asset for Columbia Pictures.

Cohn traveled to Europe in 1945. He was terrified at the prospect—not because of any danger; the war was over. Cohn was one of several film leaders who were asked by the government to tour the war-ravaged countries of Europe for two purposes: to investigate possibilities of future films of propaganda value, and to speed the reopening of theaters in the Allied and occupied countries, some of which had not seen American movies in six years.

Cohn's terror stemmed from the fact that he would be thrown into close contact with such men as Jack Warner of Warner Brothers; Eddie Mannix, a top official of M-G-M; Barney Balaban, president of Paramount; Cliff Work, president of Universal; and Darryl Zanuck of Twentieth Century-Fox. These were men that Cohn had combated throughout his history as a studio head. He insisted that Sidney Buchman accompany him on the trip.

Cohn and Buchman were outfitted by the studio wardrobe department in officers' uniforms, and they set out in the company of their fellow moviemakers. As the Air Force plane touched down in each European capital, the moguls were met by their representatives, and there was intense competition for the best suites in the leading hotels. The quarters were in the Grosvenor House of London and the Ritz in Paris, both places attempting a semblance of their prewar elegance.

The European trip made a profound impression on Cohn— especially a visit to Buchenwald, where some bony inmates still remained. Returning to Paris, Cohn decided he had seen enough and declined a trip to Italy with the others.

Before his departure Cohn agreed to see Garson Kanin, the man who had read him the script of *The More the Merrier* four years before. Under the close supervision of General Eisenhower, Kanin and Carol Reed had assembled from 10,000,000 feet of combat film a documentary of the war in Europe, *The*

True Glory. The film companies rotated the release of documentaries made by the government, and *The True Glory* had befallen Columbia. Kanin was assigned by his commanding general to confer with Cohn about the release.

When Kanin reported to the Ritz Hotel, he was detained by a pair of sentries who asked for his pass. Kanin had none, and he was forced to identify himself at the desk, then to be announced to Mr. Cohn. After five years of Army service, Kanin was in no mood to wait in a hotel lobby before being ushered into the presence of Harry Cohn.

Finally, he was permitted to see Cohn. He found the suite occupied by a number of hangers-on, some of whom were proffering supplies of perfume, champagne, and other rarities.

Cohn was in an anteroom playing gin rummy with Sidney Buchman. "Wait a minute until I finish this hand," Cohn told Kanin.

The offhanded remark infuriated Kanin.

"Put down those goddam cards!" he snapped. "Don't you know you're in the midst of history? This city has been liberated only a short while. There's not a dog, not a cat, in Paris; they've all been eaten. There's not a movie house open; at least that might intrigue you. Do you have to go on with that stupid card game?"

Cohn gazed up in surprise at the Army officer. "You drunk or something?" he asked.

He concluded the game and then turned to Kanin. "Now what is this all about?" he asked.

"It's about a documentary called *The True Glory*," said Kanin.

"Oh, yes," said Cohn. "We drew straws to see which studio would release it. Columbia lost. Come on, let's have a drink."

Cohn went to the main room, where the operators were milling around. Kanin accepted a glass of champagne, but the drink only increased his anger.

"Aren't you ashamed of yourself?" he said to Cohn. "Here you are behaving in a reprehensible manner, playing the black market and swilling champagne. Then you make sarcastic cracks about a picture that thirty-two men gave their lives to film."

Cohn bristled at Kanin's remarks. "That's no way to talk to the president of Columbia Pictures," he declared.

"What's that?" Kanin asked.

"What's what?" Cohn said.

"Columbia Pictures?"

"You know damn well what it is."

"You're the president?"

"You're damned right."

"If you're the president, can you tell me how to spell Columbia?"

"Of course I know how to spell Columbia!"

"I'll bet you a hundred dollars you can't spell it."

"Okay, wise guy." Cohn muttered to the onlookers, "This is one of those smart-ass writers trying to show off."

Kanin brought $100 in bills out of his pocket, and Cohn scurried to find a like amount in his luggage. He said defiantly, "Now I'm going to take that hundred dollars from you."

"All right," said Kanin, "but first spell Columbia for me."

"Very well. Columbia: C-O-L-O—"

Kanin picked up the money and departed. Years before he had been briefed by his friend Norman Krasna that in excitable moments there was a fifty-fifty chance that Harry Cohn would be unable to spell Columbia. The odds seemed favorable to Kanin.

11
THE POSTWAR BOOM AND THOSE
WHO HELPED MAKE IT

*T*he prosperity of Columbia Pictures was even greater in peace than it had been in war. Gross receipts leaped $10,000,000 between 1942 and 1944, and profits surpassed $2,000,000 for the first time in 1944. Two years later the gross had grown another $10,000,000 to $46,501,910, and profits stood at $3,500,000.

It was a happy time for Harry Cohn. He remained as autocratic and combative as ever but in general he was pleased with his life. He had been blessed with a second son, and Joan had assumed a position as one of Hollywood's most gracious hostesses. The constant growth in business volume and profits kept the East at bay. The AA and A pictures were almost invariably profitable, and so were the B's.

A major reason for Cohn's good feeling was the fact that he now had the aid and support of two individuals who were enormously creative and sympathetic to his foibles. One was Sidney Buchman; the other was Virginia Van Upp.

She had first known Harry Cohn when she was a child actress at Universal, and he was Carl Laemmle's assistant. She met him again during the 1920's, when she worked in Edward Small's casting office. One day Cohn telephoned Small in a frenzy. Unless he had $2,000 to meet the payroll, C.B.C. would go under. Virginia Van Upp delivered the money to Cohn.

Later she turned to screenwriting and formed a successful team with E. H. Griffith to produce smart comedies for Paramount with such stars as Carole Lombard, Fred MacMurray, Madeleine Carroll, and Ray Milland. Impressed with Miss Van Upp's skill in fashioning vehicles for actresses, Cohn hired her to assist in the making of *Cover Girl*, a crucial film in the career of Rita Hayworth.

The first altercation with Cohn was always the important one, and Miss Van Upp's came when Cohn had returned from a trip to New York. He summoned her and said accusingly, "Is it true that you have discarded fifty thousand dollars' worth of clothes for Miss Hayworth in *Cover Girl?*"

"That's right—I did," Miss Van Upp replied. "Would you like to come to the wardrobe department and see them for yourself?"

Cohn accompanied her to view the gowns, and he conceded, "You're right; they're terrible."

Thereafter relations between Cohn and Miss Van Upp were cordial. He admired her professionalism, her ability to survive in a man's world without losing her femininity. She was immensely stimulated by his vitality; at the end of a tiring day she purposely visited his office to revive her energies by listening to him. She understood his drive, the way he always walked with his right shoulder thrust forward: to make his way through the crowd. She also understood that his one terror was to be vulnerable.

Miss Van Upp wrote the screenplay for *Gilda*, Rita's greatest hit. Such was Rita's faith in her that she refused to play Gilda unless Miss Van Upp produced the film, too. She did so, and Cohn was so impressed that he asked her to be executive producer.

From time to time in Columbia's history Cohn established the post of executive producer. Usually he did so at the behest of the East, which constantly urged him to delegate duties and to groom a successor. The executive producer assisted Cohn in an active, creative way and oversaw the entire AA and A product. Unlike other studio bosses who chose yes-men for the post, Cohn always selected strong personalities: Walter Wanger, William Perlberg, Sidney Buchman, Jerry Wald. Because of Cohn's nature, none remained in the job.

Buchman vacated the position to go into independent production. Miss Van Upp did not want to assume the heavy duties of executive producer because she had a husband and daughter. But she succumbed to Cohn's overwhelming persuasion.

Cohn announced the appointment in singular style. Speculation had been rife among the ten producers at Columbia, each of whom believed he was under consideration for executive producer. None had conceived the possibility that the post would go to a woman.

The subject of the appointment came into the conversation one day at the lunch table in the executive dining room. All ten of the male producers and Miss Van Upp were seated at the table when one of the men mentioned that a prominent producer had left his studio and hence might be available for the second-in-command at Columbia.

"Not interested," said Cohn. "I've made my choice."

Interest at the table quickened. "No kidding, Harry?" said one of the men. "Can you tell us who it is?"

"Yes," answered Cohn, "it's Virginia."

The news was received in astonished silence. There was no comment, no congratulations. Cohn obviously enjoyed the surprise of his announcement. He arose and walked completely around the table, sticking out his tongue at each of the ten producers.

That night he telephoned his new executive producer. "How many of those men called you to offer congratulations?" he asked.

"One," she replied.

"Who was it?"

She told him. By the time she had finished her duties as producer and had moved upstairs to the new office, the one man who had congratulated her was the only producer remaining under employment to Columbia. Cohn had fired the other nine.

Cohn renovated an office next to his, and Miss Van Upp moved into it. One evening he dashed into her office and exclaimed, "Oh my God, I never should have done this!"

"I told you that at the beginning," she replied.

"No, I don't mean your job; it's the office. You'll have to share the can with Ben Kahane!" Cohn solved the situation by permitting Miss Van Upp to use his own bathroom, a rare concession.

As with his secretaries, Cohn took a Victorian attitude toward protecting Miss Van Upp from the vulgarities of male conversation. He chastised anyone who employed obscene language in her presence. Conversely, she would not allow him to excoriate an employee when she was in the room. He consequently waited until she had left.

Despite the seeming rapport with Miss Van Upp, Cohn was uneasy with the relationship, as he was with all human relationships. He needed to find one area of vulnerability. It wasn't drinking. It wasn't any secret in her personal life; she was happily married to a radio director, Ralph Nelson. It wasn't even money, the temptation with which Cohn had snared many a victim.

He could conceive of only one other possibility: sex.

Miss Van Upp merely laughed at his offers of lovemaking; she was convinced that he was merely a verbal rapist, who had no intention of going through with the affair.

"Why, I wouldn't think of it," she once replied to his entreaty. "A man with your blood pressure? I couldn't bear the responsibility."

"Supposing I get it down," he suggested.

"When it gets to be one hundred thirty, I'll consider it," she said.

One day she was summoned to his office. He sat smugly behind his desk as he announced, "My blood pressure is one hundred twenty-eight."

"I don't believe you," she replied.

For proof, he sent for the studio doctor. Cohn watched Miss Van Upp intently as the doctor wrapped the arm and observed the pressure.

"It's pretty good today, Mr. Cohn," the young doctor announced cheerfully. "Only one hundred seventy-eight."

Cohn exploded. "Goddammit, you call yourself a doctor!" he shouted. "I *know* it's lower than that. Now take it on the other arm!"

The frightened doctor did so and announced dutifully that the reading was 130.

"See!" said Cohn to Miss Van Upp.

"Yes, but even if half of you is one hundred thirty, the other half is one hundred seventy-eight, and I'd still be scared," she said.

When Miss Van Upp's new contract was being prepared, she announced to Cohn that she was demanding a clause that prohibited him from verbal rape.

"Now what do you think they'd say if they saw that in New York?" he pleaded.

They argued the issue for nearly two hours until Cohn finally said, "Have I ever broken my word?"

"No," she admitted.

"Do you want to shake on it, and I'll consider it a part of the contract?"

"Yes," she replied. They shook hands, and he never introduced the subject again.

In 1947 Virginia Van Upp was weary from the job of overseeing the entire Columbia product and felt the need to resume her marriage. She took an extended leave of absence, during which she inspected Latin American operations for Cohn. When she returned, Cohn's need for her was over. She went back to Columbia for script assignments and once performed a delicate foreign mission for Cohn. But the intimate, creative relationship never resumed.

In the period following the war, many film creators felt the urge for independence. Sidney Buchman was one of them. He believed he had performed his service for the glory of Columbia Pictures. Now he wished complete creative freedom, as well as more substantial returns from the attractions he created.

Cohn was strangely unreceptive to Buchman's wishes. Although he still esteemed Buchman as a man and as a producer and writer, Cohn could not countenance Buchman's operating on the Columbia lot without the direct supervision of Harry Cohn. But most of all, Cohn could not tolerate the intrusion on his proprietorship.

Buchman asked for a deal that would give him $100,000 to write and produce a script; then he would receive 50 percent of the net profits. He wanted to make one picture a year.

Cohn proposed that Buchman receive $50,000 for each film, plus 50 percent of the profits, and that he would be required to produce two pictures a year.

"It's not in the cards," Buchman argued. "I'd be cheating you and myself; I'd be doing inferior work. I wouldn't wreck my own career that way. You're putting the pressure on me to make two pictures a year. Well, I can't do it, and I won't do it."

Cohn was completely intractable. All the camaraderie of working on pictures from *Theodora Goes Wild* to *The Jolson Story* suddenly disappeared. Buchman was merely another Columbia employee trying to get the better of Harry Cohn.

Buchman coolly laid his plans. He fired his agent and hired tough, able Lew Wasserman, aide-de-camp to Jules Stein at MCA. Wasserman telephoned Cohn with the news: "I'm representing Sidney Buchman."

"The hell you are," said Cohn.

"Well, I am, and he's leaving your lot," Wasserman announced.

Cohn maintained a stony silence with Buchman. Meanwhile, Wasserman was lining up a contract for Buchman with Louis B. Mayer, who was eager to have him work for M-G-M. After a week Cohn buzzed Buchman and asked him to come to the office. Cohn asked about the M-G-M deal, and Buchman explained it to him. As they talked, Cohn received a telephone call from his wife.

"I got a dirty bastard in my office," Cohn said.

When Mrs. Cohn learned he was speaking of Buchman, she insisted that he come for dinner at the house that night.

"She's killing me on this thing," Cohn complained to Buchman. "She keeps telling me I'm making the mistake of my life."

Buchman agreed to go to dinner. The three ate the meal in the immense Cohn dining room, and the atmosphere was funereal. Mrs. Cohn continued telling her husband he was foolish to let Sidney go. Cohn said little.

At the end of dinner Mrs. Cohn remarked to Buchman, "I guess we won't be seeing you anymore."

Buchman replied cheerfully, "If the dinner's free, I'll come back every Friday night."

"It's a deal," Mrs. Cohn said with a smile.

The conversation dribbled out, and at ten Buchman took his leave. Cohn followed him out to the courtyard, where Buchman's car was parked. Buchman started the motor, but Cohn continued leaning against the car door. He seemed unable to speak, yet unable to let Buchman go.

"Harry, take your arms off the door," Buchman said. "I'm leaving."

Then Cohn said something that was hard for him to say, "Pal, where did we go wrong?"

Buchman was so taken aback by the plaintiveness of the inquiry, so out of character with Harry Cohn, that he could scarcely reply. Finally, he said, "Harry, you're too shrewd a man to kid yourself. You know where we went wrong. You know what the whole gambit is about. I haven't written a script for fifty thousand dollars for twelve years. But you want me to go back to where I started."

"What do you want?" Cohn asked quietly.

"You know what I want: a hundred thousand a picture, one a year, and fifty percent of the profits."

"You've got it."

"It's too late. I haven't the face to tell Wasserman and Mayer that I can't take their deal. They'll think I've been stringing them along, trying to get the terms out of you. There's only one way to do it: you've got to call Wasserman and Mayer and explain to them what happened. You may have to ask Mayer to do it on a favor basis."

Cohn made the necessary telephone calls, and although it was painful to him, he asked Louis B. Mayer for the favor. And so Sidney Buchman remained at Columbia.

A Chrestomathy of Legends

*E*ddie Buzzell was one of a long series of intimates on whom Cohn relied for constant companionship. Such men were called on to accompany Cohn on trips to New York and for weekends on his yacht or to play cards, watch films, or merely talk in the early hours of the morning, Cohn wishing never to be alone.

During the period of Cohn's marriage to Rose, Buzzell came to Hollywood and lived at the Cohn house. He had been a Broadway star, and now he had ambitions of becoming a film director. Cohn hired Buzzell to make a series of shorts for Columbia. The director was proud of the results, but he couldn't convince Cohn to look at the films. One night he scheduled a preview of his most promising comedy, and he persuaded Cohn to see it at a downtown theater.

The two men took a pair of actresses to dinner at the Brown Derby, then drove to Los Angeles. The preview went well, Buzzell thought, and Cohn laughed heartily, along with the rest of the audience.

The foursome was waiting for Cohn's yellow Rolls-Royce to be delivered in front of the theater when a ragged-looking man crossed the street, climbed a lamppost, and dived headfirst to the sidewalk. The crowd on the street watched the suicide in horror.

The party mood of Cohn, Buzzell, and the two actresses was shattered; all sat in silence as they rode back to Hollywood.

The stunned Buzzell finally said, "My God, Harry, why would a man do such a thing?"

"He must have seen your picture," Cohn replied.

During a studio meeting Jack Cohn suggested that Columbia make a biblical film.

"Why don't you just take care of the selling and keep your nose out of my end of the business?" Harry replied.

"I just thought we should make a Bible picture, that's all," Jack continued. "After all, they're a standard item, like Westerns or Foreign Legion pictures. DeMille makes big money with them. There are a lot of good stories in the Bible."

"What the hell do you know about the Bible?" Harry asked. "I'll bet you don't even know the Lord's Prayer."

"I sure do," Jack replied.

"The hell you do! I'll bet you fifty bucks you can't recite the Lord's Prayer. Come on—put up or shut up."

"Okay, it's a bet," said Jack, and both brothers laid down $50.

"Okay, say it," Harry said.

"Now I lay me down to sleep—" Jack began.

Harry interrupted him and handed over the $50. "That's enough," Harry said. "I didn't think you knew it."

After the birth of his first son Cohn was so overjoyed that he told a studio underling, "You know something? I'm so goddam grateful for being a father I'n not going to be a son of a bitch anymore."

A few days later, he passed the same employee in the hallway. "I can't stand the strain anymore," Cohn grumbled. "I gotta go back to being a son of a bitch again."

Cohn enjoyed finding small errors in scripts so he could hold them up to the writers and producers as examples of ignorance. One day he summoned the writer and producer of an important film to his office.

"What the hell is this?" he demanded, slapping his hand on a script page. "Here you got the boss telling his secretary, 'Will you type this letter, *please*?'"

He waited expectantly for an explanation.

"But what's wrong with that Harry?" asked the puzzled producer.

"What's wrong with it?" Cohn scoffed. "I'll show you." He pressed a buzzer to summon his secretary, at that time a long-suffering young man.

"Yes, Mr. Cohn," said the secretary.

"Let me ask you," said Cohn. "When I ask you to do something, do I ever say please?"

"No, Mr. Cohn, you never do," was the answer.

Cohn gazed exultantly at the producer and writer and said, "See!"

Cohn often summoned top studio employees and gave them a dressing down as an exercise in authority. A favorite victim was Rudy Maté, a director-cameraman of whom Cohn was personally fond. Yet Cohn was impelled to berate Maté on occasion. Maté, a gentle, sensitive man, became tongue-tied during these outbursts of Cohn's and could barely stammer his replies.

While Maté was directing a film, he received the inevitable call to visit Cohn, and he stood before the inquisition with his usual nervousness. As Cohn continued the tirade over some minor infraction, Maté felt the need to wipe away the sweat that was accumulating on his forehead. The director had a habit of picking up nails on his movie sets and fingering them in his pocket as a symptom of nervousness. As he pulled out his handkerchief, several nails clattered to the floor.

"You son of a bitch," Cohn continued, "you're also stealing my nails!"

Fashioning a script about big business, a writer needed a grandiloquent speech for a tycoon to deliver to his board of directors. The writer reached back into his childhood and chose Spartacus' oration to the gladiators. When the script pages arrived at Cohn's desk, he sent for the writer and his producer.

"What the hell is this?" Cohn asked.

The writer tried to explain the historical background of the oration, but Cohn grew impatient.

"I don't want any of that crap," he declared. "I want a speech that every person in the audience will recognize immediately."

"You mean like Hamlet's soliloquy?" suggested the writer.

"No, no!" said Cohn. "I mean something like 'To be or not to be'!"

All Columbia workers were trained to assume attitudes of intense activity when word spread that Harry Cohn was headed in their direction. Film cutters were especially alert. Upon hearing that he had left his office, they scurried off the iron balconies where they smoked and talked shop. An exception was a young cutter from New York who had no fear of Harry Cohn or anyone else.

One day as Cohn approached, the other cutters vanished inside the cutting-room doors. Only the young New Yorker remained in sight; he was nonchalantly shaving with an electric razor.

Cohn strode by with his usual deliberate pace until he heard the electric hum above him. He looked up and saw the cutter shaving himself.

"What the hell are you doing, shaving your beard on company time?" Cohn demanded.

"Well, I grew it on company time," replied the cutter.

"That's very funny," Cohn replied. "And you're a very independent young man. You're fired."

Once each year Harry Cohn endured the ritual of the Christmas Eve party in his office. It was the one day of the year when the barrier between boss and workers was down. Cohn had no relish for the event, since one or more workers inevitably got drunk and tried to bawl out the boss. Cohn was uneasy under this reversal of circumstances, and it was one of the few occasions when he had several drinks himself, in order to tolerate the proceedings.

Writer James Poe brought his secretary to a Christmas party in Cohn's office. She was a singularly buxom and unintelligent young woman, and she was soon the object of attention from the bolder males who filled the long office.

Cohn himself took note of the secretary, and he led her by the hand to his desk, where he installed her in his own chair. Her large bust was outlined in a tight sweater, and Cohn stood behind the chair and swiveled it back and forth with machine-gun noises, as if he were spraying the room with bullets.

The celebrators in the room were amused by this horseplay, but Cohn tired of it. His voice rose in a manner that commanded the attention of everyone. "You've been in this studio long enough to know who you like and who you don't like," he said. "I'll tell you what I'm going to do. I'm going to let you point out anyone in the room, and I'll fire him. That'll be your Christmas present."

The room suddenly fell silent and everyone studied Cohn to determine if he were truly joking. He wore an enigmatic smile that gave no hint of his intention, but the threat seemed real enough to make several people ease toward the door.

"Close the door!" Cohn ordered. "Nobody leaves." He spoke to the secretary: "Now, young lady, who will it be? Anyone you say—just point him out to me."

All eyes studied the blank face of the secretary as she gazed about the room. Then she giggled and said, "Gosh, Mr. Cohn, I just love everybody."

"Aw, get the hell out of my chair," said Cohn disgustedly, and the frivolity resumed.

Harry Cohn preferred simple food, and when he was in New York, his favorite restaurants were Lindy's and Gallagher's. The urbane Nate Spingold was always seeking to improve Cohn's habits and attitudes, and he urged Cohn to try the more elegant meals at Le Pavillon.

"After all, you're staying at the St. Regis," Spingold reasoned, "Le Pavillon is right across the street in the Columbia building. Why go all the way over to Fifty-first and Broadway to eat at Lindy's, when one of the great restaurants of the world is within a few steps?"

Spingold offered to make a reservation, and Cohn grudgingly agreed to try Le Pavillon.

Cohn arrived for dinner and was ushered to a table near the kitchen. Observing the parade of dirty dishes that went past the table, Cohn asked his waiter to send over Henri Soulé, operator of the restaurant. The waiter replied that Monsieur Soulé did not speak to ordinary diners.

"Yeah?" said Cohn. "'Well, tell him his landlord wants to talk to him."

The waiter returned with the message that Monsieur Soulé was not available. Cohn stood up and marched out of the place.

As he passed Soulé, he muttered, "I'm going to look into your lease."

On the following day Soulé was notified that his monthly rental of $17,500 would henceforth be doubled. Furthermore, he would be denied the use of his wine cellar; Harry Cohn had decided that Columbia needed the space to store film. During return visits to Le Pavillon, Cohn was accorded special attention by Soulé.

On rare occasions Harry Cohn assumed the unnatural role of peacemaker. Having formed a close friendship with Charles Feldman, Cohn tried to seek accord between Feldman and Louis B. Mayer, who had banished the agent from M-G-M.

After much persuasion, Cohn convinced Feldman to accompany him on a peace mission to Mayer's office. The two men drove to Culver City in Cohn's Rolls-Royce, and Cohn delivered words of advice during the journey.

"When I started out in this business," said Cohn, "I let anyone spit on me as long as I got what I wanted. One time I had to beg for money to meet the studio payroll. I would kowtow to anyone, so I could keep the company going. You're starting out in business, and you can't afford to make an enemy of a powerful man like Louie B. Now I want you to go up to his desk and shake his hand and tell him how sorry you are."

Feldman followed Cohn's instructions up to that point. Then Mayer made a slighting remark, and the meeting ended in a fistfight between Mayer and Feldman. Cohn pulled them apart, and he drove back to Gower Street with resolutions to avoid the peacemaking role in the future.

13
A PUBLIC VIEW OF THE "FICTITIOUS, FABULOUS, TOPSY-TURVY, TEMPERAMENTAL WORLD"

*H*arry Cohn's most notable excursion into the public consciousness came in 1946, when a lawsuit was brought against him by Charles Vidor, Columbia director. For the first time Cohn's conversational style and business methods were exposed to full public view, affording a commentary on the operations of a studio dictator. It was a spectacle that shook the foundation of the Columbia Pictures Corporation and the power structure of Hollywood.

Charles Vidor was a handsome, brilliant Hungarian, who possessed the legendary Hungarian faculties for charm and opportunism. He had worked in German studios before he came to Hollywood during the invasion of European film creators of the 1920's. He had directed minor films at M-G-M, Paramount, and RKO before he went to Columbia in 1939.

Cohn was quick to see Vidor's promise and gave him increasingly important films: *Ladies in Retirement* with Louis Hayward and Ida Lupino; *Adam Had Four Sons* with Warner Baxter and Ingrid Bergman; *Together Again* with Irene Dunne and Charles Boyer. During the first half of the 1940's Vidor became Columbia's most serviceable director. Although he lacked the originality of Capra or Stevens, he was more versatile than either of them. He could invest quality in a musical like *Cover Girl*, a costume romance like *A Song to Remember*, or a comedy like *Over 21*. Most valuable of all, he evoked creditable performances from Rita Hayworth, as he demonstrated in *Gilda*.

Vidor had married well. He was husband to Karen Morley and Evelyn Keyes while each was a prominent actress in films.

With his next wife, he ascended to the very citadel of Hollywood power; she was Doris Warner Le Roy, daughter of Harry Warner, president of Warner Brothers.

The love-hate that marked many of Harry Cohn's relationships was nowhere more evident than in his dealings with Charles Vidor. The two men were often on the most intimate terms socially. They were also capable of the most violent encounters in matters of studio business.

His marriage to the Warner heiress increased Vidor's discontent with his Columbia contract and he sought means of escape. He filed suit against Columbia Pictures for release from his contract and $78,000 in damages. His contention: Cohn had employed abusive language against him and had overstepped his rights as an employer.

Important figures in the film world attempted to dissuade Vidor from his suit, reasoning that Hollywood's reputation would suffer because of the disclosures. But Vidor was adamant, and the Warner dynasty appeared eager to have the litigation successfully concluded. The case was called on December 9, 1946, before Federal Judge Ben Harrison, an austere man from provincial California who was unfamiliar with the sophisticated language and erratic dealings of the film milieu.

The aggrieved Vidor was the first to take the witness stand. He recited the words of abuse that Cohn had hurled at him, and the testimony was explicit enough to cause several women to leave the courtroom. Vidor declared that on one occasion Cohn told him, "You're a Hungarian ———-—— who would do anything for money."

Judge Harrison was visibly pained by the repetition of the obscenities. He asked Vidor how long he had endured such epithets. When the director answered that it had been almost three years, the judge asked, "And you took the insults all these years?"

"Yes," said Vidor, "I always thought he was joking."

He was asked if he had complained to other studio officials. Yes, he had protested to Virginia Van Upp and Ben Kahane and had been told merely to stay away from Cohn. Vidor had also taken his grievance to Jack Cohn. The brother's reply: "Oh, I've been taking the same from that ——--—— for many years. What do you expect from him?"

Vidor seemed to indicate the real seeds of his discontent when he discussed Cohn's opposition to his marriage to Doris Warner Le Roy. "He said the most terrible things about Doris," complained Vidor, who then proceeded to repeat what Cohn had said. Observers of the trial theorized that therein Vidor lost his entire case, only minutes after he had begun it. Judge Harrison bristled as he heard the Hungarian director repeat in open court the accusations against his wife.

"He called me into his office on October 10, 1945, and told me she would ruin my career," Vidor testified. "Cohn said, 'You're putting yourself in an icebox. Her family will drive you crazy. Her father will drive you crazy. Her aunts will drive you crazy, and you will blow your brains out if you marry her.'"

"Did you defend the girl?" the judge asked.

"How can you defend a person against such statements?" Vidor replied. "I loved her."

Later Cohn shifted strategy, Vidor testified, and he wanted to be best man at the wedding. Vidor refused. But he did want to borrow $25,000 from Cohn (a revelation that also mitigated against Vidor's case). Cohn refused, but he offered a $50,000 wedding present if Vidor extended his contract another eighteen months. Vidor refused.

Vidor continued outlining the Cohn iniquities. Cohn invited Vidor and his bride to dinner at the studio, but when the Vidors arrived a few minutes late, he became so incensed he instructed his secretary to "give him a drink and throw him out." The Vidors left and refused Cohn's orders to return. The next day Cohn accused Vidor's wife of insulting Mrs. Cohn by not appearing for dinner.

Once, said Vidor, Cohn told Mrs. Vidor on a movie set, "You know, this guy has never been faithful to any woman. If I see him look at another woman, I'm going to call you."

Vidor added that Cohn accused him during the making of *Gilda* of using too much film, quitting early, and shooting excessive retakes. The director added, "I told Mr. Cohn that the delays were due to the fact that Miss Hayworth got tired at five o'clock in the afternoon and was unable to give her best performances. I also told him that his abuse was upsetting me, that I could not sleep, that I had to have doctors give me injections, and that I was very nervous."

Cohn's assemblage of attorneys attempted to damage the Vidor testimony in cross-examination. Didn't Vidor want his release so he could make films for Warner Brothers? He denied it. Didn't Vidor once borrow $4,400 from Cohn and not repay it? He had. Hadn't Cohn refrained from calling Vidor any bad names for a fifteen-month period following *A Song to Remember*? He had.

On the second day of the trial Judge Harrison indicated his growing impatience with the remark to attorneys: "We've got to get this thing over as this man [Vidor] is earning two thousand dollars a week, and we can't afford to waste his time."

Vidor's agent, Bert Allenberg, testified that the director had been assigned a minor film, *Johnny O'Clock*, as punishment by Cohn.

"Can a director pick and choose a picture at his own pleasure?" the judge asked. "Hasn't his employer anything to say about it?"

Allenberg tried to explain how directing a cheap film would be a demotion, but Judge Harrison cut him off with: "You're wasting the court's time in testimony such as this." When the Cohn lawyers protested that *Johnny O'Clock* cost more than $1,000,000, he added, "I don't care if it cost only four bits. You're still wasting the court's time."

Another agent, Milton Bren, testified to the vile names he had heard Cohn call Vidor and his wife. The judge bristled. "I wouldn't believe a witness who would carry such a tale. A man who would do that isn't a man, even if it's true. Court's adjourned."

Vidor's attorney, Martin Gang, protested that he had another question to ask Bren.

"Ask it tomorrow, if you wish, but I won't believe it," said Judge Harrison, leaving the bench.

Mrs. Vidor, pregnant with her first child by Vidor, took the stand on the following day to describe how Cohn had warned that Vidor would maltreat her if she married him. She had replied, "If he hits me, I'll hit him back." Cohn's comment: "Well, he's a Hungarian, and you don't know him as well as I know him. He's had affairs with every woman on this lot—all my actresses." Mrs. Vidor repeated the incident of "give him a drink and throw him out."

There was an air of expectancy as the time arrived for Harry Cohn to testify. It was virtually the first public appearance of the legendary film magnate, and the press was alert to the significance of the event. Cohn had always avoided contacts with newspapermen, but before testifying, he visited the press room of the Federal Building and exerted his charm on the reporters. He had the prudence to send a case of bourbon and a case of Scotch to newsmen covering the trial.

Cohn offered disparate versions of incidents Vidor related in his testimony. Cohn testified he offered the director $50,000 if he would extend his contract eighteen months, and Vidor first accepted, then rejected the deal. Instead, he asked for the loan of $25,000 "because that way I won't have to pay any income tax."

Cohn said that when he protested, "But Charlie, you'll have a note outstanding," the director replied, "What's the difference? I'll never pay it anyway."

The $25,000 was never lent.

As for the office incident, Cohn testified: "When I walked in, Mr. and Mrs. Vidor were sitting on the couch necking. I said, 'Charlie, if you want to do that, go in the other room.' I was kidding. I went over to my secretary, who was mixing drinks, and said, 'Go on, give them a drink and throw them out.' I was still joking. Mr. and Mrs. Vidor got up and walked out, but I didn't pay any attention to that. I thought they'd gone upstairs to the dining room."

Cohn added that he had received complaints of Vidor's behavior on sets from such actors as Gene Kelly, Phil Silvers, Jess Barker, and Paul Muni. After having worked nights to perfect a dance number for *Cover Girl*, Kelly performed it, only to have Vidor turn his back and walk away afterward. Said Cohn, "I told Mr. Vidor that was a hell of a way to treat an artist."

Judge Harrison seemed as intrigued by the impressive figure of Harry Cohn as were the other spectators in the courtroom. The judge listened intently as Cohn described the atmosphere in the executive dining room: "It was a kind of freemasonry. Everybody said what they liked. They could bawl out the boss, too." He denied having fired anyone for what had been said in the dining room.

Cohn was asked if he ever used bad language to Vidor.

"Oh, I might have called him a Hungarian son of a bitch," said Cohn, "but we were good friends. That's the way I expressed my friendship."

"Did he express his friendship the same way?" the court inquired.

"Sure. The same way. That's the kind of relationship we had."

"Did he call you a Hungarian?"

"No. I am not a Hungarian."

Judge Harrison grew impatient when Vidor's lawyers tried to introduce twenty-three variations of "son of a bitch" employed by Harry Cohn.

"It is very apparent that Mr. Cohn uses language which is no credit to himself or the motion picture industry," said the court. "He uses this language to accomplish whatever he has in mind. Some persons pass out salve, with an occasional pat on the back. But Mr. Cohn figures to use rough language to gain his ends."

The defense brought forth a parade of Columbia executives to establish that Cohn's language to Vidor was not unusual. Ben Kahane explained that Cohn's use of "son of a bitch" was elemental, and he illustrated by examples of employment of the phrase: (1) to express surprise: "I'll be a son of a bitch!" (2) as a superlative: "It's a son of a bitch of a scene!" and (3) to express exasperation: "You stubborn son of a bitch!"

Sidney Buchman testified that Cohn had called him a son of a bitch, but he had learned to parry such epithets with irony. D. A. Doran admitted that he had acquired a case of ulcers while employed by Cohn; Doran added that he considered them an occupational hazard. Max Arnow declared that he himself had called Cohn a son of a bitch, yet he remained under employment at Columbia.

Joan Perry Cohn took the stand to confirm her husband's version of the affair in the office. Then she donned horn-rimmed glasses to quote from her household log, a large volume bound in red morocco. It revealed that the Vidors had dined at the Cohn house eight times before and after their marriage. In addition, the Cohns and Vidors had dined out together on several occasions.

Vidor's lawyers brought forth a Universal executive, Rufus LeMaire, in an attempt to refute Cohn's testimony about the dining room. LeMaire said he indeed had been fired by Cohn after this exchange over lunch:

Cohn: "Hey, LeMaire, I bet you didn't vote today, did you? I know you didn't vote. You couldn't register because you can't write!"

LeMaire: "It seems to me you ought to go to school, too. You might learn how to be president of the company."

Cohn admitted the exchange but said LeMaire was not fired; he resigned.

Even Frank Capra, long departed from Columbia, was called to testify. Vidor had claimed that Cohn had spitefully barred Mrs. Vidor from the preview of *Gilda*; Cohn declared wives were banned from previews by company policy. Capra testified that he had always taken his wife to previews during his years at Columbia.

Two actors ended the testimony. Stephen Geray declared that during the filming of *Gilda*, Vidor berated him about his performance in a scene. When Geray tried to explain, Vidor shouted, "Shut up, goddammit!" and took him in a corner to continue the attack in Hungarian.

Glenn Ford confirmed the Geray incident and added that there were several goddammits from Vidor during *Gilda*, "addressed mostly to the little people on the set who couldn't answer him."

The testimony was over, and Judge Harrison expressed relief, declaring that he didn't know why the two parties hadn't consulted psychiatrists instead of lawyers. He sighed, "I don't know whether this is a lawsuit or a publicity stunt."

There could be no doubt that he lacked sympathy for the plaintiff. He shot a hard glance at Vidor and commented, "A man who is willing to smear his wife's reputation to break his contract is just as bad as the one who uses vulgar language. Cohn at least denied making statements against Mrs. Vidor."

After having deliberated for nine days, Judge Harrison did indeed decide against Charles Vidor. The verdict: "The court finds that Harry Cohn was accustomed to and in the habit of using obscene language in talking to Mr. Vidor and others. Such language was part of Mr. Cohn's speaking vocabulary. It was used by him as superlative adjectives, not intended by him as insulting or used for the purpose of humiliating the plaintiff, and the plaintiff so understood that."

The judge suspected that Vidor had filed the suit merely because he found the contract no longer attractive. The peroration summed up the entire affair: "Both [Cohn and Vidor] inhabit a fictitious, fabulous, topsy-turvy, temperamental world that is peculiar to their way of life. Their standards are not my standards. Let them be judged by those people of decency who inhabit their world of fantasy and fiction."

It was to be expected that Harry Cohn would devise an exquisite punishment when Vidor's appeals failed and he was forced to return to his Columbia contract. Cohn assigned Vidor to direct *The Man from Colorado*, a Western starring William Holden and Glenn Ford, the actor who had testified against the director in the trial.

The first meeting between Ford and Vidor took place at Billingsley's, a Sunset Boulevard restaurant where Columbia employees lunched. Ford offered his hand in reconciliation. "I'd rather shovel garbage," Vidor spat.

Cohn made the most of the incident, hoping that Ford would insist on removal of Vidor as director. But the producer of *The Man from Colorado*, Jules Schermer, convinced Ford to endure Vidor's ill-treatment. When shooting began, Vidor refused to speak to the actor. Instead, he instructed the assistant director or wardrobe man, "Would you tell Mr. Ford to stand over here?"

Cohn admitted that Vidor, with his control of the filming, held the advantage. "You watch," he told an aide. "That Hungarian will find some way to —— me up."

The prediction proved correct. Columbia directors were barred from printing more than one take of any camera angle. Vidor printed take after take of the same scene, altering the camera angle to a slight degree each time. As the interminable variations of the same scene played in the projection room, Cohn became increasingly furious.

Finally, he suspended Vidor with the explanation that *The Man from Colorado* was thirteen days behind schedule after twenty-two days of shooting. Vidor was replaced by Henry Levin.

Vidor employed the same device on other films and was replaced by Levin. Once Vidor passed Levin in the hall of the executive building and announced, "I'm starting our new picture next Monday."

The attrition continued until Cohn in fury assigned Vidor to direct a twelve-day *Crime Doctor* picture. Before the film could be made, Cohn was convinced by his top advisers that the feud was harming studio operations. Vidor was offered a new contract that would allow him to produce independently for Columbia release. He accepted with one proviso: Harry Cohn would have to apologize to him.

Cohn fretted about the apology for days. Then one Friday he called a Columbia writer, Michael Blankfort. "Get your things; you're coming on the yacht with me this weekend," Cohn said. He added with a note of irritation, "I have to apologize to Vidor. I want you to be my witness."

Blankfort reported to the main entrance at six that evening, bag in hand. Vidor was also there with his bag, and Cohn breezed through with the command, "Let's go."

The three men entered Cohn's limousine, and Cohn and Vidor sat at opposite sides of the back seat. Blankfort took his position between them. As the limousine drove southward to the harbor at San Pedro, not a word was spoken.

Finally, Vidor made a comment about the weather. Silence resumed. Cohn remarked about the traffic. Again, silence.

As they neared the dock where the *Jobella* was moored, Cohn turned to Vidor and said, "They tell me I'm supposed to apologize. If you think I'm going to say I'm sorry, you're out of your ——ing mind."

Vidor smiled victoriously. Cohn's admission of his obligation was all that Vidor needed, and he said, "That's all right, Harry."

When the limousine arrived before the dock, Cohn said to Blankfort, "You're the witness; you heard me apologize." Then Cohn announced to both, "I don't need you two this weekend; I've done what I had to do." He sent the two men back to Hollywood.

The uneasy truce lasted two years, during which time Vidor directed Rita Hayworth and Glenn Ford in *The Loves of Carmen*. The old antagonisms erupted again, and Vidor threatened another public airing of the methods of Harry Cohn. To prevent another scandalous trial, Louis B. Mayer acted as peacemaker and arranged a settlement by which Vidor purchased his freedom for $75,000.

A curious figure in the entire Cohn-Vidor affair—and its principal victim—was Lewis Meltzer.

His history with Columbia dated back to *Golden Boy*, which he and Daniel Taradash had been imported from Broadway to write. When Meltzer had been at the studio for two months, he was overcome by curiosity to meet the legendary president of Columbia. Cohn agreed to an appointment.

The writer walked directly to Cohn's desk and leaned across it to shake hands. This startled Cohn, whose passion for cleanliness prompted him to avoid handshaking; the wide desk between him and visitors allowed him to avoid it.

After a few disparaging remarks about the "Armenian rug peddler," as Cohn termed Rouben Mamoulian, Cohn asked Meltzer, "What are you?"

"I'm an American and a Jew," the writer answered.

"I like that: American first," said Cohn. He asked Meltzer more about himself, then announced, "Okay, don't kill it; the conference is over."

"Wait a minute," Meltzer interjected. "'What about you? Tell me about the *Hall Room Boys* and all that."

Cohn was taken aback, but he launched into a reminiscence of his early days on Poverty Row. As he spoke, Meltzer interrupted with: "Want a Coke, Harry?" The startled Cohn shook his head. Meltzer disappeared down the hall and returned with a bottle of Coca-Cola, which he gulped as Cohn continued his account of the C.B.C. era.

Meltzer was Cohn's kind of man: imaginative, erratic, fearless, fallible. After *Golden Boy*, Meltzer remained under contract, whereas Taradash was released.

Meltzer proved to be an extremely facile and versatile screenwriter, if an unpredictable one. His penchant for riotous living sometimes made his output sporadic, but during periods of productivity he was amazingly prolific. His inventiveness caught the attention of Charles Vidor, when he was a rising director at Columbia, and Vidor insisted that Meltzer work on all his scripts. The two men became close friends.

One noontime Vidor and Meltzer were locked in serious and confidential conversation. Harry Cohn demanded to know what they were talking about. Meltzer admitted it concerned the fact that he was $10,000 in debt. Later Cohn sent for Meltzer and handed him a check for $10,000.

"Take this, and pay off your debts," Cohn ordered. "I make you only one condition: that Milt Pickman, who advises me on management, will be your manager and straighten out your affairs. One other thing—cash that check right away, and forget about it. If you mention it to anyone, I'll deny it."

Meltzer's resolves to live a better life lasted for a while, but then he returned to his familiar ways. He became restive under his Columbia contract, especially since Cohn was lending him to other studios at a profit. Meltzer repeatedly asked for a release from the contract, but Cohn refused. When an offer came from Paramount for double his $1,000 salary, Meltzer employed the last resort to achieve his freedom from Columbia. He went to the office of the president and insulted his wife.

"Why did you say that?" Cohn demanded.

"So you'd break my contract," Meltzer said.

"It's broken."

Before Meltzer left the office, Cohn shook his hand for the second time in their acquaintance. "You had a good time here," Cohn said sadly. "You learned a lot. You could be one of the greatest writers and producers in the business if you weren't such a bum."

Meltzer turned to leave. As he went out the door, Cohn called to him, "Dress nice. Let the other studios know we trained you well here."

The change of studios did not improve Meltzer's habits. In 1946 he was living at the Garden of Allah Apartments, earning $2,000 a week and dying from malnutrition. He preferred to drink, and by the time that doctors were called in, there appeared to be little chance to save him.

A constant visitor during his illness was Charles Vidor. One day Vidor came by the Garden of Allah and remarked, "Lew, I'm in terrible trouble."

"Look who's in trouble!" Meltzer cracked.

"I'm serious, Lew," Vidor insisted. "I'm suing Harry Cohn to break my contract, and I can't get anyone to testify for me. Will you do it?"

"What the hell could I say?"

"That Harry Cohn caused you to have a nervous breakdown."

"Oh, hell. I went to the hospital—sure. But it was only to get away from the studio. I'll testify for you, but get me something logical."

"I'm also charging that Cohn used obscene language."

"I'll testify to that. But I think you're crazy. I think you're both crazy."

Vidor wanted Meltzer to come to court on a stretcher, but the writer refused such "theatrics." Although his doctors protested, Meltzer agreed to a deposition. "What's the difference? I'm dying anyway," he said.

Rumors of the deposition reached Harry Cohn. He called Meltzer to demand, "Are you going to testify against me?"

"Sure" said Meltzer. "If you had asked me first, I would have testified against Charlie. You both use the same language. The whole thing is child's play."

Cohn was to remember Meltzer's treachery. A few years later Meltzer was signed to a high-paying contract to write a series of

Alan Ladd pictures that were to be made independently in Europe and released by Columbia. Cohn was ready to abrogate the deal unless Meltzer was removed. Meltzer withdrew.

Meltzer had survived malnutrition, but his health failed once again. Doctors despaired for his life unless he could be treated with a new drug that had been developed by the Schenley Distillers. The Korean War was under way, and the military had tied up supplies of the drug. Meltzer's physician reasoned that the only man who would be able to acquire some of the drug was Harry Cohn.

"I'm not going to beg him," said Meltzer.

The physician telephoned Cohn and told him the urgency of the matter. "What he did was stupid," said the physician, "but that doesn't matter now. He's dying, and that medicine is the only thing that can save him."

"I couldn't care less," said Cohn. But on the following day the medicine arrived by air. Cohn refused payment for the expense, nor would he admit that he had acquired the drug.

Meltzer escaped death once more and returned to screenwriting. Years later he was invited by William Goetz to write a Joan Crawford vehicle, *Autumn Leaves*, one of several films Goetz was producing for Columbia. Meltzer doubted that he would be allowed to work for Columbia, and he asked for an appointment with Harry Cohn.

"Come right up," said Cohn.

When Meltzer arrived in the long office, he noted that Cohn had no one else with him; it was his usual custom to have witnesses present during negotiations.

"Sit down," Cohn said jauntily. "I understand you're going to work for Bill Goetz."

"Only if it's okay with you," Meltzer said.

"Why?" asked Cohn.

"It's your studio."

"Look—I don't butt into Bill Goetz's business. You're welcome here. I want you to feel at home."

Meltzer was astounded, but he was more so when Cohn said, "I want you to help me get Charlie back."

Meltzer gazed at him in disbelief. "I'll be a son of a bitch!" he said. "You want Charlie Vidor back? What about what happened ten years ago?"

"Oh, that's in the past," Cohn replied. "I never let bygones interfere with business, and we could use Charlie back here."

Through Meltzer, Cohn resumed his relationship with Vidor, and the two men were discussing film projects as Cohn's career ended. The Cohns and the Vidors became good friends once more, just as if the spectacle in Judge Harrison's courtroom had never occurred.

14

ALL THE KING'S MEN
HELPS PUT HUMPTY-DUMPTY
BACK TOGETHER AGAIN

*T*he corporate structure of Columbia Pictures suffered a tremor in 1948, as did all film companies. After an all-time high of $3,706,541 during fiscal 1947, Columbia profits suddenly plummeted to $500,000. Blame was placed on the increasing costs of studio labor and the nation's preoccupation with television. But there were also rumblings in the East that Harry Cohn had lost his touch. In truth, it had been two years since Cohn had been able to conjure an attraction that could electrify the industry. By now Columbia had assumed the proportions of a major company, with a contract list of players, writers, and directors that approached those of the bigger concerns, and there were indications that Columbia was producing the same kind of standardized product that had long emanated from the majors.

Harry Cohn had in no way mellowed, and with the end of the postwar boom he once again explored the bounds of creativity that had been the source of Columbia's vitality in the past. Cohn had long admired the work of Robert Rossen, who had written a string of impressive screenplays during eight years at Warner Brothers. When Cohn was having script problems with *Johnny O'Clock,* a vehicle for Dick Powell, he sent for Rossen. Both Cohn and Powell liked Rossen's work on the script. They agreed to let him direct it, Charles Vidor having refused the assignment.

Word circulated that Rossen had performed creditably, and Charles Einfeld of the newly formed Enterprise Pictures considered him to direct John Garfield in *Body and Soul.* But first Einfeld asked Cohn for permission to view *Johnny O'Clock.*

"—— you," Cohn replied. "I never saw any film by Rossen; I took a chance on him. Why shouldn't you?"

Cohn admitted to Rossen later that he would have been willing to show the film to Einfeld. Rossen was hired by Einfeld, and his direction of *Body and Soul* provided the best film ever made about boxing.

Rossen had sought to buy *All the King's Men*, a novel based on the Huey Long saga, by Robert Penn Warren. Before he could acquire it, the book had won the Pulitzer Prize. *All the King's Men* was purchased by Columbia at the instigation of Nate Spingold, who suggested that the company's sagging prestige would profit from such a property. The purchase price was $250,000.

When Cohn suggested that Rossen return to Columbia, the director said he would do so only if he could make *All the King's Men*. Cohn gave him the assignment.

Cohn was considering Spencer Tracy for the role of Willie Stark, the Southern demagogue, but Rossen argued for a lesser-known actor. The director had been influenced by *Open City* and other neorealistic films of Italy, and he was determined to make *All the King's Men* without the usual trappings of a Hollywood production. Rossen had seen Broderick Crawford in *Of Mice and Men* on Broadway and favored him for the role. Eastern executives opposed the casting, arguing that a top star was needed as box office insurance for such a controversial film. Crawford was a character actor most noted for Universal westerns.

Cohn permitted Rossen to test Crawford. The actor was prepared for the challenge. He delivered two and a half pages of forceful dialogue with such vitality that Rossen failed to note that the camera had run out of film.

"I don't need to see the rushes," the director announced. You're Willie."

"I'll believe it when I see it in the papers," Crawford answered dubiously.

Cohn was impressed with Crawford's test. The actor was so eager to play the role that he cut his usual salary in half and signed a term contract. The next day he was on his way to the location at Stockton.

Rossen had written a script for submission to the Columbia executives. On the train north he threw it out the window. He reasoned that he couldn't improve on a Pulitzer Prize novel, so he commenced shooting the film from the book.

The studio hierarchy became alarmed as the rushes arrived from the Stockton location. Rossen was filming scenes that were nowhere to be found in the finished script. The photography had none of the polish of the usual Columbia product. What's more, many of the performances by townspeople recruited by Rossen were downright amateurish.

Cohn took note of the criticisms and forwarded them to Rossen. The director exploded, firing off an angry telegram in reply. Cohn telephoned him.

"What you're saying is 'Go —— yourself,'" Cohn suggested.

"That's right," said Rossen.

"Okay, go ahead with the picture."

Cohn had faith in the project for a simple reason: he understood Willie Stark. He and Willie were similar in more ways than their passion for power. Indeed, Rossen injected Cohn characteristics into Crawford's Willie, particularly Cohn's method of working one person against another during conferences.

Rossen completed *All the King's Men* for less than $1,000,000, receiving only $25,000 for his services as writer, director, and producer. When the film was assembled, Rossen believed it had a chance for the Academy Awards. He urged Cohn to release the film in Los Angeles before the year-end deadline for Academy consideration.

"Okay," said Cohn, "but don't expect me to put on a campaign."

Rossen himself paid for some publicity, but the reviews were such that little was needed. A few weeks later Cohn telephoned Rossen to say, "I just thought I'd tell you that much to my surprise *All the King's Men* won the best-picture award of the New York Film Critics."

All the King's Men went into the Academy Awards as the favorite, but Harry Cohn declined to attend. He told Rossen, "It's your show."

Academy voters named *All the King's Men* the best picture of 1949 and also gave awards to Broderick Crawford as best actor and Mercedes McCambridge as best supporting actress. The achievement began a renaissance of quality that brought new glory and profits to Columbia Pictures in the following decade.

15
DEALINGS WITH ACTORS: RONALD COLMAN, ROSALIND RUSSELL, MARILYN MONROE, LUCILLE BALL, LORETTA YOUNG, DAVID NIVEN

*D*id Harry Cohn insult Ronald Colman? Indeed he had, said Colman. His wife, the actress Benita Hume, agreed. Harry Cohn said he didn't give a damn whether he had or he hadn't.

Colman had reluctantly returned to Columbia for *Talk of the Town*; he feared that his role would be overshadowed by those of his costars, Cary Grant and Jean Arthur. But because of the sensitive direction of George Stevens, Colman had enjoyed making the film.

After *Talk of the Town* had been completed, Cary Grant requested a private showing for himself and his bride, Barbara Hutton. Harry Cohn grudgingly assented to the use of his private projection room, a privilege he disliked granting to anyone, particularly actors. Colman heard about the showing and was invited by Grant to attend.

When Colman and his wife arrived at Cohn's office at the hour for the screening, Cohn summarily sent out word that they would not be admitted.

Colman was offended by Cohn's action, and his feelings were expressed through intermediaries to Cohn.

"Harry, you've got to apologize," said Stevens.

"That's right," agreed Sidney Buchman.

"Goddammit," snapped Cohn, "why should I get down on my knees to an *actor*?"

Stevens and Buchman continued their arguments that the

president of Columbia Pictures could not afford to offend one of the screen's most distinguished actors. A telegram of abject apology was composed by Stevens and Buchman, and they finally persuaded Cohn to sign it.

On the following day Colman telephoned Cohn's office for an appointment. He said that he and his wife wanted to drop in on their "old friend."

Colman told Cohn upon his arrival, "Over the many years I have spent in the motion picture business, I have never met an executive with your graciousness and sensitivity."

Cohn delighted in quoting Colman's remark for months afterward.

Harry Cohn thrived on combat, but he seldom enjoyed fighting with women, who employed tears and other unfair weapons. In Rosalind Russell he found a splendid adversary, and the pair jousted fondly over a twenty-year period.

Their admiration for each other was apparent but unexpressed. Cohn liked her professionalism, her adherence to principle. She was impressed by his zest for picture making, by his uncanny taste. Both profited from the association, in such films as *Craig's Wife, His Girl Friday*, and *My Sister Eileen*.

After completing a Columbia picture during the war, the actress was anxious to embark on an entertainment tour of Army camps. She went to Harry Cohn to request use of the gowns she had worn in the film. They were glamorous creations by Irene that were well designed for service audiences.

Miss Russell began the conversation with a peroration she sometimes employed in negotiations with Cohn: "Now, Harry, we're going to have a little talk. Let's just speak in a normal manner and not raise our voices. Don't try to outshout me because I have one of the most powerful voices in the history of the theater; I could be heard in the highest balcony. So just keep your voice down."

Cohn reacted instinctively with an expletive, causing Miss Russell to caution, "My father used to say that swearing was a sign of a limited vocabulary. So let's just stop that."

She then told of her mission.

"No clothes," he replied flatly. "No clothes are going out of this studio."

"Now you know I'm going to get those clothes," she replied calmly. "So why don't you just give in and save all the argument?"

"Don't you know there's a war on?" Cohn asked.

"Of course, I know there's a war on," Miss Russell replied. "That's why I'm going to the camps, and that's why I need the clothes."

"Impossible. Those fabrics are too hard to get. Rita Hayworth and Jean Arthur asked to buy the clothes they wore in pictures, and I turned them down."

"All right, Harry," she said, starting to leave. "Tomorrow morning it will be on page one of *Daily Variety* and *Hollywood Reporter* that Rosalind Russell had to cancel her camp tour because Harry Cohn refused to give her gowns for her appearances.

Cohn stared at her in disbelief. "You wouldn't do that," he said.

"Oh, yes, I would," she assured him. "That's how badly I need those gowns. They're just right for the boys—sexy but tasteful."

Cohn contemplated her threat and decided it was genuine.

"Wait a minute," he said, pushing a button that connected him with the wardrobe department. He asked her what outfits she wanted and she replied, "The gray traveling suit, black beaded dress, pinstripe suit, and white evening dress."

Cohn asked for the cost of the wardrobe. "All right," be said to Miss Russell, "you can have them for the full price—thirty-three hundred dollars and fifty cents."

"I want them now," she said.

Cohn ordered the wardrobe department to deliver the clothes to his office.

"Give me a blank check," she asked.

"Now she wants a check!" Cohn said in exasperation. "What am I running here—a bank?"

He produced a check, and she asked, "Whom shall I make it out to?"

"Not to Harry Cohn; to Columbia Pictures!" Cohn instructed. She completed the check and said, "Okay, bring in the clothes." They arrived, and she started to depart with them. Then she paused.

"Just a minute," Miss Russell said. "You know, I thought you might be difficult about this. It so happens that in the picture I wore my own fur coat. I went to a fur company—the same fur company that makes your wife's coats—and I asked them how much rent they would get for a fur like mine. They told me a hundred dollars a day. I wore it in the picture for twenty-seven days, so that comes to a rental of twenty-seven hundred dollars."

His anger rising, Cohn rang for the production manager on the film and asked if her report was true. He was assured that Miss Russell had worn her fur in the picture.

"I'd like the check, please," the actress said sweetly.

"Doesn't your agent pick up your checks?" Cohn asked.

"This one I'll take myself, thank you," she replied.

In a complete fury, Cohn scribbled out the check for $2,700. Miss Russell swept up the gowns and started for the door, fanning herself with the check.

As she went out the door, the red-faced Cohn shouted at her, "Jew!"

After she had been dropped by Twentieth Century-Fox in 1949, Marilyn Monroe was signed to a contract at Columbia for $175 a week. She was timorous and inexperienced, but Max Arnow, Columbia's talent executive, and others saw qualities of a starlike nature in her. Harry Cohn was unconvinced, but at that time Columbia was able to maintain a contract list of many such untrained girls.

Harry Romm, who was producing a B picture called *Ladies of the Chorus*, chose Marilyn for the role of a dancer who appeared in the same chorus with her mother, a former burlesque star, played by Adele Jergens.

Marilyn was placed under the tutelage of Fred Karger, a handsome young member of the music department. With gentleness and understanding, he coached her for long hours until he believed she was ready for the challenge of her two numbers, *Anyone Can Tell I Love You* and *Every Baby Needs a Da Da Daddy.*

Harry Cohn had issued the edict that all performers in *Ladies of the Chorus* would have to deliver their own songs, and he sent for Marilyn Monroe to determine her capability. Karger called for Marilyn at the modest room that was her home and drove her to the studio. By the time she arrived, she was quivering with fear, and she asked to be excused to make a telephone call. She called her Christian Science practitioner for words of encouragement. Then Karger took her to Cohn's office.

Cohn was gruff. "They tell me you can sing; well, Let's see if you can."

He sat defiantly behind his desk while the frightened girl stood beside the rickety piano at the far end of the room. Karger played an introduction, and she started her song.

"I can't hear her," Cohn complained.

Karger replied acidly, "There is such a thing as a microphone, you know."

He began the number again, and this time Cohn came from behind his desk to hear Marilyn. As he walked toward the piano, he brushed a folder that she had brought with her. It fell to the floor, and out dropped an issue of the *Christian Science Monitor.* Cohn's attitude changed immediately. His wife Rose had taken up Christian Science at one time, and he himself had dabbled in the religion. Now he was conciliatory toward the girl who sang frightenedly at the other end of the office, and he agreed that she could do her own singing in *Ladies of the Chorus.*

But when her sixth-month option came up, Cohn ordered her dropped from the contract list. "The girl can't act," he declared.

Some of his bolder associates never allowed Cohn to forget that he had dismissed Marilyn Monroe. After she had become a star, they sent him huge photographs of her with an inscription such as: "To my benefactor, Harry Cohn, Love, Marilyn."

The pranks so irritated Cohn that he later ordered Max Arnow, "Get me another blonde who can be a star."

After Lucille Ball had come to Hollywood as a Goldwyn Girl in 1933, she was signed to a term contract at Columbia Pictures at $75 a week. Her principal assignment was to play a foil for the Three Stooges in two-reel comedies. After three months an economy wave struck the studio, and she was discharged, along with the rest of the stock players.

She achieved stardom at RKO and M-G-M, then returned to Columbia in the late 1940's for three pictures at $85,000 apiece. She made two films produced by S. Sylvan Simon, *Miss Grant Takes Richmond* and *Fuller Brush Girl*, and was scheduled for another. Then Simon died, and the film was canceled.

Harry Cohn was anxious to escape paying Miss Ball for the third film. She was just as anxious to have him pay her. Meanwhile, she instructed her agent to search for another film. He found a promising one: *The Greatest Show on Earth*, to be produced and directed by Cecil B. DeMille.

The prospect of working with the great DeMille was a thrilling one for Miss Ball, and she was stimulated by her initial conferences with him. She assured him she could get free from her Columbia commitment in time to assume the role of the elephant trainer.

Miss Ball reported to Harry Cohn that she would like to postpone her commitment to Columbia so she could accept an outside picture; she did not reveal that it was for DeMille. Cohn refused to release her. Instead, he handed her a script of a Sam Katzman quickie called *The Magic Carpet*.

"That's your next picture," Cohn announced.

Miss Ball took the script home and read it. She was assigned to the role of a belly dancer in the featherweight Arabian Nights farce. She sought counsel from veteran director Edward Sedgwick.

"Cohn handed you a lease breaker," Sedgwick told her. "He expects you to turn it down; then he's automatically free of paying you eighty-five thousand dollars. Tell him you'll do the picture. It'll break Katzman. His whole budget is less than your salary."

Miss Ball telephoned Katzman and said, "This is Lucille Ball. I just read your script of *The Magic Carpet*, and I loved it. I'm ready to go to work."

"Oh, no!" Katzman exclaimed. "You don't want to make that picture!"

"Indeed I do. I'm sending you a letter to that effect tonight."

When Katzman was assured by mail that she intended to make the film, he invited her to confer with the writers. When she arrived for the appointment, she found the two men had no office at the studio. She met them by chance in the parking lot on Gower Street.

They were overjoyed that a star of Miss Ball's prominence would be appearing in their script and offered to write additional scenes for her.

"No, no, don't change a word," she insisted. "I like it just the way it is."

The Greatest Show on Earth was drawing closer to the start of production, and Miss Ball assured DeMille she would be able to report for it. She was outfitted with lavish costumes for the spectacle. Meanwhile, she was also being fitted with scanty harem outfits for *The Magic Carpet*. One day the Columbia designer, Jean Louis, noted that she was putting on weight.

"I guess I'll have to diet a little," she said.

But her weight continued to mount, and furthermore, the smell of bacon sickened her in the morning. She went to her doctor and heard the joyous news: she and Desi Arnaz were expecting their first baby after almost a decade of marriage.

"Don't tell anyone; don't even tell your nurse," Miss Ball instructed the doctor.

When she reported for the first day of work on *The Magic Carpet* the wardrobe woman commented, "My goodness, but you're putting on weight."

"Just let out the costume, honey," Miss Ball answered.

Her role extended only five days in the ten-day picture. After she had finished her final scene, she went home and telephoned Harry Cohn.

"Harry, this is Lucille Ball," she said.

"Yeah, what do you want?" he asked gruffly.

"I wanted you to be the first to know: I'm going to have a baby."

Cohn exploded. "Why, you son of a bitch, why the hell didn't you tell me before the picture?"

"I just found out, Harry."

All that remained was to relate the disappointing news to DeMille that she would be unable to appear in *The Greatest*

Show on Earth. She was accompanied to the confrontation by her husband and agent.

"What is all this?" DeMille asked.

"Mr. DeMille, I'm going to have a baby," Miss Ball announced.

"Well, do something about it," said the director.

"But you don't understand," she said. "Desi and I have been hoping for this for ten years."

DeMille sighed wearily. He rose and said good-bye to the visitors. As Arnaz was going out the door, DeMille added, "Congratulations—you're the only man in history who screwed Lucille Ball, Columbia Pictures, Paramount Pictures, Harry Cohn, and Cecil B. DeMille, all at the same time."

Loretta Young was discontented with her contract with Twentieth Century-Fox. She contended that Darryl Zanuck performed ably as a producer for male stars but failed to devote the same care and attention to actresses in his films. At the conclusion of her contract she resisted Zanuck's offer of a renewal. "I'll never be anything but Mrs. Alexander Graham Bell to you," she said in a moment of pique.

Her contract ended, Miss Young embarked on a free-lance career. Months passed without offers from other studios. She puzzled over this. After nine months of inactivity she concluded that she had been blacklisted by the industry because of her defiance of Zanuck. She expressed her suspicions to her agent, Myron Selznick. He made cautious inquiries and discovered that the major studios had indeed subscribed to a gentleman's agreement not to hire the actress who had defied a fellow employer.

"There's only one man in town who has the guts to break the blacklist—Harry Cohn," said Selznick. "He'll do it—if he gets a bargain."

"That's all right with me," said Miss Young. "You're the one who has said I had to work at one hundred and fifty thousand dollars a picture. I'll work for Columbia at half that amount, just to work."

Those were the terms under which Harry Cohn hired Loretta

Young for three pictures. The first was *The Doctor Takes a Wife*, a successful comedy with Ray Milland. She followed with another success, *He Stayed for Breakfast*, opposite Melvyn Douglas.

For her third film at Columbia, Harry Cohn proposed costarring Miss Young with Fredric March in *The Bedtime Story*. Both stars' contracts specified top billing, but March gallantly agreed to allow her name to precede his.

Miss Young's wardrobe was created for her by Irene, but as production approached, she lacked one dress for an important scene. The actress told Cohn she would supply one and charge the studio accordingly. As was her custom, she visited Magnin's at sale time and chose a variety of dresses. One seemed ideal as the needed gown for the film. Its cost was $155, but the designer suggested changes amounting to $400. Miss Young ordered the gown delivered to the studio. Since Irene charged between $600 and $800 for her creations, the actress submitted a $700 cost for the gown.

One night at ten o'clock, Cohn called Miss Young in a rage. "You're not going to make money on your clothes at the expense of my studio," he ranted.

"Now wait a minute, Harry," she answered. "Tell me what this is all about."

"You know what it's about! You pick up a dress for a hundred and fifty-five dollars, and then you try to palm it off on me for seven hundred."

"But how did you know what it cost?"

"The price tag was still on it!"

Miss Young tried to explain the circumstances, but Cohn would not listen.

"Nobody's going to try to cheat me and get away with it," he continued. "I'm taking away your top billing. And you're not going to wear that dress in the picture, either. You'll wear what I tell you to wear."

Cohn carried out his threat of removing top billing, and he ordered the wardrobe department to devise a new dress. In retaliation, Miss Young submitted to fittings only when the wardrobe department was working on overtime. She continued changing the design at her whim, so that the new dress eventually cost $5,000.

The incident placed a frost on the relations between Loretta Young and Harry Cohn. Each refused to talk to the other. This presented social discomfort, since they frequently attended the same party. Many an evening was ruined for Miss Young because Harry Cohn sat glowering across a crowded living room.

Years passed, and Miss Young received the recognition of the industry with an Academy Award. Still, the silent feud continued. One evening she entered the home of Mervyn Le Roy to find the familiar broad back of Harry Cohn at the other end of the room. Unable to face another uneasy evening, she approached his back and said, "Harry, don't turn around. This is Loretta, and I want to say something to you. It's been a long time; but I finally want to tell you that I was wrong and you were right, and I'm sorry we had a misunderstanding. Now if you forgive me, you can turn around. If you don't, just stay the way you are, and I'll go away."

Harry Cohn remained fixed for a few moments. Then he turned slowly around, a smile on his broad face.

"That's the nicest thing I've ever heard," he beamed.

Cohn thereafter made intensive efforts to woo Miss Young's services. Circumstances prevented her making another film for Columbia, but she and Cohn remained cordial friends.

During their early years as bachelors in Hollywood, David Niven and Errol Flynn shared a Malibu house they dubbed Cirrhosis by the Sea. Flynn also owned a boat on which the two actors cruised Southern California waters during their days off from filming.

One Sunday afternoon Niven and Flynn were returning from Catalina Island when they encountered a drifting yacht in mid-channel.

"Ahoy!" Flynn hailed, "Give you a lift?"

"Yeah," answered a solidly built man on deck. "The goddam motor won't work." It was Harry Cohn, adrift on the *Jobella*.

Flynn towed Cohn's yacht into harbor. That evening Niven devised a prank: he would have his lawyer send a formal letter to Cohn claiming the *Jobella* as salvage. Flynn agreed it was a capital idea.

A week later Niven's agent, Leland Hayward, asked him, "What have you done at Columbia?"

"What do you mean?" asked Niven. "I've never placed a foot on the Columbia lot."

"Then why have you been barred from the studio for life?"

Niven puzzled over the news, then remembered his prank. Obviously Cohn hadn't seen the humor, so Niven decided to explain it to him. But Cohn would neither answer Niven's telephone calls nor return them.

The actor became worried. His contract option with Samuel Goldwyn was approaching, and he feared that Cohn might influence Goldwyn to fire him. The only solution was a face-to-face encounter with Harry Cohn. Niven called for an appointment.

He arrived at Cohn's office at 9 A.M. The actor sat throughout the morning without being admitted to the inner office. Cohn departed for lunch and returned, and still Niven remained. Not until 6:15 was he finally allowed to see Cohn.

"What do you want?" Cohn growled.

"Do you remember the day Flynn and I gave your boat a tow?" Niven asked.

"Yeah."

"Do you recall receiving a letter from my lawyer about it?"

"Yeah. Do you want to apologize?"

Niven was astonished. "Are you really mad because of it?"

"Do you want to apologize?" Cohn repeated.

"Well, I suppose I do—if you think an apology is in order."

"All right, I accept your apology. Now get your ass out of here!"

Niven never worked at Columbia during Cohn's lifetime.

16
A Prince for Cinderella

*A*s in all her unmarried periods, a relative quietude descended on the relationship of Rita Hayworth and Harry Cohn following her separation from Orson Welles. It appeared inevitable that Rita would find another man and that the quietude would end.

Rita's marriage to Welles prompted a curiosity about what was going on outside the boundaries of Hollywood, and in May, 1948, she decided to make her first visit to Europe. Cohn had no film in readiness for Rita, and he saw the publicity value of sending his star to the Continent. He aimed to send along his trusted aide, Evelyn Lane, to guard Columbia's most valuable asset.

"How long do you plan to stay?" Cohn asked Rita.

"Three or four months," she replied.

"Then Evelyn can't go with you," he said. "I can't spare her that long."

And so Rita embarked for Europe with only her secretary for protection. It was a miscalculation that Harry Cohn was later to regret.

The meeting occurred under the auspices of Elsa Maxwell. She had arranged a dinner party in Cannes, and she chose the occasion to bring together Rita and Aly Kahn. Rita reluctantly agreed to attend, and she was charmed by the dashing, smooth-talking man. She hadn't the faintest notion of who he was.

She learned. The French newspapers gave much attention to the new romance between the Hollywood star and the playboy son of the famed Aga Khan, spiritual leader of Moslem millions. Word of the romance traveled quickly to Harry Cohn, and he was displeased.

He became more displeased as the romance progressed from the Riviera to Toledo and Madrid, then to Lisbon and back to

Biarritz and Cannes, the international press in constant pursuit. Rita returned to Hollywood, and Aly followed soon after, renting a house across the street from her Beverly Hills mansion.

The storybook nature of the romance was tempered by the fact that neither Rita nor Aly was free to marry. Her divorce from Orson Welles had not become final; Aly was long estranged from but still wed to his first wife. This caused cluckings from churchmen, editorialists, clubwomen, and other guardians of American morals. Harry Cohn also expressed to Rita his disapproval of her association with Aly and the publicity it aroused. Cohn's objections were not on moral grounds, but because such publicity might damage her box office draw, then at its peak.

As always when she was in love, Rita heeded only her heart. She went off to Mexico City with Aly and then to Acapulco. The headlines continued.

Harry Cohn continued to fume. He had plans for Rita, and they did not include marriage to a Moslem prince. Cohn decided to send an emissary to Rita, someone who might convince her of the folly of her course and the wisdom of returning to her career at Columbia Pictures. No man could perform a mission of such delicacy. It had to be a woman, and no woman was more respected by Rita than Virginia Van Upp.

Miss Van Upp agreed with some misgivings to make the trip to Mexico City, where Rita and Aly were staying, and to attempt to reach some understanding with Rita about her contract with Columbia. She arrived to find the famous pair beleaguered by the press. Both Rita and Aly complained bitterly that they were virtual prisoners in the Hotel Reforma.

"It's your fault; you wanted to be a movie star," Miss Van Upp told Rita. Then she turned to Aly and added, "It's your fault, too. You're not exactly John Doe."

"Who is this John Doe?" Aly demanded, staring at Rita. Miss Van Upp tried to explain the expression to him, but he remained unconvinced that John Doe had not been one of Rita's lovers.

Miss Van Upp made no overt gestures on behalf of Harry Cohn. She merely observed and waited. In time, Rita expressed a desire for a heart-to-heart talk with her friend from Hollywood.

Unable to find any other place where they would remain unobserved, they met in the suite of the hotel proprietor. The two women sat on the mink-covered bed of the opulent apartment, and Rita told of her love for Aly.

Miss Van Upp quickly recognized that Harry Cohn had dispatched her on a fruitless mission; no one on earth could convince Rita to abandon her romance with Aly Khan.

As Rita concluded, she sighed deeply. "I love him," she said, "but I'm worried."

"About what?" Miss Van Upp asked.

"It's your fault."

"Why?"

"Because you wrote *Gilda*. And every man I've known has fallen in love with Gilda and wakened with me."

Rita and Aly continued on to Cuba, then back to Hollywood, where she claimed her final decree of divorce from Orson Welles. She also informed Harry Cohn she would not be reporting to work, and he promptly took her off salary; her annual pay was $248,000.

She didn't pause for regrets. She hurried off to Europe with Aly, as well as her secretary and her daughter, Rebecca Welles. The headlines continued, the tone becoming strident. A banner in London's *The People*, circulation 4,500,000: THIS AFFAIR IS AN INSULT TO ALL DECENT WOMEN. The *Sunday Pictorial*, with a 3,800,000 circulation, agreed it was "a very sordid business." Back home, William R. Wilkerson, publisher of *Hollywood Reporter*, editorialized that Hollywood should "wash its hands of Rita Hayworth."

The criticism diminished after Aly secured his divorce from his first princess. Then, on May 27, 1949, H. H. Prince Aly Salomone Khan was married by the Communist mayor of Vallauris, France, to Margarita Carmen Cansino Judson Welles. Harry Cohn declined an invitation to attend the ceremony.

V

Twilight of the Gods:
The Fifties

• • • • •

THEY DON'T SCARE EASILY. They are tough, these pioneering giants, and they have endured the patents fight, a war, the revolution of sound, the Depression, and another war. Why should a flickering tube endanger their empires?

But in 1950, 5,000,000 Americans own television sets. By 1960 it is ten times 5,000,000.

The effects at first are subtle: the closing of neighborhood theaters here and there; the failure of reliable stars to draw audiences; the decision of film company directors to pay no dividends.

The downward trend accelerates. Suddenly theater attendance is cut in half. Scores of stars are rendered obsolete.

The pioneers remain cool. There's nothing wrong that good pictures and showmanship cannot cure, they say.

Technology saved the business before; it can do it again. The way seems clear when Cinerama makes its debut on Broadway on September 30, 1952, dispatching customers on a roller coaster ride to the edge of vertigo. Two months later audiences are attacked by clawing lions and hurled spears in *Bwana Devil*, first of a spate of three-dimensional films. Then Twentieth Century-Fox gives the screen clarity and width with CinemaScope. Paramount follows suit with VistaVision.

But 3-D gives people headaches, and the novelty of big screens passes. The public remains enamored with the seventeen-inch screen in the living room.

The dark years bring mighty changes. Louis B. Mayer is eased from the company that bears his name. Then Dore Schary is removed; then Nick Schenck himself. Darryl Zanuck tires of the burden of power and leaves command of Fox for the pleasures of Europe. Howard Hughes loses interest in his toy, RKO, and tosses it aside. It is picked up by tiremakers, then turned into a television lot by Lucille Ball, who was once fired there. Republic rides into the sunset, and

Universal is purchased by agents.

The majors are releasing 320 films a year at the start of the decade, 189 at its end. A quarter of the nation's theaters have closed forever.

Stars and agents are on the ascendant. The few stars who remain box office no longer work for the studios; they are partners. It is the time of the independent. Long-ailing United Artists, unhampered by studio overhead, now becomes a giant. M-G-M, the "beached whale," gasps for life.

The studios buy time. They sell their old movies to television, thus creating their own competition. They film *Cheyenne* and *How to Marry a Millionaire* and *Father Knows Best*, also for television. Fox drills for oil.

There is death in the air. Louis B. Mayer makes a last try at regaining control of M-G-M, then succumbs to leukemia. Cecil B. DeMille delivers himself of *The Ten Commandments*, then dies in his bed. Humphrey Bogart takes a drink of orange juice and feels the rasp of mortality in his throat. Tyrone Power steps out of his dressing room in Madrid and falls dead. The promise of James Dean is smashed on the highway near Salinas. Errol Flynn faces death with his last nymphet. The King is dead, and Coop, too. And soon, Marilyn.

But life remains. It is not the golden time; the boom is long past. It is not the world that Hollywood would have chosen for itself. But the essential thing is survival, and it appears contrary to all consensus that Hollywood will survive.

● ● ● ● ●

I

"Do Me a Favor, Will Ya, Harry? Drop Dead."

*B*efore leaving Paris, Harry Cohn had another, more friendly conference with Carson Kanin. Cohn's anger at being humiliated was tempered by his memory of the bargain of acquiring *The More the Merrier* from Kanin. Cohn asked if Kanin had any new stories, and the writer outlined one. Cohn liked it, and he agreed to pay $100,000 for the finished script. But after Kanin emerged from the Army and presented the script, Cohn had misgivings and reneged on the deal. The story was eventually filmed by Universal-International as *A Double Life*, and it won an Academy Award for Ronald Colman.

Kanin would not deal with Columbia after that, and for years he refused to talk to Harry Cohn. Cohn was unconcerned—until Kanin had something he wanted.

It was *Born Yesterday*, a comedy that Kanin had written for Jean Arthur. She had withdrawn from the play during the out-of-town engagements, and Kanin had replaced her with a nightclub comedienne, Judy Holliday. Miss Holliday as the dumb-blonde mistress and radio announcer Paul Douglas as the boorish junk dealer became immediate stars when the brilliant comedy opened on Broadway.

It was no mere coincidence that the junk dealer was named Harry Brock. Kanin had borrowed characteristics of Harry Cohn for the character and later told him so. As with Willie Stark in *All the King's Men*, Cohn became infatuated with Harry Brock. He needed a strong property to buoy Columbia's fortunes in the face of a falling market, and he was determined to secure *Born Yesterday*.

But Kanin had instructed his agent, Abe Lastfogel of William Morris, "The only studio you can't sell the play to is Columbia."

Lastfogel related the information to Cohn, who was unde-terred. He continued pestering the agent to make a deal.

One day Lastfogel and Al Jolson were in Cohn's office when a call came from Mark Hellinger. The producer had just negoti-ated a deal with Cohn to bring his production company, which had commitments for the services of Humphrey Bogart, to Columbia.*

"What do you think of Bogart for *Born Yesterday*?" Cohn asked.

"I think it's great," replied Hellinger.

"I'll see what I can do," said Cohn.

He hung up the phone and asked Lastfogel, "Did you hear that?"

"They could have heard it in Pasadena," the agent replied.

"If I offered you a million dollars, would you accept?" Cohn asked.

"Are you prepared to make such an offer, with the under-standing that it will be a license deal for ten years only—then the property reverts to Kanin?"

"I'm telling you right now: I offer you a million dollars," said Cohn. He motioned to Jolson and added, "Al is my witness."

"All right," said Lastfogel. "Give me forty-eight hours to dis-cuss it with Garson. I'll break his arm if he doesn't accept."

Lastfogel telephoned Kanin in New Haven, where he was opening another play. "What do you think?" Kanin asked.

"There aren't too many offers," the agent admitted. "I think we'd better take it."

The pair agreed to accept Cohn's offer. They also agreed to stand firm against a last-minute counteroffer they knew would be forthcoming; it was an ancient technique in studio negotiations.

Kanin and his wife, Ruth Gordon, were dining with Thorn-ton Wilder and his sister at a restaurant in New Haven when a call came from Lastfogel. Kanin answered it in the kitchen.

"Well, here it is," the agent reported. "Cohn wants the rights to a musical remake. What do you think?"

---

* Hellinger died before the deal could be concluded.

"Let's refuse him," said Kanin. "We can make the picture ourselves, if necessary."

"Are you sure you want to risk it?" asked Lastfogel.

"Yes," Kanin replied firmly.

"Have you had a drink?"

"Yes."

"Have you started dinner?"

"Yes, I'm perfectly sober. Why pussyfoot around with Cohn? He made a deal; let him stick to it."

To Lastfogel's immense relief, Cohn dropped his demand the following day, and the deal was concluded. The industry was startled that Cohn would make such a deal at a time when business was on the wane. That was precisely the time for it, reasoned Cohn, who was proud to be the first studio head to pay $1,000,000 for a screen property.

Cohn now expected Kanin to write the screenplay for $75,000, half of what he usually received. "It should be a labor of love," Cohn argued.

Kanin would have written the script for less than Cohn offered, but he was irritated by Cohn's intransigent attitude. Kanin maintained the fee should have been a matter of negotiation.

"Harry, more than any man I know, you confuse principle with stubbornness," Kanin told him. It was a line that Cohn became fond of; years later Cohn applied it to Kanin himself during a negotiation.

Cohn hired Julius and Philip Epstein to write a script, and he tried to induce Kanin to read it.

"How much will you pay me?" the playwright asked.

"You money-grabbing son of a bitch!" Cohn exploded. "You don't care about anything but your pound of flesh."

George Cukor had been signed to direct *Born Yesterday*, but he balked when he read the Epstein script. He induced Kanin to read it. Kanin dispatched a letter to Cohn declaring the nuances of the two leading characters had been destroyed by jokes. "You own the *Blondie* series; why not just shoot it as *Blondie Goes to Washington*?" Kanin concluded.

Cohn summoned the Epstein twins and threw the letter down on his desk. "What about this?" he demanded.

The Epsteins read the letter, and Philip replied, "If we had written the play *Born Yesterday*, and Garson Kanin had written the script, we would have said the same thing."

"That's fair enough," said Cohn. He released the Epsteins from their contract.

Cukor continued trying to convince Kanin to write the script. "All right," agreed Kanin, "but I won't be employed by Cohn." Another screenwriter received the credit, but Kanin composed most of the scenes himself, submitting them surreptitiously to Cukor.

"I screwed Harry Cohn," Kanin crowed afterward. "I wrote his script for nothing!"

The casting of *Born Yesterday* was a matter of controversy from the time that Cohn purchased film rights to the play. He rejected Kanin's suggestion to cast Judy Holliday in the role she created. Cohn referred to her as "that fat Jewish broad" and refused to entertain the suggestion that she could be a candidate for film stardom. Meanwhile, he negotiated with many top stars for the role of Billie Dawn. But his intentions were opposed by a conspiracy of Garson Kanin, Ruth Gordon, George Cukor, and Katharine Hepburn.

Cukor was scheduled to direct Miss Hepburn and Spencer Tracy at M-G-M in *Adam's Rib*, written by the Kanins. The script contained a rare comedic role for a young actress, and the Kanins and Cukor wanted Judy Holliday to play it as a test for *Born Yesterday*. She balked, claiming the role called for her to appear overweight and sloppy; she was certain that Harry Cohn would not reward her with Billie Dawn after seeing it. But the trio assured her they would inject a final scene in which she would appear svelte and glamorous.

Miss Hepburn was privy to the plot, and she assisted by asking M-G-M press agents to inject items in the trade press reporting that Judy Holliday was stealing *Adam's Rib*. Miss Hepburn believed the items would impress Harry Cohn. She was right.

All the plotters repeatedly urged the discipline of diet on Miss Holliday, who remained overweight. As he passed her on the set, Kanin sang softly, "Judy's busting out all o-ver—" She was convinced. As her glamour scene approached, she refrained from eating for three days and lost ten pounds. The scene was photographed with the utmost care. Cukor rejected the studio's proposal that a gown be purchased for Miss Holliday at a department store; he insisted on a designer's creation.

Miss Holliday appeared radiant in the scene, and she provided brilliant comedy throughout the film. The ruse succeeded. Cohn saw *Adam's Rib* and agreed to sign Judy Holliday for Billie Dawn.

Kanin had also urged Paul Douglas as Harry Brock in the film version, but an accident of fate had prejudiced Cohn against Douglas. During almost three years in *Born Yesterday*, Douglas had veered from his impeccable performance only once. That was at a matinee during the second year, when Douglas had a brief argument with the management. He went to a nearby bar for a couple of drinks, returned to the theater, and gave a slovenly performance. In the audience was Harry Cohn.

"The guy's got no vitality," Cohn told Kanin. Cohn favored Broderick Crawford, who had recently won the Academy Award for *All the King's Men*.

Kanin continued his arguments to team the original costars, thus creating two new screen personalities for Columbia. Cohn was finally convinced. Then Douglas turned down the role. He contended that his role had been subordinated to Billie Dawn in the film script. No amount of argument could dissuade him, and Crawford was awarded the role of Harry Brock.

For the role of Billie's intellectual tutor, Cohn wanted William Holden, whose career was slowly building since his return from the Air Force. Holden was reluctant to accept the part, realizing he would be overwhelmed by two showy roles. Both Kanin and Billy Wilder urged him to accept, arguing that his presence in such an auspicious film could only further his career. "I'll find something good for you later," promised Wilder. His *Stalag 17* won Holden an Academy Award.

With the start of production approaching, the time had come for a confrontation of Harry Cohn with his new star, Judy Holliday. She arrived from New York by airplane at eleven one evening and was met by a Columbia publicity man. A limousine rushed Miss Holliday to the studio for her meeting with Harry Cohn.

Miss Holliday displayed signs of nervousness during the long ride from Los Angeles Airport to Sunset Boulevard and Gower Street. She became more nervous as she tramped down the long office and approached Cohn's desk.

"Mr. Cohn, may I present Miss Judy Holliday?" the press agent burbled.

The actress smiled and stretched out her arm. Cohn ignored it. He rose from his chair and walked completely around her. He sighed deeply and muttered, "Well, I've worked with fat asses before."

His comment was shattering, but it produced the desired effect: Miss Holliday reduced fifteen pounds in three weeks.

The stars rehearsed their roles and presented *Born Yesterday* in play form before studio audiences every night for a week. The resulting intimacy contributed to a brilliant exhibit of ensemble playing, and all three performers registered strongly. But it was Judy's picture.

Harry Cohn, who had been berated by the East for the $1,000,000 deal, had his biggest comedy hit since the Capra-McCarey-Stevens-Hawks era and a bright new star as well. When the 1950 Academy Awards approached, the race for best actress seemed to be narrowed to a pair of veteran stars in dazzling comebacks: Bette Davis in *All About Eve* and Gloria Swanson in *Sunset Boulevard*.

But the Academy voters selected a new star: Judy Holliday.

Garson Kanin continued to do business with Harry Cohn, his scripts including two more vehicles for Judy Holliday: *The Marrying Kind* and *It Should Happen to You*. Always the procedure was the same; Cohn insisted on it.

Kanin and Miss Gordon attended dinner with the Cohns in the formal dining room. They all retired to the living room, where Joan Cohn knitted as Kanin read the finished script, from first to last. As he had with *The More the Merrier*, Cohn remained a perfect audience, laughing at the comedy and crying in the love scenes.

2

THE WINDS OF CHANGE

*C*olumbia Pictures recovered quickly from the skipped-heartbeat of 1948, and by 1950 gross business had climbed to a record of almost $60,000,000 with profits of $2,000,000. The company suffered none of the pains of withdrawal experienced by the studios that had been ordered to divest themselves of their theater chains.

The film business was shifting in other ways, and the changes disturbed Harry Cohn. He was nearing his sixties as the decade began, and his patterns of operation had solidified. It frustrated him to discover that he could no longer control the destiny of Columbia Studios with the sureness he had always exhibited. His own stars had become less tractable. He was repeatedly at odds with William Holden and Glenn Ford; Larry Parks was suing for a release from his contract; Rita Hayworth had jumped her contract to marry a Persian prince. Now the free-lance stars, on whom Columbia had long relied for casting important films, were growing difficult to deal with. Not only were their agents demanding immense salaries, but they even wanted a percentage of the profits, creative control over scripts, and choice of directors. Harry Cohn had always dictated such matters, but now the stars would not be dictated to.

Television, too, was bringing new and mystifying changes to the men who controlled the film industry. They had learned to cope with the competition of radio; during the early craze over *Amos 'n' Andy*, theaters broadcast the program before starting the evening performance. But now movie houses were empty on Tuesday night, when Milton Berle was appearing on *Texaco Star Theater*, and there was no way to compete.

As television stations continued to proliferate, the new industry was faced with the problem of how to fill the home screens with hours and hours of entertainment. At first the viewers were undiscriminating and peered happily at puppet shows, parlor games, and English movies. But as the novelty declined and advertising dollars began pouring into the new medium, the need for more sophisticated entertainment became apparent.

In the beginning nearly all network shows were performed before electronic cameras in New York. This provided the vital quality of immediacy, but it was a wasteful and unsatisfactory process. The only method of duplicating the shows for other time zones of the United States was by kinescope film, which was indistinct. After one showing the kinescope was usually discarded, and the performance was lost forever. Also, the obvious limitations of live performance precluded the use of outdoor scenery, crowds, animals, realistic action, and all the expansive elements that audiences had come to expect from motion pictures. Television viewers were becoming claustrophobic from an endless succession of living-room scenes.

The answer to the problem lay in film and hence Hollywood. But the major studios were badgered by the militancy of theater owners, who threatened retaliation for any film company that fed entertainment to the competing medium. The studios dutifully maintained a hands-off policy. No contract players were allowed to appear on television. When movie decorators dressed living-room scenes, they were forbidden to include television sets, even though millions of American homes now had them.

The vacuum created by the majors' reluctance to enter television production was filled by independents, ranging from veterans like Hal Roach to newcomers to film making, such as Jules Stein's MCA. Some executives in the major studios believed that companies should defy the theaters and enter television production. Among them was Ralph Cohn, eldest son of Jack Cohn.

Ralph proposed to his father that Columbia establish a subsidiary to make television commercials and programs. Ralph asked for $50,000 to start the venture. Jack relayed the request to his brother.

"All right, give him the fifty thousand," replied Harry Cohn, "and see what he can do. But he's to get no more than fifty thousand."

Harry Cohn had another motive for approving the request; it meant that Ralph would be transferred from the studio to New

York. Cohn had no fondness for Ralph, perhaps because he and his nephew were so much alike. "One bastard at the studio is enough," said Harry Cohn.

Ralph applied his energies to the wooing of advertisers, and he enjoyed such immediate success that he had no need to ask his uncle for money beyond the initial $50,000. On June 12, 1952, Ralph was able to announce a historic deal. Columbia's subsidiary Screen Gems—a name resurrected from the studio's short-subject program in earlier years—would produce thirty-nine *Ford Theater* programs for the Ford Motor Company. The half-hour films were budgeted at $25,000 apiece, with Ford paying 75 percent of the cost in return for first-run rights and an option for additional showings. Columbia retained ownership of the negative and would earn its profit on a second sale to Ford and reshowings thereafter.

Thus, Columbia became the first big studio to break the policy of noninvolvement with television. The $1,000,000 deal awakened other companies to the riches that were available in the new medium. Soon Columbia took another major step: it began selling old feature movies to television. In time, all the companies would follow.

Screen Gems grew fast, and its value to Columbia was apparent. The sale of new television films and old movies brought much-needed revenue in the face of the dwindling box office. And television production helped maintain studio staffs and pay for the crushing overhead at a time when the number of Columbia's feature films was shrinking—from sixty-three in 1951 to thirty-five in 1954.

Harry Cohn took no particular pride in Screen Gems. He viewed the new enterprise as a necessary adjunct to the company. But he gave the television arm no more attention than he accorded B pictures or shorts. His business was still the making of topflight movie entertainment.

Harry Cohn had long been a friend and admirer of Howard Hughes, the shadowy, eccentric industrialist who dabbled in motion pictures. In 1948 Hughes staged a major return to the movie industry by purchasing control of RKO, long the sick studio of Hollywood. Hughes' absentee ownership had not improved RKO's health.

In searching for a solution to his problems with RKO, Hughes turned to Harry Cohn, whose operation of Columbia had long been a model of economy. Hughes asked Cohn to run RKO in conjunction with his own studio.

Cohn was immensely flattered by the proposal. He sought conversations with Hughes on the matter. This was a problem because of Hughes' penchant for secrecy. Such a negotiation called for special security measures, since news of talks between Hughes and Cohn might stir activity in the stocks of two corporations.

The solution was easily arrived at, since both men conducted business in the early morning hours. Hughes drove to Cohn's house in his vintage Chevrolet, arriving after midnight, when most of the Hollywood community was asleep. The two men held their discussions for two or three hours; then Hughes drove away.

In the end, Cohn decided against the Hughes proposal. He concluded that the growing problems of operating Columbia were enough to occupy his entire energies.

Over the years Harry Cohn received several offers to sell his interest in Columbia. He never issued an immediate rejection of such offers, even though he had no intention of relinquishing control of the company. He preferred to hold the prospective buyers in abeyance while he supposedly considered the deal. In reality, he wanted the enjoyment of savoring the fact that he could sell his holdings for millions.

As the studio problems grew, he required more time to reject the offers to sell. Turning sixty, he felt a diminution of his energies. The prospect of laying aside his immense responsibilities as president and production head of Columbia Pictures held attraction for him. For the first time he actually considered a proposal that he sell out.

"No, I won't do it," he finally decided. "Sitting behind this desk, I can always press the buzzer and get somebody to talk to me. If I wasn't head of the studio, who would talk to me? Who would come to my house for dinner? No, I won't do it."

During the late 1940's and early 1950's Cohn gave serious consideration to the terms of his employment by Columbia Pictures. On December 9, 1943, he had signed a contract with the company providing a salary of $3,000 a week plus $300 expenses; that was what he had been earning prior to that time without a contract. The contract expired on July 1, 1945, and Cohn continued on the same basis. Efforts to negotiate a satisfactory contract failed.

Arnold Grant, an attorney Cohn had invited to join the Columbia board and an expert in executive contracts, argued that Cohn had reached the age when he should start providing for his heirs within the framework of his working arrangement with Columbia. Cohn was reluctant to do so, declaring that his stock would provide enough death benefits. Grant countered that it was the company's responsibility as well, and Cohn conceded.

The board hired Grant to prepare a brief for the proposed contract. Grant suggested the same terms of Cohn's employment—$3,500 a week plus $300 expenses—with the addition of benefits of $961.54 weekly for his survivors to be paid for 260 weeks following his death.

The Grant brief offered voluminous documentation that provided insight into the operation of Columbia Pictures and other motion picture studios during the prime business years of the 1940's.

The brief began by citing a statement of Joseph P. Kennedy, who himself had headed film companies. Kennedy had argued that too much business interference with production of motion pictures was wholly undesirable and added, "Movie production requires producers—men with a flair for showmanship and an instinct for dramaturgy, men who could orchestrate the sound and fury of which pictures are made."

Columbia Studios, the brief reported, employed 1,910 employees at the time (1947) with an annual payroll of $18,226,881.62. Twelve of the executive personnel earned more than $500 weekly. Columbia also maintained 107 distribution offices in 107 cities, employing 3,070 employees with a payroll of $6,650,000.

Grant compared Cohn's annual compensation of $197,600 with the salaries and benefits allotted the heads of other film companies. Louis B. Mayer received $755,840 as production boss of M-G-M, and the president of the parent company, Loew's, Nicholas Schenck, was paid $599,460; the total was $1,355,300 for performing the same functions Harry Cohn did for less than $200,000. The totals for the other companies were: Twentieth Century-Fox, $917,480; Universal, $527,960; Paramount, $582,803; RKO, $436,999; average, $764,108.

The growth of the company under Cohn's leadership was outlined in detail: gross income doubled between 1940 and 1946; operating profit increased thirteenfold in the same period; net profit up six and a half times; and net worth doubled to $25,000,000 between 1937 and 1946. Great emphasis was placed on the increase of profits on A and AA pictures, which were Harry Cohn's particular province.

The brief was presented to the board and then to the stockholders for a vote. Seventy-three percent of the stockholders voted to approve the new agreement with Harry Cohn. Neither the board nor Cohn considered the vote "substantial, satisfactory, and generally representative" of stockholder feeling, and the agreement was abandoned. Later Cohn accepted lesser terms. The rejection was a severe blow to Cohn, who didn't feel that his leadership of Columbia needed a defense. He was to suffer further humiliation from an outgrowth of the affair.

The Columbia board of directors had authorized payment of $40,000 in legal fees in connection with the negotiation for the new contract. This outlay was questioned by three stockholders owning 473 shares of the more than 600,000 shares of common stock. They filed a stockholders' suit on April 11, 1950, charging that the board was so dominated by Harry Cohn that it had entered into an improvident employment contract with him, allowed him to charge the company $40,000 in legal fees he should have paid himself, and wrongfully permitted him to profit at the corporation's expense.

The suit fired a broadside of charges against Cohn and his way of life. A referee of the New York Supreme Court ruled in

1952 that Cohn had been able to answer all the charges satisfactorily. Among them:

1. That Cohn maintained a yacht at company expense. In reality, he owned and maintained the *Jobella* himself.

2. That Cohn charged the company for a projection room in his home. The referee ruled that the room, which cost $129,000, was necessary to the performance of Cohn's duties.

3. That the company paid for changes and repairs in the Cohn residence. No such evidence.

4. That Cohn charged the company for entertainment in his home. The Cohns' New Year's parties, one of which cost $3,728.76, were paid for by Columbia, But the referee ruled, "Undoubtedly, such parties are necessary and proper in order to foster good relationships between the motion picture companies, the stars, and other persons in the industry."

5. That Cohn used company automobiles on noncompany business. No evidence.

6. That company personnel used company materials to make clothes for the Cohn family. Mrs. Cohn, like a few stars and executives' wives, received clothes made at Columbia for cost, plus 10 percent, the work being done only in slack periods of production.

7. That excessive wages were paid to friends and relatives of Harry Cohn. A list of those whose employment was sponsored by Cohn and an explanation of their duties disproved the allegation.

8. That a golf instructor was paid by the company to coach Harry Cohn. A former golf instructor was in the company's employ, and he sometimes played weekend games with Cohn. "But this occasional golf game does not justify the accusations made."

9. That a family portrait was painted at company expense. No evidence.

10. That Cohn diverted secret profits to himself. No evidence.

11. That Cohn purchased bogus literary and dramatic properties. No evidence.

Because of the stockholders' suit, Cohn was advised by his attorneys not to visit New York, and he was exiled for two years. Weary of the whole matter, he offered to pay half of the $40,000 legal fee. The decision of Supreme Court Justice Eder on October 7, 1951, declared the offer was fair.

Justice Eder supported Cohn throughout his decision:

> Cohn admittedly is an executive and production manager of a very high degree. That is well established by the fact that during his incumbency and administration as president of the company, and as its production head, he acting in this extraordinary dual capacity, the corporation's gross business has increased from $7,000,000 to over $57,000,000. . . .
>
> There is nothing wrong in the corporation agreeing under the employment contract to pay death benefits to members of Cohn's family, nor in paying required premiums on the policies. Cohn was a very valuable asset to the corporation; it greatly desired to have him remain; to accomplish this it was necessary that it agree to his terms in order to induce him to continue in its employ for a definite three years' period. By so agreeing and having him continue in its employ the corporation gained a distinct and highly valuable benefit.

The decision vindicated Harry Cohn, but he remained shaken by the whole affair. For the first time the value of his services to Columbia Pictures had been subjected to serious questioning. Regardless of the eventual victory, his self-esteem had been dealt a damaging blow.

Another disturbing change faced Harry Cohn in the 1950's: he discovered that a small group of men could tell him whom he could or could not employ. This group was composed of congressmen, congressional investigators, professional Red hunters, and other self-appointed guardians of Americanism.

Being oblivious to political matters, Cohn gave no consideration to the inadvisability of hiring suspected Communists or supporters of Communist causes. His criterion was talent, and a man's political views were of no concern to him.

In 1945 Ben Kahane and Mendel Silberberg came to Cohn's office with grave faces. Kahane announced, "Harry, you've got to fire John Howard Lawson immediately. Don't ask questions; don't argue. Just get him off the lot—fast."

"But why?" Cohn asked.

Kahane lowered his voice to a confidential tone. "The House Un-American Activities Committee is coming to town for hearings," he said, "and Lawson will very likely be named a Communist. We've got to be in the clear."

A massive frown encompassed Cohn's face. Lawson was one of his valued writers; he had written *Sahara* for Humphrey Bogart and was now working on another war film for Bogart. Cohn walked to the window and gazed out on Gower Street for a full five minutes while Kahane and Silberberg waited expectantly.

Finally, Cohn turned and announced, "No, I'm not going to fire him."

Both men protested that circumstances forced him to do so.

"No," Cohn reasoned, "I've got —— —— on the lot, and *he's* a fairy." He mentioned the name of a noted songwriter.

By the 1950's McCarthyism was in full flower, and Cohn could no longer ignore the Red baiters. Encouraged by the Washington extravaganza of 1947 that had flushed out the Unfriendly Ten, investigators hunted down every Hollywood figure who had ever displayed friendliness toward Red-tinged causes.

In 1951 the House Un-American Activities Committee turned up a real prize: a star who had been a bona fide member of the Communist party. He was Larry Parks, portrayer of Al Jolson. Parks appeared before the committee and admitted that as an idealistic youth, he had been drawn into the party in 1941, but he had left in disillusionment in 1945. Pressed for names of fellow members, Parks replied, "I wish I did not have the choice of going to jail for contempt or crawling through the mud as an informer. I don't think this is American justice."

His interrogators insisted on names, and Parks reluctantly complied. The actor concluded, "It is doubtful whether my career can continue, extremely doubtful, because I came here and told you the truth."

Parks' fears were realized. He had no unreleased pictures, and only two remained to be made under his Columbia contract. He told Cohn through an intermediary that if the studio didn't want him to make the two films, he was willing to cancel the contract. Cohn accepted the offer, and Parks' film career was ended.

After completing *The Brave Bulls*, Robert Rossen was subpoenaed by the House Un-American Activities Committee. Cohn asked him what his intentions were, and Rossen said that he would tell of his membership in the Communist party from 1937 to 1947, but that he would invoke the Fifth Amendment rather than reveal names of his fellow members.

"You're a fool," Cohn told him.

Rossen testified as he said he would, and he was released from his Columbia contract.

As their activities continued to reap headlines, the Washington Red hunters accelerated their efforts to uncover celebrities who might have erred in the direction of the Left. One of those under suspicion was Harry Cohn's new comedy star, Judy Holliday.

Cohn heard rumors that Miss Holliday would be questioned about her political activities. Through his connections in Las Vegas, Cohn made representations to Senator Pat McCarran of Nevada, whose Internal Security Subcommittee planned hearings on subversive infiltration of the radio, television, and other entertainment industries. Cohn sought time from the Senator—time to release Miss Holliday's second starring film, *The Marrying Kind*, without the damaging effects of bad publicity.

The Senator was obliging. Miss Holliday appeared before the committee in March 1952, a month before the release of *The Marrying Kind*. Senator McCarran withheld release of her testimony until the following September.

As it turned out, she was as ingenuous before the senators as she had been in *Born Yesterday*. She confessed that her eyes had been opened when she learned she had given her name and money to Communist-front organizations. She added, "I have been awakened to a realization that I have been irresponsible and slightly—more than slightly—stupid."

To Harry Cohn's vast relief, the appearance did no harm to her popularity.

Because of Harry Cohn's practice of disregarding an employee's politics, Columbia had more of its talent caught in the Red hunt than any other studio. Cohn was bewildered by the issues and the methods involved, and he accepted the judgment of Nate Spingold, who told him that those who refused to cooperate with congressional committees would have to be fired. Cohn was able to weather all the losses, except one.

Sidney Buchman was called before a House Un-American Activities Subcommittee during its hearings in Los Angeles. He testified that he had joined the Communist party in 1938 because he felt it was the only force working against Fascism. He left the party in 1945 because he decided Communism was "stupid, blind, and unworkable for the American people."

Representative Francis E. Walter then asked him to submit to the customary expiation: to name his colleagues in the party.

Buchman replied that he could not. He argued that such people never plotted subversion, that most of the names had already been made public, and that "it is repugnant to an American to inform."

The congressman persisted. Buchman maintained his stand; he would not name names, nor would he exercise the Fifth Amendment. His attorney then rose to point out that one of the members of the subcommittee had left the hearing room; hence, there was no quorum. The hearing ended in confusion.

Buchman was furious that his attorney would use the tactic, and he later waived the lack of quorum, thus placing himself open to a citation for contempt of Congress.

The Columbia hierarchy was distressed by Buchman's action. Harry Cohn was deeply disturbed and uncomprehending.

Buchman instructed Spingold, "Don't let Harry get involved; keep him out of this." Cohn did not become involved. He remained in the background, and those who viewed him intimately had never seen him so disturbed.

Buchman was subpoenaed before the committee once more. He refused to appear; instead, he filed suit to kill the subpoena, arguing that he had already acted in good faith by appearing before the committee in Los Angeles. He was cited for contempt of Congress and eventually fined $150 and given a one-year suspended sentence.

Obviously, Buchman's employability by a major studio was ended by his appearance in Los Angeles. There was no final parting between him and Harry Cohn, no farewell. Cohn was absent from the studio the day that Buchman cleared his desk and left of his own will. He was pleased he could spare his friend the embarrassment.

In the troubled years ahead Harry Cohn often came to the point in a difficult conference when he shook his head and muttered, "Dammit, I wish Sidney was here!"

Buchman never returned to Columbia.

3
THE OTHER SIDE OF THE COHN

Robert Mitchum: "You don't seem like such a son of a bitch to me."

Harry Cohn: "That's because you've never worked for me!"

*T*hroughout his career Cohn strove to create an image of himself as a rough, rugged, unscrupulous man with charity toward none. During the 1950's Hollywood was beset with scandal magazines, and one of them printed a story about Cohn, "The Meanest Man in Hollywood." Cohn telephoned Phil Silvers at three o'clock one morning, laughing hysterically. He had just seen the magazine, and he insisted on quoting the entire article to Silvers, punctuating the reading with roars of laughter.

The pose as Hollywood's meanest man was a convenient one for Cohn. It permitted him to act tough in contract negotiations and in day-to-day dealings with studio personnel. It allowed him to maintain a distance between himself and the myriad of persons who sought his favor for a story sale, a job, or a handout or those who merely desired proximity to a man of such wealth and power.

In reality, not only was Harry Cohn capable of acts of charity, but he also performed them throughout his tenancy as president of Columbia Pictures. Veteran employees were aware of dozens of instances in which Cohn personally assumed the expenses of lengthy illnesses or funerals for Columbia workers.

His mode of bestowing such beneficence followed the same pattern. He never expressed sympathy over the person's plight, since he was incapable of doing so. The typical Cohn gesture was to summon an employee and begin: "You no-good son of a bitch, how did you get yourself into this lousy jam? If you had saved your money instead of blowing it on the races, your wife wouldn't be in the County Hospital. You ought to know better, you stupid bastard. Now get your ass down to Cedars of Lebanon Hospital, and tell them to send an ambulance for your old lady. Yes, I'm picking up the tab, you son of a bitch, but if you tell anyone about it, I'll can you—understand? Now get the hell out of here!"

If the employee was familiar enough with the Cohn nature, he left immediately with only a brief expression of gratitude. Nothing embarrassed or unnerved Cohn more than to be thanked profusely.

A trusted Cohn aide in the production department was stricken with cancer. Cohn arranged for the man's mother to be flown from New York to California. When it appeared that the aide could get the best treatment at the Sloan-Kettering Institute in New York, Cohn sent the entire family there at his expense and instructed the New York office to wire him daily bulletins on the aide's progress. Cohn paid the hospital bill but instructed the recovered aide gruffly, "You can pay the doctors yourself."

A black man had long been Cohn's personal chauffeur and handyman. When illness forced the amputation of the man's leg, Cohn paid all the medical expenses. After his recovery Cohn installed him as operator of the snack-stand concession on the Columbia lot.

Cohn's treatment of actors was often brutal, but he could also be beneficent in his own way. During the filming of *Born Yesterday* Broderick Crawford telephoned Cohn and said, "Arrange to shoot around me this afternoon. I've got to bring my son home from the hospital; he just had an eye operation."

"You leave that set, and I'll sue you for seven million dollars," Cohn replied.

Crawford fumed all morning. He told of the exchange to Judy Holliday and William Holden, and both advised him to leave the set that afternoon. Crawford vowed he would do so.

Shortly before the lunch break a siren was heard outside the stage. The stage door opened, and an ambulance drove inside. Crawford's son was on a stretcher in the rear.

Harry Cohn appeared from behind a backdrop. Before Crawford could ask for an explanation, Cohn barked, "Now you go home with the boy." Cohn added threateningly, "And don't you ever *tell* me you're going to leave a set!"

Cohn was especially soft where mothers were concerned. Larry Parks' mother was dying as *The Jolson Story* was being completed. Cohn arranged to have a print of the film prepared, so she could see her son's triumph before she died.

One day Jean Louis, Columbia's fashion designer, came to Cohn with a cablegram that bore the news of his mother's critical illness in Paris.

"You go—right now," Cohn declared.

"But I have no passport, no ticket," Louis replied.

"That will be taken care of," Cohn said. "You go. You only have one mother."

Frank Sinatra and Harry Cohn became good friends during the years when Sinatra was enjoying his initial burst of fame in Hollywood. Cohn, who preferred to seek favors of no one, made a request of his friend Frank Sinatra. The singer, then at the zenith of his popularity with the youthful audience, had been scheduled for a four-week engagement at the Capitol Theater in New York. Cohn asked if he would view a Columbia picture, *Miss Grant Takes Richmond*, starring Lucille Ball and William Holden, with the possibility of taking the movie on the bill at the Capitol.

Sinatra saw the film and found it a mild comedy, but he agreed to request that it be booked into the Capitol during his engagement. He did so, over the objections of the Capitol management. Predictably, the Sinatra engagement was an enormous success, achieving a first-week gross of $122,000. Thus, Cohn was able to advertise to the trade that *Miss Grant Takes Richmond* collected a $122,000 gross in its first week at the New York Capitol.

During the third week Sinatra was stricken with a strep throat. He was ordered to a hospital by his doctors, but he refused, preferring to remain in the apartment of his close friend, Manny Sachs, at the Gotham Hotel. Doctors enforced a complete rest, and an oxygen tent was installed for Sinatra's use.

It was the first time since his rise to fame that he had been seriously ill, and he was surprised to learn how few of his so-called friends responded with offers of sympathy and aid. A singular exception was Harry Cohn. Cohn flew to New York and spent the morning with Sinatra from 10 o'clock to 1:30. Cohn went off to business appointments and returned at 5 in the afternoon. He remained with Sinatra until his time for sleep at 9:30. Cohn read to the patient, reminisced of his early days in films, told jokes, and delivered numbers recalled from his days as a song plugger. Cohn continued the daily routine until Sinatra recovered.

Cohn's parting remark was in character: "You tell anybody about this, you son of a bitch, and I'll kill you!"

Although he spoke disparagingly of his relatives, Cohn was solicitous of their welfare and personally supported ten families. He insisted on being the sole support. When a relative sought funds and mentioned that he was also going to solicit brothers Jack and Nat, Harry Cohn said, "No, don't do that; I'll give you the full amount."

Although his private charities were many, Cohn resisted efforts to enlist him for organized drives in the Hollywood community. His resistance continued until his late years, when he became acquainted with the charitable activity of Harry Karl and his parents. One day Karl induced Cohn to accompany him to the City of Hope, a hospital in Duarte, California, for the treatment of cancer and related diseases. Cohn emerged with tears in his eyes. He agreed to join Karl and Alfred Hart as guests of honor at a banquet for the City of Hope.

Cohn became an official of the City of Hope and even participated in a telethon to benefit the hospital. It was his first appearance on television, and he stage-managed the show with his usual authority.

His secretary, Dona Holloway, was watching the show at her home, and she telephoned a message to the station: if Mr. Cohn would play a number on the piano, she would donate an entire week's salary to the City of Hope. The master of ceremonies showed the note to Cohn. He flared at the suggestion that he abandon his dignity. "She will be fired tomorrow morning," be snapped, tearing up the note. "She's fired."

Miss Holloway saw the entire action on television, and she was bewildered. At three o'clock that morning she received a telephone call from her boss. "Will you ever forgive me?" he asked. "I don't know why I did that."

At 4 A.M. Harry Cohn sat down to the piano before the television cameras and played *The Missouri Waltz*, in honor of another president named Harry.

Cohn had an immense fondness for Humphrey Bogart. The actor made films at Columbia on loan-out from Warner Brothers, later brought his Santana Productions to Columbia, and eventually sold his interest to the studio for $1,000,000. When Bogart was making *The Harder They Fall* for Columbia, he was dying of cancer. Harry Cohn and a few others knew it.

Bogart underwent an operation and submitted to cobalt treatments in a vain effort to halt the cancer. Harry Cohn made repeated announcements that Humphrey Bogart would star in *The Good Shepherd*, from the best-selling novel by C. S. Forester.

Cohn telephoned Bogart every week.

"The part's great for you, Bogie," Cohn enthused. "Better than *The Caine Mutiny*. Now I want you to get your ass over to the studio as soon as you can, so we can talk about the script. We want to start rolling as soon as you're okay."

Bogart confided to a friend, "Tell you why I think I'm going to beat this rap. It's Harry Cohn. He keeps calling me about going to work. Now you know that tough old bastard wouldn't call if he thought I wasn't going to make it."

Cohn continued the charade until Bogart's death on January 14, 1957.

4

"WHY WOULD HARRY COHN
BUY A DIRTY BOOK LIKE
FROM HERE TO ETERNITY?"

*T*he answer to the joke was; "He thinks everybody talks
that way."

The purchase by Harry Cohn of the James Jones novel *From
Here to Eternity* for $82,000 seemed a folly to many people,
including the executives of Columbia's New York office. The best
seller was notorious for its obscene words and scenes of raw sex.
Even if the story could be laundered enough to pass the still-
powerful industry censors, there were other forbidding problems. The Jones plot, although powerful in its cumulative effect,
was sprawling and undisciplined. Most of all, there was the
Army. The Hollywood studios still functioned under the wartime
system of submitting screenplays for military approval in return
for the right to photograph troops, equipment, and installations.
As a result, war films contained nothing critical of the military.
From Here to Eternity, with its depiction of sadism and favorit-
ism in the Army before Pearl Harbor, scarcely jibed with Pentagon policy. Yet Cohn needed Army installations and personnel to
lend authenticity to the film.

The first problem was licking the story. Cohn hit on a plan
that was unusual in film studios: he hired the author. The
unorthodox Jones came to Hollywood and did his writing from
midnight to seven in the morning, leaving his finished pages on
Cohn's desk before he departed. His treatment for the movie
script proved impractical, but he and Cohn established a warm
rapport. When Jones departed, he penned an inscription in a
copy of his book to Cohn: "From one ——off to another."

Cohn searched for screenwriters to adapt the massive novel.
Many refused the assignment, deeming the subject unconquer-

303

able. Others made attempts at treatments and failed. Cohn's executives urged him to abandon the project, but he refused. *From Here to Eternity* had become a cause with Harry Cohn.

A writer who had recently returned to Columbia suggested ways of solving the script problems. He was Daniel Taradash, who had come to Hollywood with Lew Meltzer to write their first screenplay, *Golden Boy*. Buddy Adler, who had been assigned to produce *From Here to Eternity*, was enthusiastic about the proposals by Taradash and arranged a meeting with Cohn and Columbia executives in Cohn's bedroom.

Cohn was also impressed, and he offered Taradash the assignment. The writer accepted, on condition that he receive 2.5 percent of the profits. Cohn agreed.

Taradash produced a detailed 100-page treatment that interwove the characters and solved the problems of censorship. Just as important, he discovered a way to mollify the Army: he injected a scene in which the corrupt captain was given an opportunity to resign his commission, rather than be promoted, as in the novel.

The treatment was enthusiastically received, and Taradash began work on the shooting script. Cohn remained apprised of the progress at all times, and he had numerous script meetings with Taradash and Adler. Cohn hammered away at each scene. His constant attack made Taradash and Adler question every line of dialogue, every piece of action.

The result was a script that was lean and hard. Then Cohn insisted that ten more pages be removed. Taradash answered angrily that Cohn could remove ten pages at random.

"Dan, I don't want to cut this script," Cohn said plaintively. "But we've got to."

Finally, the script was in order, and then Buddy Adler performed a delicate mission. A lieutenant colonel in the Signal Corps during the war, he maintained important connections in the Pentagon. He took the script to Washington, and within two days he had complete approval of the script and permission to film at Scofield Barracks in Hawaii, where the story took place.

Next came the selection of a director. Taradash had long favored Fred Zinnemann because of his sensitive portrayals of

GI's in *The Search* and *Teresa*. But Zinnemann had made a picture at Columbia that Cohn hated, *Member of the Wedding*. He argued that Zinnemann was an art house director who had never made anything commercial. Cohn was urged to see the recently filmed *High Noon*, which Zinnemann had directed for Stanley Kramer. Cohn saw the film but was unimpressed; it had not yet been tightly cut and lacked the highly effective score.

Taradash made an impassioned plea for Zinnemann, concluding with: "Maybe I won't make this picture with him, but I'll make one someday, by God." Cohn was impressed by Taradash's conviction, and Zinnemann was hired.

Zinnemann, soft-voiced and slight of stature, proved resolute in artistic matters, and he offered a good match for Harry Cohn. They clashed immediately on the casting of the boxer, Prewitt. Cohn insisted on Aldo Ray, since the role could make him a valuable star for Columbia. Besides, he had been on salary for ten weeks without working.

Zinnemann declared he wanted Montgomery Clift for the role. Cohn argued violently against Clift.

"Thank you, but if I can't have Clift, it's no deal," the director announced.

"I'm president of this company!" Cohn shouted. "You can't give me ultimatums."

"I'm not giving you ultimatums," said Zinnemann. "I want to make a good picture, and I don't see how I can make this picture without Monty Clift."

In the end, Cohn agreed to the casting of Clift.

For the role of Karen Holmes, the officer's wife who slept with enlisted men, Cohn wanted Joan Crawford. Adler, Zinnemann, and Taradash argued against her, but Cohn prevailed. Then Miss Crawford became disconcerted over her wardrobe and withdrew from the film.

Agent Bert Allenberg called on Harry Cohn to suggest in a hesitant manner the casting of his client, Deborah Kerr, as Karen. "Why, you stupid son of a bitch," yelled Cohn, "get out of here." Miss Kerr's Hollywood career had largely been limited to the playing of aloof British ladies at M-G-M.

When Cohn met with Adler, Zinnemann, and Taradash later that day, he scoffed, "You know what that crazy son of a bitch Allenberg suggested? Deborah Kerr for Karen."

The three visitors looked at one another and said almost simultaneously, "Yes!" Each saw the wisdom in casting an actress whose portrayal of promiscuity would offer the element of surprise. She was cast as Karen, and three weeks of coaching helped remove her British accent.

All parties agreed that Burt Lancaster should play Sergeant Warden. But Lancaster was in partnership with Harold Hecht to produce their own films and was unavailable. The only chance lay in acquiring an old commitment with Lancaster that producer Hal Wallis owned. Wallis was not inclined to sell. With production six weeks away, Columbia tentatively assigned Edmond O'Brien to the role of Warden.

Cohn's assistant, Milton Pickman, arrived at a formula for acquiring Lancaster. Columbia would pay Wallis $150,000 for Lancaster, who would earn $120,000 for the Wallis commitment. In addition, Columbia would pay $40,000 for a Wallis script, *Bad for Each Other*, plus the services of Lizabeth Scott and Charlton Heston in the film.

Donna Reed was the first to test for the role of Lorene, the prostitute. She was under contract to Columbia after eight years at M-G-M, and Cohn, always eager to prove Louis B. Mayer wrong, wanted her to play the star-making role. But Zinnemann was not in favor. He wanted Julie Harris, whom he had directed in *Member of the Wedding*. Cohn scorned her as a "child frightener."

Cohn asked Miss Reed to play a scene with Aldo Ray, when Cohn was still promoting him for Prewitt. Zinnemann photographed the test entirely on Ray's face, Miss Reed being seen only in profile or from the back of the head. Three months later Cohn asked her to test again, this time with black hair. A few weeks afterward he wanted her to test once more in the same scene.

"But why?" she asked. "I've already done that scene twice."

"Don't ask questions," Cohn ordered. "Just do it."

Miss Reed did as instructed, this time playing opposite Clift. It was the scene in which the prostitute spoke of returning home to lead a respectable life, and Zinnemann conceded a bourgeois quality in Miss Reed that gave dimension to the role. Cohn's device had worked. Since he had given in and allowed the other roles to be filled by outsiders, it was important to him to have one role cast with a Columbia player.

Zinnemann wanted Eli Wallach to play the role of Maggio, and the Broadway actor performed excellently in a test as the warm-hearted soldier who died in the stockade. All the production minds agreed Wallach should be hired, although Taradash had reservations that the actor seemed almost too muscular, too self-sufficient for the vulnerable Maggio.

Frank Sinatra had read the novel *From Here to Eternity* and was convinced the role of Maggio could alter the bad fortune that had befallen his career. A series of personal mishaps had brought him adverse publicity, and nervous tensions had reduced his singing voice to a pale approximation of its onetime glory. He had failed on a television network variety show, film offers had dwindled, and even his nightclub engagements were second-rate. Lacking any promising offers for his services, Sinatra had accompanied his second wife, Ava Gardner, to Africa for the filming of *Mogambo* with Clark Gable and Grace Kelly.

Harry Cohn was unpersuaded by Sinatra's entreaties to be considered for the role of Maggio. Only when Ava Gardner made a personal plea to Cohn did he agree to test Sinatra. The singer flew from Nairobi to Hollywood at his own expense and sat outside Cohn's office for two hours before being admitted.

"I'll pay you if you'll let me play the role," said Sinatra.

His test proved impressive, but Sinatra had little hope that he would win the role; he had heard that Wallach was virtually cast for it. Then Wallach discovered the film conflicted with a commitment he had made with Elia Kazan to appear in *El Camino Real* by Tennessee Williams on Broadway. Rather than renege on his promise to Kazan, Wallach declined the role of Maggio. Sinatra won it by default.

Cohn offered Sinatra $1,000 a week for eight weeks, a fraction of what he had previously earned in films. Sinatra and his agents agreed to the terms, especially since Cohn demanded no options on future pictures. They asked for assurance that Sinatra would be billed together with the other stars. It was a concession Cohn was reluctant to give, since he wanted to avoid any suggestion that *From Here to Eternity* was a musical. But in the end he billed all five stars above the title.

Cohn continued to work with Adler, Zinnemann, and Taradash in honing the script to a sharp edge. He insisted that they work at night in preparing for production, and one evening he magnanimously offered to take them to dinner at Perino's, an expensive Los Angeles restaurant.

"But I have no tie," Zinnemann protested.

"Don't worry about it," said Cohn. He buzzed the wardrobe department and ordered, "Bring me up three ties for Mr. Zinnemann to choose from."

The four men had dinner at Perino's, then returned to the studio to continue working on the script until after midnight. When the session was finally concluded, Zinnemann prepared to leave.

"Just a minute," Cohn said sternly. "Give me back the tie."

Cohn decreed that *From Here to Eternity* could cost no more than $2,000,000. Despite an expensive cast and a location in Hawaii, Adler was able to keep within the budget. The entire company was transported by charter airplane to Hawaii, arriving at 5 A.M. By midmorning, shooting had begun. Cohn denied Zinnemann's request that the company be given a day for sightseeing in the islands. As soon as location scenes were completed, cast and crew were flown back to Hollywood to finish the film. The entire picture required only forty-one days of shooting.

One languid evening shortly before location shots were completed, Zinnemann was filming the drunk scene between Clift and Sinatra before the officers' barracks at Fort De Russy. Cohn had declared that the two actors should play the scene standing up. But as they rehearsed the dialogue, both Sinatra and Zinnemann agreed that it flowed more easily in a sitting-down position. An informant on the set relayed the information to Harry Cohn, who was dining at the Royal Hawaiian Hotel with an Air Force general.

As Sinatra and Clift were enacting the scene, a siren was heard. An Air Force limousine swung into view and sped up to the camera position before the barracks. Out stepped Harry Cohn, an ominous scowl on his huge, tanned face. The general, also formidable in size and bearing, emerged after him. Both men wore white dinner jackets, and the general's was festooned with decorations.

Cohn strode up to Zinnemann and demanded an explanation of why his orders concerning the scene had been countermanded. The director explained that he had agreed with Sinatra that the scene seemed more effective if both soldiers squatted on the ground.

"You shoot it the way I tell you, or I am going to shut down the picture!" Cohn announced.

Zinnemann stared at the imposing, defiant figure of Cohn, then at the clusters of officers and other Army personnel who were observing the scene. Rather than create any further acrimony before the onlookers, he acquiesced to Cohn. The two white-jacketed leaders drove off in the limousine, leaving Zinnemann to complete the sequence. He later regretted having given in to Cohn. Zinnemann and Sinatra were estranged because of the incident.

Filming concluded in Hollywood, and Zinnemann began assembling a rough cut. Once again Cohn issued a ukase: *From Here to Eternity* could be no more than two hours in length. There was more to this than his usual demand for compact, tightly cut movies. Theater men then shunned overlong films, which cut down audience turnover.

The two-hour limit pained Zinnemann. He was forced to abandon two prized scenes: one in which Clift believed the Pearl Harbor attackers were Germans; another in which half a dozen soldiers in the barracks improvised a blues number, which Zinnemann wanted to use as a theme similar to the *High Noon* ballad.

Cohn remained adamant, and Zinnemann cut the film to its final 118 minutes. He permitted no interference in his right under the Directors Guild contract to edit the first cut himself. When Cohn surreptitiously edited a scene before Zinnemann had reviewed it, the two men had another confrontation of power. This time it was Cohn who relented; he restored the edited scene to its original condition.

Cohn recognized the greatness of *From Here to Eternity* sooner than anyone connected with the production. When the film approached release, he did a remarkable thing. For the first time in his history he allowed his name to appear in an advertisement for a Columbia picture. A message to the public over his signature conveyed the pride with which he was presenting *From Here to Eternity*.

The film became the biggest money-maker in Columbia history. Final cost, including prints and advertising, was $2,406,000; the first release brought $19,000,000 to the company. So great was the demand for seats at the Capitol in New York City that the theater remained open almost around the clock; it was closed briefly in the early morning so that janitors could sweep the floor.

Reviewers were as enthusiastic as the public. The New York Film Critics gave awards to *From Here to Eternity*, Lancaster, and Zinnemann. All five leading players were nominated for Academy Awards. Eight Oscars were won by the film, tying the record held by *Gone with the Wind*.

From Here to Eternity provided a golden touch to the careers of all the principals connected with it, especially Sinatra, whose Academy Award as supporting actor dramatized his conquest of failure. No one was more pleased with the film's success than Harry Cohn. At a time when all studios were dabbling with wide screens and three dimensions, he had electrified the industry with a film in black and white at the normal screen ratio.

Furthermore, he had demonstrated to his brother Jack and the other businessmen of the New York office how a single film, made under the close supervision of the company president and production head, could help Columbia's fortunes. In fiscal 1954, which reflected the earnings of *From Here to Eternity*, gross income leaped $20,000,000 to a record total of $80,000,000, and profits quadrupled to $3,500,000.

5
THREE COHN SUCCESSORS . . . AND
THEN THERE WAS NONE

*D*uring the 1950's, Jack Cohn, Abe Schneider, and others of the New York power complex applied increasing pressure on Harry Cohn to select someone to relieve himself of a portion of the burdens of studio leadership and to be his eventual successor. Harry Cohn recognized the necessity of grooming such a person, but he was incapable of doing so.

Three producers of recognized ability made programs of films at Columbia during the 1930's. All three possessed the qualities of leadership and creativity that qualified them to head the production of a major studio. All three vanished from Columbia for the customary reason: estrangement with Harry Cohn.

E. Maurice (Buddy) Adler had every requisite to command a major studio. He had the looks and grace of a leading man. The scion of a New York mercantile family, he was well spoken and mannerly, yet he could speak the primitive language of the self-made movie pioneers. Buddy Adler had learned film making from the ground up; he had risen from the M-G-M shorts department, as had Fred Zinnemann. After serving with distinction in the Signal Corps during World War II, Adler joined Columbia as a producer.

Harrry Cohn was remarkably fond of Buddy Adler, but as with most persons for whom he displayed fondness, he could not refrain from punishing Adler.

After the preview of *No Sad Songs for Me*, starring Margaret Sullavan and Wendell Corey, Cohn and entourage returned to his office for the usual assessment. Cohn pointed his finger at fourteen persons in the room, asking each for an opinion of the film's reception at the preview. He interrogated everyone in the room except the producer of *No Sad Songs for Me*, Buddy Adler.

Early in their relationship, Cohn discovered Adler's area of vulnerability. Adler's habits were exemplary; he was happily married to Anita Louise, who had been a Columbia actress. He did not drink to excess, nor was he susceptible to the lure of money as were others Cohn employed.

But Adler had a past. As the playboy member of the Adler family, he had become involved in a number of scrapes that made his advent to Hollywood a virtual exile. Cohn played on this repeatedly. "You know what you are, Buddy," Cohn hurled at him at the climax of an argument, and Adler was defeated.

Cohn exercised his verbal sadism on Adler again and again in conferences. During one savage cross-examination in the presence of a writer, Adler fell to his hands and knees and wailed, "Harry, what do you want of me?"

Victorious, Cohn remarked, "Oh, Buddy, you're so high-strung!"

Despite such treatment, Adler was intensely loyal to Cohn and commented many times, "Harry taught me everything I know about picture making." But ambition took precedence over loyalty, and with *From Here to Eternity* Adler saw the opportunity to establish his own name in the industry. He instructed the publicist on the film, Walter Shenson, "Whenever you have a member of the press on the set, bring him to see me first."

Shenson did as he was instructed, and Adler reaped much publicity during the filming. This did not escape the notice of Harry Cohn. When Adler was departing for the New York opening, Cohn told him, "Don't forget whose picture it is."

The Academy Awards brought the issue of credit more clearly into focus. Under rules enforced by the Screen Producers Guild, the actual producer of a film, rather than the studio head, was entitled to accept the Oscar for best picture. Cohn declined to attend the ceremonies. As Cohn watched the Awards on television, his elation at the victory of *From Here to Eternity* was tempered by the fact that Buddy Adler, not Harry Cohn, received the Oscar for best picture of 1953.

As a result of the triumph of *From Here to Eternity*, Adler drew offers from every major company. His contract with Columbia was expiring, and despite his treatment at the hands of Cohn, he was willing to remain at the studio if his terms were improved.

"I'll give him a thousand dollars a week for five years; take it or leave it," Cohn announced flatly to Adler's attorney.

Adler was astounded. The offer was no more than he had been receiving at Columbia. He accepted a contract at Twentieth Century-Fox to make a series of important films at a salary of $200,000 a year, plus $50,000 for each film and a percentage of the profits.

The departure of Adler upset Cohn, who had expected him to remain. The two men and their wives continued to be friendly on a social level, and Cohn expressed his pride when Adler ascended to head of Fox production upon the withdrawal of Darryl Zanuck.

Stanley Kramer had established himself as the most promising young independent producer through a string of well-made, successful films: *Home of the Brave, Champion, The Men, Cyrano de Bergerac,* and *High Noon.* He preferred to remain an independent, fashioning a picture a year with care and precision. But economics interfered with his plan. He had acquired as partners a financial expert, Sam Katz; the brilliant writer of the Kramer hits, Carl Foreman; and the man who had achieved an inordinate amount of publicity for the films, George Glass. All owned stock in the Kramer company, and a film a year was not enough to support the organization.

Impressed by Kramer's performance as a film maker, Cohn invited him to bring his company to Columbia. His offer was supported by the New York executives, who sought the infusion of young blood into the company. The move was favored by Katz, a founder of the theater chain of Balaban and Katz and a former executive at M-G-M. He envisioned a new empire with himself behind the throne as Kramer assumed leadership from Cohn.

Kramer was reluctant to move to Columbia. He had spent his youth in the big studios, and he detested the authoritarian rule. He agreed to the deal only after receiving assurances of complete autonomy.

Cohn demonstrated his enthusiasm for the contract by posing for photographers at the signing on March 19, 1951. Kramer was to deliver thirty motion pictures in five years. Cohn declared, "This is the most important deal we have ever made. Never before has an arrangement of this kind been concluded between a major corporation and a completely self-operating independent organization."

He could not, of course, abide Kramer's independence. Fearful of being swallowed by Cohn, the young film maker avoided him. This confused and disturbed Cohn. He was especially upset because Kramer declined to join him for lunch in the executive dining room. Kramer recognized it as the focus of trouble for Cohn's underlings.

Uncomfortable in the position of a "miniature Zanuck," Kramer nevertheless set his company in motion by purchasing a number of plays and books as story material. His contract required him to make his films for less than $980,000 apiece, unless Harry Cohn gave special permission. Most of Kramer's independent films had cost less than half that amount, but now he was faced with the addition of studio overhead charges. Although he gave the films the same thoughtful preparation as before, he was unable to cast them importantly. Lacking big names and other box office values, the films were pushed out by the Columbia sales organization along with the rest of the product; they failed to receive the special handling that Kramer films had required.

The returns were uniformly poor. Deficits were amassed by _Death of a Salesman_ (which Cohn especially hated), _The Happy Time, Member of the Wedding, My Six Convicts, The Four Poster, The Juggler, Eight Iron Men, The Sniper_, and _The Wild One_. The greatest fiasco was a musical fantasy, _The 5,000 Fingers of Dr. T_, which Cohn had allowed to achieve a $1,631,000 cost. Its gross was $249,000.

The Cohn-Kramer relationship deteriorated with each failure. Kramer realized the fallacy of trying to pursue a role he was unsuited for, and he yearned for escape. But he wanted to leave on a note of success.

The Caine Mutiny had been published to reviews that were mild to uncomplimentary. Many reviewers ignored the Herman

Wouk novel entirely. But screenwriter Stanley Roberts saw possibilities as film material and urged Kramer to buy it. He did so, paying $60,000.

Kramer sought to film *The Caine Mutiny* as his last film for Columbia. To do so, he had to overcome two formidable opponents: the United States Navy, which refused cooperation on the ground that it had never had a mutiny in its history; and Harry Cohn, who was increasingly unfriendly to the Kramer cause and retained the $980,000 cost limit. Kramer journeyed to Washington and went over the heads of lesser officers to plead his ease before the Secretary of the Navy and the Chief of Naval Operations. They believed Kramer's argument that he planned no damage to the Navy's reputation, and the producer was permitted the use of three destroyers, three tenders, aircraft carriers, and 2,000 marines in landing barges.

Cohn was more difficult to negotiate with. He recognized the potential of the project, especially after *The Caine Mutiny* had become an immense seller. But Cohn decreed that the film could cost no more than $2,000,000, had to be shot in fifty-four days or less, and could run no more than two hours on the screen. The limitations placed strains on Kramer and his director, Edward Dmytryk. The Roberts script had to be cut from a compact 190 pages down to 110, thus eliminating many transitional scenes. Since Kramer planned an expensive cast—Humphrey Bogart, Fred MacMurray, Van Johnson, and José Ferrer were among the leading actors—economies had to be made elsewhere.

Kramer met the Cohn restrictions, and the film suffered accordingly. *The Caine Mutiny* was released at a time when elaborately produced films of three hours or more in length were proving commercially sound.

Although it may not have achieved its potential, *The Caine Mutiny* was a big success—an $11,000,000 gross versus a complete cost of $2,414,000. It wiped out the deficits created by the previous ten films made for Columbia by Kramer. But by this time there was no basis for his continuance at the studio. Columbia bought all rights to the films, and his contract was ended.

Cohn and Kramer had an acrimonious parting.

"You cost the studio a lot of money," Cohn declared.

"Yes, I did," Kramer replied defiantly.

"We are glad to see you go.

"I'm glad to be going."

A year later Kramer had produced and directed *Not as a Stranger* independently. He encountered Cohn on a flight to Las Vegas.

Cohn slipped a fatherly arm around Kramer's shoulder and said warmly, "I hear you've got a great picture. I want you to know I'm proud of you.

Harry Cohn wanted to hire Jerry Wald during the time Wald was producing films at Warner Brothers, but he was deterred by fears that Jack Warner would learn of such a move. Again, he wanted Wald when the producer combined with Norman Krasna in an abortive effort to rescue the fortunes of RKO, but Cohn was afraid Howard Hughes would resent having his production boss lured away. Cohn grew bolder when reports circulated that Hughes was going to sell RKO.

Wald met with Cohn dozens of times, often in Cohn's bedroom late at night. Finally, they arrived at an agreement that Wald believed would preserve his independence and freedom of action. He moved from RKO to Columbia on October 29, 1952.

The Cohn-Wald rapprochement reached its peak in the first week and declined thereafter. By the end of a year it was apparent that the arrangement would not work. Wald was presumably in charge of production, but Cohn thwarted him in every project.

"Working for Cohn," Wald once complained, "is like playing for a football coach who trains you to the utmost, then sends you on the field with the wrong signals."

Wald, an ebullient man who sparked ideas and liked to hurry into movie columns with them, was restrained by Cohn's ukase against publicity for producers. When he attempted to bootleg items to columnists, Cohn found him out and confronted him with the violation of rules. Cohn constantly humiliated Wald in story conferences, disparaging the producer's ideas in abusive terms.

"Why does he do that to me?" Wald once exclaimed as he left Cohn's office after another rebuke.

"Why do you let him do it to you?" asked the writer who had been present.

One of Wald's favorite projects was *The Harder They Fall*, a story of corruption in boxing. Wald wanted Budd Schulberg to adapt his novel to the screen, but Schulberg was not eager to work for Cohn. His father, B. P. Schulberg, had been hired as a producer at Columbia after his fall from leadership of Paramount. The elder Schulberg, having been head of a major studio, had been an ideal target for Cohn's abuse, and his tenure at Columbia had been a miserable one.

Wald tried to overcome Budd Schulberg's objections to working at Columbia and assured the writer he could do the script without entering the studio. Cohn would not permit it.

"Goddammit, I want my writers on the lot," Cohn said. "They are to check in at nine, take an hour for lunch, and work until six, just like anyone else." Schulberg declined the assignment.

In 1956 Wald made his escape, joining Twentieth Century-Fox with his own production company.

To Schulberg, author of *What Makes Sammy Run?*, Wald remarked, "For years I have been fighting the Sammy Glick image; people thought that I was Sammy. Let me tell you something: Sammy Glick was a Boy Scout leader compared to Harry Cohn."

6

THE TROUBLE WITH
LOVE GODDESSES

*R*ita Hayworth returned to the United States after less than two years as Aly Khan's princess. During the interim she had acquired a second daughter, Yasmin, and had managed to lose her entire savings of $300,000. It was imperative that she return to work. She instructed her agents at the William Morris office to inform Harry Cohn she was resuming her contract. Hence, she was once more under salary at $3,500 a week.

Her sudden return caught Harry Cohn by surprise. He immediately assigned writers to work on a story, but weeks went by without a usable script. The Hayworth salary continued, and the East was clamoring for Cohn to put her to work. He sent for Vincent Sherman, a facile director who had made a creditable remake of *Craig's Wife* with Joan Crawford.

"How would you like to direct Rita Hayworth's first picture since her divorce from Aly Khan?" said Cohn.

"I'd love to," said Sherman. "Got a script?"

"No, but I've got a great story," said Cohn. He gave the director twenty-five pages of a Virginia Van Upp original story concerning a man who returned to Trinidad to discover his brother murdered and the brother's wife suspected of the crime.

They agreed on terms and shook hands. Cohn explained the urgency of the film. "Do the best you can, but get me a picture," said Cohn, offering these instructions: "Don't give her too much dialogue. Cut to her face and have her say, 'Who me?' Play to her reaction—she's a great reactor. Give me ten to twelve reels of film, a couple of dance numbers, some conflict between her and Glenn Ford, and some exotic backgrounds. If you do that, I'll give you a deal for another picture."

Cohn promised to equip Sherman with a fancy office, stock it with flowers, and invite Louella Parsons to witness the announcement of Rita's returning film. Cohn carried out his promise and ordered Rita to be present.

Rita's appearance was the first signal of the impending trouble between her and Cohn.

"How do you like that!" Cohn muttered afterward. "I give you a big office and lots of fanfare, and she shows up in jeans and blouse!"

"I thought she looked charming," Sherman said.

"She's a princess!" Cohn protested. "She should dress like one!"

Rita became cognizant of the hurried nature of *Affair in Trinidad*. She balked at reporting for the start of production and insisted on more adequate preparation of the script. Cohn was furious at the further extension of her salary.

Affair in Trinidad was completed by Sherman for $1,200,000, and Cohn released it hurriedly, since Rita had been off the screen for more than two years. The film did good business, but drew less than previous Hayworth pictures. Cohn did not stint in the next two films for her. The first was *Salome*, an opulent biblical drama, and *Miss Sadie Thompson*, an updated version of *Rain*. Both films were marked by wrangles between Cohn and his star. He accused her of malingering, while she declared he was shunting expenses for other movies to her company, Beckworth.

Cohn's troubles with Rita were compounded when she decided impulsively to marry once more.

Her husband number four was singer Dick Haymes. She felt sorry for him when he came to visit her in Hawaii during the filming of *Miss Sadie Thompson*. The trip brought him under the threat of deportation since he was an Argentine citizen and had not notified authorities that he was traveling to an American territory. Rita married him to eliminate the possibility that he would be deported.

Soon Dick Haymes was dictating the style of Rita's hair, her costumes in films, the kinds of roles she should play. Haymes also volunteered to produce Rita's pictures and to costar opposite her. It was more than Harry Cohn could bear.

Harry Cohn's disenchantment with his princess was accompanied by a realization that her stardom had waned. Some eroding element—the escapades with Aly, the absence from the screen, or merely a new generation of moviegoers seeking their own favorites—had caused Rita's popularity to diminish. The films she made after her return from Europe, which were no better or worse than the hits she had made in the 1940's, brought smaller returns. The blame could not be placed on the falling market for films; *From Here to Eternity* proved that the proper combination of elements could still produce a bonanza.

After Rita Hayworth walked out on another script, Harry Cohn made his solemn announcement: "We will make a star."

Her name was Marilyn Novak, and she was touring the country as Miss Deepfreeze in a promotional campaign for Thor appliances. During her visit to Los Angeles she attended a party where she met a young man who worked in the casting department at Columbia Studios. He suggested that she drop in to talk with his boss, Maxwell Arnow.

Marilyn visited the studio, and Arnow was impressed with the raw beauty of the young woman. He gave her tips on grooming and suggested that she return for coaching and a screen test after she finished the tour.

She went back home to Chicago, where her father worked as a clerk for the Milwaukee Railroad, then returned to Hollywood. Instead of reporting to Arnow, she found work amid an assemblage of other anonymous beauties supporting Jane Russell in a Howard Hughes musical, *French Line*. An agent named Wilt Melnick saw her on the set and gave her his card, suggesting that she call at his office, the Louis Shurr-Al Melnick agency.

Marilyn arrived and signed an agency contract. Melnick put it in his desk. "It stays there until you take off weight," he declared. She lost fifteen pounds in ten days.

She revisited the agency one day when Maxwell Arnow happened to drop by on his vacation. When Louis Shurr started to introduce Marilyn, Arnow said, "I've met her. I want her to make a test."

She tested in a two-minute scene from a Benn Levy play. Being totally unschooled in acting, Marilyn was at a loss to know what to do with her hands. "Lean against the mantel with your arms outstretched behind you," suggested Arnow. It was a fortunate posture, not only immobilizing her hands but also accenting her most apparent assets.

Harry Cohn was not visibly impressed with the test footage. "I can't hear what she's saying," he complained.

"Don't listen; just look," suggested Jerry Wald.

"What can I do with her?" said Cohn after the test was over. "She can't act."

"A lot of stars in pictures can't act," Arnow argued, "but they're great personalities. That's what this kid is. She'll never be able to act, but that doesn't matter. She's got star quality."

Cohn recognized the fact, but as always, he was testing the confidence of his executives. He agreed to sign the girl to a contract, but at no more than $125 a week. Her agents reluctantly accepted.

Now, as always, Cohn set about to create Marilyn Novak in an image of his own devising. First, the name.

Cohn announced that the new actress would be called Kit Marlowe. Marilyn protested, and he learned at the outset of his relations with her that she was to be no acquiescent star.

"I don't like this Kit Marlowe thing," she declared.

"What have you got to say about it?" Cohn snapped. "We're deciding."

"Well, it's my name, she replied. "How can you expect me to be around this business long when you give me a gimmick name? I'm no Marlowe. The name has to fit the girl."

"So what do you suggest?"

Obviously she could not retain Marilyn, since it was already the possession of a famous blonde. "I like Kim," she announced. "It's close to Kit, which is what you wanted, and it's got three letters, too. And I like my own last name, too."

Cohn grudgingly agreed to Kim Novak. He then assigned the Columbia departments to glamorize her. Clay Campbell devised a makeup that softened her Bohemian features. Helen Hunt fluffed Kim's hair into a halo of silvery blonde tinted with lavender. Jean Louis designed a wardrobe to accentuate her most appealing feature, her bust.

But Kim again demonstrated her qualities of independence. She altered the makeup to suit herself. She disappeared inside her dressing room and appeared later with her hair in a style she pre-ferred. She declined Jean Louis's insistence that she wear a brassiere.

"She has no bust!" shouted Cohn when he saw test films of the new Kim Novak.

"That *is* her bust," Jean Louis said resignedly.

Cohn instructed the designer, "I want her to wear a brassiere."

"Impossible; she refuses," said Jean Louis.

"I don't care. You put a brassiere on her."

Realizing the gravity of the Cohn ultimatum, Jean Louis argued the issue with Kim. She became hysterical in her refusal, and the designer declared, "You must wear the brassiere in the fitting; what you do after that is your own affair." She wore brassieres thereafter.

Searching for a vehicle to introduce his new star, Cohn decided on a melodrama called *Pushover*. It was not an AA pic-ture, but it offered Kim a showy role and a chance to play oppo-site a polished performer, Fred MacMurray. Cohn realized that Kim would need a director who was sensitive to her inexperience and could give her the patient instruction she needed. Cohn tested several directors in scenes with Kim and MacMurray before deciding on Richard Quine, a former actor whom Cohn had developed as a director. Despite budget limitations, Quine photographed some of Kim's scenes again and again until she delivered a creditable performance.

The reception to Kim in *Pushover* convinced Cohn that he now had a star of sufficient caliber to replace Rita Hayworth. He was determined not to commit the same errors of permissiveness that had made Rita a continual headache to him. All of Cohn's possessive instincts exerted themselves on his new star, and he attempted to dictate her life at the studio and away from it.

Cohn insisted that Kim live at the Studio Club, a YWCA-sponsored rooming house for aspirants to the movie business; there she had to conform to the curfews, as in a college dormi-tory. When she began gaining weight, he made her live in her stu-dio dressing room and eat slimming meals prepared by the studio chef. Cohn refused to allow her to date except on weekends while she was working, and he placed a guard outside the Studio Club to make sure she didn't.

Kim's principal escort was a builder and theater owner named Mac Krim. Cohn kept himself apprised of the romance and made it clear to Kim that she should not acquire the distraction of a marriage during the vital, formative years of her career. Once Cohn reluctantly accepted an invitation to dine with Kim and Krim at Krim's house. Kim and Mrs. Cohn withdrew after dinner, and Krim left Cohn alone for a few minutes. When Krim returned, he found Cohn searching the closets.

"Can I help you with something?" Krim asked.

"No, Cohn replied. "I was just looking to see if any of her clothes were here. I wanted to make sure she wasn't living with you."

Kim made overtures of friendship to her gruff, unrelenting boss. One Christmas she had returned from her first personal appearance tour. Unable to afford presents for her friends, she had cooked some fudge at the Studio Club and wrapped it in colorful packages. She took one to Cohn.

"What's this?" he demanded, staring at the box.

"It's some fudge, Mr. Cohn," she replied. "For Christmas."

"Well, you don't think you're going to get anything from me, do you?"

"No, sir."

"All right. And another thing. I heard when you were on radio during your tour you told an interviewer that I was really a nice man."

"Yes, sir, I did."

"How dare you say that? You've only met me a few times. How do you know whether I'm a nice man or not? Don't you go around talking about me like that anymore. Understand?"

"Yes, Mr. Cohn."

Kim complained to her friends at the studio that Cohn never called her anything but Novak, and the way he said it made it sound like an insult. Outside her hearing, he referred to her as "that fat Polack."

Despite their lack of warmth toward each other, Kim's career progressed rapidly under Cohn's direction. He gave her another showcase role, this time in a more important film, *Phffft*, starring Judy Holliday and Jack Lemmon. Then she played a lead in *Five Against the House.*

Now Cohn believed she was ready for an acting challenge, and he chose to star her with William Holden, Rosalind Russell, Cliff Robertson, Betty Field, and Arthur O'Connell in *Picnic.* Joshua Logan, who was accustomed to directing experienced performers on the stage, objected to including Kim in the picture.

"Take her, or I'll get a new director," Cohn decreed.

Logan acquiesced. But after interviews with the stolid Kim he despaired of achieving any fire from her performance in the role of the small-town girl awakening to life. Logan directed her in a test of a love scene with Aldo Ray. The director told Ray, "Get some emotion from her any way you can, short of rape." Ray followed instructions, and the result was a torrid scene that proved Kim could exhibit emotion on the screen.

Picnic was an ordeal for her. She was terrified by Logan and fearful in the company of such accomplished actors. She reacted with balkiness. Once, on the sweltering Kansas location, Logan was filming the picnic sequence with the entire cast and thousands of local extras. Kim would not emerge from her dressing room across the park lake. Emissaries were sent to notify her, but still she did not appear. Logan fumed, then grabbed a bullhorn, and broadcast the message: "Kim, you get over here right now!"

Her dressing room door remained shut. Finally, Logan stormed across the bridge to her dressing room, threw open the door, grabbed Kim by the wrist, and marched her to the camera.

"Now, goddammit, you act!" he ordered.

Picnic established Kim as a star, but her confidence did not increase. Her behavior on *The Eddy Duchin Story* caused Tyrone Power to comment, "Confusion between temperament and bad manners is unfortunate."

The major and minor crises involving his new star were a source of irritation to Cohn, but he had accomplished his purpose. The value of Kim was established in cash terms when Otto Preminger sought to borrow her to appear opposite Frank Sinatra in *The Man with the Golden Arm*. Cohn bargained toughly with Preminger and exacted a $100,000 fee, a handsome profit for Columbia, since her salary was $750 a week.

Kim also began to realize her value. She found it inequitable that she should be starring in the title role of *Jeanne Eagels* for $13,000 while her leading man, Jeff Chandler, was paid $200,000.

Kim fired her agents and signed with the William Morris office. She made it clear that she expected to be paid more for her work. She refused to report for her next assignment, and Cohn placed her on suspension.

Cohn had long used the suspension to bring actors to submission; usually they lacked the savings to hold out for long. But the economic sanctions failed with Kim; she was being paid by her agency while denied her Columbia salary. This infuriated Cohn more.

His fury was so great that he did an unusual thing: he granted an interview. *Time* magazine was planning a cover story on Kim Novak and sought an interview with her warring boss, Harry Cohn. To the surprise of his publicity chief, George Lait, Cohn agreed to see reporter Ezra Goodman.

Among the rambling statements by Cohn:

> Great parts make great pictures! Great pictures make great parts! This girl has had five hit pictures. If you wanna bring me your wife or your aunt, we'll do the same for them. . . . [concerning Kim's worth] You can't put a figure on her. Star salaries are astronomic today. We've got twelve to fifteen million dollars invested in her. She's the number-one woman star in Hollywood. Audrey Hepburn is the only one else. The public has accepted this girl. . . . [The stars] believe that publicity after a while. There's nothing you can do about it. I have never met a grateful performer in the picture business. . . . Hayworth might be worth ten million dollars today easily! She owned twenty-five per cent of the profits with her own company and had hit after hit and she had to get married and had to get out of the business and took a suspension because

she fell in love again! In five years, at two pictures a year, at twenty-five per cent! Think of what she could have made! But she didn't make pictures! She took two or three suspensions! She got mixed up with different characters! Unpredictable!

Eventually, Cohn came to terms with Kim—her terms.

7
DEALINGS WITH ACTORS: ALDO RAY, DONNA REED, KATHRYN GRANT, JACK LEMMON, MARLENE DIETRICH, BRODERICK CRAWFORD

*A*ldo DaRé was a former constable of Crockett, California, who had been chosen more or less by accident to play a football player in *Saturday's Hero*, starring John Derek and Donna Reed. DaRé's masculine inelegance appealed to Harry Cohn, who decreed the usual name change. His own Italian name would read "Dare" instead of "DaRay" to the general public, argued Cohn, who proposed the name of John Harrison, after his two sons. DaRé won a compromise as Aldo Ray.

Cohn took personal charge of Ray's career. The young actor's teeth were straightened, his voice was trained to be less raspy, and he was fitted for five suits by Cohn's tailor, all at Cohn's expense. He assured Ray he would never need an agent, because Harry Cohn would always take care of him.

Indeed, Aldo Ray was given a starring role in his second picture, opposite Judy Holliday in *The Marrying Kind*. Proud of his discovery, Cohn sent Ray on a personal appearance tour throughout the country.

The actor was earning only $200 a week, and he saw in the tour a chance to improve his financial position. He signed his name to charges for clothes for himself and presents for his family in Crockett. When he returned to Hollywood, he received no check on the following payday. Another week passed with no check. On the third payday he went to the cashier's window and was handed a check for 24 cents.

Ray, a hearty extrovert, was convulsed by Cohn's retaliation for his tour extravagance. He went from department to department in the studio, displaying the check and laughing uproariously. One of those he showed it to was Jonie Taps, a music department executive who was close to Harry Cohn. Taps offered Ray $1 for the check, and the actor quickly accepted.

As Ray was leaving the studio, the gateman told him, "Mr. Cohn wants to see you.

Ray reported to Cohn's office and was admitted immediately.

"You want to see me, boss?" Ray asked.

"Yes! Sit down!" Cohn said fiercely. He waved the 24-cent check in Ray's face and asked, "Have you seen this before?"

"Sure—that's my paycheck," Ray said.

"How dare you show that around the studio?" Cohn demanded. "Don't you know you're making the studio a laughing-stock? Don't you realize you're holding me up to ridicule?"

"Don't get mad," Ray said lightly. "What about me? I can't even buy a hamburger with that check."

Cohn continued his tirade while Ray tried to explain that he had merely thought it was a good joke. Cohn dismissed him.

On the following day Cohn's secretary called Ray to tell him to report to the office. Ray feared he was to receive another reprimand, and he approached Cohn with caution.

"Sit down!" Cohn said gruffly. "You did a good job on that tour. Take this."

He handed Ray a check for $10,000. The actor was dumbfounded.

"Now don't go out and spend it," Cohn instructed. "Put it in the bank."

As Ray left the office, Cohn added a final note of caution: "And don't go around biting the hand that feeds you."

Relations between Cohn and Ray remained good for a year, after which time the actor felt he was being underpaid and ill-used. Cohn had promised him Prewitt in *From Here to Eternity*, but the role had gone to Montgomery Clift. Ray was shunted to loan-outs for high prices while he received only his usual Columbia salary. The actor hired an agent.

The cordiality between Ray and Cohn vanished. The actor took suspension after suspension rather than perform in films he believed inferior. Cohn became increasingly furious. He barred Ray from the studio when he wasn't employed in a picture.

The nadir of their relations came one day when Cohn was being shaved in the Columbia barbershop. Ray strolled in.

"What the hell are you doing here?" growled Cohn.

"I'm here to get a haircut, like I always do," said Ray.

"Get out! Get out!" Cohn commanded.

"What the hell do I have to do to get the right kind of treatment at this studio—be a relative?" Ray asked.

Cohn exploded with a burst of expletives so violent that a producer and director in the shop urged Ray to leave. Long afterward Ray regretted the incident and the unexplained estrangement from Cohn. He could not forget that Cohn had once wanted to name him after his, Harry Cohn's, own sons.

Donna Reed believed she knew Harry Cohn. Her husband, Tony Owen, had worked intimately with Cohn, and she had known Cohn as a social friend and as an employer. She knew that one of his great fears was that the recipient of his generosity would not be grateful. So she did not complain at the beginning of *From Here to Eternity* when Fred Zinnemann, who had not wanted her cast as Alma, neglected to shoot any close-ups of her scenes with Montgomery Clift. She merely kept a list of the camera angles she knew would be needed.

In conversation with the film editor, William Lyons, she learned that he, too, had kept a list of shots that Zinnemann had neglected. Lyons presented his list to Harry Cohn, who ordered the necessary shots filmed.

Cohn was protective of Miss Reed in other ways. Since she was the only Columbia player in the cast, he directed the publicity department to emphasize her in the press releases and interview assignments. Realizing she had an excellent chance to win an Academy Award, he continued the publicity campaign.

After she had completed *From Here to Eternity*, Cohn cast her in a fifteen-day picture.

The actress was astonished. She could not imagine that Harry Cohn would ask her to follow *From Here to Eternity* with a B picture. When she refused the film, he assigned her to Westerns.

Miss Reed could not fathom the reason for the treatment, except that perhaps he feared her ingratitude. She received cryptic messages from Cohn's secretary: "You know, you're welcome to have lunch in the executive dining room."

On another occasion a Cohn aide asked her, "Have you thanked Harry for *From Here to Eternity*?"

"Of course, I have," she replied. "What else can I do?"

Miss Reed could find no solution for Cohn's attitude. Four days before the Academy nomination she realized her situation was desperate. Unless she escaped Columbia, her life would be miserable. She instructed her agent, "Ask for my release; this is a matter of life or death."

Harry Cohn granted her one final kindness: he gave her the release.

Max Arnow saw possibilities in an acting hopeful named Kathryn Grant, formerly Kathryn Grandstaff of Houston, Texas. Arnow asked Jean Louis to choose a proper dress for Miss Grant, then saw that she was carefully made up and coiffed before presenting her to Harry Cohn.

The studio boss was telephoning, and he continued his conversation as the young girl stood uneasily, then angrily before him. He merely gave her a sidelong glance and continued talking. By the time he hung up the phone, she was furious, and she stalked out of the office when the interview was over.

Miss Grant was tested and signed to a contract, and Cohn arranged for her to continue taking college courses with the studio teacher and eventually to receive her degree from the University of Texas. Cohn enjoyed arguing with the Sprightly Texan, except when she used large words.

"Don't use your damned education on me," he said.

"Why not? You gave it to me," she replied. He appeared to be pleased.

Cohn was also pleased when a romance developed between his young actress and Bing Crosby, then a widower. Columnists had rumored a marriage, and the press was alerted when the pair flew off to Hayden Lake in Idaho for a wedding. All the churches in the area were covered by reporters and photographers. The publicity-shy Crosby flew with his wife-to-be to Las Vegas and then to Pebble Beach, but the press was everywhere. He decided against the wedding.

The distraught actress flew home, and Harry Cohn directed her to report to his office.

"Miss Grant, what may I do for you?" he asked.

"I would like to work very hard—right now," she replied.

"I will send you on a personal appearance tour in two days," he announced.

Cohn ordered her outfitted with a glamour wardrobe and sent her on an extensive tour of the country with publicist Muriel Davidson. When the actress returned, he kept her at work in important pictures.

On October 23, 1957, Harry Cohn received a telephone call from Kathryn Grant in Las Vegas. "Mr. Cohn, I have some news for you," she said.

"You don't need to tell me," he interrupted. "You're going to marry Bing tomorrow."

"How could you know? We've only told three or four people!"

"A little bird told me," he replied happily. He had received a telephone call from a Las Vegas informant half an hour earlier.

Max Arnow had been delegated to locate a new leading man for Judy Holliday in *It Should Happen to You*, and he found an ebullient young television actor who seemed a distinct possibility. The director, George Cukor, saw a film of the actor and agreed that he should be signed.

Jack Lemmon completed *It Should Happen to You* without meeting Harry Cohn. The actor returned to his New York home, then came back to the studio for dubbing and retakes. Meanwhile, he was negotiating with Columbia for a contract that would give him what other studios had failed to offer: opportunity to do plays and outside films.

After Lemmon had finished his final dubbing, he received a message from Arnow: "*He* wants to see you."

"Okay," said Lemmon, "but it's five o'clock, and I've got to catch a seven o'clock plane."

Lemmon reported to the office of the president, and Cohn viewed him with caution. Here was a new breed of actor: independent, unafraid of studio authority, devoted to the stage, even Harvard-educated!

"We're going to change your name," Cohn announced.

"The hell you are," replied Lemmon.

"How the hell can I put a name like Jack Lemmon on a picture?" Cohn demanded. "The critics will murder you."

"I'll take my chances."

"Let me tell you a story, young man. Once a girl walked into this office, and she was unknown. I changed her name, and she became a star."

"Who was that?"

"Ann Sothern," Cohn said proudly.

"And what was her name before you changed it?"

"Harriet Lake."

"That does it! Harriet Lake is much better. Ann Sothern is the most theatrical name I ever heard. I can see it in lights on Broadway."

The argument continued with neither man giving ground.

"What would you change my name to?" Lemmon asked.

Cohn spelled it out: "L-E-N-N-O-N."

"And how would you pronounce it?"

"Lennon."

"Great! Just like Lenin, the Russian. They'll say I'm a Commie!"

"Hah!" Cohn replied in triumph. "I looked up Lenin, and it's pronounced Lay-neen."

The conference ended in an impasse. Lemmon flew East and embarked on a motor trip through New England with his wife. During the drive he became even more resolute in his determination to retain his name. His motivations were basic. All his life he had endured taunts and jests because of his name; the temptation for playmates to make sport of it was increased by his middle name of Uhler, thus encouraging cries of "Jack U. Lemmon!" Retaining the name had become a matter of pride.

Also, Lemmon went to Hollywood with a stage actor's normal suspicion that movie moguls would try to mold him into the traditional image of a movie star. If Cohn could change his name,

Lemmon reasoned, Cohn could change him in other ways as well. Lemmon was determined to maintain his individuality.

Cohn dispatched telegrams along the Lemmons' route of travel. "Awaiting decision on contract" Cohn messaged. Lemmon did not reply. "Received no answer to yesterday's telegram," Cohn wired. Lemmon remained silent.

Finally, Lemmon reached Campobello Island and dispatched his reply to Cohn: "Have been taking this much time to give special consideration. I am not changing my name."

Having tested the actor's mettle, Cohn gave in.

Cohn held no grudge over the actor's recalcitrance. He even rewarded Lemmon with special "Introducing" billing on *It Should Happen to You*. He continued to receive important films: a musical with Betty Grable and Marge and Gower Champion, *Three for the Show*; another comedy with Judy Holliday, *Phffft*; and *My Sister Eileen* with Janet Leigh.

Relations between Cohn and Lemmon were remarkably smooth. Whenever the actor felt he was not suited for a role, he explained his reasons to Cohn, and he was excused for the assignment. "I won't force you to do it," said Cohn, "but *you* go tell the producer, director, and writer why you don't want to do the picture." It was difficult for Lemmon to explain to a film's creators why he declined to be associated with it, but he always carried out his end of the agreement with Cohn.

Cohn was unable to believe that an actor could continue to deal with him in a calm, straightforward, and honest manner, and he maintained his suspicions. When Lemmon asked to be lent to Warner Brothers for *Mister Roberts*, Cohn agreed because of his affection for the director of the film.

"I give you my blessing out of respect for John Ford," said Cohn, adding, "but don't come back here complaining about the size of your dressing room and thinking what a big man you are."

Lemmon's performance as Ensign Pulver won him an Academy Award as best supporting actor of 1955, but his attitude never changed. He remained a source of wonderment to Cohn, who often remarked, though never to Lemmon, "That's the nicest actor we've ever had on the lot."

After *Pal Joey* had been first produced on Broadway, Harry Cohn purchased the film rights, the character of the conscience-less John O'Hara hero appealing to him. For years Cohn tried to produce *Pal Joey*, but he was always thwarted by script and casting difficulties. During the 1950's Cohn sought Marlene Dietrich for the role of the rich, mature woman who contributed to Joey's support. Dietrich agreed to play the role if Frank Sinatra played opposite her in the title role. Cohn was still angry with Sinatra for the affair at Fort De Russy, when the actor and Fred Zinnemann had tried to defy Cohn's orders. Cohn proposed Jack Lemmon as Dietrich's leading man. She refused, stating that Jack Lemmon was "a nobody," and she withdrew from *Pal Joey*.

Cohn was incensed because his hopes of filming *Pal Joey* were once more disappointed. He vowed vengeance against Dietrich.

The actress had been earning huge salaries with her appearances in Las Vegas gambling houses, and her favorite designer for onstage gowns was Columbia's Jean Louis. Cohn decreed that Jean Louis could no longer supply costumes to Dietrich.

She was not easily dissuaded. She notified her employers in Las Vegas, and they spoke with their liaisons in Chicago, who made representations to Harry Cohn.

Jean Louis received a telephone call from Cohn, who said, "You can go ahead with the stuff for that Dietrich dame. But she is not to enter the studio by the front door—understand? She comes in the side door only."

Dietrich got what she wanted, and Cohn was defeated. But he was later to call on the gentlemen of Chicago to return the favor.

During his long years as president of Columbia Pictures, Harry Cohn knew no stormier or more generally satisfactory relationship with an actor than the one he had with Broderick Crawford.

It was perhaps inevitable that the two should experience such conflict and affinity with each other. Both were blustery men, big in size and appetite; both practiced individualism as a near-religion. Crawford did his best work for the studio in two

Cohnesque roles: Willie Stark in *All the King's Men* and Harry Brock in *Born Yesterday*.

The first meeting presaged the nature of their relations. Crawford had made an impressive test for *All the King's Men*, and all that remained was for him to come to terms with Columbia. A meeting was arranged between Cohn and Crawford, along with his agent, Al Melnick.

"I hear you're going to be with us," said Cohn.

"Don't be too sure," the actor replied.

"What do you think of the script?" Cohn asked.

"I think it's the best I ever read."

"Then what are you worried about?"

"I figure to get screwed on the contract."

Crawford agreed to a contract at half his usual salary, with the promise that it would be improved if his performance warranted it.

After *All the King's Men* had been released, Cohn telephoned Crawford with the news: "You've just been voted the New York Film Critics Award."

"That's fine," said the actor. "I'm going to New York to receive it."

"No, you're not," Cohn warned. "You're in the middle of a picture with Glenn Ford."

"Herschel—" During moments of anger Crawford always called Cohn by that name.

"You cannot interrupt production!"

"Herschel, New York is my hometown. I know all those critics from long ago. Think what they'll say if I tell them I can't receive their award because Harry Cohn won't let me."

"I'll call you back."

Cohn telephoned Crawford back with his permission. "Why don't you take your wife?" said Cohn, who paid for both plane fares, as well as a suite at the Waldorf-Astoria Hotel.

A strict regulation at Columbia decreed that actors could not use telephones on movie stages, lest they waste time and money in calling their agents or bookmakers. One day Broderick Crawford had an urgent personal call to make, but he was told by the assistant director and the production manager that he was forbidden to telephone from the set.

"Excuse me, then," said the actor. "I'll go outside to make the call." He left the stage and returned four and a half hours later.

Cohn in a dudgeon called Crawford that evening. "I have a full report on you," said Cohn. "You left the set and didn't return for four and one-half hours. Is that right?"

"That's right," the actor admitted.

"What the hell did you do?"

"I went out to make a phone call."

"Then what took you so long?"

"The line was busy."

Crawford was permitted to use the telephone on the set thereafter.

The director of a Crawford picture complained to Cohn that the actor had twice walked off the set at six in the evening. Cohn demanded an explanation from Crawford.

"If you'd bother to read my contract, you'd see a clause that says I will not be required to work after six o'clock," Crawford declared.

Cohn pondered.

"Well, the next time you leave," he said, "say good-night."

Their relations continued on a give-and-take basis until Broderick Crawford was cast in *Born Yesterday*. As the result of his Oscar, he was receiving munificent offers from other studios. He wanted a nonexclusive contract and fulfillment of Cohn's promise of more satisfactory terms after he proved himself.

Cohn refused to discuss the matter. Crawford managed to engender minor ailments that kept him from reporting to a western he was making, and Cohn finally agreed to a meeting. But he refused to entertain suggestions that Crawford's contract be revised.

"Herschel, I can walk out of here any time and go back to the stage to earn my living," said Crawford.

"Oh, no you can't!" said Cohn.

"Oh, yes I can. Ask Judge Roth."

Cohn called his legal adviser, who reported that Crawford's contract permitted him to work in other media.

"I don't care if I never make another picture," said Crawford. "For openers, —— you!"

"—— you back!" growled Cohn.

He then offered a proposal. Crawford countered with his own.

"—— you!" said Cohn.

"—— you back!" said Crawford. He offered another proposal.

"—— you!" said Cohn.

"This time I won't say —— you back,'" declared Crawford, "but I'm going to break that contract."

On the following day Cohn and his wife were leaving for their annual vacation at the Phoenix Biltmore, where he liked to lie in the sun, mingle with Eastern business magnates, and attend exhibition games of big-league baseball teams in spring practice. When he arrived in Phoenix, he discovered that Crawford and his agent, Melnick, had taken an adjoining room. After an initial encounter Crawford and Melnick only nodded in passing Cohn, who was obviously disturbed by their war of nerves. When Crawford left the hotel after a ten-day stay, he was surprised to discover Cohn had paid his bill.

Upon his return to the studio Cohn sent for Crawford.

"I want to thank you for the vacation," the actor said cheerfully.

"—— you for openers," Cohn grumbled. "What kind of a deal do you want? You've already cost me a quarter million dollars."

"I want out," Crawford said.

"Out you get." Cohn offered to tear up the contract and replace it with a nonexclusive deal for two pictures a year at an increased salary.

"I'll take it—but you've got to give me thirty days' notice before the start of a picture."

"Is that a promise or an Irish threat?"

"You've got a deal, Herschel."

"Then don't call me Herschel," Cohn said. "That means you're mad at me."

The new contract proved satisfactory to both parties, although Cohn often invited Crawford to his office just for argument's sake. They always found excuses to shout at each other.

While filming *The Violent Men*, Crawford fell during a stunt and broke two vertebrae. Cohn sent his own doctor to see the actor in the hospital, but Crawford refused to be examined by him, believing him to be an insurance doctor. He learned later that Cohn's interest was personal, not in pursuance of his duties as head of production.

Cohn went to the hospital to visit Crawford, who admitted that his condition was grave.

"Yes, I know," said Cohn. "I've seen the X rays." He mentioned that the picture had only three days of shooting without Crawford, and the cost of replacing him would be $540,000.

"It's my fault; I'll give you the money," said Crawford.

"You'll what?" said Cohn incredulously.

"It's my fault," Crawford repeated. "They told me not to try that stunt, but I went ahead and did it. I'll pay you the money."

"That'll be the ——ing day!" Cohn scoffed.

Crawford's check for $540,000 was delivered to Cohn's desk. Cohn drove back to Cedars of Lebanon Hospital, marched to Crawford's room, and threw the check in his face. Then Cohn turned around and walked out.

Downstairs he had an afterthought. He returned to Crawford's room and said, "Incidentally, thank you very much. But I'll hold up the picture until you come back."

He added, "And the next time you're told not to do a stunt, goddammit, you follow orders!"

One day Cohn called Crawford to his office to read a passage from a well-thumbed book. The key phrase was: "Any man who makes you famous, some day you will spit upon."

Crawford remained in embarrassed silence.

"Everybody I've made famous has done this to me," Cohn remarked. "You'll do it, too."

"Never," said Crawford.

"Yes, you will. You may not even know you're doing it, but someday you'll cut my heart out."

When Crawford's contract had finally ended, he went to Cohn's office for a farewell. He found Cohn more mellow than he had ever seen him.

"You're the only one who never spit on me," said Cohn, adding, "But you hated my guts, didn't you? Tell me you did."

"Okay, Harry, I hated your guts," Crawford said.

Cohn seemed pleased. "You have a problem," he observed. "You don't hate enough."

"Why should I hate?" Crawford protested. "I'm an actor. My vitriol comes out in acting."

"But you don't hate enough."

"Neither do you."

Cohn grinned. "Yes, but don't tell anyone. It was fun fighting with me, wasn't it?"

"Hell, yes. I used to go home and try to figure out what I could do to Harry Cohn. One night I lay awake for three hours before I thought of something."

Cohn was delighted. "We've had our fights, but nobody will be able to say a word against you in front of me."

"Same here," said Crawford. "And I'll never say anything against you—except that you were the biggest —— I ever worked for."

Again Cohn was pleased. "You promise?"

"Absolutely. I'll take full-page ads in *Variety* and *Reporter* if necessary. You know something? You taught me more about acting than I ever knew before. And my family has been at it for four generations."

"You taught me more about handling actors than I ever knew before," Cohn conceded.

"Harry, I'm going to do something for you. I'm going to do a picture for free. I don't want any salary. Just give me unlimited expenses. This is my farewell present to you."

Cohn accepted his offer, and Crawford performed in a film for the total cost of $275 in expenses. Cohn in return gave 500 shares of National Cash Register stock to Crawford's two sons. Even with the one actor he liked and understood, he could not bear to be obligated.

8

A MATTER OF LIFE AND DEATH

*O*n March 4, 1954, Harry Cohn entered Cedars of Lebanon Hospital after working a full day at the studio. Although an operation had been urged on him, he resisted giving approval for the surgery even after his admittance to the hospital. One of his doctors sat drinking with him most of the night, and only at the end of the session would Cohn agree to submit to the operation. It was announced as minor throat surgery for removal of a nodule on the thyroid gland. Not revealed was the fact that the nodule was cancerous.

The operation marked the beginning of the decline of Harry Cohn's incredible energy. No longer did he race about the studio, climbing stairs two and three at a time. No longer could he work at top speed for sixteen hours a day. Yet the shifting patterns of the movie business demanded even more of his energy and resourcefulness.

Disappearing from Hollywood was the one-man studio rule that Cohn had pioneered. Studios were becoming clusters of independent producers and of stars who lent themselves as full partners to the film corporations. The East was constantly prodding Harry Cohn to adjust and conform to the new order. He made attempts to do so, but often his irascibility interfered.

Columbia's New York executives had arranged a loan of $630,000 to Mike Todd so he could finish his all-star extravaganza *Around the World in 80 Days*. Todd was told that as a matter of protocol, he would have to go to Hollywood and secure the approval of the president of the corporation.

A Teletype message was sent to Harry Cohn telling of the deal and of Todd's journey to see him. Cohn was not impressed by the Todd enterprise. He knew Todd as a flamboyant producer of girly shows and believed that Todd had reneged on a $2,000 bet.

Todd breezed into Cohn's office to a frigid welcome. Todd could not easily be daunted, and he sat down and placed his feet on Cohn's desk. Because of Cohn's passion for cleanliness, he considered his desk inviolate.*

"Take your ——ing shoes off my desk," Cohn ordered.

Todd calmly removed his feet from the desk, discarded his shoes, and placed his stockinged feet on the desk.

"You welshing son of a bitch, get the hell out of my office," Cohn ordered. "The deal is off."

Todd left the office and sought financing from United Artists. *Around the World in 80 Days* became the fourth largest money-maker among films to that time.

Abe Schneider and Nate Spingold of the New York office negotiated an independent deal with Sam Spiegel for *On the Waterfront*, a film about corruption on the New York Harbor docks. Harry Cohn was not in favor of the film, but he did not interfere with the contract. He objected when Spiegel insisted on filming on real locations in the East; Cohn argued that the picture should be made in Hollywood. Since his contract granted him complete independence, Spiegel prevailed over Cohn.

Cohn viewed the finished picture in his home projection room with the director, Elia Kazan. Cohn's only comment concerned the scene in which Marlon Brando, as the punch-drunk longshoreman, told the Catholic priest, played by Karl Malden, to go to hell.

"Boy, are you going to have trouble with the Breen Office over that 'go to hell,'" he said. "They'll never pass it."

But the industry censors did approve the scene. Cohn was furious and demanded to know why other Columbia films had been censored for lesser offenses.

Cohn gave grudging admiration to *On the Waterfront*, especially after it grossed $9,500,000 (its total cost: $902,000). The film won eight of the 1954 Academy Awards, including those for

---

* Once, at the climax of a dressing down by Cohn, an alcoholic actor named Warren Hymer had urinated on the desk; Hymer was banished forever from Columbia, and the desk was burned.

best picture, best actor (Brando), best actress (Eva Marie Saint), best direction (Kazan), and best screenplay (Budd Schulberg, who would work for Spiegel, if not for Cohn). It was another of a long series of triumphs for Columbia at the Academy Awards, but it was a hollow victory for Harry Cohn. It was the first such winner that did not bear the stamp of his personal supervision.

With the help of *On the Waterfront* and *The Caine Mutiny*, the Columbia gross in fiscal 1955 reached another high of $88,311,113, and profits achieved a new record of $5,000,000. But the figures did not reveal the whole story. A large share of the profits also came from the television arm, Screen Gems, including the sale of old movies to television. The operation of the studio for production of feature movies was becoming increasingly hazardous from a financial standpoint. Studying the charts of studio expenditures and income, the financiers of the East decreed that costs had to be reduced. Since Columbia had been operated since Poverty Row days with an absolute minimum of waste, the principal savings had to come in reduction of personnel.

Cohn approached the task with heavy heart. Although he could fire an actor or writer quixotically, the jobs of the lesser-paid studio workers were almost sacrosanct. Workers were divided between Old Columbia and New Columbia, the line of demarcation being the time when the studio emerged from minor to major status, circa 1940. No Old Columbia worker could be discharged without Harry Cohn's approval. With the East-ordered economy wave, both Old and New Columbia employees had to be dismissed. Cohn customarily secured other employment for veteran workers before they were removed from his payroll.

Cohn encountered increasing frustration in his efforts to maintain a production program at the studio. Project after project died because Cohn could not interest producers or acquire stars for them. The source of his greatest grief was *Joseph and His Brethren.*

Clifford Odets had written what many considered a monumental screenplay, but Cohn could find no actor of sufficient stature to play Joseph. Cohn continued in his attempt to keep the production alive, passing it from one producer to another. Otto Preminger agreed to attempt *Joseph and His Brethren* only to decide three weeks later that he was unsuited for it. Cohn responded with a flood of vituperation.

At one time the start of production was scheduled, and expensive sets had been built. But Rita Hayworth, who was to play the female lead, failed to appear, and the entire project was canceled.

Finally Harry Cohn believed that the salvation of *Joseph and His Brethren* lay with the man who had thrust Columbia to greatness, Frank Capra. Casting aside any bitterness that had resulted from their parting, Cohn brought Capra back to the studio. But Capra found Cohn unresponsive and distant, and again the film was abandoned.

Eventually *Joseph and His Brethren* was written off as a loss of $1,700,000. Columbia made a degree of restitution by exacting the promise of two final pictures from Rita Hayworth because she had failed to report for the film.

Cohn continued to be frustrated on projects he wanted to film. Once he called an independent producer to come to the Cohn office to discuss a favorite script of his.

The producer, who had once been fired as a director by Cohn, enjoyed complete autonomy under his new Columbia contract. He issued a Cohnian reply to the invitation: "—— you." Cohn was unable to retaliate.

Cohn found more willing attendance from two new confidants, Mr. and Mrs. George Sidney. Significantly, both came from M-G-M. Lillian Burns Sidney had been drama coach and adviser to many M-G-M stars: Louis B. Mayer had once said of her, "She is the only woman I know who could run a major studio." This, plus the aura of the M-G-M tradition, impressed Cohn, and he hired her as executive assistant. Later, George Sidney came to Columbia as director of *The Eddy Duchin Story, Jeanne Eagels*, and *Pal Joey*. He was the son of an old Cohn friend and longtime M-G-M executive, L. K. Sidney.

The Sidneys became inseparable companions of Harry Cohn at the studio and at his home. Mrs. Sidney read scripts to Cohn and advised him on sundry matters, and some of his producers and directors complained that she exercised an almost mystic influence on him.

Relations between Harry Cohn and his brother Jack had solidified into constant bitterness. The Teletype that carried messages between the studio and the New York office became a daily arena. Harry Cohn stood behind the Teletype operator in the room next to his and dictated curt messages to his brother, punctuating them with finger thrusts at the shoulder of the teletypist. If Harry did not enjoy the reply that was coming from Jack, he would order the operator to jam the machine. Then Harry would offer his own reply to the unfinished message.

Cohn viewed most emissaries from New York with suspicion. He preferred them to make their trips to the Coast in sleeper planes; hence, they would not waste a day's work in transit. When Easterners arrived, they could tell how they stood with Cohn by the automobile that had come from the studio for their use. Columbia had an arrangement for the use of Chrysler Corporation cars in return for displaying them in movies and television shows. If Cohn sent an Imperial to the airport, the Eastern visitor knew that he stood in Cohn's favor at the time. The arrival of a Plymouth meant impending trouble.

Cohn's visits to New York followed a rigid pattern. He arrived at the airport in the morning, to be greeted by his own representatives in the New York office—Spingold, Harry Romm, Milt Pickman, etc.—never by any of the Jack Cohn team; that would have been a sign of conciliation and weakness. Cohn went to his suite at the Sherry-Netherland Hotel, where he entertained visitors and arranged for theater tickets, which had to be on the aisle in Row B or C. After lunch, Cohn reported to the Columbia office, where he operated from the boardroom. Jack preferred never to meet alone with Harry, and conferences usually involved several of the top executives. Little was accomplished in the meetings because either brother usually picked on some minor and extraneous matter for a lengthy tirade.

After his throat operation, Cohn was subject to moments of almost manic irascibility. One day George Seaton, then president of the Academy of Motion Picture Arts and Sciences, called on

Cohn to ask permission to use film clips of Columbia pictures on the Academy telecast. Cohn flatly refused.

"I'm not going to give them a goddam thing," he declared. "What the hell has the Academy ever done for me?"

"Harry, is that a swivel chair?" Seaton asked calmly.

"Yeah," Cohn grunted.

"Can you turn a hundred and eighty degrees?"

"Yeah." Cohn turned completely around and faced the banks of golden Oscars behind his desk. He whirled back to Seaton and became red-faced and shrill.

"Every one of those *I* earned!" he shouted. He launched a tirade against the film makers who had helped earn the awards for Columbia over the years. He ended with: "Let the Academy get me up there and give me what I deserve."

He also knew times of mellowness. Despite the long history of his battles with Rita Hayworth, William Holden, and Glenn Ford, he grew sentimental when the contracts of all of them came to an end. "There go my three kids," he said wistfully. "It's the end of an era."

Cohn found increasing solace in his family. He was proud of Joan and often remarked after a large party, "She was the most beautiful woman there." He approved of her conversion to Catholicism and her plans to rear their children as Catholics.

One day he came home from the studio to find a birthday party for one of his sons in progress. As he gazed down from his bedroom window at the frolicking youngsters in the garden, tears ran down his cheeks.

"What's the matter?" asked his secretary, Dona Holloway.

"It breaks my heart because I will never see my sons grown," he said.

Cohn had a fixation that he would die at the age of sixty-seven. His mother and two brothers had done so, and he was afflicted with a weakness of the heart that had claimed other Cohns. Despite the condition, he continued his schedule of work and play.

He had found a new and absorbing interest: Las Vegas. Almost every weekend Cohn and his close personal companion, Jonie Taps, boarded an airline for the Nevada fun capital. Cohn first made his headquarters at El Rancho Vegas, operated by his former nephew-in-law, Beldon Katleman. Later Cohn stayed at the Sands Hotel, where he became close friends with Jack Entratter.

Cohn adored Las Vegas. He was treated like a visiting pasha, hotel help and entertainers seeking his comfort and pleasure, with never a bill presented. The hotel operators enjoyed having a personage of his eminence as their guest. They never profited from Cohn's gambling; the Saratoga fiasco had ended his plunging days. He occasionally fed quarters into the slot machines or bet a few dollars at blackjack. Most of the time he merely observed, standing behind the pit bosses and watching the suckers lose their money. He enjoyed seeing the Las Vegas shows and offered avuncular advice on songs, costumes, and timing to favorite performers like Ernie Kovacs and Edie Adams.

He liked the around-the-clock activity of the gambling houses, the presence of glittering, handsome people, the intimacy with the figures who owned Las Vegas. All this exhilarated him and caused him to lay aside the problems of Columbia Pictures and of his health.

Irving Mills, who had once been an intimate of Cohn's, came upon him one night in a noisy Las Vegas cocktail lounge. Cohn was surrounded by showgirls, and he looked old and tired. Mills drew his old friend aside and urged, "Harry, go to bed; you don't look well."

"It's none of your ——ing business," snapped Cohn.

Cohn enjoyed trips to Hawaii, which bore pleasant memories of his first visit there for *From Here to Eternity*. During one of his returns an enterprising reporter named Cobey Black from the Honolulu *Star-Bulletin* found Cohn in an expansive mood. He granted what he termed the only personal interview of his career.

The setting was the most palatial hotel room of Waikiki, the Diamond Head suite of the Surf Rider Hotel. Cohn occupied it with his wife and three children. He spoke of his fondness for the islands and commented, "My observation of Hawaii is, shoot an arrow into the air and where it lands, buy property."

The *Time* cover article on Kim Novak had recently appeared, and the reporter asked if Kim Novak was as temperamental as the magazine reported.

"I should say she is," replied Cohn, "but that's a part of the business. Nobody takes credit for Novak's success. The success of Novak is due to great pictures. Any girl who gets six pictures like Novak got has got to be a star. Talent is only as good as the picture."

It was during a Honolulu trip that Harry Cohn almost sold out his interest in Columbia Pictures. Aware that his health was not as vigorous as it had been, Mrs. Cohn had urged him to accept an offer of several millions from a New York banking house. His close friend, Alfred Hart, a liquor and banking milionaire who served on the Columbia board of directors, urged him as well.

Cohn signed the papers authorizing the sale of his stock and mailed them to California. As soon as he had done so, he was a different man. He seemed to have nothing to live for. Recognizing this, Mrs. Cohn agreed that he should send a message to his attorney, Mendel Silberberg, rescinding the sale. Cohn's interest in life returned.

9
THE LAST HURRAH

*I*n 1956 Jack Cohn underwent an operation to correct a hernia. He seemed to be recovering from the surgery; then he developed an embolism and died suddenly.

Harry Cohn wept at the news. When he arrived in New York for the funeral, officials of the New York office noted an immense change in him. His ruddy color had paled; his leathery voice had gone flat.

He went to see Jack's widow, Jeanette, who had witnessed forty years of bitterness between the two brothers. Harry took her in his arms, and both sobbed of their loss.

"Jeanette, the bottom has fallen out," he said sorrowfully.

With close friends Cohn spoke darkly of the number sixty-seven. Jack had died at that age, and the year was approaching for Harry Cohn.

Cohn was subject to periods of depression, something his longtime associates had never witnessed before. Inexplicably, he had lost the ruby ring that Charlie Lombard had given him. He had always considered it a talisman of good luck, and its loss disturbed him deeply.

He possessed a terror of being alone. Once he telephoned Tony Curtis at two in the morning. Cohn had developed a fondness for the young actor and had declared he would never make *Joseph and His Brethren* without him.

"Get over here right away!" Cohn said urgently.

Curtis sleepily assented, and he dressed and raced his car to the Cohn mansion. He arrived to find that Cohn merely wanted to chat about the movie business.

Abe Schneider, who had risen from bookkeeper to financial mind of the company, succeeded Jack Cohn as head of the New York operation. Harry Cohn respected Schneider's financial judgment, but he was uneasy with the new relationship with the

East. He missed the uninhibited give-and-take he had known with his brother.

Now, for the first time, Harry Cohn was certain that he was subject to actual threats to his power; he was convinced that moves were under way to unseat him as president and head of production. He spoke of evidence that a power play was in the making, and he became more secretive in his executive decisions.

Harassed by a market that continued its fall and by the threat—real or imagined—to his power, Cohn struggled to keep the studio in operation. He placed great hopes in a film made by his old friend John Ford and starring Tyrone Power, *The Long Gray Line*. It was a sentimental pageant of life at West Point, and Cohn was certain it would be a success. It performed well—a gross of $5,635,000 against a cost of $1,748,000, but not as well as Cohn hoped.

Next, Cohn realized his long ambition to film *Pal Joey*. He wanted Frank Sinatra to play the title role, and he opened negotiations with the singer's agent, Abe Lastfogel. This time Sinatra was not available for $1,000 a week. Lastfogel outlined the terms: $125,000 plus 25 percent of the profits.

"You're nuts," exploded Cohn. But in the end he accepted the terms. Cohn stinted on nothing. To enhance the project, he cast both the Cohn-created Love Goddesses, Rita Hayworth and Kim Novak. George Sidney directed with the same lavish touch he had applied to musicals at M-G-M.

At the same time New York had entered into another production with Sam Spiegel, *The Bridge on the River Kwai*. Cohn disapproved. He believed it was madness to take a film company halfway around the world to Ceylon. The fact that the picture featured no women made the venture seem even riskier to him.

Cohn took the final print of *Pal Joey* to New York on his annual trip to the stockholders' meeting. He arrived on a Monday morning and showed *Pal Joey* to the New York office for a good reaction. Spiegel arrived from London the following day with a print of *The Bridge on the River Kwai*. The salesmen of the East were jubilant.

"It's a good picture," said Cohn of Spiegel's film. "But it's too long. It shouldn't be an inch longer than *Pal Joey*." In all his conversations he continued injecting *Pal Joey*. But the talk in the New York office was of *The Bridge on the River Kwai*.

Joan Cohn had come to New York with her husband, and she met with Jack's widow, Jeanette. "You know Harry is not a well man," said Joan. "We don't know how much longer we'll have him with us. Let's make life as pleasant for him as we can." Jeanette agreed, and she spent much time with Harry, reminiscing about Bella Cohn and her freshly baked coffee cakes and all the warm memories of Eighty-eighth Street.

Harry Cohn presented his usual gruff, assured manner at the annual stockholders' meeting of Columbia Pictures in November, 1957. But there was bad news for the stockholders. Abe Schneider reported that the first-quarter earnings of the fiscal year were poor, and the corporation faced a possible loss. He expected the second quarter to be slightly better, and the second half of the year would be excellent because of expected earnings from *The Bridge on the River Kwai* and *Pal Joey*. Schneider assured the shareowners that Columbia would continue its efforts to cut costs.

A stockholder inquired if the bulk of first-quarter earnings had come from the operations of Screen Gems. "You can make that assumption," said Schneider. Ralph Cohn reported that his Screen Gems operation was proving to be enormously successful.

Harry Cohn told the gathering that it continued to be difficult to secure the services of important stars. "There's nothing we can do about these star deals," he admitted. "If Marlon Brando will make a deal with me tomorrow for fifty percent of a picture, I'd kiss him."

Before leaving New York to return to California, Cohn took his wife late one evening to Gallagher's, a restaurant he had known since his song-plugging days. There he encountered Sidney Buchman.

Buchman had made no films since his appearance before the congressional committee four years before; unlike others who could not be hired openly by the film companies, he refused to bootleg scripts under assumed names. He had been living in New York, and he was sitting with friends in Gallagher's when Cohn passed by and said hello. Later a waiter came to Buchman with the message that Mr. Cohn would like to see him.

The reunion of the two old friends was warm and cordial. Buchman was shocked by Cohn's appearance. The China-blue eyes no longer danced, and they had lost their color; now they seemed a lifeless gray.

"What's it going to be, pal?" Cohn asked imploringly.

"Only what it has been, Harry," said Buchman. "It's over."

Throughout the conversation Cohn held Buchman's hand tightly in his. Cohn loosened his grasp with reluctance when Buchman mentioned that he had to leave.

10
"Get Me a Box"

*I*n the chill December evening Evelyn Lane stood on the runway at Los Angeles International Airport waiting, as she had dozens of times before, for the arrival of her boss, Harry Cohn. Beside her was the studio limousine that was permitted on the field by airline officials because of the eminence of the president of Columbia Pictures Corporation.

When the big plane lumbered to a halt, Miss Lane looked expectantly to the cabin entrance; always Harry Cohn was the first to emerge. To her surprise, he was not standing in the doorway when the hatch was opened. Three other travelers came out, and then Cohn appeared at the door.

Miss Lane was shocked by his appearance. She had worked in intimate association with Harry Cohn for fifteen years, and she had never seen him with such pallor. She instructed an assistant to telephone Mrs. Cohn to have the family physician at the house when her husband arrived home.

Harry Cohn stood in the doorway as if transfixed. He carried a large package that contained a piece of Steuben glass, a gift for his wife; it had been sent by Jeanette Cohn, with whom he had spent much of his time in New York. He had gone there for the premiere of *The Bridge on the River Kwai* and to attend a dinner in honor of her late husband and Harry's brother, Jack Cohn.

"Thank God you're here," said Harry Cohn as he approached Evelyn Lane. "I didn't think I would make it."

She led him to the studio car, and on the drive to Beverly Hills he told her what had happened. At the banquet in his brother's honor Cohn had been told a startling piece of news by a high Columbia official: Kim Novak was having a romance with Sammy Davis, Jr.

Cohn had been thunderstruck. He returned to the Sherry-Netherland after the banquet and swallowed nitroglycerin pills that had been prescribed for his heart condition. He boarded the plane, and over the Rocky Mountains he suffered severe chest pains. The airline stewardess proposed that the plane land in Denver for medical assistance, but Cohn would not permit such a thing. That could only endanger the Columbia stock, he reasoned, and he insisted that the plane continue to Los Angeles.

Cohn's doctor examined him at his home and insisted that he go to the hospital. Still wary of the effect on Columbia stock, Cohn flatly refused. He insisted on being treated at home. An electrocardiogram was administered by a heart specialist, and it revealed no unusual damage to Cohn's heart. But he was seriously ill.

The studio learned of the illness when, for the first time in the memories of the oldest Columbia employees, the Christmas party was not held in Cohn's office.

Cohn's visits to the studio were brief and infrequent. He seemed curiously distant from the everyday operation of the studio. Kim Novak's romance with the black entertainer continued to concern him; he believed the news would destroy her value as a Columbia star.

"I can't understand it," he fretted. "If she had taken up with Harry Belafonte—yes. But Sammy Davis, Jr.!"

He scouted a solution to his problem. A call was placed to his friends in Chicago, and their attorney was placed at his disposal. The attorney went to see Davis in Las Vegas. No threats of physical violence were made. Davis was presented with the simple alternatives: end his romance with Kim Novak, or find himself denied employment by any major nightclub in the United States. On January 10, 1957, Sammy Davis, Jr., was married to Loray White, a black dancer in a Las Vegas revue.

Cohn's interest in studio affairs continued to diminish. He had long been intrigued with a screen story about wartime Italy. It was the tale of a former American gangster who had been deported to Italy and had then found himself in the war zone during the American invasion. The American authorities were eager to enlist his services in saving a bridge that was vital to the approach to Rome, and they sent an officer, the gangster's brother, to seek his help. The gangster agreed to help the invasion, but only if the American government would accord him the pardon and respect he yearned for.

It was the kind of tale that held fascination for Cohn, and he had spent much time trying to develop a shooting script. But he could interest no producer in the project, and in the end, he was forced to abandon it.

Harry Cohn now prepared himself for death.

He directed the preparation of a new will, which would grant his fortune, valued at $14,000,000, to a foundation, with adequate allowance for the support of his widow and children to the end of their lives. He legally adopted the young girl he and his wife had taken into their home, to assure her participation in the legacy. As for the ceremonies attendant to his death, Article Second of his Last Will and Testament, dated February 14, 1957, stated, "I direct and request that no funeral services be held at the time of my death."

Cohn still found no credence in the existence of God. Many years before, he had entertained Rouben Mamoulian on the *Jobella*, and he had said to the director, "You're an intelligent man; will you answer me a question?"

"I will if I can," said Mamoulian.

"What happens to us after we die?"

Mamoulian was momentarily startled. "Well, there are various beliefs. Some people believe that death is the end of everything; some believe that life goes on."

"What do you think?"

"My personal feeling is that there is another life."

"What proof can you give me?"

"I can only say that between the two hypotheses, I prefer to believe that there is a link between this life and the next. It makes more sense than the theory that we are in something that is just temporary. People who suffer in this life can expect a better life next time."

"Rouben, I want you to prove it to me!" Cohn insisted.

"Alas, I cannot prove it. Some of the most important things in life cannot be proved."

Lacking proof, Harry Cohn did not believe.

The time was approaching for Cohn's annual vacation at the Biltmore in Phoenix. Having arranged for other matters concerning his death, he decided to prepare his monument. Some of his friends owned stock in the cemetery where Al Jolson had been buried, and they urged Cohn to buy space for his own resting place. Cohn visited the cemetery and found it too distant from the studio. Instead, he chose Hollywood Cemetery, six blocks due south of Columbia.

"I picked out a great plot," he enthused later that day to a friend. "It's right by the water, and I can see the studio from it."

Cohn had been told by his doctors that his heart ailment might be cured by surgery. He pondered the possibility and even acquired films of heart operations from universities and medical schools. He ran the films hour after hour in his projection room before deciding that he could not face the surgery.

He departed on February 22 for Phoenix with Mrs. Cohn. He seemed extremely tired as he left, but his spirits rose as he arrived at the Biltmore. He was met by Harry Romm, his good friend and New York representative. Romm and his wife had spent their vacation with the Cohns for several years.

Cohn talked jauntily of picking out his burial place and a marble monument and said with a wink, "I'll be close by; I'll be watching them at the studio."

Then he remarked seriously to Romm, "Harry, I'll give you a million dollars if you can get me through this next year."

"Why talk that way?" Romm said.

"Because it will be my sixty-seventh year, and I'm afraid of it," said Cohn.

Cohn cast off his gloomy talk and entered into the social atmosphere of the Biltmore. During the day he sat in the sun, watching the tennis players and swimmers, or read in his room while the Romms played double solitaire to keep him company. He dozed off in brief naps, and when the Romms tried to leave the room, he awakened and bade them stay.

One night Cohn received a telephone call from George Sidney in Hollywood.

"Harry, I want you to do something for me," said Sidney.

"Anything you want," said Cohn. "Tell me what it is."

"Is that a promise?"

"Yes."

Sidney then said that his father, L. K. Sidney, had died.

"Oh, my God!" exclaimed Cohn. "I'm coming to the funeral."

"No, that's the promise," Sidney insisted, "that you stay there."

"What will people say?" Cohn replied. "I'm coming home."

Cohn and his wife flew to Los Angeles, and they went directly to the Sidney residence. As he sat talking with the director, Cohn asked, "Did you get L. K. a box?"

"A casket? Yes, Harry."

Cohn stared intently at Sidney and said, "Get me a box."

Sidney refused to entertain such a notion. "I'll get you a box in about thirty-five years," he scoffed.

That night Cohn telephoned the studio switchboard. Wilma Addie, who had been his night operator for a dozen years, received the call.

"Any messages?" Cohn asked.

"Why, Mr. Cohn," she said, "I didn't know you were back."

His usual vigor had vanished. After a pause he said quietly, "Now you know."

"No, there are no messages, Mr. Cohn," she reported.

"If anybody calls, I'm at the George Sidneys," he said, hanging up the telephone.

The Cohns attended the Sidney funeral at Temple Israel on the following day. They left by a side entrance, and Cohn stood at the curb waiting impatiently for his limousine. A Columbia press agent named Robert Yeager saw Cohn make a comment to a nearby aide. A man with a sense of history, Yeager suspected that in view of Cohn's ill health, the appearance might be his last on the Hollywood scene. After Cohn and his wife had been driven off, Yeager asked the aide what Cohn's final words had been. They were: "Where is that son of a bitch?"

Howard Hughes had put his private plane at Cohn's disposal for the return to Arizona. Because the plane was not pressurized, Cohn's doctors advised him to take a regular flight. Hughes ordered a TWA passenger plane to delay its departure until Cohn arrived from the funeral.

It was one of the evenings that Harry Cohn enjoyed. Each night one of the Biltmore guests acted as host at a reception for other distinguished visitors, and this was Harry Cohn's night. He was dressing in his room before dinner. Harry Romm was with him.

"Would I be imposing if I asked you to get me a piece of roast beef from the table over there?" Cohn asked.

Romm was surprised by the request. Cohn had always insisted on doing such things himself. Romm replied with the gruffness the two men often affected with each other, "Why don't you get it yourself?"

"I don't feel good," Cohn admitted.

"Why didn't you say so?" Romm said. He brought Cohn a sandwich from the hors d'oeuvre table.

Cohn finished eating and asked, "Is it warm in here?"

"No, not particularly," said Romm.

"I feel groggy. Mind if we wait in the lobby for the ladies?"

The walk in the cool desert air seemed to revive Cohn. The wives joined the two men, and all went into the dining room.

During dinner Mrs. Cohn noticed her husband take out his gold pill case and swallow six nitroglycerin capsules. She whispered to Romm, "Get an oxygen tank to our room, and bring a wheelchair here."

"Why?" Romm asked.

"Because Harry is only supposed to take just *one* of those nitroglycerins."

A bellboy brought a wheelchair to the table. Cohn scowled at it and said, "Get that goddam thing away from here!"

"Would it be all right if I take it over to the kitchen and help you over there?" Romm asked. Cohn consented.

But when Romm offered his arm, Cohn slammed it away. He would walk out of the dining room on his own power.

Cohn was wheeled to his room. He refused entreaties to go to the hospital, and a nurse was hired for him. He appeared to be resting comfortably.

"Don't call off the party," he urged, but Mrs. Cohn did.

Cohn's physician, Dr. Stanley Imerman, and George Sidney were notified of his illness. They were unable to get a flight from Los Angeles that evening, and they left in the morning. Harry Romm met them at the Phoenix airport and rushed them to the Biltmore. As they arrived, they learned that an ambulance had been sent to the Cohn cottage.

The three men reached the cottage as Cohn was being carried out in the stretcher. He looked ashen, but his voice was as strong as ever. "I don't want to be carried out this way," he insisted. "I want to sit up."

Before Cohn was placed in the ambulance, Sidney attempted to place a nitroglycerin capsule under his tongue. Cohn spat it out. "Get the box," he said to Sidney.

With siren screaming, the ambulance sped toward the hospital with Mrs. Cohn and Dr. Imerman at Cohn's side. Cohn resisted the physician's efforts to give him aid.

"It's no use," said the toughest man in Hollywood, adding, "It's too tough. It's just too tough."

He died a block from St. Joseph Hospital.

After the ambulance arrived at the hospital, Mrs. Cohn conferred with a priest. She told him that her husband had invoked the name of Jesus Christ in his extremity. For that reason, the priest declared it would be suitable to baptize Harry Cohn into the Christian faith. The rite was performed.

Epilogue:
Rosebud

EPILOGUE:
ROSEBUD

*D*uring a research trip to New York, I made a point of searching out Whitney Bolton, whom I had known when he was head of publicity for Columbia Pictures from 1943 to 1947. He was a handsome man with tanned face and trimmed blonde mustache, elegant in tailored suits that hid his ample middle, the result of good living on a liberal expense account. A well-spoken man with a mellow voice, he had seemed miscast as press agent to the explosive, profane Harry Cohn. Yet he lasted longer than most Columbia publicity heads, parting with Cohn on friendly terms, hired immediately by David O. Selznick.

Born in Washington, D.C., in 1900, Bolton had enjoyed a privileged youth. He was educated in Mexico and at Staunton Military Academy and the University of Virginia. Instead of entering the business world, he was attracted to Broadway, and he became drama critic and columnist for the New York *Morning Telegraph* and a member of the Players Club. In 1938, he moved to Hollywood as correspondent of the New York *Herald Tribune*, serving for five years until he was lured by the better salaries of studio publicity departments. When the studio system broke up in the 1950's, Bolton returned to New York, where he wrote drama criticism for a minor paper and announced news for the Mutual Broadcasting System.

Like motion pictures, network radio had declined rapidly with the onslaught of television, and Mutual, always the struggling fourth network, had suffered the most. When I arrived at Mutual's makeshift offices at 1440 Broadway, I could hear Bolton's voice over a loudspeaker, announcing the 5 o'clock news. His tones were deeper than before, but the diction retained the same polish. He emerged from the studio with a warm welcome. I hadn't seen him for a dozen years, and he seemed grayer and somewhat stouter, but he still exhibited a press agent's outgoing manner. He led me to a small, cluttered office dominated by a large clock with a sweep second hand.

We talked for forty-five minutes, reviewing old times, telling of our current lives; then I questioned him about his tenure at Columbia. He responded in entertaining style, though he was too much the gentleman to disclose anything scandalous. I felt the interview was drawing to a close when he glanced at the clock and said, "I've got to do the six o'clock news. Stick around."

Hoping to acquire something more substantial than what he had related, I asked when he returned: "Is there something you can tell me that would help people understand why Harry Cohn behaved as he did?"

Bolton sighed deeply. "Bob, you're a hard man," he said. "All right. I'll tell you a story I have told to only a handful of people. You can do whatever you want with it." And then he began.

During the mid-1940's, Bolton spent an evening with a psychiatrist friend, Dr. Samuel Stern (not his real name), who specialized in psychosomatic medicine at Cedars of Lebanon Hospital in east Hollywood. The conversation was wide-ranging, since Bolton's interests extended beyond the world of motion pictures. At one point Dr. Stern asked, "You work for Harry Cohn, don't you?"

"That's right," Bolton replied.

"I met him the other night."

Bolton was surprised. "You met him? Professionally?"

"More or less. I'll tell you about it."

Stern had been awakened at 2 A.M. by a Beverly Hills doctor who asked that Stern come to see a patient. "Why?" Stern asked. "Is he violent? Does he need restraint?"

"No, but he is in a very disturbed state. I beg you to come."

"Who is the patient?"

"Harry Cohn."

As a psychiatrist, Stern was intrigued by the prospect of examining a mogul who ruled his studio with total control yet apparently had a secret vulnerability. He drove through the dark empty streets of Beverly Hills until he arrived at the Crescent

Drive mansion. The butler admitted him, and he was met by Cohn's physician, who led him through the marble hall and into the paneled library. The patient was seated in a deep leather chair, his blue silk pajamas darkened with sweat. He acknowledged the introduction with a grunt.

"Who the hell sent for you?" Harry Cohn demanded, his leonine face scowling in defiance.

"Your doctor sent for me, on the chance that I could help you," Stern replied calmly. "If you don't think so, I'll leave. I don't need you."

Cohn's tone changed. "All right," he muttered, "don't get on your high horse, pal. Sit down."

Seeing his patient relatively calm, the other doctor departed.

There was a momentary silence between Cohn and Stern, then the psychiatrist remarked, "You make a lot of money, Mr. Cohn. I could use a lot of money. Tell me why I'm here. What makes you so upset?"

Cohn's face turned serious. "I'm afraid they're going to take it away from me," he said.

"Who will take it away from you?"

"You know—they. The powers that run this town."

"That's your anxiety?"

"Yes."

"That's perfectly normal. Many executives feel that way. Maybe you want to get rid of your responsibilities."

Anger clouded Cohn's face. "I'm going to show you something, Doc," he said. He led Stern to stairs descending to the basement. At the bottom, he switched on a light that revealed a large storeroom crowded with furniture and file cabinets. Cohn turned over a rug to reveal a safe imbedded in the floor. He turned the dial and opened the door, extracting a gold wedding ring and a faded $25 United States savings bond.

"These were my mother's," Cohn explained. "My father gave her the ring; when she was dying, she gave it to me. When I first started making money, I bought her this savings bond. She never cashed it."

"All right, Mr. Cohn," Stern said. "What have these things got to do with your anxieties?"

"Just this. After I started earning some money, making a few pictures, this woman whose ring I hold compelled me to success."

"Most mothers help their sons."

"But she didn't help me!" Cohn protested. "I did everything I could to win her approval, and she would never give it to me. Even when I made Columbia an important studio, she still wouldn't admit that I had turned out all right."

He was talking liberally, without the customary gruffness, and Stern made no effort to interject. Cohn continued with a story from his childhood. He had been a mischievous youngster, repeatedly engaging in scraps with other kids. His parents often were faced with complaints from neighbors. One day when he was five or six, his mother became exasperated by his latest offense, and she shouted, "You were born in a shithouse and I should have left you there!"

Her outburst haunted Harry throughout his youth. Finally, when he was seventeen and supporting himself, he pleaded with his mother to explain what she had meant. Reluctantly, she told him the story. The Cohn family had lived in a tenement with no bathrooms; the tenants had to use a privy between the buildings. One night when she was eight and a half months pregnant with Harry, she visited the privy and strained to relieve herself. To her horror, the baby was born and fell into the pit. Mrs. Cohn screamed, and the neighbor women rushed to retrieve the baby and wash him off.

"I live in constant fear that someone will know my secret," Cohn continued.

"That's hardly rational, since there is probably no one alive who knows that story," Stern answered.

"You're talking 'rational,'" Cohn snapped. "I'm telling you what my fears are. When I became the rich Harry Cohn, I was invited to dinners and cocktail parties by the bigshots, and every time I was drenched under the arms, afraid that somebody there would know my secret. Once I was at a producer's house in London, and I met the Duke of York. Just the three of us, the producer, me, and the future king of England. I was totally wet with sweat. That's why I take showers four or five times a day. That's why I wash my hands over and over again all day."

"It's not unusual for a patient to indulge in excessive cleanliness in an effort to wash away traumatic memories," Dr. Stern remarked.

"Don't give me that head-doctor crap," Cohn said angrily. "I don't need your help."

"I'm sure you think you don't. But by telling that story, you may have helped yourself. I'll leave you now."

"The butler will show you out," Cohn said, dismissing him. "And send your bill to this address, not the studio. I don't want any sneaks to see it."

"Dr. Stern never did send Cohn a bill," Whitney Bolton told me. "And since Cohn was not a patient, Stern figured he was free to tell me the story. And now I have told it to you. Maybe it will help you understand Harry Cohn. Then again, maybe not."

INDEX